AF654455

ISLAM: FAITH, STATE AND LAW

ISLAM
Faith, State and Law

By
Rais Siddiqi

ANMOL PUBLICATIONS PVT. LTD.
NEW DELHI - 110 002 (INDIA)

ANMOL PUBLICATIONS PVT. LTD.
4374/4B, Ansari Road, Daryaganj
New Delhi - 110 002
Ph.: 23261597, 23278000
Visit us at: www.anmolpublications.com

Islam: Faith, State and Law

© Reserved

First Published, 2005

ISBN 81-261-2222-6

[Responsibility for the facts stated, opinions expressed, conclusions reached and plagiarism, if any, in this book is entirely that of the Author. The Publishers bear no responsibility for them, whatsoever.]

PRINTED IN INDIA

Published by J.L. Kumar for Anmol Publications Pvt. Ltd., New Delhi - 110 002 and Printed at Mehra Offset Press, Delhi.

Contents

Part - II
The Comparison

Part - III
Real Law

Part - V
Diplomacy

Preface

Islam is a complete and final faith. It's not merely an ideology or philosophy, but it is a perfect code of conduct, which commands all aspects of human life, in this world and leads to the next world too. Islam, not only teaches its followers, how to lead a successful life, but, it also controls them. And for the purpose, this progressive and scientific religion has a flawless law, with its original source in Holy Quran and Prophets' traditions. In the course of time, scholars of high calibre have codified all Islamic principles, laws and rules and regulations.

Islam, not only shows its followers, the path of spiritual and religious aspects of life, but, it also guides them, regarding their social and political acts. Islam has well-defined directive principles for polity—formation and functioning of state and diplomacy. It's directions also cover inter-state relations and domains, like international law.

Islamic political system is distinct from other systems and its social philosophy is also different from all worldly ideologies. Islam does not believe in the sovereignty of man. According to Islamic tenets, the whole universe (including this world and the earth) belongs to God, All Mighty. He is the real ruler and sovereign authority. The head of government in an Islamic state is merely God's deputy (Caliph) and not the head of state, as the sole power rests in God's hands, alone. The ruler acts in the name of God and strictly in accordance with Divine commands.

In a logical manner, Islamic law, in an Islamic state, applies to all its citizens, including non-Muslims. However, the non-believers are bestowed upon with certain privileges and do enjoy guaranteed protection, under the Islamic government.

This book—comprehensive and exhaustive in itself—covers three major aspects—faith, law and polity and polity, in turn, includes governance and diplomacy. The foundation, protection, governance and development of a state and building of nation, all have been discussed in detail. And it has all been discussed in the light of Islamic philosophy, ideology, logic, law and jurisprudence. Hence, the first part is devoted to faith only. In Islam, faith is the foundation of all the institutions.

The undersigned is confident that this work of his would satisfy the scholarly urge of all those, who may prefer to read this book and would also prove to be a ready reference for all researchers, working on the related subjects.

Editor

Part - I

True Faith

1

Introduction

What is religion? Is it a set of dogmas, mythological beliefs or mere rituals? Is it a mere slogan? Is it a cult? Is it a body of rules and regulations formulated by some individual or group of individuals? Is it ritualistic worshipping and no more? Is it a *mantra* for turning poverty into riches? Is it a money-purchased ticket for paradise? "If it is not all this, then at best it is one's personal affair," the modernist will say and he may further add: "Since it is my personal affair, you need not bother about it".

This attitude has become fossilized over the centuries and has come to be the accepted viewpoint the world over, even in the Muslim countries. You may claim to be a Muslim, well and good. But whether you conform to the basic fundamentals of your religion in actual practice or not, no one bothers. Rather, no one dares to offend you by questioning you about your personal affair. None has a right to interfere in the personal affairs of others. This is the prevailing situation the world over. But has this the sanction of any true religion? Let us examine critically.

What is Faith ?

First of all let us review how this attitude came to be popular. No true religion ever confines itself to the spiritual aspect of human personality only to the exclusion of its intellectual and temporal aspects. All religions lay down rules for the spiritual as well as temporal guidance of man as much in his relations to society as in his relations to his soul or to the ultimate reality.

True Faith

True religion knows no duality of body and soul. It encompasses man's whole personality in all its manifold aspects and varied relations. Religion deals with man as a whole and supervises all his activities, physical, intellectual or spiritual. In the early history of all great religions this unity of man is observable. It was only later on when ease-loving persons found it difficult to maintain a coherence between their secular and sacred activities that a bifurcation came to be accepted between the two. Religion crystallised into lifeless dogma that could be safely entrusted to the clergy. The common worldly-wise man was left to do as he wished with little danger of interference from the other side. Religion and politics came to be segregated and the result in Allama Iqbal's words, was barbarism. This cleavage between religion and politics was more pronounced in Christianity where the Church was officially separated from the State some centuries back. Religion was no more a dynamic force in human society. It was just a personal affair of the individual. The hint was quickly picked up by all European nations and with the passage of time the attitude was accepted by the Muslim societies as well when the latter came under European domination and influence.

The result was evident. People lost sight of the true teachings of their religion and the slogan "religion is a personal affair" came to be accepted by all—Muslims and non-Muslims alike. This state of affairs practically put an end to call to do right and dissuade from doing wrong and the sporadic attempts of some zealous religious leaders and workers as well as some good Muslims to bring youth back to religion were often met with ridicule or went unheaded. This ultimately led our society to moral bankruptcy.

The Torn World

The present-day world is torn between the materialistic philosophies of Marxism and Capitalism. It becomes all the more pronounced with the advancement in science and technology. Modern science is materialistic in theory and mechanical in its practical approach. In framing theories about its subject-matter, it relies upon sense perception as the only source of knowledge and considers material phenomena as the only knowable, i.e. scientifically demonstrable, reality. In practice, its main interest is to develop machines, or handle machine-like things, by applying its theories to material objects.

Material Objects

It has the same approach towards human activities. The method applied to the study of material objects is also used, with necessary modifications, to frame scientific theories about human behaviour. An attempt is made, in the light of these theories, to control man as a naturally-built machine. Whatever aspects of human behaviour can be observed through sense perception are accepted as the data of human sciences, but the aspects which are not so observable are rejected or ignored as "unscientific." For example, man's creative experience of self, the visionary experience of a poet or a philosopher, and religious experience of a prophet or a saint are considered to be beyond the scope of scientific inquiry, and without any scientific content. Either their truth is altogether denied as a distortion and unreality as by the strictly materialist philosophy, *or* they are believed, as by the idealist philosophy, to imply a truth which is not scientifically demonstrable.

Modern philosophy, which has developed on the lines of modern science and claims to be "scientific in spirit basing its conclusions on facts rather than religious beliefs," does not fully recognise to be a "hand-maiden" of religion, it has become the interpreter of science. Its new job is to organise the results of various natural and social sciences in a picture of the world as a whole, not allowing any place of importance to religion. Based on "pure" science and pursuing a course independent of religion modern philosophy has been led to two distinct world outlooks, i.e. the dialectical materialist outlook and the Western idealist philosophy.

Materialist Philosophy

The dialectical materialist philosophy totally rejects the truth of religion and believes in the sense-oriented science like a religious faith. True to the materialist and mechanical spirit of science, it views the ultimate Reality as Matter in Motion, i.e., a big moving machine which can be scientifically studied and mechanically handled through human brain, itself a highly evolved matter. However, this big machine is not a single mechanical device, but consists of diverse mechanisms (i.e. motions of matter) which are qualitatively different from each other. These mechanisms, or "forms of motion", as they are called by this philosophy, are classified as mechanical, physical, chemical, biological and social—the quality of individuality missing in them because there is no room for it in a mechanical set-up. The term "dialectics" is used to associate the element of change and growth with motion, but this does not change the predominantly mechanical character of the material dialectics. A motion of matter, which is devoid of voluntary self or creative individuality, is necessarily mechanical and cannot be called dialectical in the true sense. The true dialectics must involve a creative factor, which alone can make forward movement and dynamic growth possible.

A mechanical motion is one which results from a specific mechanism, i.e., a specific collective arrangement or apparatus of material objects, and not from an inherent creative factor that may be controlling or moving material objects from within. Dialectical materialism is predominantly mechanical because although it recognises an element of growth and change in phenomena, yet it tries to interpret it to be the result of specific material conditions rather than an inherent creative factor that may be moving the matter from within. It denies that the element of change and growth can be injected into the material motion only through a creative will. For example, it believes that a social movement or revolution is caused by a specific mode of material (economic) conditions and not by the creative will and consciousness of an individual or a group, or by the religious awakening of a people. No doubt, man's will and consciousness are also said to play a role in the social revolution, but this role is merely that of a superstructure, or a by-product, and not that of a prime mover of the revolution. Even a prophet's message is interpreted to be a by-product of material conditions rather than a revealed Word of God. The failure on the part of material dialectics to comprehend the creative role of will and consciousness is mainly due to an anti-religious prejudice, and the strictly materialistic outlook inherited from science. A socialist form of economic planning, which is the ultimate goal of this philosophy, may force the people to work like a machine, but it can never inspire them to be willing partners in social reconstruction unless it also recognises the creative and determining character of their will and consciousness.

Labour is believed, by the dialectical materialists, to be the prime mover of social dialectics, but the concept of labour is confined to the production of such material and "spiritual" (i.e., of the character of a mere superstructure or by-product) values as are needed for man's material, rather than his creative or religious survival. Moreover, the labour process of the production of material and "spiritual" values, according to this view, can be mechanically controlled through socialistic planning, and does not involve any creative or religious factor that may inspire the individuals to be selfless "co-workers" of God.

Believing that man basically strives to fulfil his material (metabolic-economic) needs dialectical materialism considers him selfish by nature, as also taught by modern science. That is why this philosophy is reluctant to give man's self the role of a free agent—an agent that can decide and direct its own course of action—thus, depriving it of any opportunity to usurp other's rights by its selfish pursuits. The only way to check man's materialist-selfish nature, according to this philosophy, is to make him work under a socialist mode of production where no room is left for self-seeking and exploitative activity and every individual is forced to work, willingly or unwillingly, for collective good. However, it is not quite correct to consider man as basically materialist and selfish "by nature". He can be made a selfless and willing participant in social reconstruction if his religious consciousness is also awakened and recognised as a reality. Having no vested interests to serve, the dialectical materialistic philosophy can very easily see through the religious truth if only it broadens its epistomological outlook to include the religious experience along with the sense perception.

Second World Outlook

The second world outlook, the Western idealist philosophy, does not outright reject the truth of religion like dialectical materialism, but it also bases its conclusions on scientific discoveries rather than religious beliefs. It does not give religion its due place in world outlook and accepts it, at the most, as mere ritualism or another worldly affair of human soul. And that too because religion, in such a position, can be used as an instrument of exploitation, and this philosophy has to serve the capitalist exploitative system by all means, scientific or unscientific.

The Western philosophy is idealistic in so far as it believes that it is man's consciousness and self that determine the course of events and not the course of events—the material conditions—that determine man's consciousness and self. But this idealism is not based on the creative or religious concept of man's self, according to which he is a selfless vicegerent of God on this earth or a spirited selfless worker. Instead, it is based on the narrow scientific concept of man's self which views him as selfish by nature—always running after his material gains and motivated merely by his animal-like instincts. According to this view, every individual has the right to work for his own benefit even at the cost of others' rights. Such a concept of self gives exploiting classes, as the dialectical materialists rightly allege, a free hand to exploit and the working classes a mental justification for being exploited. True idealism, based on the deeper anti-exploitative nature of man's self can, however, come only through religious consciousness. The Western philosophy remains blind to it partly because of its sense-oriented outlook and partly because of its exploitative interests. It never dares to probe into the revolutionary meanings of religion, which is against all exploitation, and tries to maintain it in its present distorted form. If at all "scientific" investigations are made into religious consciousness, they deal merely with the whereabouts of human soul after death and not with its requirements in this life, which is as real as life after death. The human soul, in these investigations is visualised to be a sort of non-observable material object rather than a directing force which "proceedeth from my Lord's *Amr*".

So the failure of the Western idealist philosophy to comprehend the true nature of "idealism", which should be based on a deeper concept of self, and the inability of dialectical materialism to realise the true nature of dialectics, which should also include the creative and religious aspect, is mainly because of their total allegiance to the sense-oriented science and disregard for religious truth. It is strange that while they claim to be based on facts and to be scientific in spirit they adopt a very unscientific attitude towards religion. They fail to recognise that the religious truth at its own level of experience, is quite scientific, although it may look unscientific, superhuman, supersensible, or even non-existent at the ordinary level of sense experience. "Religion is not physics or chemistry" says Iqbal, "....it really aims at interpreting a totally different region of human experience". The conflict between religion and science, he adds, "is due to the misapprehension that both interpret the same data of experience. We forget that religion aims at reaching the real significance of a special variety of human experience."

Total View

Although religion is a total view of Reality and not sectional and piecemeal like various sciences, yet it has all the characteristics of a scientifically true knowledge and can provide as scientific a world outlook as the modern philosophy claims to do—an outlook which is, however, epistemotogically wider than modern philosophy. Let us now briefly see how and why the religious truth can be called scientific.

The first characteristic of a science is that it is based on experience. And so is religion. As Iqbal writes: "Religion is essentially experience—known in this sense by the unfortunate name of mysticism and recognised the necessity of experience as its foundation long before science learnt to do so. It is as critical of its level of (religious) experience as naturalism (science) is of its own (sensory) level". But whereas science excludes religion from its limited view of reality, religion being an expression of the whole truth, does not reject science as a true form of knowledge and establishes the truth of sense perception as a part of man's total knowing self besides his religious faith.

The second characteristic of the scientific truth, based on sense perception is that it is communicable and verifiable. Being a special inner capacity of varying stages (the prophetic experience being the highest stage, unattainable by saints and ordinary individuals), religious experience also reveals a truth which can be communicated and verified. If that was not so, prophets and saints would never have been able to communicate their message and there would have been no individuals and communities following and verifying the truth of their message. The religious communities could not be organised on the basis of a mere blind faith. Religious experience, no doubt, is primarily subjective, but its contents can be made objective through words and deeds and verified to be true by others, according to their capacity.

The third characteristic of the scientific truth is that it can successfully be put into practice because it corresponds to the real nature of things. "The question whether objective truth can be attributed to human thinking," says Karl Marx, "is not a question of theory, but is a practical question. In practice, man must prove the truth of his thinking". The only proof of the truth of an idea a scientific theory or an ideology, according to modern philosophy, is provided in practice, i.e., the scientific experiment or the socio-political life of a people. Religion also, throughout the ages has proved its truth through practice i.e., the "pragmatic test," in the words of Doctor Muhammad Iqbal. How could religious communities exist till today, and their beliefs still inspire their individualist religion, being in accord with the true qualities of human nature, had not practically solved their various problems?

The fourth characteristic of a science is that it is a systematic knowledge organized on the basis of general principles about a particular section of natural phenomena as framed in the light of sense perception. Religious knowledge is also systematic, based on certain fundamental principles about the nature of man and universe and their relationship with God as revealed through religious experience. Not only is this knowledge systematic itself but, being revealed within, it has also the dialectical power to organise individuals and communities into well organised systems, which move from within creatively rather than mechanically. Man has not to apply religious knowledge like scientific theories, on external objects from outside but he applies it to himself from within; and the truth of religion is proved by its practical suitability for such an application to various aspects of man's life, individual, socio-political, economic, educational etc., etc.

Now let us examine unity and diversity of religions. All true religions have been proclaiming Oneness of God. From this viewpoint there is a basic unity in all true religions. They all have a common origin. Outwardly, there have been many differences in various religions, but inwardly they all have preached the same basic realities. Their names, details and rituals have varied over the ages but their essence has always remained unchanged.

There are only two basic religions in the world. The one is *Deen-e-Batil* (the False Religion) and the other is *Deen-e-Haq* (the True Religion). The false religion, in whatever form it may appear is man-made. The true religion has been revealed by God through His prophets in different ages and at different places. Right from Prophet Noah to Prophet Muhammad (peace be upon them all) all Apostles of God had preached this True Religion, which is characterised by two basic concepts: the Oneness of God and the Accountability of man for his actions in the life hereafter. Apparently one may ascribe different religions to the prophets who preached them. One may talk of the Religion of Abraham, of Moses, of Christianity, or of Muhammadanism, but in reality they are only different versions of the same True Religion.

Concept of Diversity

The concept of diversity of religions has been created by Western scholars. These people cannot think of various religions as creations of the prophets who preached them. They speak of prophets as 'founders' of their religions. Clearly, when one bases one's studies and observations upon superficial things, one loses sight of the common thread running through them all. This leads to the study of various religions as segregated from one another, with the result that when these scholars notice any point of similarity between two religions they hasten to conclude that the 'latter' religion has borrowed the idea from the 'former' religion. Naturally they notice similarities between the teachings of the Quran and the older Scriptures, and accuse the Prophet of Islam (peace be upon him) of having borrowed the various concepts from Christianity or Judaism or Zoroastrianism, and of composing the Holy Quran himself. They lose sight of the fact that all True Religions have basically preached the same two concepts: the Oneness of God and the Accountability of man for his actions. No prophet has ever declared to be 'founder' of his religion. All have declared that they are 'Messengers' of God and have come to remind the people of the two basic concepts. The Prophet Noah preached "Worship Allah, fear Him and follow me" (71:3). But the people replied: "(O comrades) do not forsake your idols" (71:23). The Prophet Hud delivered this message to his nation, the Aadites: "O my nation, worship Allah besides Whom there is no God, you are only putting forth false claims" (11:50). His people replied, "We shall not forsake our idols simply because you say so and we are not going to believe you". (11:52). The Prophet Saleh said to his people the Thamud, "O my nation, worship Allah besides Whom there is no God" (11:61). They replied, "Do you forbid us from worshipping those (idols) whom our forefathers have been worshipping, we have doubts about what you are calling us to believe" (11:62).

The Arguments

The Prophet Abraham said to his father and his nation, "In place of Allah do you worship these idols who can neither benefit nor harm you in any way. Damn you and those whom you worship besides Allah. Don't you see reason? (21:67). The people said, "Burn him down and support your idols" (21:68). This same true Religion was stressed by Abraham and Yaqub for their descendants, "O my children, this is the religion chosen by God for you, so do not die except as Muslims (sincere followers)" (2:1 32). The same lesson was taught by Prophet Joseph to his companions in prison, "O my co-prisoners, is it better to have so many gods or to have One All-Powerful God. Those besides Him whom you worship exist only in names coined by yourself or by your forefathers. God has not sent any authority for them. Power only belongs to Allah. He has ordered you not to worship anything except Him. This is the firm religion" (12:39-40). The Prophet Lot preached the same thing but was threatened by his people with banishment (26:167). Prophet Shoaib preached in Medina: "O my people, worship Allah besides Whom you have no god" (11:84). The people replied "O Shoaib, does your prayer order you to impel us to forsake our idols whom our ancestors have been worshipping" (11:87).

When Prophet Moses delivered his message to Pharaoh, he threatened, "If you talk of any god except me, I shall put you in prison" (26:29). Again when Jesus Christ came with explicit signs he said, "I have come to you with wisdom so that I may make clear to you the things in which you have been differing. So fear God and follow me. Allah is my Lord as well as yours, so worship Him only. This is the Right Path" (43:63-64). Last of all Prophet Muhammad (peace be upon him) was sent with the same message: "You (O Prophet) have been told the same things that Messengers before you were told" (41:43). And the teachings of Islam need no elaboration here. Islam is no man-made religion nor is it new. It has been in existence since the times of Noah. All prophets were Muslims (sincere servants of God). It is said of the *Shariah* of Muhammad (peace be upon him): "He has guided you to a *Shariah* (path) which was stressed by Noah; and what has been revealed to you, the same has been enjoined upon Abraham and Moses and Jesus, that uphold this religion and do not create differences in it" (42:13).

These were the prophets well-known to the Arabs. But the True Religion has been preached in all ages and all nations. "We sent a messenger to every nation that worship Allah and keep aloof from idols" (16:36). "And before you whosoever was sent as a Messenger was instructed with the same revelation that there is no god besides Me so worship Me only" (21:24-25). This message was delivered to all nations by their prophets unamended because "No man has the authority that when God gives him the Book and the Decision and prophethood that he should say to the people 'leave Allah aside and worship me:' rather he would always say, Be sincere worshippers of God as you read and learn and teach the Scriptures; neither would he order you to take the angels and the prophets as your gods; would he order you to disbelieve after you have become believers" (3:79-80).

All True Religions, One

It is quite clear that all True Religions are basically one. They are, so to say, only different editions of the same 'Book'. The last and the most comprehensive edition is Islam. That is why Islam always enjoins upon its followers to keep this Unity of religions in view and to believe in all prophets and Sacred Scriptures. "Say, we believe in God and in the Book sent down upon us and in whatever was sent down upon Abraham and Ismail and Ishaq and Yaqub and their descendants, and in whatever was given by God to Moses and to Jesus and to other prophets, we do not discriminate one from the other, and we are sincere servants of God" (3:84).

Now compare this broad-mindedness of Islam with other religions. "The Jews say 'Christians have nothing' and the Christians say 'the Jews have nothing' whereas both these groups read the Scriptures" (2:213) Say: "We believe in God and the Book sent down upon us" (3:84) fully quoted above. And they say:

> "None will enter paradise except those who are Jews or Christians" (2:111). In contrast with this narrow-mindedness Islam declares that every true religion ultimately leads to success. Indeed those who believe (in Islam) and those who turn Jews or Christians or Sabeans (etc.), among them whosoever believes in God and in the Hereafter and performs good acts, he shall find his reward with his Lord. These people will have nothing to fear, nor shall they feel sorrow" (2:62). Again, "Those who stick to their Scriptures and keep up prayers, so We shall not let the reward of the virtuous to go waste" (7:10). That is why Islam calls to itself and mankind, not because there is inherently any superiority of Islam over other religions but because Islam reminds the followers of other religions those basic teachings of all true religions which they

have lost sight of—be it due to passage of time, or be it due to the fact that their clergy have passed on to them the Divine message in a distorted form.

> "O People of the Book, come to a point common between you and us that we should not worship anything except God, that we should not make anything His partner, and that we should not take one another as our Lord except Allah, now if they turn away their faces, say: anyhow we are true believers" (3:64).

Final Settlement

The Prophet Muhammad (peace be upon him) was sent for this very purpose that he should settle down for ever the differences that had appeared in the True Religion over the centuries. "Call them to this very thing and be steadfast as you have been ordered. Do not go after the wishes of these people; rather say: I believe in the Book revealed by God. I have been ordered to do justice between you. Allah is our Lord as well as yours. We are responsible for our actions and you for yours. There is no dispute between you and us. Allah will bring us together one day and we have to return to Him" (42:15).

Islam, being the religion of all humanity, has been declared to be the only religion chosen by God (3:19). Here Islam is not just another name for Muhammedanism (as western scholars say), but it is the essence of all true religions. Its connotation is in its literal meaning of obedience and submission, and not as a technical term in the history of religions.

The Unity and continuity of the true religion is testified by the Holy Quran. "In the beginning people were one group. Then Allah sent the prophets as announcers of good tidings and as warners, and with them He sent True Book so that they may settle according to it those things in which people had created differences. These differences were created by none else than those very people who were given the Book and that too after they had received the clear orders, just out of mutual enmity. So Allah guided the believers towards that (Reality) about which the people had differences.

Verily Allah guides to the right path whomsoever He desires" (2:213).

Let us now see the points of diversity in various religions. Verses 2:213, 2:253, 3:18, 10:19, 10:98, 11:119, 23:51-53, 41:45, 45:17 and 98:4, of the Holy Quran throw much light on the reasons and philosophy of diversity in religion. True religion, as has been shown above, is one, and has continued and has been revived by the Prophets throughout the ages. Whenever people lost sight of the teachings of the True Religion, God sent a prophet to remind them of the Truth. The differences were created by the people themselves and not by the prophets. The Diversity among religions relates only to the details of law and rituals as dictated by the exegencies of time and place. They are only different versions of the same Divine Message; different editions of the same book, so to say. All prophets delivered the same basic message. Those who accepted their message were called believers, others were disbelievers. Thus, two basic groups were created. Later on, each group split up into various sects and creeds. Among Believers the rift was created by mutual prejudices and biases. Each group of scholars claimed to have the monopoly of understanding and teaching the Scriptures. Lust for popularity, power and material benefits led them to make changes in the World of God, omitting whatever was against their interests, adding whatever would add to their power over the people. Much the same happened among disbelievers. Various cults of worship sprang up. The number of gods kept on multiplying. Each tribe had its own set of idols. True religion—differences, reminders through prophets—the cycle was repeated throughout the centuries from the time of Noah to that of Muhammad (peace be upon him), when the Divine Message was preserved in its minutest details in the hearts of believers. Now that there was no longer any danger of change in the Divine Message there was no longer any need for sending a new prophet. The seal on prophethood was set with Muhammad (peace be upon him). The differences among the Muslim sects are only of a minor nature. There are no differences so far as basic teachings of Islam are concerned.

The root-cause of all diversity in religion has shown to be mutual enmity. Prejudices lead us away from the right path. We become prone to exaggerating defects of others and overlooking our own shortcomings. Distorted thinking leads us to revile others, leading to mutual enmity, hate, turmoil and even war. Any discrimination between the various forms of True Religion has been condemned by the Holy Quran. "Those who disbelieve in Allah and His Messengers and those who wish to create a gulf between Allah and His Apostles, and those who say: we believe in certain things and disbelieve others, and they seek to adopt a midway; in reality these people are disbelievers" (4: 150—152). This is because such people have fallen a prey to their biases, prejudices and self-interests. They accept what suits them, reject what does not suit them. The criterion for their acceptance or rejection of a religion is not based on principles but on personal likes and dislikes. They are led astray. Since all true religions seek to create in man healthy ways of thinking based on logical reasoning, therefore such rift-lovers have been called disbelievers.

Verse 11:19 of the Holy Quran says: "If your Lord had wished so He would have made all people one group; but they would go on creating differences except those on whom your Lord has shown mercy. He has created them for this". In another verse it is said: "The people were all one group in the beginning. Then they created differences, and if it had not been decreed by your Lord earlier, the matter in which they differ would have been settled once for all" (19:19). Now the question arises: if God hates discord why does He allow disputes to arise. He could nip the evil in the bud. The reply to this objection is given in verse 5:48, "If God had wished He could have made all people one *Ummah,* but He desires to test you in what He has given you, so try to excel one another in doing good". Differences provide food for thought. If all people follow the same path it would become stereotyped. There will be no opportunities for thinking and judging. Differences provide men with the occasions to think, in order to discriminate between right and wrong. Use of these faculties is the wisdom behind disputes. A second advantage of disputes is that they provide righteous people with opportunities to call the wrong-doers to the right path (22:67). A third advantage is given in verse 10:19. If every time God comes to settle disputes the human faculties of thinking and deciding will rust. That is why settling down of religious disputes has been put off till the Day of Judgement. (22:17). God has made clear the right and the wrong. All human beings are required to use their discriminating faculties in choosing the right path.

Despite the philosophy behind diversity, human beings have been ordered to shun creating differences. The Muslim *Ummah* has been ordered emphatically: "And be not like disbelievers who created differences in their religion and divided into various sects" (30:31-32). "Be not like those who created differences and began to differ even after explicit orders have come to them" (3:105). Positively, we have been ordered to remain united. "Hold fast together the rope of Allah and get not scattered" (3:103).

2

Concept of Religion

Primitive man lived in a world which he did not understand; he was surrounded by all sorts of dangers, many of which he could not see or comprehend; so it is no wonder that he jeared nature. When he did so and conceived them as being more powerful than he, it was only natural that he should attempt to obtain their goodwill and to get them to aid him, or at least not to injure him. Primitive man thus began to worship the objects of nature that impressed him most or that he feared most. If he lived in a country where the rays of the sun were welcome, it followed that he would worship the sun. If he lived near a volcano or great waterfall, primitive man would be impressed by it and worship it. The same would be true of any high mountain, large river, huge tree, great rock, or any animals which were feared, such as the tiger, lion, alligator, or any animal upon which man depended for food or raiment, such as the cow, bear, or buffalo. If the rain brought prosperity, it might be worshipped. On the contrary, the thunder, lightening, or tornado might be worshipped through fear. The sea and fire have been common objects of worship. At a later stage animals and other objects of nature were worshipped. This was not, however, the original type of nature worship but a later development of it.

Primitive man could not realize the full meaning of death, and could not think of the person who died as leaving this world entirely. He thought that the spirit must be simply leaving the body or going upon a journey, and that it was, therefore, apt to return. Dreams might have increased this belief in spirits; in fact, Spencer declared that belief in spirits came from dreams. This conception of death, supplemented by dreams, led primitive man to believe that the spirit was able to leave the body and the dwell at a distance from it, or upon death to come back and perhaps enter into some object of nature, as a tree or animal, or to return to his old hut.

Sometimes the savage would look upon this spirit as a friend and sometimes as an enemy, depending largely upon whether the person was liked or jeared in life. Efforts were made to appease the ill will or gain the goodwill of a spirit by means of prayers, offerings, praise, and even flattery.

Evolution of Religion

While many of these customs and actions seem strange to us, the theory is logical enough. The belief in spirits seems to have been almost universal, at least the belief that the spirit lived after the body was gone. Herbert Spencer, imagining that religion originated from this belief, worked out his famous "ghost theory" of the origin of religion. He suggested that a savage, because of overeating, or from some such cause, might have a dream, perhaps of going on some hunting expedition, and yet he told next morning by his wife or by someone else that he had not stirred from his hut, but had tossed about all night; that he might see his reflection in the pool of water; and that in this way he would come to the natural conclusion that he had a double, which could leave him at will, especially when he slept. From this belief in a double personality came ancestor worship. Animal and nature worship also originated in this way, according to Spencer, as a development of ancestor worship. In fact, Spencer attempted to show that all religions originated in this fashion. The theory was, of course, built upon too narrow a foundation, for while possibly some religions began in this manner, it is preposterous to assert that all religions were thus evolved. Ancestor worship still survives in many countries, most noticeably in China, simply because the people have not emerged as yet from this stage. In some countries it preceded nature worship, at least in certain forms, but as a rule ancestor worship came later, being an outgrowth of nature worship.

In fetish worship, an object is idolized because it is supposed to be the residence of a spirit or god. In this way any striking object of nature or any unusual object might be worshipped; it might be carried around as a kind of talisman. This type of religion might be called a combination of the preceding two; it is an outgrowth of them.

Worship of Supreme

The worship of a supreme, all-powerful being was sometimes found among primitive men. This at first took the form of polytheism, or the worship of several gods, but it gradually changed to monotheism through the calling out of the minor or less important gods. Sometimes this supreme being was merely a mountain, a tree or the sun, but it stood out as supreme over other deities. Gradually, this belief became loftier and purer, the worship of the lesser divinities being abandoned. This gave the foundation for the highest form of religion.

When a savage looked upon a god as a person, he naturally thought that the god needed food and other necessities of life; so he offered them. Sometimes these sacrifices were destroyed entirely. In countries where cannibalism was, or had been, practised these sacrifices might take the form of human beings, generally slaves or children. Hindu mothers even today frequently throw their babies into the Ganges as offerings. The early Greeks before starting upon a great expedition would sacrifice a beautiful girl, and the Spartans allowed their children to be flogged to death before the temple of Diana. The sacrifice of animals succeeded human sacrifice. In this way, especially among the Jews sacrifices took the nature of a sign of atonement for sins, or as a means of warding off punishment.

Concept of Prayer

Prayer is the logical attendant of sacrifices. It is the method of telling what is the object of making the sacrifice, it states the request that is made of the gods. Its importance increases with the rise of the religion.

Because of the religious association, objects connected with worship attain an air of sacredness, especially the fetishes, temples and places of worship. Any object or ceremony or service connected with religion becomes invested with sacredness. This still continues, and at times has become more pronounced with the progress of religion.

Vitally, related to and infinitely confused with early religion was magic. Professor Thomas takes that magic with the savage is of higher importance than religion. In nearly every tribe there was some person or persons similar to the witch doctor or the medicine men of the American Indians, whose function was to interpret signs, foretell the future, exercise power over the spirits, either in warding off calamity or in bringing things desired, cure the sick, and do those things which were beyond the power of the average man. As the religion became elevated, it gradually purged itself of these impurities, although most religions are not yet entirely clear of them.

Formerly, religion was of greater social importance than it is today; it absorbed more of the life of the savage. The gods had to be consulted before any important event took place, even after the state of savagery was passed. The Romans would never undertake any war or military expedition or engage in any battle unless the signs were favourable. The king or chief was also high priest at first, and in that stage church and state were one; it was not until very recent times that they became separated particularly in Christianity. Religious dances formed an important feature in religion. Religious feasts were held in times of harvest, and on other special occasions.

The moral effect of religion was chiefly in the way of producing tribal solidarity, and in restraining the tendencies to excess. It would tolerate those things which were of help to the tribe, and forbid those things which were injurious. It developed tribal loyalty, obedience to the chief, observance of tribal customs, and submergence of individual interests to tribal interests. In practice it acted as a strong conservative force, checking and discouraging individual initiative and independence. On the other hand, it was a hinderance to reform and gave little chance for original thinking; in fact it discouraged it. While the primitive religion held the individual from excess, it often was an impediment to progress.

Of the three seats of early culture, Chaldea (or Early Babylon), Egypt, and China, Chaldea was in all probability not only the earliest but the centre from which the other two spread out. The Hebrews, borrowed heavily from Early Babylon, the Jewish Legal Code being traced back in many particulars to the Code of Hammurabi, which antedated the laws of Jews by many centuries. The people of Early Babylon were cosmopolitan; in fact, Hammurabi, the first great king, ruled a collection of many peoples, who spoke many tongues. As a consequence their religion was not a pure religion but a mixture of many beliefs. There was a belief in spirits; the world was thought to be full of such spirits, which could be controlled only by means of charms and magic. These spirits were supposed to be responsible for all pains and disease as well as misfortune. Nature worship was also interwoven into the spirit worship. There was a vast number of gods, both great and minor. Most of the gods were represented by animal emblems. The religion was too complicated to develop into a real state religion. When Babylon was absorbed into the Persian Empire, it lost its religion, which was not sufficiently developed to survive.

Earliest Religion

The earliest religion which we find in Egypt was the resultant of many still earlier religions. It contained remnants of animal worship, particularly the ibis, cow and cat, and by the fact that those animals were sacred in the provinces in which they were worshipped. Alongside of this was the worship of higher gods, such as the sun, moon and sky. Chief among these gods was *Ra,* meaning "sun". There was a family of gods similar to the Greek family of gods, consisting of *Osiris,* the sun god of *Abydos,* his wife and sister, *Isis,* and brother, Set. While *Osiris* was the embodiment of height and purity, *Set* was supposed to represent the opposite; he was the embodiment of all evil, particularly the desert, darkness, the hot south wind, sickness, and, what seems strange to us, red hair. Between *Osiris* and *Set* there was constant hostility, and we have the story *of* the death of *Osiris,* the search for the body of *Iris,* and the avenging of the death *of* the son, *Horus.* Egyptian religion approached monotheism through the survival of the stronger gods and the predominance of one god in each city or province. Egyptian temples were residences of the gods, rather than places of worship, images being placed in the temples so that the gods might enter them. The worship of the gods was celebrated being a public rather than a private function. Egyptian religion included a belief in future existence. The pyramids were erected as tombs for the kings. The belief was that the soul accompanied the sun god to the underworld, where its lot depended upon how its possessor had lived or had treated the god during life. While Egyptian religion was an advance over what had preceded, it showed possibilities of becoming a pure spiritual faith, and embodied in it many ideas of correct living and of duty to neighbours, it became degenerate and corrupt with the decay of Egyptian civilization and the crumbling of that nation as a political state.

However, both the Babylonian and Egyptian cults show how religions develop through the coming together of many religions. The Babylonian and Egyptian religions were too cold and formal to become great, although they exerted some influence upon the development of other religious beliefs.

Greek Religions

The religion of Greece passed through the same stages as other religions; however, because of the high state of culture attained, the rapid growth of civilization, and the favourable environment, which stimulated the imagination and the philosophical and religious development, it developed much more rapidly than the religions of other countries. While nature and spirit worship at a certain stage existed in Greece, they were early abandoned. The gods were functional gods and had distinctly human attributes; they had not only human bodies but even human passions; they hated, loved, were jealous, and even stole like human beings, despite the belief that they were endowed with super-human powers. The Greek gods formed a family, Zeus being the father and Hera the mother. The Athenians after establishing a vast number of temples and shrines, erected one to the "unknown god" for the fear that they had omitted one. Each city had its patron god or goddess; also each divinity represented a particular function.

With Greek religion went a belief in a future world inhabited by spirits who received rewards or punishments, particularly the latter. Perhaps the greatest effect of Greek religion was the inspiration it gave to art, specially sculpture and poetry. The religious festivals and games offered an incentive to physical development. While the gods were supposed to be guardians of justice, righting wrongs and meeting out punishments, and in this way to hold men in restraint, the moral effect was almost negligible, for the gods represented the prevailing standards of morals. The Greek religion did not hold out a goal to be attained, such as the Nirvana of Buddhism or the Heaven of Christianity which easily supplanted the Greek religion when the early Christian apostles preached the new faith.

Roman Religion

Rome offers perhaps the best example of the survival of the fittest in regard to religion. Early Roman religion was animistic, the nature spirits were worshipped or appealed to; sacrifices and worship was given in exchange for protection and help as it was bargain or contract, not a feeling of love. There was the worship of *Lares,* or household gods, who were the spirits of the ancestors. This led to the introduction of the worship of defied persons, like *Romulus* and later *Julius Caesar*. Roman religion became a part of the state, no war or enterprise being undertaken without consulting the gods and then not carried out unless the omens were favourable.

The religion was so complicated that it required a priestly class to interpret the will of the gods or the wishes of the spirits. However, the Romans took over almost entirely the Greek worships, especially their conception of the gods, only giving the Greek gods and goddesses Latin names, and carried out their worship to such an extent that many people think of the Roman religion merely as an outgrowth of Greek religion.

However, through competition the best elements of the different religions survived until finally Islam emerged not only as a religion but as a beacon light to humanity. Prior to that a stage had come when Christianity became the dominant religion; increasing in force after the fall of Rome as a world power, it became incorporated into the state and ruled Europe for a long time through the Catholic Church, which later split into the Roman and Greek Catholic Churches.

While there are many religions in the world, five stand out above all others, not only in the number of adherents but in their social influence. To complete this study of the evolution of religion, we must discuss the essential features of Confucianism, Brahmanism, Buddhism, Christianity and Islam.

Chinese Religion

The most influential of the three religions of China—Confucianism, Taoism, and Buddhism—Confucianism is an integral part of Chinese civilization, which has been looking backward for centuries. While named after Confucius, a Chinese sage and philosopher who is supposed to have lived from 550 to 478 B.C., it antedated him by many centuries, for Confucius was chiefly a collector and preserver of the wisdom of the past, although he did add somewhat to it. He collected this knowledge and handed it down in written form, of which there are now preserved five or six books. To those books is added a second set of classics edited by disciples of Confucius, especially Mencius, which are supposed to contain teachings of Confucius. The worship of Confucius himself is the chief addition to the worship of the time prior to him. Confucianism in reality is not much of a religion according to the general conception of religion, being more a system of philosophy. There is nothing cruel or revolting or degrading in the worship, no mythology, no idols, no priestly class. Everything is dignified and well arranged. It is essentially a religion of form, in which doctrine counts for very little and action is not governed by any code of ethics. The main thing is to do the proper thing at the proper time in the proper way.

The objects of worship are of three classes :

(a) heaven, the principal Chinese deity, by which is meant the sky—the blue air—which is conceived of as a living force, and worshipped for itself and not as the residence of some other power;

(b) the spirits, all good, generally spoken of in the plural sense, there being one for each object of nature, and conceived of, not as moving around, but as being organized into a priesthood, and worshipped in a body;

(c) ancestors, the worship of whom is the prescribed working religion of each individual. Belief in the future world is centred in the idea of the continuation of the family; it is thought to be the duty of everybody to marry and rear descendants in order to carry on this worship. Tablets are placed in the home to the memory of these ancestors; and to these tablets the spirits of the ancestors are supposed to come when properly invoked. The emperor must sacrifice to all the emperors who preceded him, and the magistrates to all who have held the office before them. This homage is given, not for the sake of peace or aid, but because of gratitude and devotion. The person offering sacrifices prays to be worthy of offering them. There is no self humiliation, for the Chinese take their religion complacently.

Under Confucianism religion is not separated from daily life; it is a ritual fixed by tradition and carried out by custom and habit. As taught by Confucius religion becomes a theory of government and morals. In the way of social influence Confucianism is largely responsible for the complacence of the Chinese; it was one of the causes of the backwardness of China in the past. Closely akin to Confucianism is Taoism, a cult founded by Lao-Tsze, which in its early days consisted by a higher code of morals and self-discipline than Confucianism. It degenerated, however, into magic and, while it later borrowed the apparatus of religion from Buddhism and became recognized, it has never obtained a vital hold upon the people. Confucianism never grappled with the social problems of the day or attempted to reform things; it has merely tried to hold them as they were. Its effect has been to keep its adherents from advancing. Unlike many religions it has not degenerated or become corrupt, but has remained much the same as it was two thousand years ago.

Vedic Religion

One of the old religions is Brahmanism. It is the direct outgrowth of the anterior Vedic religion, which was brought into India by her conquerors. The Vedic religion was an advance over the previous faith of Babylon, but was a combination of spirit and nature worship. Upon this Vedic faith was based Brahmanism, which cast aside the old ideas of nature worship in favour of an inward subjective religious attitude. New gods were introduced, chief of whom is *Brahma*—the creator, *Vishnu*—the preserver and *Siva*—the destroyer. The conception of *Brahma* is not only an external deity, but is also present in one's own experience. Brahmanism teaches that service to religion is done by getting away from mankind, by isolation and separation of self from the sin of the world. There is no distinction between good and bad deeds, for to be holy one must keep clear from all that degrades or confuses. Salvation is a matter of individual concern, there being no desire to spread the light or to save others. Religion is gained through isolation, to be holy one must be alone.

Connected with Brahmanism are sacred books, including the sacred Vedic literature, supposedly inspired writings, hymns, treatises and law books; there are also the famous laws of Manu, compiled about 2000 B.C., a collection of rules designated to govern the entire Hindu population. There is also required of the Brahmans a complicated system of sacrifices, which have become a matter of form. The social effects have been great, but since only the individual is concerned, group morality has not been fostered. Brahmanism has not attempted to relieve the sufferings of the people or lay hold of the problems of society. It has allowed the people of India to live in poverty and misery; it has made no attempt to break down the caste system, but on the contrary has upheld it and encouraged it, because the priestly class are on top of the social pyramid. Neither it has attempted to elevate the position of woman; it has held her down. These failures indicate its great weakness, because a religion to be successful must aid humanity. Brahmanism has simply not done it. Its key-note is isolation and self-salvation. It has, however, paved the way for Buddhism, which was an outgrowth of it and which is the culmination of Indian religions.

Buddhism was originated in India but it has flourished as a religion in China, Japan, Tibet, Java, Sumatra, Siam (Thailand), Burmah and Ceylon (Sri-Lanka) and is divided into northern and southern branches. While considered a revolt from Brahmanism, it is simply the evolution of Brahmanism into a higher form.

Buddhism

Buddhism is a religion without a god, without prayer, without a priesthood, without worship. It is a religion which owes its success not to its theology or to its ritual, for it has neither, but to its moral sentiment and to its external organization. The term "Buddha" means the Enlightened One or the Enlightened; there were supposed to have been twenty-four of these Enlightened Ones before Gautama, the founder of Buddhism, appeared. They were human but were supposed to have reached a super-human condition by passing through periods of renunciation and of compassion for man's suffering and to have entered human life and borne the burden of man's sufferings. It is not negative like Brahmanism, but positive and constructive. One achieves happiness through a life of right living; thus the religion has an extremely high code of morals and ethics. It offers Nirvana, a place of liberation and freedom, which one can reach even before death. The way of reaching it is by a life of self-renunciation and by suppression of the desires and passions. Under Buddhist morality, which includes equality towards all and respect for all living beings, are five rules of righteousness, which resemble the ten commandments; they are binding on all followers of Buddha. They are:

(1) not to kill any living being;

(2) not to take that which is not given;

(3) to refrain from adultery;

(4) to speak no untruth; and

(5) to abstain from all intoxicating liquors.

Devout members and the following:

(1) not to eat after mid-day;

(2) not to be present at dancing, singing, the playing of music, or acting;

(3) not to use wreaths, ointments, scents, or personal ornaments;

(4) not to use a high or broad bed, and

(5) to possess no silver or gold.

Because there is no god, prayers, sacrifices and priests are not necessary. Man must save himself by his own efforts. While under Buddhism there are no priests, there are wanderers who leave home and travel about, teaching and practising the religion. They resemble the monks and friars of the Catholic Church.

Buddhism became marvelously popular because of its simplicity, morality and broad humanity. But because of its openness and freedom it has degenerated, becoming contaminated with magic and superstition in every land where it has gone. It was too lofty to be appreciated, and therefore was not suitable as a working religion to the people with whom it dealt. While a lofty religion, Buddhism even at its best is a sad religion, regarding human life as evil. While having deep compassion for the sufferings of man, it has taken no means of reforming the world, concerning itself only with winning individual adherents; so it has had little social effect, although it has not been reactionary as Brahmanism has been. On the whole, it is an exceedingly free religion, allowing its followers to worship as they see fit or not to worship at all.

Christianity

After discussing these religions, we focus our attention on Christianity. Any treatment of Christianity should be prefaced by one of Judaism, of which it is an outgrowth, but because of lack of space and general familiarity with the principles of Judaism—such a treatment may be omitted. At the time of the coming of Christ, Judaism had become hardened into mere formality and needed rejuvenation. Christianity fulfilled that need by replacing the religion of form by one of love.

When Christianity appeared, the world was in need of a higher religion, hence its rapid rise and influence. It, later, became hardened into too definite a system under the Roman and Greek Catholic Churches, and still later under many of the Protestant sects, perhaps most noticeably under the Puritans and the Church of England, but its constant trend is to throw off the control of individuals and the opinions of a few, and allow greater and greater individual freedom, especially in the Protestants denominations.

To sum up, Christianity is the religion proclaimed by Jesus Christ. Its principles are set forth in the New Testament, and its churches abound all over the world. Although Christianity has had a great influence on Western civilization, the West is finding it increasingly difficult to live up to her own Christian principles.

Islam

Islam, last of all the religions but by no means the least, came in the sixth century A.D. as the climax and the crowning glory of all the religions known to this world. It is the eternal source of light to the humanity which was still groping in pitch darkness. The dawn of Islam saw the rays of its light all over the globe like the rising sun and continued as an unending and ceaseless battle against want and hunger, ignorance and disease and a pleothora of problems with which humanity has always been suffering. It aims at establishing a Welfare State. It is a religio-political concept of State in which temporal and spiritual are not kept in water-tight-compartments. It is the very negation of the Christian dogma which preaches: Render unto Caesar the things that are Caesar's and render unto God the things that are God's. In Islam Caesar and God are not two separate entities. It is not torn by the dualism of state and church whose separation has been deemed an absolute dogma in Christianity. In Islam God and Universe, spirit and matter, church and state, are organic to each other. Man is not the citizen of a profane world to be renounced in the interest of a world of spirit situated elsewhere. To Islam matter is spirit, realizing itself in Space and Time. To sum up, unity of God and catholicity of Islam are the corner stones of this great religion which have made it universal for all times and climes spreading to each and every nook and corner of the world.

Muslim World

The followers of Islam constitute one-fifth of the entire human race. The Muslim world straddles over vast regions of the continents of Asia and Africa. This region has been the cradle of a large number of higher civilizations. Economically, its potential is great. Politically, it is "the great third of the world." And, to crown them all, it is the world of Islam— it is the upholder of a great ideology which is not merely a religion but a way of life.

For long Islam has been misunderstood and misinterpreted in the West. It is one of the most queer facts of history that despite West's strides in quest of knowledge and learning, despite the centuries of contact between the world of Islam and the West, Islam is perhaps the best known and the most misunderstood religion in the West.

However, it is a happy augury that now there are welcome moves to develop correct understanding between Islam and the West. This is a very pleasant mission indeed. But this is not possible without a proper understanding of the causes of conflict and distrust which have separated the two. Therefore, a sincere attempt should be made to find out the causes of the discontent, conflict and distrust of several centuries. If we succeed in doing so, new vistas of cooperation and concord will open up to the entire humanity, which in fact will be a great service to the humanity as well as to the religion.

3

The Eternal Religion

Islam is an Arabic word and like many Arabic words, has no single word equivalent in the English or any other language. As for the meaning of the word, it connotes profoundest security and, therefore, peace obtained through submission. And since such peace and security can be derived only through submission to the Will of God, it implies total Submission of God.

Such being the literal meaning of Islam, man's awareness of submission to God must not be dated as commencing with any particular era, philosopher, prophet or scripture. The Holy Quran itself clarified this beyond a shadow of doubt. All the prophets from Noah to Muhammad (peace be upon them) are the Messengers of God and therefore the prophets of True Religion *(Deen-i-Haq)*. Obviously, the best of media for learning the ways of such submission is the education imparted by those inspired from the Divine Source.

Islam for All Times

The reason why Orientalists and those we speak of as Muslims refer to Islam as the religion of the illustrious Prophet Muhammad (peace be upon him) is that he is the last in the lineage of the prophets, the Book revealed to him is the last revealed word of God, and his pattern of life is the only one worthy of being followed in practice, because far more is known about him than about any other prophet and therefore it can be said with authenticity that every act and deed of his is the matchless example of piety and righteousness. This finality, both of the Book and prophethood has established the fact beyond any shadow of doubt that Islam and Islam alone shows the Light of Allah to the entire humanity which has been groping in pitch darkness. Some great Western thinkers, for instance Thomas Carlyle in his *"Hero and Hero Worship"* looks upon the Prophet of Islam (peace be upon him) as his idea! of a true prophet and Islam equated with submission to God as the ideal religion. Goethe believed the same, though it is not on record that he subscribed to the same estimate of the Holy Prophet (peace be upon him). To his question: "If this be Islam, do we not all live in Islam?" Carlyle answers, " yet we that have any moral faith, we all live so." So much for the literal meaning of the word Islam, and it is this sense that the Quran and its Prophet (peace be upon him) use the word.

Having established the meaning of Islam, we proceed to the implication of the word submission. Submission is obedience-in-action. There is no such thing as believing in submission but no submitting in action. Ignorance of this simple logic—or wilful evasion of it—underlies the tragedy of those who pretend to be Muslims but just as the implications of Islam are ignored so also are those of being Muslim. The general belief conveniently developed is that if you recite the words " There is no god save Allah and Muhammad is the messenger of Allah" you are a Muslim, and you need trouble yourself no more about deeds or misdeeds, the fire of hell being now forbidden on you. There could be no greater mistake.

Oath of Allegiance

During the Holy Prophet's (peace be upon him) lifetime and for at least some decades after him, the recital of these words was no more than an equivalent to an oath of allegiance, and it was understood by the convert that having conceded and acknowledged the Holy Prophet's (peace be upon him) Divine-messenger status, the convert would do as the messenger bade him do. For instance, as long as the authority of the messenger was not acknowledged he could not reasonably expect one to demolish one's idols, but once that authority was acknowledged, his orders and counsels were acted upon in word and spirit in all matters. It was never taken for granted that having accepted the validity of his Messenger-of-Allah status there was no change required in deeds and practices. If it were otherwise his claim to prophethood would have been acknowledged by everyone the first day he made the announcement. On the contrary, we find that he is offered immense bribes of wealth, position, and beautiful women, if only he would let them continue to do as they wished to do. But this condition was not acceptable to him. The objective of his mission was not to get himself acknowledged but to get humanity do the right things.

But today, it is regrettable indeed, the Holy Quran, its arguments, words and spirit have all been modified to suit the conveniences of those having vested interests. The *'kalima'* has been given a technical significane, made a magical chanting and regard to the practice of the Holy Prophet's (peace be upon him) councils has been consigned to oblivion.

In not a single instance does the Holy Quran commend belief or acknowledgement of its Prophet (peace be upon him) without action. The words repeated again and again are:

"Those who believe and do good work, for them are gardens below which rivers flow...." Paradise is never held out to those who merely believe or recite *'kalima'*.

"Forgiveness" says the Holy Quran is incumbent on Allah only towards those why do evil in ignorance and then turn quickly in repentence to Allah. These are the ones toward whom Allah relenteth. Allah is ever Knower, Wise. Forgiveness is not for those who do ill deeds until when death attends one of them, he says I repent (4:17-18). "He who does wrong will have the recompense thereof and he will not find against Allah any protecting friend or helper. And who does good works, whether male or female and is a believer, such will enter paradise" (4: 123-124). "For those who do good is the best reward and more thereto. Neither ignominy nor dust cometh near their faces. Such are rightful owners of the garden" (10:26).

That a believer is not necessarily a Muslim the Holy Quran clarifies:

> "O you who believe; observe your duty to Allah with right observance and do not die save as Muslims: (4: 102). Here the Holy Quran is directly addressing those who already believe, not disbelievers, in the Messenger-of-God status of the Holy Prophet (peace be upon him) telling them that such belief or acknowledgement is not necessarily to be equated with Islam. To be Islamic they shall have to be performers of submission to God even unto death; Again the Prophets Ibrahim and Yaqub (peace be upon them) are quoted as advising their sons not to die except as performers of submission (2: I 32). The sons of Ibrahim and grandson Yaqub and the latter's many sons were always believers in the unity of God and the messengership of their prophet-fathers, yet their belief or assumption was not enough. What was still required and would be constantly and always required was submission-in-action. The advice quoted was a reminder to them and is to all others.

Not Mere Belief

It is clear that mere belief is not looked upon by the Holy Quran as qualifying one to the status of being Muslim. There is a good reason for this. Belief unaccompanied by action can be very deceptive, a person may think quite sincerely that he believes while he really does not believe. True, genuine belief is a state of the mind that firmly grips the substrata and conscious levels of it. When belief comes into total possession, it becomes impossible for the mind so possessed to do anything but what the belief directs. The validity of belief can be tested only by deeds. If the deeds are not right, the belief too is not right. People who assume that though they are habitual sinners, they do have *Iman,* only victims of self-deception. Faith and deeds cannot contradict one another.

There are not a few people today who observe the five daily prayers, fast and even perform *Haj.* At the same time, if they are Government servants, they live on bribe-accumulated wealth, even after retirement. Or, if in business, they may be smugglers, or landlords, and in *every* case live in violation of the Quranic injunctions in respect of *Riba*, their excuse being that since they perform the elementary prescribed rituals and offer contributions to various *mazars* (shrines), salvation is assured to them. Not content with the sins of their own bribes they try to bribe the souls of dead saints.

The Holy Prophet (peace be upon him) like the Quran, does not offer any assurance to mere observer of ritualistic prayers, fasting or pilgrimage *(Haj)* but he does guarantee paradise for him from whose preserves his modesty. He commends giving water to a thirsty dog, and declares that the acquisition of learning or keeping a night's watch at the frontier is better than many a night of prayers. All this is not to say that prayers, fasting or the Annual Pilgrimage to Makkah are valueless. They are of immense value but like priceless pearls, are fragile and quickly demolished by the stroke of wrong deeds. Helped by good deeds they are polished imbued with lustre and become meaningful. Deeds and rituals act and react on one another. Wrong deeds indicate that the rituals are not being effective.

Of course, there are levels of submission, surrender. Human nature being what it is, weaknesses being inherently compulsive, it is not to be expected that one may never stray off the straight and narrow path. God does not expect the same calibre of devotion, say, from a man of humble capacity and means with modest ambitions, of common pursuits and little learning as He does from one capable of high thinking and commanding greater resources and leisure. The level of Islam or Submission differs from man to man. Thus, the Holy Quran tells certain Bedouins who came to the Holy Prophet (peace be upon him) declaring they had *Iman* (faith):

> "Do not say that you have faith *(Iman)* because faith has not entered your hearts yet: but say rather: We have acknowledged with preliminary submission. Yet if you act in obedience to Allah and His Messenger, He will not withhold from you the reward of your deeds. Allah is Forgiving, Merciful."

And the Book goes on to define faith:

> "The full of faith are those only who believe in God and His Messenger and afterwards do not waver but strive with their wealth and their lives for the cause of God. Such are the sincere." (49:14-15).

The test of true faith, that is striving with one's wealth and even life. Money is the anvil on which *'Iman'* is hammered out.

On one occasion, while sitting in the company of his companions the Holy Prophet (peace be upon him) exclaimed:

> "Who is it that will carry out four behests?"

Abu Huraira said, "I will, O Messenger of Allah". Then the Holy Prophet (peace be upon him) grasped his hand and said:

> "If you are content with what you have, you will be rich. If you do good to your neighbours, you will be a *momin* (truly imbued with faith); and if you wish for others what you wish for yourself, you will be a Muslim. And do not laugh much, for too much laughter dulls a man's intellect."

Test of a Muslim

The Supreme Being in one instance tells us that the test of a man being a true Muslim is that he spends his wealth and his life according to the revealed commandments, and in the other, the Holy Prophet (peace be upon him) defines a Muslim as one who makes no difference between what he desires for himself and what he desires for his fellowmen. Salvation is elevated to a superordinary level namely doing to others what one would have others do to him. The highest submission is that of the Prophets (peace be upon him).

Just as doing good has levels, so has doing evil. There is the evil that God forgives. This is what might be called a slip. A man going along the *sirat-i-mustaqim,* the straight path, strays off but realising his error, returns immediately to it. Misdeeds that are planned and persisted in do not fall in the category of forgivable sins. Sins that are crimes which corrupt society victimise millions of human beings. A judge or police officer, for instance, who takes a bribe, primarily deprives someone of his right. This is the first wrong. But the fact that he sets an example for corruption, that he becomes an abettor in the economic inflation—to note but one result— thereby causing prices to rise and, consequently bringing hardship to the poor in short, becoming a corrupter of social conditions, the extent of his misdeed is surely not one that God overlooks.

Their professions have the sanctity of law behind them. But does the Holy Quran justify their activities? Does the Holy Quran justify or condemn profiteering? Does the Holy Prophet (peace be upon him) countenance the renting out of land or building property? Does the Holy Quran forbid turning any wealth into a commodity of circulation among the rich? It is permissible to market the free gifts of nature, pre-eminently land? Is exploiting labour Islamic? Is dividing humanity into wealth-based classes not against the words and spirit of the Holy Quran and the *Sunnah* of its Holy Prophet (peace be upon him)?

Finally, what then is our religion? The religion of wrong-doers is wrong-doing, not Islam. Such people take shelter behind the shield of the slogan that religion is a personal affair. In the present day world this has become the rule rather than the exception. You may claim to be a Muslim, well and good. But whether you offer your prayers or not, whether you observe fasting during *Ramazan* or not, whether you pay *Zakat* or not, whether you perform *Haj* or not, no one bothers. It is presumed to be your personal affair. None has a right to interfere in the personal affairs of others. This is the prevailing situation the world over. But has this the sanction of Islam? Nothing that the slogan: " Religion is a personal affair" is a creation of the anti-Islamic forces, let us examine this attitude in the light of Islamic teachings.

Liberal Religion

Contrary to the hostile propaganda Islam of all the religions of the world, is perhaps the most tolerant though not compromising religion. There is no compulsion in matters of faith is its basic proclamation of Human Rights. It not only proclaims the human right of freedom, but extends to all mankind the fullest freedom of thought, of action, of speech and expression. "Say, O people; Truth has reached you from your Lord, so whosoever seeks guidance, does so for his own benefit, and whosoever goes astray is himself responsible for it and I am not a supervisor on you" (10:108). Again, "Say, Truth is from your Lord, So whosoever wishes may believe and whosoever wishes may disbelieve." (18:29). Also, "Act as you please, verily Allah sees what you do" (41:40).

Islam preaches without being in the least coercive. It brings to light the inherent weak-spots in various systems of thought. It lays bare before our eyes the final outcome of the right or wrong ways of life. It distinguishes for us what is good and what is bad. It unfolds the mysteries of the universe and holds before our eyes a unified view of cosmos. It urges us to observe, to think to mediate to infer and to do justice to ourselves not deceiving ourselves by making false decisions knowingly not to be misled by biases, prejudices, self-interests.

Everything has been made as clear as day. Yet there is no compulsion. You choose the right path, well and good. You feel inclined to tread the wrong path? Well that is your own outlook and choice, Islam gives you the basic freedom. But please have the courage to declare your faith or your faithlessness. Be clear in your mind. Do not mix up things. Do not hesitate. Choose any system and stick to it. Own it boldly. Let there be no hypocrisy, no showing off, no lip-service, no contradiction in your thought and action.

But once you have exercised your option, your choice is automatically curtailed. You are bound to act in a specified way you have no option to claim to have certain faith and to disobey the injunctions of your faith. "Where God and His Apostle have decisively laid down (the course) in any matter, it does not behove a believer man or woman to act on their own sweet will in that matter" (33:36). This is for Muslims, for the Jews and the Christians a similar law has been laid down. "And whosoever does not decide (his affairs) according to what God has laid down, he is an unbeliever" (544: 5.47).

Here your choice is curtailed. Option is still there, but in one direction only. You may offer prayers night and day, but you cannot cut them down to less than five times a day. You may observe fasting for most of the year, but you cannot disregard fasting during the month of *Ramazan*. You may give away all your wealth to the poor and the needy, but you cannot withhold *Zakat*, if it is due from you. You may perform *Haj* as many times in your lifetimes as convenient, but you cannot forego it altogether if you are liable under *Shariah*. The option you see, is now on the positive constructive side only. There is no option on the negative, destructive or regressive side.

Practising your religion is no more your personal affair. It becomes a state affair as well. Now that practice of religion becomes partly a State affair, let us see how an Islamic State should deal with it. According to the Holy Quran, there are four classes of people to deal with by a State internally. First there are True Muslims, the *Mo'minin.* These are the people who have willingly accepted Islam as their religion and practice it faithfully out of a love for it. This class seldom causes any trouble to the State.

True Muslim

Next come the Muslims—ordinary Muslims who profess Islam mainly through inheritance to some extent consciously. Before preoccupied with worldly affairs, they often neglect to observe the injunctions of Islam meticulously, mostly because of their preoccupations, lassitude or heedlessness or even ignorance, with no intention of repudiating such injunctions. How should the State deal with them? Islam's preferred course seems to be educative rather than coercive. Islam believes in inner self-discipline more than an outer imposed discipline through legal measures.

The Holy Prophet (peace be upon him) is said to have expressed his indignation at those who do not fast in *Ramazan* by saying, "Were it not for children and the sick ones, I have an urge to set fire to those houses from which smoke rises during daytime in *Ramazan*". Imam Abu Hanifa has labelled those who give up their prayers intentionally as expelled from Islam. Similar expressions of wrath, indignation and dislike are met with against those who show laxity in the observance of Islamic injunctions. However, if non-observance of Islamic injunctions become massive and widespread and poses a threat to true religious thinking by setting up bad example for the masses, the State may take suitable steps to ensure that religious injunctions are followed faithfully or at least not flouted publicly. No punishment has been prescribed by the Holy Quran for drinking, but Hazrat Omar prescribed 80 lashes for drinking perhaps with a view to nipping the evil in the bud.

Thirdly there are the Hypocrites. These are a dangerous class. They follow no rules except the dictates of their self-interest. They claim to be Muslims not out of any love for Islam, but because of a likelihood of sharing the benefits accruing to the Muslims. Should tables turn on Muslims, they will not hesitate to join anti-Islamic and anti-State forces. For these the course to be followed by the State has been laid down in the Holy Quran. "O Prophet; fight against the infidels and the hypocrites and be stern with them". (66:9). Muslim history provides examples of tackling these people.

In the days of Caliph Abu Bakr (God be pleased with him), for example, some tribes made an open attempt to make the practice of religion a personal affair by refusing to pay *Zakat*. Hazrat Abu Bakr's keen foresight saw in this attitude a danger for the State and decided to wage a war against them disregarding their observance of prayers and other injunctions of Islam. This example provides a hint for an Islamic State to interfere in the so-called personal affairs of the Muslims to ensure that Islam is followed by the Muslims in its entirety and not piecemeal. But State intervention is warranted only when non-observance of Islamic injunctions becomes massive and widespread and poses a threat to Islam or State. Short of that the preferred course is one of educating the masses in religious teachings and setting right patterns of behaviour at the top levels of society from where they shall automatically percolate to the levels of the masses.

Fourthly, there are the minorities. As hinted earlier, they too are expected to follow faithfully their own religious injunctions. Islamic State can provide them help by proper legal administrative and organisational measures.

Holy Quran, the Guide

Islamic polity in modern times will always be guided and inspired by the teachings of the Holy Quran and by the sayings and traditions, acts and deeds of the greatest benefactor mankind has known, the Holy Prophet Muhammad (peace be upon him). Blessed by and chosen of God, his was a divine mission, one of lifting humanity from the depths of moral and spiritual degeneration and guiding its steps towards a new destiny, a new life of peace, equality and brotherhood. All world historians are agreed that there has been no revolution greater than the one the Holy Prophet (peace be upon him) brought about. If there has ever been a total revolution it was this. Unlike so many incomplete ideologies of later ages, it at once gave its followers moral elevation, economic emancipation and political freedom. It brought peace; it brought equality; it banished racism, it ended exploitation; and it founded a society which by its orderliness, discipline and progress dazzled the entire world. There is for the modern man the beautifully worded but largely ignored U.N. Charter. But Islam gave a much more comprehensive charter of human freedom some 1400 years ago and, what is more, unlike the present day got it fully implemented wherever it held sway. Islam has played a pioneering role in the evolution of human civilisation in the sense that it was the first to rise above the considerations of race, colour, language and ationality—problems that still afflict humanity—and did not just give a call but actually established a world brotherhood, based on its lofty ideals.

Islam, an Answer

It is no self-righteous claim that given its moderation and balanced approach, Islam provides an answer to the spiritual and material problems of 20th century society as well. Islam is not a static ideology. It is a dynamic force, forever evolving to meet the new demands of the times and guiding the faithful on the basis of its eternal, God-ordained principles. Nothing better illustrates the undiminished vitality of Islam than the creation of Pakistan itself and lately the revolution in Iran. Avoiding the extremes of the various isms in vogue today and steering a middle course, Islam alone can lead the world out of its present turmoils and act as a vehicle for the establishment of a new international order. This is acknowledged by some of the leading thinkers in the West too. After the failure of both outdated Capitalism and repressive Communism a disillusioned world is increasingly turning towards Islam in search of salvation. Witness the reawakening in the length and breadth of the Muslim belt and a new interest in and respect for the message of the Holy Quran among non-Muslims. The revival has most significantly coincided with the advent of the 15th century of Hijra which, according to tradition, is the century that will see the final triumph of Islam. At this juncture in history, clearly a special responsibility devolves on us Muslims. We have to act as the vanguard of the coming revolution and it is only fit that we prepare ourselves suitably to play our ordained role.

No doubt, some preliminary measures towards uniting the Muslim *Ummah* and realising its hidden potential have been taken, but the fast changing times demand of us to make still greater efforts. There is need to bring together the disparate Muslim countries into an unbreakable bond of politico-economic unity; there is need to create a new machinery for the united defence of the Muslim lands; there is need to achieve greater diplomatic co-ordination for the attainment of common goals. Above all, there is need to hold fast to Islam and revert to its spiritual and moral basis, for recording our individual and collective lives, but once made Muslims an irresistible force in Africa, Asia and Europe. Needless to say, it is only by reviving the spirit of early Islam that Muslims can win back their lost glory and the leadership of mankind Almighty Allah has promised them. This we can do by bringing about a revolution in our minds, in our thinking and attitudes, in the light of the eternal teachings of Islam and the Holy Quran.

In modern times when territorial nationalism is the order of the day and material and economic considerations almost wholly shape people's outlook and policies, what is unique about the Islamic polity is the fact that it is the triumph of an ethical concept and a cultural ideal. In this context, it should be kept uppermost in the mind that Islam is not merely a religion in its narrow import. It is not a set of dogmas, mythological beliefs or mere rituals. It does not divide life into watertight compartments. There is no dichotomy in Islam between the temporal and spiritual; the structure of Islam is essentially religio-political. In this system the state forms an integral part at the apex and as Allama Iqbal points out "is only an effort to realise the spiritual in human organisation". Lectures on *Reconstruction of Religious Thoughts in Islam,* (page 115). Thus, Islam presents the whole of reality to man and wants to give him guidance in every walk of life. It requires him to discriminate between the right and wrong and to accept a path because it is right and not because it is secular or non-secular. It attempts to bring the realities of this world in harmony with the ideals that provide security for this world and the Hereafter. It is a complete code of conduct. It is a way of life and a philosophy of life. It is a social, economic and political system. It is with this background that the tradition of Islam is considered a better ideal for the entire mankind than any other way of life, religion or ideology. As Toynbee aptly puts it: "In a world in which distance has been annihilated by the progress of Western technology, or in which the Western way of life is having to compete with the Russian way of life for the allegiance of all mankind, the Islamic tradition of the brotherhood of man would seem to be a better ideal for meeting the social needs of the times than the Western tradition" (Arnold J Toynbee: The *World and the West,* section: Islam and the West).

4

Basic Philosophy

The basic philosophy of Islam revolves round a set of beliefs and concepts. The Unity of God, Prophethood and the Hereafter are the irreducible fundamentals of this creed. These concepts are rooted in the basic awareness of man and the realities of human experience.

Human awareness springs from a sense of being which is inherent to man and his comtemplation of the physical universe. The Quran dwells on the reality of human consciousness generated by an interaction of the inner self of man and the outer world of nature. Sura Zariyat states:

> "On earth, and in yourselves, there are signs for firm believers. Can you not see? Heaven holds your sustenance and all that you are promised. I swear by the Lord of heaven and earth that this is true, as true as you are speaking now" (51:20-23).

The cardinal beliefs of Islam are not figments of imagination made sacrosanct by supernatural sanctions but emanate from deeper levels of human thought and experience.

As man delves into his own self and contemplates about his whereabouts he is irresistibly drawn towards four basic realisations which point to the reality of God. The universe is a vast mechanism of infinite complexity but it is perfectly ordered and regulated. Man has a limited vision and potentialities.

Understanding the Faith

There are many areas of life and dimensions of the universe which defy his understanding. Man cannot comprehend the universe as a whole, much less control it. Sura Yunus states: "The unbelievers ask: Why has no sign been given him by his Lord? Say: Allah alone has knowledge of what is hidden. What if you will: I too am waiting. It is he who guides you by land and sea. You embark and as you set sail, rejoicing in a favourable wind, a raging tempest overtakes you. Billows surge upon you from every side and you fear that you are encompassed by death. You pray to Allah with all fervour. Deliver us from this peril and we will be truly thankful. Yet when he has delivered you, you commit evil in the land and act unjustly. Men, it is your own souls that you are corrupting" (10: 20-23).

Beneath the complex exterior of the universe lies a design, a pattern, a system. The Quran dilates on the impeccable order of the universe as a sign of divine being who presides over it. This is described being who presides over it. This is described as Hikmat Sura Yasin says:

> "Let the once-dead earth be a sign to them. We gave it life and from it produced grain for their sustenance. We planted it with the palm and the vine and watered it with gushing springs, so that men might feed on its fruit. It was not their hands which made all this. Should they not give thanks?

The night is another sign for men from the night We lifted the day—and they are plunged in darkness.

The sun hastens to its resting place: its course is laid for it by the Mighty One, the All-Knowing, We have ordained phases for the moon, which daily wanes and in the end appears like a bent and withered twig.

The Sun is not allowed to overtake the moon, nor does the night outpace the day. Each in its own orbits runs" (36: 36-43).

The Universe provides for man and caters to his purposes and requirements. This fact is epitomised by the Quranic term *Raboobiyat* *Sura Qaf* cogently states:

> "We spread out the earth and set upon it immovable mountains. We brought forth in it all kinds of delectable plants. A lesson and an admonition to penitent men. We send down blessed water from the sky with which We bring forth gardens and the harvest grain, and tall palm trees laden with clusters of dates, a sustenance for men; thereby giving new life to some dead land. Such shall be the Resurrection." (50: 7-11).

The universe holds out many benefits to man which are not accidental but form part of the cosmic design. This aspect of universal experience is embodied in the Quranic term *Naymat.* The mercy of God who has made the universe as the abode of man is not only unlimited but also continuous. The boundless mercy and munificence of God is described as *Rehman* while its continuity and timelessness as *Rahim. Sura Waqiah* states:

> You surely know of the first creation. Why, then do you not reflect? Consider the seeds you grow. Is it you that give them growth or We? If We pleased We could turn your harvest into chaff.

Consider the water that you drink. Was it you that poured it from the cloud or We? if We pleased We could turn it bitter. Why then do you not give thanks?

Observe the fire which you light. Is it you that create its wood or We? We have made it a reminder for man (56: 58—74).

The awareness generated by human contemplation of the universe underpins the reality of God. Deep down the recesses of human psyche lies the evidence of a reality higher than man himself. The objective universe offers many hints and clues for the existence of a mighty power.

The concept of Prophethood flows from the concept of God with irresistible logic. God, who is the creator and sustainer of man enjoins upon him a certain way of life. The values and principles of life which God has framed for the salvation of man are communicated through revelation. The prophets are the messengers of God and teachers among men. They convey by word and deed the infallible message of God. The message of God was conveyed to man gradually. Islam marked the perfection of Divine communication and its apostle Muhammad (peace be upon him); embodied the finality of prophethood.

Although the fundamental beliefs of Islam are rooted in the introspective reaches of human personality and the many splendoured reality of physical universe, there are many queries and questions which agitate the mind and require a satisfactory answer. The prophets disabused the minds of men of erratic beliefs and mistaken notions. Apart from this, history bears proof of many societies which were so sunk in abysmal ignorance and superstition as to disallow any opportunities of contemplation. The prophets admonished such people to the right path and exposed their misconceptions.

Reality of God

The prophets drew the attention of ignorant and confused men to the reality of God and offered for human weal a full-fledged system of life. They were not day-dreamers but men of action who braved with courage and steadfastness the opposition of the uninformed. They were dynamic persons who changed the destiny of man by conviction and consistency. They were not closeted away from the ordeal and challenge which their environment posed. The prophets brought despairing men a message of hope and infused them with a noble purpose. Sura *Araf* states:

> Whenever, there come to you apostles from amongst you rehearsing my signs unto you. Those who follow them will be rewarded and those who reject them will be punished.

Sura Mujadala bears out the dignity and stature of the prophets:

> Believers, when you converse in private, do not speak with wickedness and enmity and disobedience towards the apostle, but with justice and piety. Have fear of Allah before whom you shall be brought together. Believers, when you confer with the apostle, give alms before such conference. That is best and purest for you. But if you lack the means, know that Allah is forgiving and merciful. (58:9-10).

How would the prophets be recognised? The Quran states that the first man on earth was a prophet, therefore, he needed no proof of himself. Thereafter, every prophet foretold the signs of his successor. Jesus told his people that he was the messenger of God as proclaimed to them by Moses. The Bible contained many hints and references about the advent of the Prophet (peace be upon him). The chapter of New Testament captioned Matthew makes many statements about the prophet who would follow Jesus. Prophesy reached its perfection and came to fulfilment in Muhammad (peace be upon him).

Triumph of God

The Quran guarantees the triumph of good represented by Prophet (peace be upon him) over evil embodied in ignorant persons whom he confronts with the divine message. The prophets over-came by faith in God and personal resilience the storm of opposition raised by vested interest they sought to abolish. Those who persisted in evil despite the warning and admonition of apostle were exterminated from the face of earth by natural calamity. The Quran is unambiguous on this fact.

Those that oppose Allah and His Apostle shall be brought low as have been before them. We have sent down clear revelations. A shameful punishment awaits the unbelievers.

Do you see those that have befriended people with whom Allah is angry? They belong neither to you nor to them. They knowingly swear to falsehood. Allah has prepared for them a grievous scourage. Evil indeed is that which they have done. They use their faith as a disguise and debar others from the path of Allah. A shameful scourage awaits them (58.5: 14— 16).

Akhrat (Hereafter) is another cardinal concept of Islam. It has a basis in sound human experience. Man has limitless desires and aspiration. His self craves for the infinite. He has a natural urge to transcend the confines of time and space and rise above the transitoriness of life. The belief in *Akhrat* fulfils human promptings for and eternal life; it provides a point of certainty in flux and unending change.

Secondly, human beings live in communities. Social life entails a system of rights and responsibilities. No society exists in a perfect form. Here men are being deprived of fundamental rights and there responsibilities are being shrugged aside. Exploitation of man by man is a fact of life. The short span of life and human ways of doing things preclude the possibility of dispensing perfect justice. How can a person responsible for massacre be punished in this life? These facts provide a rational basis for belief in the Hereafter.

Bounty of God

Picking up threads from the concept of God discussed above, emphasis was laid on the bounty of God. If God has offered men certain benefits and previleges, why should man not be accountable for it? *Sura Naba* recounts the gardens of luxurious growth given to man and draws attention to the day of sorting out. The Quran dwells on the concept of *Akhrat* at great length:

About what are they asking?

About the fateful tidings—the theme of their disputes.

But they shall know the truth; before long they shall know it.

Did we not spread the earth like a bed and raise the mountains like pillars?

We created you in pairs and gave you rest in sleep.

We made the night a mantle, and ordained the day for work. We built above you seven mighty heavens and placed in them a shining lamp. We sent down abundant water from the clouds, bringing forth grain and varied plants, and gardens thick with foliage.

Fixed is the Day of Judgement. On that day the Trumpet shall be sounded and you shall come in multitudes. The gates of heaven shall swing open and the mountains shall pass away like vapour (78: 1-12).

The *al-Qiyamah* is variously described by the Quran as Day of Judgement, Day of Reckoning, Day of Sorting Out.

A rational interpretation of fundamental beliefs of Islam has been attempted. The Quran makes a cogent and convincing statement of how concepts like unity of God, Prophethood and the hereafter are rooted in human observation and experience. It rejects the view that religion is based on the instinct of fear latent in man and demonstrates that the roots of religious faith in positive aspects of human life.

Islam has made unique contributions to human civilisation; and among these is the concept of the dignity of man. According to the Holy Quran man is the noblest of God's creation, as it says; "Certainly, We created man in the best make". (95: 4). At another place the Holy Quran declares: "And surely We have honoured the children of Adam and We carry them in the land and the sea, and We provide them with good things, and We have made them to excel highly most of those whom We have created". (17: 70). Man was made Allah's vicegerent on earth, and he was destined to rule everything around him. The Holy Quran says: "And when thy Lord said to the angels, I am going to place in the earth one who shall rule in it". (2: 30).

The idea of man being the ruler of the universe is repeated in many verses of the Holy Book: "And He has made subservient to you whatsoever is in the heavens and whatsoever is in the earth, all, from Himself. (45: 13). "Allah is He Who made subservient to you the sea that the ships may glide therein by His Grace, and that you may give thanks". (45: 12). "He has made subservient to you the sun and the moon; each pursues its course till an appointed time". (31: 29). "And He has made subservient to you the night and the day and the sun and the moon. And the stars are made subservient by His command. Surely there are signs in this for a people who understand"(16:12).

According to Islam, man's position in nature was that of a conqueror. He was created to control all the forces of nature and to rule in the earth and not to bow before them. But man degraded himself to the utmost when started worshipping the earth, rivers, trees, fire, the sun and the moon and the stars, and all those objects of nature which were made subservient to him. He even worshipped unhewn stones, and sometimes carved out idols with his own hands and worshipped them as if they were Divine, or as if they controlled good or evil for him. As the Holy Quran says: "Do you worship that which you knew not? And Allah has created you and what you make" (37: 95-96). And as Abraham asked his Sire: "Why dost thou worship that which neither hears, nor sees, nor does it avail thee in the least" (19:42).

The gravest of sins, according to the Holy Quran is *Shirk* or associating others with Allah. This is not due to feeling of jealousy on the part of Allah, but because *Shirk* demoralises man, while Divine unity brings about his moral elevation. That is why Islam has laid so much emphasis on *Tauheed* or oneness of God, which is the most fundamental principle of the Islamic faith.

Man was endowed with vast capabilities for attaining knowledge. In the first place, he was given knowledge by Allah as the Holy Quran says: "And he gave Adam knowledge of all things" (2: 31). The Arabs were an illiterate people, and reading and writing was so rare among them that it may be said not to have existed at all. The Holy Prophet (peace be upon him), himself did not know reading and writing and is called Unlettered Prophet (peace be upon him), as stated in the Quran: "And thou didst not recite before it any book, nor didst thou transcribe one with thy right hand (29: 48). Yet the first Divine message received by him was about reading and writing. As the Quran says: Read in the name of thy Lord who created. Creates man from a clot. Read and thy Lord is most bounteous, Who taught to write with the pen. He taught man what he knew not". (96: 1-5).

Read and write, was thus His first message; and to these two means of gaining knowledge of things, the faculty of observation was also granted to man. The Holy Quran has repeatedly invited the attention of man to the creation of this universe and the various phenomena working around him. He asked to observe and reflect. To quote one instance from the Quran: "In the creation of the heavens and the earth and the alternation of the night and the day, there are surely signs for men of understanding. Those who remember Allah standing and sitting and (lying) on their sides and reflect on the creation of the heavens and the earth. Our Lord, thou hast not created this in vain"; (3: 189-90). The process of observing and reflecting convinces man that every thing made by God is perfect. He sees no incongruity in Allah's creation, and this naturally leads him to His glorification. "Glorify the name of the Lord, the Most High; Who creates things, then makes them complete: And who makes things according to a measure then guides them to their goal". (87: 1-3).

Man, before Islam, was at the lowest ebb of human civilisation.

He was just a slave of nature's forces. The Holy Prophet (peace be upon him) raised him to the dignity of the master and the ruler, and it was due to this realisation of man's position to the universe that the Muslims in their very early history took vigorous strides towards the expansion of knowledge and the advancement of the sciences. Reading and writing was within a few years spread throughout the whole of Arabia and other countries which came under the influence of Islam and the Muslim State so encouraged the pursuit of study and scientific research, that centres of learning and universities sprang up throughout the empire of Islam.

According to Islam, every child is born in a state of sinlessness; and it is afterwards in life, that a person becomes a Jew or a Christian or anything else by following the religion of his parents. The Holy Prophet (peace be upon him) said: "Every child that is born conforms to the true religion (Allah's *fitrat;* and it is his parents who make him a Jew or a Christian or a Magian" *(Bukhari,* 32: 79). Every child is, thus, recognised by birth to be a Muslim, and the purity of human nature is not affected by his being born of non-Muslim parents. The Holy Prophet (peace be upon him) once related a vision in which he had seen the Prophet Abraham in paradise with children all around him, and he added that those children were all the children that had died in the state of nature, i.e. before they attained the age of discretion. Some of the companions of the Holy Prophet (peace be upon him) asked him if the children of the polytheists were also included? The Holy Prophet (peace be upon him) replied: "Yes, the children of those who set up gods with God *(mushrikeen)* as well" *(Bokhari,* 91:48). The doctrine of the sinlessness of man by birth is an aid to his leading a sinless life. If a man does good and avoids evil, he is true to his nature. It further strengthens him to overcome sin, because he knows that nature had fitted him for this task. And step by step he can further rise to very high spiritual levels.

Not only that no impurity is attached to man by birth, but he also partakes of the Divine nature, for it was the Divine Spirit that was breathed into man, into every human child. As the Holy Quran says: "Who made beautiful everything that He created, and He began the creation of man from dust. Then He made his progeny of an extract of worthless water. Then He made him complete and breathed into him of His spirit" (32: 7-9). The Divine Spirit spoken of here is something distinct from the animal soul. It shows a mystic relation of the spirit of man with the Divine Spirit, and refers to the higher life of man. The destiny of man, according to Islam, is thus higher than mere conquest of nature, it is to seek union with the Divine Spirit. The goal of life is "Liqa Allah", or the meeting of God. In the language of the Holy Quran: "O man; thou must strive hard striving (to attain) to thy Lord until thou meet Him" (84: 6).

Entire Human Conduct

Islam encompasses entire human conduct. Justice is the *sine qua non* of Islam. Like other religions Islam is not satisfied with just transformation of the moral viewpoint of the individual or society, leaving man to his own sweet whim of what to obey and what not to obey as per the dictates of his convenience.

Islam is concerned with all sides, all sectors and all levels. As such, it aims at making a compact, homogenous, steel-cast *'Millat'* with definite laws of do's and don'ts and, what is more important, with a sovereign enforcing authority backed by all powers of reward and punishment. It gives laws in all sectors of human conduct at levels of family, society and polity, trade, politics, social manners, citizenship, agriculture, industry, foreign relations, health, public finance, public works, education, civilisation and what not. And it gives justice to see that they are practically enforced.

After declaration of prophethood, for full 13 years in Makkah, the Prophet of Islam (peace be upon him) preached the best principles of individual and social conduct, presented the best logic and arguments, demonstrated the best powers of oratory and persuasion, gave the best specimens of personal virtues, quoted the commandments of the Holy Quran, discussed the life-after-death. More than 95 per cent of the inhabitants of Makkah and of the places around remained infidels showing intenser enmity towards the Holy Prophet (peace be upon him), his Companions and Islam. When, however, the scene changed to Medina with Islam becoming a state, a government, a political and military force, new people came within its fold and Islam could set up a model in all sectors for all times and climes.

At Medina, the Prophet (peace be upon him) blended the ever-warring tribes into one compact fraternity, changed hearts, values and viewpoints, reformed society and polity, created an atmosphere of dependable safety, peace and goodwill and overthrew the governments of oppression and tyranny whose game was to play one set of people against another.

The Holy Quran puts all emphasis on the suppression of oppression and enforcement of justice.

"Verily Allah orders you to give the due to whomsoever it belongs and when you sit in judgement, be just and upright—" (4: 58).

"O people of *Eimman* (Faith) give all support and perseverance to the cause of justice in the way of Allah. And do not trespass for fear of this nation or that. And catch full hold of justice as it is close to *Taqwa.* And fear none but Allah. Verily He knows every action of yours". (5: 8).

"Tell them, O Prophet, that your Allah has commanded justice."

"Sure, we have sent to you this Book of Rights so that you may pronounce judgements between peoples as per the commandments of Allah. And do not be among those who unjustly take sides" (4: 105).

Only 227 verses of the Holy Quran discuss laws and they pertain to no more than 11 sectors of human activity. Of course, this is the core and kernel, the nucleus. All the remaining parts of the structure of the Islamic polity have been furnished by the *Sunnah,* the sayings and doings of the Prophet (peace be upon him).

As regards the two evil courses of bribe and recommendations the Holy Prophet (peace be upon him) said that he who gives and he who takes bribe will both go to Hell. He has cursed the giver and taker of bribe.

True Judge

The Holy Prophet (peace be upon him) had to deal with hundreds of cases between persons belonging to erstwhile opposite camps. The least favour or disfavour on his part would have broken the oneness and unity of *Millat.* But it was his impartial justice that gave no loophole of criticism to anyone that kept the *Millat* intact, that is the model par excellence to all posterity.

He has prescribed the special qualifications of the judge, the *Qazi.* Once he said: "Judges are of three kinds-one of which will go to Paradise, recognises the right of one *vis-a-vis* another and pronounces judgements accordingly. The other is one who recognises the rights but due to any worldly consideration does not act accordingly. And the third kind is one who does not care to recognise the rights and acts unjustly".

"When a judge does his best to know the truth from untruth and finds the truth, he would get two rewards. But one who does not find the truth in spite of his best efforts would get one reward only."

As regards the court-procedure, he said: "None is to pronounce judgement if he is in wrath and anger."

"Both the parties are to be present before the judge."

"I am but a human being. I try legal disputes. It is possible that one of the party is more adept in presenting his side of the case and under the impression of his being rightful, I judge in his favour. So if a party secures such a favour by trampling the right of another party, the former is taking nothing but a piece of Hellish Fire. It is for him to take it or leave it."

He has ordered the judge to hear equally attentatively both the parties and to deliver judgement only when the truth comes out. Similarly, the Holy Prophet (peace be upon him) has laid down the essential qualifications of the court witness. He had refused to accept the evidence of (1) person guilty of breach of trust, (2) person guilty of immoral sex; (3) person who has previously been inflicted with court punishment; (4) person who harbours feelings of revenge or hate against his brother, including the party in question; (5) person who has been guilty of giving false evidence; (6) person who is related to or in service of one of the parties or is a flatterer to one of the parties.

He said that giving false evidence is equivalent to committing *Shirk.*

The Holy Prophet (peace be upon him) while awarding judgement took full notice of the condition of health, of finance and of other factors of the guilty and gave relaxations accordingly. He always pardoned whenever it could be. He always arranged for compromise and *Qasas* whenever it could be. He gave punishment only when it had to be.

Islam considers the whole humanity as one family and treats mankind as one community. The Holy Prophet (peace be upon him) was first to demolish narrow visions of geographical and political nationhood, and taught the lesson of broadmindedness and international brotherhood to the world at large.

Paying his tribute to the Holy Prophet (peace be upon him) the French poet Lamartine wrote: "Muhammad is the one great man without whom the world would appear incomplete. Truly, Muhammad stands to this day, and for all time to come, at the peak of humanity.

Every nation at sometime or other, in its history, had its superman, the luminary who gave it light, the reformer who inspired it with noble ideals, and the Prophet who raised it morally, intellectually and spiritually on a high pedestal. But no other prophet of any religion has exercised so deep and lasting an influence in the religious, historical and social history of mankind as the Prophet of Islam (peace be upon him).

As a prophet and reformer, entrusted with the noble mission of raising mankind from the depths of degradation and the dungeons of moral, political, social and religious bankruptcy and decadence into which it had fallen in the sixth century, Prophet Muhammad (peace be upon him) could not be otherwise than a revolutionary in the fullest sense of the term. The lofty ideals he preached not only brought about a complete change in the political situation but also had an equally important and a more enduring bearing on the social conditions of the people.

To consider that the advent of the Holy Prophet (peace be upon him) on the Arab horizon merely heralded the birth of a politically unified Arabia is to pay but poor tribute to him and confess shocking ignorance of the implications of the message and his dynamic personality which ushered in a revolution of considerable magnitude in the thought and actions not only of the Arabs but of mankind itself.

Concept of Nation

Islam, the religion the Holy Prophet (peace be upon him) preached, introduced the conception of the nation as a unit and a vital stage in the organisation of human society. It is lofty in the conception of the relationship of man to God and noble in its doctrine of duty of man to man to the lower creation. It was the first religion that preached and practised democracy in its true sense.

It was Islam which for the first time proclaimed liberty to mankind, and introduced universal brotherhood in humanity. It does not recognise differences of class, caste, race, nation, or geographical and political boundaries and territories of the world. No one in Islam is better because of creed or colour. "An Arab has no superiority over a non-Arab, nor a non-Arab over Arab except piety". Islam laid down the ideal that nobility depends not in belonging to a particular family or tribe but upon being noble in personal conduct and character. The Divine Message has come down to us in the form of the Holy Quran which is the basic source of guidance for humanity.

It is a great charter of the freedom of humanity. As a book of ethics, and a code of conduct, clear, concise and simple in terms, there is no other sacred book in the world to replace it. It is "a stupendous monument of solitary legislation", to quote the words of Washington Irving. No wonder it has exercised a most potent and powerful influence over mankind throughout the ages.

Islam's institutions are unique: they do not compromise with materialistic dogmas. They stand firm on individual piety and individual freedom a close-knit family devoted to the welfare of a classless, benevolent society.

The principle of equality and brotherhood, justice and freedom which the Holy Prophet (peace be upon him) defined as integral elements of faith have engendered a righteous character and a noble spirit in society.

Distinguishing the essence of piety from the mere form of ceremony of righteousness, the Holy Prophet (peace be upon him) made faith in Allah and benevolence towards man the essential features of religion. He brought to perfection the grand idea of unifying the whole human race and gathering it together under one banner.

His was "a life consecreted, from first to last, to the service of God and humanity". He preached that a true Muslim is one from the danger of whose tongue and hands all Muslims are immune and that the best occupation is service to mankind, that knowledge is a valuable legacy, manners and courtesy the various ornaments, and carefulness a clear and transparent mirror and that spiritual virtue consists in adoring Allah.

The Prophet of Islam (peace be upon him) denounced vehemently meanness and slander, hypocrisy and untruthfulness, superstition, gambling, drinking, oppression of the weak by the strong and other evils, and gave new light and guidance to mankind.

The supreme place he gave in the faith to the duty of alms-giving and charity to the poor is another praiseworthy feature of religion he preached. He told us that every good act is a charity, an exhortation to your fellowmen to do virtuous deeds is equal to alms-giving; guiding the wanderer to the right path is charity; assisting the blind in crossing the street is charity; removing stones and thorns and other obstructions from the road is charity; giving water to the thirsty is charity, and so on. There is hardly a religious duty which is more sacred and benevolent to the Muslims than that of charity to the poor. The Holy Prophet (peace be upon him) preached that true poverty is not merely lack of wealth but lack of desire for wealth.

Living Faith

The strict observance by the Muslims of the daily prayers for five times is another testimony to the value of a living faith and the spirit of universal brotherhood. One should also witness the congregational prayers offered by the faithful to see for himself the atmosphere of equality, brotherhood and love. In the presence of Allah, all stand shoulder to shoulder, the rich and the powerful with the poor and the lowly, the master and the servant offering prayers and bowing themselves before Allah in abject submission. Can there be any more levelling influence in the world?

The Holy Prophet (peace be upon him) upheld the dignity of women and gave them an honoured place in society. The economic and cultural position of women was raised to a high status, and recognition of women's right to property marked the beginning of a new era, which is now the recognised feature of every civilized society. With his far-sighted vision, the Holy Prophet (peace be upon him) laid down a complete social system containing minute regulations for man's conduct in all circumstances of life.

His love for, and human treatment of, animals are too well-known. According to a *Hadith,* the Holy Prophet (peace be upon him) is reported to have said: "If you behold three mounting an animal, stone them until one descends".

The Prophet of Islam (peace be upon him) will for ever remain the symbol of the most exemplary human conduct. All his efforts were aimed at elevating man's mind and soul, and giving him an exalted position. He preached righteousness and toleration, and in his own self presented the most accomplished model of his teachings. In his own lifetime he moulded the character of his fellowmen, reformed them, changed their thoughts, put new ideals before them, elevated them to a higher plane and let them onwards, towards the path of progress and to the fullness of a better and nobler life.

With the passage of time, Western writers, in spite of their ignorance and prejudice, began to assess the position of the Holy Prophet (peace be upon him) and the revolution brought about by him. In the case of some honest and fair appraisal and objective considerations have been dominant. A case in illustration is that of Dozy where truth found to favour: "We see then that the Arab conquests of the seventh century have continued to play an important role in human history, down to present day. It is this unparalleled combination of secular and religious influence which I feel entitles Muhammad (peace be upon him) to be considered the most influential single figure in human history". (The 100: *A ranking of the Most Influential Persons in History*— Michael H. Hart). In this list the name of the Holy Prophet (peace be upon him) is on the top. Jesus Christ is number three.

Lamartine in his "*History* de *La Turquie*", Vol. II, says about the Holy Prophet (peace be upon him):

> "No person in the world had ever willingly or unwillingly, independently or under duress kept before him an object or goal higher than the goal of Muhammad (peace be upon him).

Higher Goal

This goal was much higher than general human level, much above human intellect. What was this goal? To do away one by one with the curtains of superstition that were hung between God and man to fill the heart of man by his presence and dye man in colours of God's attributes, to present in the crowd of false deities the sacred and reasonable concept of God free of any defect. Up to now no man has dared to undertake such a stupendous and grand task, which is beyond human reach and then its sources should be so limited. This is so because neither when he conceived the idea of this responsibility, nor when practical steps were taken to implement it, he had only his person or a few residents of a corner of the desert at his disposal. There were no sources, no support, nor necessary arrangements. With this sort of paucity of resources, no man in the world, up to now, has brought about such a glorious and splendid revolution.

"A revolution of such dimensions that within two hundred years, Islam practically as a religion ruled over Arabia. In the name of God, it had conquered Iran, Khorasan, Western India, Syria, Egypt, Ethiopia, territory of North Africa known at that time, many islands of Mediterranean and Spain. If the loftiness of the goal, absence of resources and brilliancy of results is the criterion of human genius, then where is the man who can dare present any other human being to compete with Muhammad (peace be upon him). Great men in the world have piled arms, codified laws and ruled over extensive empires. At the most they created material powers and resources which in most cases were reduced to ashes. But this man did not shake only the armies and battalions, legislative assemblies, big empires, nations and families but also the hearts of millions of people living in one-third area of the known world of that time.

"And more than that. This personality shook places of sacrifices, deities, religions and rituals, conceptions and convictions and as a matter of fact shook the very souls of men. On the basis of a book, whose every word has a legal significance, he built up a community which in its turn fused different languages and races into one single nation. This everlasting nation, rebellion and hatred against false gods and overflowing love for one God are the legacies of this great personality. In the midst of a plethora of false gods the proclamation of conception about one God in itself was such a miracle that as soon as these words were uttered by him all places of worship of false gods were destroyed. One-third of the world was set on fire.

"His life, his devotion, his relentless efforts against superstition and the great courage to scoff at the fury and anger of false gods is known. His life at Makkah ar.d thirteen years' tribulations and severe opposition were met with supreme fortitude and courage. He gladly bore the ridicule and denial of the opponents. All these troubles and then migration by him, his continuous preaching and invitation, his supreme efforts, his full confidence in the success of his mission and in unfavourable circumstances his supernatural calm and collected disposition at the time of victory and success, amnesty and forgiveness not for the sake of statecraft, but for the success of his divine goal and object. His wishes and hopes in the world of deep strance, his regular prayers, his supplications, secret contacts with his God, his life, his death and his popularity and influence after his demise, all these facts provide evidence for what kind of life? Do these facts show a life of a deceitful fabrication or the life of a person who had unshakable confidence and trust in his claims. It was his this very iron-clad confidence and faith generated in him a very strong current on power and strength by which he made his belief ever-living and everlasting. What was this belief?

"First Oneness of God and the second to explain what God is not. This *"illa"* and the other *"illa"*. One part to wipe away the false gods in the world (even use of sword if pressed by necessity) and the other part to lay out the carpet of one true God's majesty. A great thinker, orator of a high order, prophet law-giver, military leader, victor of beliefs and convictions, responsible for presenting correct ideology of life with reason and clarity of vision; the founder of a system, in which false gods cannot enter man's mind; twenty worldly states and above them the sovereignty of One God. This is Muhammad (peace be upon him).

"Bring all of your criteria, all of your tests by which the greatness of human beings is checked and measured and then reply if the world has produced any man greater than him?"

The views of another Western author, viz., Pringle Kennedy should be taken into consideration. After dealing with the subject of social, religious and cultural condition of the world he says: "It is a matter of surprise that this new culture was born in Arabia at a time when it was urgently needed.

"For those among us who think man is everything, Muhammad (peace be upon him) is a great example of what a man can do. Those who believe that changes and revolutions in history are not the result of one man's efforts but are more dependent on the peculiarities of environments and the ability of human mind to accept them cannot deny that if a revolution had to come (as it came in Arabia) it could not take place without Muhammad (peace be upon him) and would have remained pending for an indefinite period". (Pringle Kennedy— *"In Arabian Society at the Time of Muhammad")*.

The Eclipse of Christianity in Islam by L. E. Brown bears testimony to the fact that: "Due to influence of Muhammad (peace be upon him), Arab clannish pride and exclusiveness came to an end. They became members of a brotherhood which they never knew. This link was the faith of Oneness of God. If brought them to a centre and conquests followed easily.

Hitti opines in his book *"History of the Arabs"* as under: "This was the first time that the Arabs were brought together not in the name of blood-relationship but in the name of religion. Allah was the supreme sovereign of this state. The Prophet (peace be upon him), throughout his life was His representative and ruler of the country. For this reason Muhammad (peace be upon him) in addition to his spiritual responsibilities, directed the affairs of the state like state officials. In his nation after forsaking all tribal preferences and old relationship became brothers."

The Reverend Stephenson is of the opinion: "It must be freely admitted at first that for his nation the personality of Muhammad (peace be upon him) was the source of many and great benefits. He was born in a country where political set-ups, reasonable beliefs and ethical behaviour were unknown. He brought about these three things. Through his mature intelligence, he reformed all these three simultaneously. In place of different tribes he made them one nation, similarly he preached the Unity of God in place of deities and gods. All the major unwholesome practices were done away with. As Islam flowed out of old Arabia, barbarians were gathered in its fold and they became the possessors of the benefits of Islam. Islam is an instrument to lead human beings from darkness to light and from *Satan* to God.

The Reverend Bosworth Smith observes: "On account of such a good fortune which has not parallel in history, Muhammad (peace be upon him) is the founder of three elements. One nation, one state and one religion. The founder himself was unlettered but he gave the world a Book which has poetic and musical stance in it as also complete code of conduct and law. This is the miracle of Muhammad (peace be upon him), permanent miracle and actually a miracle."

Unprecedented Revolution

They all write about an unprecedented revolution not only political but social, religious, moral, ethical and in short all matters covering life of man. They all pay tribute to Quran. At this stage it is necessary we should know what was there in the world at that time that was swept away to make room for higher and bright set up and a new world was created.

Pringle in his *"Arabian Society at the Time of Muhammad"* (peace be upon him) says that at that time it seemed that the grand edifice of civilisation which had been built during the last 4,000 years, was about to collapse and human beings were about to revert to the same barbaric state wherein every tribe was deadly enemy of the other and nobody had any knowledge or regard for institutions and regulated existence. Ancient tribal values had been lost, and on the lines of old methods kingship could no longer flourish. The institutions which Christianity introduced they did not inculcate spirit of discipline or unity but were being the cause of disunity estrangement and destruction. Time had come when all-round there was gross indiscipline, bloodshed and there was no horizon of man's life. It had gone down to the level of beasts of jungle. The tall tree of civilisation whose green and flourishing branches provided shadow and comfort to the world and were laden with the golden fruits of art, science and literature was shaking about to fall. It no longer received the moisture of respect and attachment. Only the outer crust remained. The holocaust of wars and battles cut it down to pieces and these pieces were supported by old customs and ceremonies. It was feared that they would fall down any time. Was it possible under these conditions to create or introduce emotional culture which could bring round humanity to one central point and save civilisation. This culture had to be of a new pattern because all old customs and usages had finished and to resurrect them needed centuries.

Says Carlyle: "The humanity like a dry jungle was waiting for a spark. That spark of electricity appeared in the form of that great personality and ignited the universe."

This is the evaluation of great revolution brought about by the Holy Prophet (peace by upon him). They could not go further for two reasons. Firstly, the prejudice and opposition generated by Pope Urban II (1042—1099) who initiated the crusades. This prejudice still exists. Secondly, the West is devoting all its energy and deploying all scientific discoveries to destroy opponents besides exploiting the weak. Deadly arms are being manufactured and sold. Humanity today stands at the brink of mass destruction. For these reasons, the West has not been able to turn its attention towards higher values, and sanctity of human life.

Historic March

Islam has always faced challenges on its historical march. It faced its first crisis when the Holy Prophet (peace be upon him) passed away from this earthly scene. This was very close to the rise of Islam as a historical force. When the Holy Prophet (peace be upon him) died, the crucial point was whether there should be any Islamic history at all. Some of the then Muslims (e.g. the Beduins) felt that the affair was now over: they had taken a vow of fidelity to a leader, he was no more, and that was the end of the affairs. Others felt the need for restoring status quo and emphasising the recognition of urban and tribal realities. Besides, it was presumed that new religious faith should take its course on those basis. But this was rejected and it was decided that to keep the followers of the Holy Prophet (peace be upon him) united as a socio-political economic unit and as one that marches forward in the world to enforce and spread as unit the message of Islam. This decision was taken not without opposition which was finally crushed and silenced. This decision was of immense significance for the later history of Islam.

The decision to keep the community intact and choose a leader for itself in place of the Holy Prophet (peace be upon him) appeared to be more pertinent than the issue (which has received immeasurable attention) of who that leader should be. Then emerged the issue of the actual development of Islamic history on earth, having understood the significance of its last success and homogeneity. The early Muslims took the whole burden and opportunity of government as well as cultural creation in the widest sense. They completed this task significantly so that when they could presently look at this society that they had constructed, they felt satisfied that it led the world. God had enjoined upon men the way to live; those who followed the path were visibly receiving His blessings.

Great Debacle

History, however, has its own inner logic. Muslims feel it to be will of God on earth.

But this period of Islam's earthly glory did not last long. The early period of Islam primarily comprised Arab elements, it lost its vigour after spending its inherent force with the fall of Baghdad in 1258, the successful Arab rule came to its formal end. The Mughal invasion gave a death blow to the Arab ascendency of Islam. Many millions were massacred; whole cities were laid waste and political rules passed into the hands of infidel barbarians. This ended the classical period of Islamic history.

This was a first great crisis of Islamic history. With the demise of the Arab Empire, Islamic history seemed to have lost its driving force. It appeared as if divine purpose as conceived by Islam was faltering, if it has not actually failed.

Great Survival

Despite this debacle, Islam on earth survived this crisis and it re-appeared in a new and rather different mould. With the drawing to a close of the European Middle Ages, Islam's mediaeval period—between its classical and modern eras—set in motion. Historians of Islam—whether Muslims or Westerns have taken much less interest in this mediaeval phase of Islam than that of the classical. In spite of it, there were new aspects which were not without significance. This phase of Islam produced constructive answers to the issues raised.

New Development

On the religious side, *Sufism* was a new major development. The *Sufi* or mystic interpretation of Islam has its germs even in the classical period. Yet at the time it was confined to an insignificant minority, comprising an elite of the pious withdrawn from the main stream of Islamic march. The mediaeval period bolstered its immensity throughout the Muslim world. The movement took an institutional form and gained popularity. There were additions also in interpretation; as for example, the *Masnavi* of Jalaluddin Roomi which was produced after the fall of Baghdad.

Besides, Islam converted the conquerors. After imposing on the Muslim alien rulers for 50 years, the Mughal dynasty which had subjugated the Muslim world, itself embraced Islam as a historical force soon asserted itself in Persian and Turkish forms. These forms were different from the preceding ones. New forms were different from the old in the government structure, social organisation and in cultural and aesthetic values. In this new era, Islam again began to march as a political force.

After its nadir in the Thirteenth Century, Islam began to touch a new zenith in the Sixteenth; which could be put forth as the Islam's greatest century uptil now. Then the Ottoman Empire was a most powerful state on earth; Europe shivered before its apparently unending series of conquests. At the same time, *Safuids* had established a family based on imperial power in Iran, the Mughals then had firmly entrenched themselves in India and constituted the greatest rule the subcontinent had seen for many a long time.

This second revival of Islam was confined not only to the building of Empires, but it was a new expansion also in geographical and spiritual senses. The second great wave of military expansion and missionary fervour brought for Islam new converts: in the Northern Asia Minor and the Balkans and Central Asia, in the South Negro Africa and in the East Indonesia. Thus, classical Islam was doubled in area and numbers. Once again, it was evident that historical Islam was a power to be reckoned with.

However, the second flowering of Islam, with the possible exception of the Turkish, has not been generally regarded by the Muslims as fully consistent with the classical Islam. What the

Muslims accomplished in it is not so keenly regarded as a complete example of Islam at work in the world, moulding into a divine pattern the flux, of historical development. But this tendency should not be overemphasised. The classical version of Islam has always remained official, and its social importance cannot be minimised. But even in this period Muslims never grudged to extol any individual who either successfully defended Islamic domain or extended it. Even then, there were many Muslims in the world who regarded conquest of Constantinople in 1453 as an example of God's power as well as Sultan Muhammad's effort.

However, it is a fact that in the sixteenth century Muslim World was again a mighty force having wealth and splendour. Whatever opinion one may hold up of it, the Muslims of this period were victorious in a history expansive and successful.

But even this success did not last long. The second wave of Islamic Revival was more short-lived than the first. The advance of Muslim society ceased and by the eighteenth century it entered a period of decline. Its military and political power underwent serious reverses; its commercial and economic life enfeebled, its intellectual efforts stagnated, its artistic talent lost lustre and religious vitality ebbed. The writings of great masters were confined to commentaries and classical systems were used to congeal mental faculties rather than as an impetus for opening up new horizons of thought. On the *Sufi* side, the orders degenerated from mystic perception to exploitable superstition.

Besides, it is a strange coincidence that this decay coincided with a new upsurge of Europe. At about the same time, Western civilisation set about its greatest venture of expansion that human history has ever seen. It accumulated vitality, skill, and power on a vast scale; with them the West was then refashioning its own life and soon the life of the globe.

Forces of West

The force of the West which was imbued with exploratory restlessness met the Muslim World in decline and subdued it. By 1800, the West subjugated such centres of Muslim power as remained on many areas and imposed its rule. During most of the nineteenth century many Muslim countries lost their freedom. The

Dutch entrenched them in Indonesia; Iran and the Ottoman Empire, though formally independent, lost their freedom to act. Muslim society, once dignified was now everywhere despondent in spirit and prey to outside forces.

Muslims uphold that Islam essentially is a religion, and as such deeply personal and also conclusively surpassing all particularities and limits of this existence and all its affairs; despite this, it has the distinction of having a deep concern for these affairs. It was essential for a true Muslim to carry out in this world the divine obligation as to how mankind, individually and collectively, should live. If this is seen from another angle, it appears that Muslims should see how that ideal society is built. In short, Islamic history is the fulfilment, under divine guidance, of the purpose of human history.

It is a fact that actual Islamic history, for some centuries, approximated to this ideal. We have also observed that in actual fact, periods of decay and regeneration in Islamic history have alternated. Besides, we have also noticed that the mediaeval period of Islamic history has ended in disorder. Although, many Muslim countries had gained independence after World War II and their economic plight has considerably improved, yet the basic problem has persisted; and the issue of internal cohesion and fear of foreign interference remained. In this age of Super Power contention for the domination at the cost of the other, fears of foreign interference and internal disorder have not vanished and then a challenge to Islam's will to carve history according to its dynamism.

The basic malady of modern Islam lies in perception that something has gone wrong with Islamic history; hence the fundamental problem of meodern Muslim is how to restore that history; and set it working in full vigour again so that Islamic society may again be luxuriant as a divinely-guided society. In the twentieth century the basic spiritual crisis of Islam results from the realisation that something is discordant between God-ordained religion and the historical development of the world controlled by God. Muslims have failed to establish any tangible interconnection between these two factors—otherwise they would have long subjugated the contemporary historical situation to the requirements of their faith.

This is not to say that the Muslims have ignored this problem. Of course, men like Abdul Wahab Najdi (1703- 1887), Jamaluddin Afghany (1839-1897), Shah Waliullah (1703-1762), and many others have tried to analyse and solve this problem. Their efforts in this direction have immense value. But the problem still persists and the Muslim world despite its area, numerical strength and potential wealth had failed to shake of fears of internal disruption and foreign interference.

This is not to say, that the Muslims did not try to adopt suitable devices for the transportation of its worldly condition. Many attempts have been made to solve the problem; firstly, liberalism was tried, but it failed. From the late nineteenth century to the First World War, European liberalism was in great vogue in many Muslim countries, but Muslims soon realised that this internal Westernising of the Islamic community constituted subtler and more dangerous version of the same threat; subversion from within. Its inherent threat to Islamic history and society was enough to alarm those who fervently cherish the realisation and embodiment of classical divine precepts as the goal of Muslim endeavour. This attitude to Westernisation has in recent decades reappeared with new vigour and vehemence.

Above all, there has been despair in the particular ties between Islam and Western liberalism itself. In the early stages of contact of Muslim world and the Western liberalism, Muslims hoped that Western liberalism could assist them in their basic enterprise of reconstructing the Islamic society, and thereby setting Islamic history on road to progress. The resulting disenchantment had led Muslims to seek new ways of fulfilling Islamic mission on earth as the Islamic Revolution in Iran, the shift in Pakistan to a new search for Islamic solution of problems and revival of Islam-oriented parties in many Muslim countries. But behind this new trend lurks the danger of an emerging new dogmatism which in its old form severely blocked the progress of Muslims for centuries. The need remains for reconciling Islam with rational modes of thought and behaviour to reconstruct Islamic society.

Part - II

The Comparison

5

Western Thoughts

The need for greater understanding of Islam in the West and for closer cooperation between the Muslim world and the West especially Europe and America cannot be overemphasized. It is, all the more, necessary because the panoramic unfolding of Islamic resurgence across the continents has attracted worldwide attention. What is needed is some sort of soul stirring and heart searching. Not only should we spotlight the prejudices which have distorted the image of Islam and Muslims in Europe and America through the centuries, but also objectively analyse the underlying reasons and categorically condemn the anti-Islam and anti-Muslim attitudes pervading the Western societies. There cannot be two opinions that for long Islam has been misunderstood and misinterpreted in the West. It is one of the most queer facts of history that despite West's stupendous strides in quest of knowledge and learning, despite the centuries of contact between the world of Islam and the West, Islam is perhaps the least known and the most misunderstood religion in the West.

The Silverlining

There is always a silver lining in otherwise dark and gloomy backdrop of misunderstanding and mistrust. It is a happy augury that now there are some very welcome stirrings in the West, for efforts are being made to improve the image and understanding of Islam and the Muslim world in the West. The realisation of this urgent need is dawning upon the leaders of thought and action. There are moves to develop correct understanding between Islam and the West. This is a very pleasant mission; but, the objective cannot be achieved without a proper understanding of the causes of conflict and distrust which have separated the two. What is needed, therefore, is a dispassionate, detached and objective study. A sincere attempt to find out the causes of the discontent must be made to open up the new vistas of cooperation and concord. Although political and economic alignments are multiplying everyday, they are not being supplemented by a correct understanding, the proper appreciation of one system of thought by another. True human-relationship is still far off. Such a disharmony is out of tune with the needs and spirit of our age and must be brought to an end if humanity is to grow and prosper and attain the highest pinnacles of peace and glory. The need of closer contact between different peoples of the world, with a view to sympathetically understanding each one of them is perhaps the greatest and most pressing need of our time. It is all too obvious that the importance of studying different religions was never insignificant, but in our age it has assumed greater importance. It has become an imperative necessity—particularly in the case of Islam.

Revealed Religion

Islam, like Christianity, is a revealed religion, universal and multi-national—nearly seventy countries, where Muslim population is indigenous, totalling into about one billion Muslims all over the world. In fact, Muslims constitute one-fifth of the entire human race. The Muslim world straddles over vast regions of the continents of Asia and Africa. This region has been the cradle of a large number of higher civilizations. Economically its potential is great. Politically it is "the great third of the world". And above all, it is the upholder of a great ideology—Islam. But unlike any other religion, Islam is a totality inseparably combing the religious and the secular. Of course, there are similarities between Islam and other revealed religions, but "similarities" are not of the essence; of the essence are "dissimilarities", which underpinned the need for a new revelation. The account in the Old Testament of how the universe was created by God had not stood, and cannot stand the scientific test, while the Quranic account is completely in keeping with the latest astrophysical hypothesis. How could an *"ummi"* (one who can neither read nor write) know nearly fourteen hundred years ago what science has taken so long to begin to understand? Divine revelation not anything else is the answer. The Prophet of Islam (peace be upon him) became a model of the Islamic teachings, a role Jesus could not come to adopt in Christianity for his relatively short stay on the scene. On cursory observation, these truisms may appear platitudinous, especially to one outside the fold of Islam, but in essence they are the fundamentals whose appreciation is pivotal to the sound comprehension of the Islamic ideology. It is no trite occurrence to point out that the Western orientalists 'shortcomings can be effortlessly traced to the misapprehension of subtle nuances of these basic essentials. Otherwise, their readiness to draw a con trast between Islam and Christianity and propensity for levying criticism against the Prophet of Islam (peace be upon him) would require some other explanations as one suggested by N. A. Daniels.

The hostile attitude of the West is evident from the views expressed by Western orientalists of Islam and Prophet of Islam (peace be upon him) in a good deal of literature on this subject produced by them. For the inherent variation in the Western perceptions due to a characteristic historical experience, the intellectual probings into this sphere may have acquired certain imbalances which lend themselves to rectification. It would be a disservice to humanity if attention is not focussed on the cases in illustration. It is, therefore, pertinent to point out that in a fit of disguised fury Professor A. J. Arberry writes:

> "The events of 26 January 1952, Cairo's *'Black Saturday'*, brought home to many, who were hitherto content to minimise the conflict between Islam and the West, that a situation existed fraught with the most serious danger. It is strange that the portents should have been so comfortably disregarded. The warning signals have been flying for a long time. When Iqbal wrote, 'Believe me Europe today is the greatest hinderance in the way of man's ethical advancement, 'he was not

> saying anything that he had not said before, and he was not seeking merely to provoke and shock; neither was he a solitary voice crying in the wilderness. The present threats to the peace and a security of the world are certainly not few; among those threats there are not many greater than the revival lately of that spirit of irreconcilable hostility which found its most dramatic and bloody expression in the Crusades."

It is evident from the wrath and fury that is seething between the lines that the relationship of Islam and the modern West is a complex one and what is needed is to avoid oversimplification of the problem which is according to the learned professor, "perhaps the besetting in of the twentieth century". Obviously, this warrants an indepth study of the entire problem. In fact, the contact between Islam and the West, during the last five centuries, has not been in a pleasant atmosphere. By and large the Muslims were in a disadvantageous position and the treatment which they have received at the hands of the surging forces of the West has left a bitter taste in the mouth. It is this peculiar background which animates the atmosphere and created misunderstandings. The relationship can be really improved, if a sincere attempt is made to understand each other's point of view in a cordial and friendly atmosphere without having doubts and prejudices. It is, therefore, necessary to take into consideration some of the factors which have made the situation so tense in the present day world.

The Imperialism

To begin with, the imperialistic designs of the West were under the garb of "civilizing mission". In the first wave of the contact, the pioneers of the West came to the world of Islam as merchants and missionaries. And in the final surge, they wielded the arms and conquered these lands as the "ambassadors of a higher civilization". The Western imperialism firmly established itself in Muslim countries by bringing them under its rule. Muslims were the most sufferers under this political hegemony of the West. Thus, Arnold J. Toynbee rightly observes:

> "In the encounter between the world and the West that has been going on by now for four or five hundred

> years, the world, not the West, is the party that, up to now, has had the significant experience. It has not been the West that has been hit by the world; it is the world that has been hit—and hit hardly by the West. The West (the world will say) has been the arch-aggressor of modern times. And certainly the world's judgement on the West does seem to be justified over a period of about four and a half centuries ending in 1950."

And Professor Phillip K. Hitti expresses his views, about the very recent past, in these words:

> "Unfortunately, during the last decade or two, in particular, the impact of the West has not been all for the good. There is a striking contrast between the humanitarian ideas professed by Western missionaries, teachers, and preachers, and the disregard of human values by European and American politicians and warriors; a disparity between word and deed; an overemphasis on economic and nationalistic values. The behaviour of the so-called advanced nations during the last two wars waged on a scale unknown in history; the ability of Western man to let loose these diabolic forces which are the product of his science and his machine and which now threaten the world with destruction; and, with particular relation to the Near East, the handling of the Palestine problem by America, England, France and other nations-all these have worked together to disillusion this man of the Near East who has been trying to establish an intellectual rapproachement with the West. It is these actions of the West which alienate him and shake his belief in the character of the Western man and his morality on both the private and the public levels."

Economic Exploitation

The economic exploitation of the Muslim world by the West is another factor responsible for the present discontentment. It is true that the East was exploited generally but Muslims, in particular, were the target of attack and exploitation. It is not an exaggeration that the exploitation of Muslims by the West is well nigh impossible to describe, for the simple reason that the political power in most of the Eastern countries was taken from the Muslims, therefore every attempt was made to reduce them, socially and economically, to the status of menials. This is what Sir W. W. Hunter admits about India:

> "It was not that *Mussalmans* were inferior to Hindus. It was British rule that had descended upon them as blight."
>
> "In fact, there is now scarcely a Government office in Calcutta in which a Muhammadan can hope for any post above the rank of a porter, messenger, 'filler of ink-pots' and menders of pens."
>
> "A hundred and seventy years ago, it was almost impossible for a well-born *Mussalman* in Bengal to become poor; at present it is almost impossible for him to continue rich."

The exploitation of the Muslims by the West was not confined to the British India, as the subcontinent was known then; but it was, more or less, true of the entire Muslim world. As a result, this naked exploitation of the Muslim countries has sowed the seeds of hatred and distrust. It is all too obvious, sociologically speaking, that when this dissatisfaction is engendered it does not remain in very reasonable confines—it generates emotional and psychological forces which vitiate the entire atmosphere.

Western Education

With the advent of the Western domination of the Muslim world, the White Masters gave top priority to the introduction of their system of education in the Indo-Pakistan subcontinent and made the new generations imbibe their ideas and culture. Lord Macaulay introduced the new system of education in India and declared its objectives in the following words:

> "We must do our best to form a class who may be interpreters between us and the millions whom we

> govern—a class of persons, Indians in blood and colour, but English in taste, in opinion, in morals, and in intellect."

This system was introduced with the underlying idea of bringing about an intellectual and cultural assassination of the Muslims. About the results of this system of education, Sir W. W. Hunter has opined:

> "The truth is that our system of public instruction is opposed to the traditions, unsuited to the requirements, and hateful to the religion, of the *Mussalmans.* It is, therefore, any wonder that the *Mussalmans* have held aloof from a system which has made no concession to their prejudices, made no provision for what they esteemed their necessities; which was in its nature unavoidably antagonistic to their interests and at variance with all their social traditions."

This system of education was confined not only to South Asia, but, in one form or the other, it was introduced throughout the Muslim world. Although Muslims willy-nilly sought education in these institutions, they had a deep realisation that this education was but a conspiracy against their faith, religion and culture. This fooling has ultimately led the intelligentsia to the revolt against the West which at long last developed into the freedom movement.

Cultural Dominance

The imperialist power made every endeavour to cut the people from their cultural moorings and make them adopt the modern Western culture. It was not possible for Muslims to accept it as dumb driven cattle because they have an ideology of their own—they have their own history and culture. The deliberate attempt to thrust the Western culture on the Muslims gave birth to a schism in the Muslim society. The spark of schism was fanned into a wide-spread fire of conflict by the ruling powers. Those who revolted against their traditions were called "modern" and "progressive" and those who refused to submit to the cultural onslaughts of the West, they were called the 'vehicles of conservatism and retrogression'. These tactics of the imperialist West succeeded in creating a small group of camp-followers of

Western culture in the Muslim society but it also gave birth to tremendous forces of anti-Westernism, which did not always remain within reasonable limits, for it is impossible to control the volcano of wrath and fury. This fooling of wrath and anger of the Muslim masses is a significant contributory factor to the conflict between Islam and the West. If the dominant powers had not resorted to cultural onslaught, the gulf between the two would have not been so unbridgeable.

Imposition of Christianity

Perhaps these factors of ill-will were not enough for creating the yawning chasm between Islam and the West, therefore, along with these came the pronouncements of conquering the East for Christianity. The Chairman of the Directors of the East India Company, Mr. Mangles, declared in the House of Commons:

> "Providence has entrusted the extensive Empire of Hindustan to England in order that the banner of Christ should wave triumphant from one end of India to the other. Everyone must exert all his strength that there may be no dilatoriness on any account in continuing in the country the grand work of making all India Christians."

In a similar vein Prime Minister, Lord Palmerstone boldly announced that:

> "Perhaps it might be our lot to confer on the countless millions of India a higher and nobler gift (Christianity) than any mere human knowledge."

These declarations were followed by contingent after contingent of missionaries who "at once saw their opportunities" and embarked upon the project what C. H. Phillips called "The cure of darkness is light;" Rev. Kennedy wrote:

> "Whatever misfortune come on us, as long as our Empire in India continues, so long let us not forget that our chief work is the propagation of Christianity in the land. Until Hindustan, from Cape Comorin to the Himalayas, embrace the religion of Christ, and until it condemns the Hindu and the Muslim religions,

our efforts must continue persistently. For this work we must make all the efforts we can and use all the power and all the authority in our hands; and continuous and unceasing efforts must be kept on until India becomes a magnificent nation, the bulwark of Christianity in the East;"

The Christian missionaries, despite their best efforts, could not succeed in converting the mass of the people to their religion. But they succeeded in making dents in the vulnerable lot of educated Muslims by driving a large number of them away from Islamic culture and into the alluring lap of the Western way of life. Strange though it may sound, the Missions delighted in doing at least this 'service' to their "holy cause". Mr. Chatalier wrote in a special missionary supplement of his French magazine *"Le Monde Mussalman"*:

> "No doubt our missionaries have failed so far indirectly undermining the faith of the Muslims. This end can be achieved only by the propagation of ideas through the medium *of* European languages. Through the spread of these languages the world of Islam could be brought in contact with European Press and paths would be paved for the material progress of the Muslims. Thus, the missionary organizations would realize their goal of destroying Islamic religious concepts which so far have preserved their identity and strength in isolation and separatism."

The writer added:

> "The political break-up of the world of Islam will open the way to Europe's civilizing mission. It is inevitable that the Muslims will degenerate politically, and before long the world of Islam will become like a city surrounded by European barbed-wire entanglements."

He also added:

> "It is not to be expected that the Muslims in general would be able to bring forth new positive attitudes and new social qualities once they have given up their

> present attitudes and qualities. With the weakening of their belief in Islam, decay and disintegration are bound to set in; and when this decay and this disintegration are bound to set in; and when this decay and this disintegration spread throughout the world of Islam, the religious spirit of the Muslims will be entirely uprooted and will never be able to re-emerge in a new form."

Western Scholars' Views

There can be no two opinions about the need and importance of better understanding between Islam and the West. It is a fact that Islam, the religion of 500 million people, is the most misunderstood religion in the West. The researchers, scholars and authors in ascertaining the facts in other realms of learning, accept even those things about Islam which do not enjoy slightest authenticity. As these things come, not from the politicians or the propagandists, but from the scholars, it has very far-reaching effects upon the attitudes of the Muslim world. It is regrettable indeed that despite the decline of the forces of imperialism, the onslaught of Western scholars on Islam continue. Some sober orientalists have, in the recent past, tried to adopt a sympathetic approach, but on the whole the situation is such that it deserves very close study and careful attention.

A critical study of the Western scholars on Islam reveals that *ignorance* and *prejudice* both have corrupted an otherwise very wholesome effort to study this religion. It seems that the bitter legacy of the Crusades is still haunting the intellectuals. The writers of the post-Crusade era indulged in mud slinging on Islam and sowed the seeds of enmity and hatred. This hostile and unrealistic attitude has been responsible for creating an atmosphere in which the relationship between Islam and the West cannot be cemented. True, that during the last several years, a change of attitude has occurred in some quarters. Dr. T. W. Arnold, Professor A. J. Arberry, Professor A. R. H. Gibb, Dr. W. Montgomery Watt have adopted a somewhat impartial and sympathetic attitude towards Islam. This is undoubtedly a welcome change, but despite the sane and sober approach of only a few, the general atmosphere still abounds with ignorance and prejudice and the background is manifesting itself even in the writings of some very sober writers. Real teachings of Islam are still foreign to the West. Even basic information about past and the present is faulty and coloured. To say the least, the general attitude is anything but sympathetic and realistic. But it is a happy augury that the interest of the West in Islam is definitely increasing day by day.

It is, therefore, necessary to build the bridges of understanding which is possible only through unprejudiced appreciation of one another's viewpoint. It must be realised by all the saner elements that understanding and cooperation can be developed in a free, frank and cordial atmosphere in which both the sides should take the initiative and come forward with an open mind. If the West persists in its bigotted approach, and then hopes that better results could be achieved, then the attempt is foredoomed to failure.

Surveying the situation from this viewpoint we find that it is not pleasant, to say the least. To substantiate our point we present extracts from the writings of some leading western scholars and present them without any comments. We have only arranged them under proper heads so that the reader may easily understand the weaknesses of the western approach to Islam.

Undervaluation of Islam's Debt

It is unfortunate indeed that, for a considerably long time, the Western scholars refused to acknowledge the real contribution of Islam to science and culture. This is now being admitted by most of the leading scholars and orientalists. William Drapper observes:

> "I have to deplore the systematic manner in which the literature of Europe has contrived to put out of sight our scientific obligations to the Muhammadens. Surely they cannot be much longer hidden, injustice founded on religious rancour and national conceit cannot be perpetuated for ever."

"Europe for centuries was unfair to Islam, in the sense that the positive achievements of Muslim civilization were overlooked, scholarship being the handmaid of religious partisanship."

It will be observed from the above excerpts that according to these scholars the partisan attitude of the West has now come to an end, but that is not the fact. J. B. Trend writes in *The Legacy of Islam.*

"The modern Spanish school of scientific historians is not favourably disposed towards the legacy of Islam. A hundred years ago the importance of the 'the Moors in Spain' was unduly exaggerated; today the subject is out of fashion among serious workers and apt to be despised by intelligent readers. This attitude may be regrettable, but there are reasons for it, and not all of them are bad reasons."

Even the leading scientist, Sir James Jeans, holds the view that the Arabs were mere "curators of the scientific knowledge". "They excelled", he says, "as translators, commentators and writers of treatises, and their aim was not so much to increase knowledge as to sweep all existing knowledge into their empire". Their original contribution is outright denied by this eminent scientist. A similar attempt is made by Professor Phillip K. Hitti who tries to minimise the appeal, role and culture of Islam by saying that:

> "The Islam conquered the northern region was not the Islamic religion but the Islamic State. The Arabian burst forth upon an unsuspecting world as members of a national theocracy. It was Arabianism and not Muhammadenism that triumphed first. Not until the second and third centuries of the Muslim era did the bulk of the people in Syria, Mesopotamia and Persia profess the religion of Muhammad. And when they were converted the people turned primarily because of self interest to escape tribute and seek identification with the ruling class. As for Islam as a culture, it developed slowly after the military conquest on a sub-stratum composed of the core and heritage of the Syro-Aramaean, Persian and Hellenistic civilization which had preceded. With Islam the Near Orient not only recaptured the whole of its former political domain but regained in the realm of culture its ancient intellectual pre-eminence."

Hatred, Enmity and Bias

It is evident from the writings of the Western Scholars that the West, from the very beginning, has nurtured an inexplicable hatred and enmity towards Islam. Dozy says that Christians:

> "Developed an instructive hatred for the *Mussalmans,* and entertained thoroughly false ideas about Muhammad and the doctrines he preached. Living in the midst of the Arabs, nothing was more easy than to instruct themselves on this subject; but they refused obstinately to go to the sources which could be found at their doors, and were satisfied with believing and repeating all the absurd fables which they retailed about the Prophet of Makkah."

And Sir Denison Ross admits:

> "For many centuries the acquaintance which the majority of Europeans possessed of Muhammadanism was based almost entirely on distorted reports of fanatical Christians, which led to the dissemination of a multitude of gross calumnies. What was good in Muhammadanism was entirely ignored, and what was not good in the eyes of Europe was exaggerated or misinterpreted."

Muslims were called by the western writers "Infidels", "Miscreants", "Paynims", "Pagans", "Heathens", "Heathen hounds", "Enemies of God," "Anti-Christ", "Gentiles", "Vandals" and what not. H. M. K. Shairani writes:

> "There are several phases through which the history of Muhammad has passed in Europe. The first idea that Christians formed of the Prophet was, that he was the God of the Saracens, to whom divine honours were accorded. In the labyrinth of popular fancy, while the title of True God was applied to Jesus Christ, Muhammad received the appellation of the False God. It was commonly believed that he was worshipped in the form of an idol. *The History of Charles the Great,* by Bishop Turpin, the source of so many songs and

> romances, can be cited as a very early work which gives us a description of this idol. The author tells us that the idol Muhammad, which the Saracens worshipped, was made by Mahomet himself, in his life-time; and that, by the help of a legion of devils, it was by magic art endued with such irresistible strength that it could not be broken. A singular antipathy towards the Christians possessed this idol, and through this they were exposed to imminent danger if they ventured to approach it. Even the birds of the air, it is said, were struck dead if they happened to alight upon it."

Then Shairani proceeds:

> "The method with which the worship of Mahound is conducted so closely resembles contemporary Catholic services, that we need not detail it here. Two or three observations may suffice. It is pretty certain that the Saracens prayed in Latin; they also allowed music in their services and sang hymns. At the close of the service, the priest gave hisbenison, and exhorted the congregation to stand fast in the 'Grace of Mahound'; then he showed them the sacred relics of Mahound, a neckbone, an eye-lid, and so on.

"The attribute and the office of Mahound next demand our attention. In the first place he is a God, a great God, Almighty God. He is also described as 'St. Mahoun,' helps the heathens, witches and rules over them, and receives their souls when they die. It appears that the mode of Christian worship grieves him; he is jealous of Christ's Godhead; hence the heathens fight with the Christians. They carry his images or pictures on their crest. The Christians, on their part, look upon him as 'Sorry Mahound', 'Mad Mahound,' and last of all, 'False Mahound'.

"The fact is not recorded, but belief is current that Mahound also suffered crucifixion. 'By the blood of Mahound,' or 'By the precious blood of Mahound,' is the common cry of all Paynims, whether Herod, the Sowdone or Babylon, the Amyral, or Saladin. The adjuration 'by Mahound' is so frequent that, in several romances, it is exclusively appropriated for this purpose. The following verses, however, contained curious variations:

> 'By Mahound's bones! had the wretches tarried Their necks without heads they should have carried; Yea, by Mahound's nose! might I have patted them in twenty gobbets I should have squatted them.'

"For a long time, it appears, Mahound alone fulfilled the duties of Godhead, and had no partner or associate. All early writings confirm this opinion, but the fourteenth century romance literature introduced new changes in this belief. The term Saracen, which was sometimes applied to the heathens of the West, perhaps gave rise to a confusion in the mind of the romancers, which led to the coupling of Mahound with Apollo or Termagant.

'And there-for, swete fader myn,

Forsake Mahoun and Appolyn;

And Termagant, my God so bright.'

"A further development was due to trinitarian views, the persons of the Saracenic trinity being Mahound, Apolyn and Termagant, See *Song of Roland,* ed J. Crossland, pp. 130, 131, 154 and 164. London, 1907. Besides these three chief gods, a number of other gods are mentioned:

'With sterne strokes and with grete,

On jovyn and Plotoun;

On Astrot and sire Jovin,

On Termagant and Appolin,

He brak hem scolle and croun;

On Termagant, that was heore brother,

He lasts to lyme hole with other,

Ne on his lord Seynt Mahoun.'

"Although Charles the Great did not destroy the idol Mahomet, possibly owing to the fear of a legion of devils, there are other Christian knights who have been more fortunate in this iconoclastic exploit; Roland and his *Peers* have achieved this fame, and Sir Bevis of Hamption is another famous knight who has been equally successful. The name of Rinaldo of Montalban can never be forgotten; his daring robbery of the golden idol of Mahomet has even been immortalised in Don Quixote. In the romance of Ortnit we find that Alberich, a dwarf, flung down the Moorish idols, Mahomet and Apollo, two enormous figures carved in stone.

"The historian, Matthew Paris, commenting on a mournful letter received from the Holy Land, observes that the Christians, at the time of the 'Fall of the Image of Mahomet at Makkah', rejoiced greatly. They exulted in the fall of the image', and to this exultation he attributes the fury of the 'Chrosmins', and the misfortunes that befell the Christians in consequence.

"Bayle quotes from the *History of* the *Holy Wars,* by Father Mabillion, that Tancred found the Statue of Mahomet in the Mosque of Omar, seated on a high throne. Six strong men could not lift it, and when he was informed that it was Mahomet, he made a very pathetic harangue to the idol, and cried out: 'It is this wicked Mahomet, who was the first Anti-Christ. If the Anti-Christ that is to come were now here with this, truly I would quickly have crushed him under my feet." '

Similarly, the famous poet-philosopher *Dante* places the Prophet of Islam as a heresiarch, in the inferno, and depicts a most despicable scene. The demons of hell tear the flesh off his body; devour it, and as soon as the wounds heel, renew the same action. The Italian painter Orcagne includes him in the trio of the great despisers of all religions and paints him in the hell of the Campo Santo at Pisa.

Such filthy calumnies were hurled upon Islam and the Prophet of Islam. Although now the tone is not so bitter and the "facts" not so scandalising, the spirit persists unchecked. A few instances are given below:

W. G. Palgreve writes:

> "No superiority, no distinction, no pre-eminence can be law-fully claimed in Islam by one creature over another in the utter equalisation of their unexceptional servitude and abasement. All are alike tools of one solitary Force, which employs them to crush or to

> benefit, to truth or error, to honour or shame, to happiness or misery, quite independently of their individual fitness, deserts or advantage and simply because He wills it and as He wills it."

Professor Margoliouth in his *Life of the Prophet* portrays him as the "bandit mystic of Arabia". The two features that come up in his biography are his mysticism and brigandage, the latter of course being the primary one! He writes that "one mode of acquiring a living is open to the very poorest, where there is impurity; and that is robbery", and adds that when persecuted by the Makkahans he migrated to Medina "even then he expected to have to fall back on plundering their caravans." According to him at Medina the prophet "was at the head of a robber community". There is no end to this kind of baseless propaganda which is not only far from the actual facts but a figment of the imagination. Joseph Gaer in his well-known book: *How the Great Religions Began* writes:

> "In order to establish his power he organised an army.
>
> "But to keep up an army it is necessary to have food and clothes and money. Where was he to get it?
>
> "Muhammad went out to the edge of the desert, wrapped himself up in a number of blankets against the chill of the evening, and meditated. As he sat there thinking of ways to support his army, he heard again the voice of the angel Gabriel, calling.
>
> "O thou who art wrapping, rise up and warn!"
>
> "And Muhammad returned to his followers and told them that the Angel of God had come to him, instructed him to go out and waylay the caravans carrying goods from Makkah to foreign lands. Muhammad and his followers went out plundering caravans. And whatever they plundered was divided equally among them. The success of their attacks on the caravans, Muhammad explained to his followers, proved that Allah was with them."

A. C. Bouquet, in his book *Comparative Religion* tells us that Christians and Jews regarded the Holy Prophet as "a nationalistic charlatan". About the revelation and the way it was conveyed to the prophet he says:

> "If this story is not fiction, we may conjecture that occurrence of some neurotic obsessional seizure, of a type which is soothed and dissipated by normal sex experience."

About Holy Quran

The views of most of the Western writers are so much coloured and their vision so much clouded as a result of their prejudice that they refuse to call the Quran as the word of God, instead they use all the force at their command to "prove" that its author was Muhammad (peace be upon him). Professor Margoliouth writes:

> "The secret of the power exercised by the book, of course, lay in the mind which produced it. It was, in fact, at first not a book, but a strong living voice, a kind of wild authoritative proclamation, a series of admonitions, promises, threats, and instructions addressed to turbulent and largely hostile assemblies of untutored Arabs. As a book it was published after the prophets, death. In Muhammad's lifetime there were only disjointed notes, speeches, and the retentive memories of those who listened to them. To speak of the Quran is, therefore, practically the same as speaking of Muhammad."

He further says:

> "The method followed" by Muhammad in the promulgation of the Quran also requires to be treated with discrimination. From the first flash of prophetic inspiration which is clearly discernible in the earlier portions of the book, he, later on, frequently descended to deliberate inventions and artful rhetoric. He, in fact, accommodated his moral sense to the circumstances in which the role he had to play involved him."

Even a research scholar and a sympathetic writer like Professor H. A. R. Gibb is led away on this point. He writes:

> "In the earliest period of his preaching, Muhammad's utterances were delivered in a sinewy oracular style cast into short rhymed phrases, often obscure and sometimes preceded by one or more formal oaths. This style is admittedly that of the ancient *Kahins* or Arabian oracle-mongers, and it is not surprising that Muhammad's opponents should have charged him with being just another such *Kahin.* For this and other reasons, his style gradually loosened out into a simpler but still rhetorical prose; and as social denunciations and eschatological visions passed into historical narrative,and that, in turn, at Medina into legislation and topical addresses, little was left of its original stylistic features but a loose rhyme or assonance marking the end of each verse, now anything from ten to sixty words long.

"Carlyle's dictum on the Quran: 'It is as toilsome reading as I ever undertook, a wearisome, confused jumble, crude, incondite. Nothing but a sense of duty could carry any European through the Quran, puts succinctly what must indeed be the first impression of any reader. But years of close study confirm his further judgement that in it there is a merit quite other than the literary one. If a book come from the heart, it will contrive to reach other hearts; all art and authorcraft are of small account to that'. Though, to be sure, the question of literary merit is one not to be judged on a priority grounds but in relation to the genius of the Arabic language; and no man in fifteen hundred years has ever played on that deep-toned instrument with such power, such boldness, and such range of emotional effects as Muhammad did.

"In trying to trace the sources and development of the religious ideas expounded in the Quran (a question, be it remembered, not only meaningless but blasphemous in Muslim eyes), we are still confronted with many unsolved problems'. Earlier scholars postulated a jewish source with some Christian additions. More recent research has conclusively proved that the main external influences (including the old Testament materials) can be traced back to Syriac Christianity."

"Arther Jaffery in *The Quran as Scripture* also offers the view that "The Quran is Muhammad's book" and tries to show that "Muhammad took over from his contemporaries a particular theory of the nature of Scriptures, and one particular form of the doctrine of a prophetic order with which scripture revelation was associated."

It has been observed that most of the English translators of Quran approach the Book with this preconceived bias. George Sale writes in his preliminary remarks to the translation:

> "I imagine it almost needless either to make an apology, or to go about to prove it a Work of use as well as curiosity. They must have a mean opinion of the Christian Religion, or be but ill-grounded therein, who can apprehend any change from so manifest a forgery. But whatever use an impartial version of the Koran may be, in other respects, it is absolutely necessary to undeceive those who, from the ignorant or unfair translations which have appeared, have entertained too favourable an opinion of the original, and also to enable us effectually to expose the imposture."

Rodwell and E. H. Palmer's approaches are not the least different.

And this bias has even spurred the historian to shower sarcasm. Professor Hitti writes:

> "Muhammad fearlessly continued to preach and by persuasion convert men from the worship of the many and false gods to that of one and true God, Allah. The revelations did not cease to "descend". He who had marvelled at the Jews and Christians having a "scripture" was determined that his people, too, should have one."

And worst of all, when some unbiased scholar tries to speak the other, other leaped orientalist rush to his throat and appeal to him in the name of objectivity, higher criticism, and historiography, to echo their bias. Just one extract from a review written by the leading orientalist, Dr. Alfred Guillaume, over

Dr. W. Montgomery Watt's book *Muhammad at Makkah* would suffice to illustrate this point:

> "It is when one comes to Dr. Watt's words on Muhammad's prophetic consciousness that one feels misgivings. He writes: 'We cannot with any plausibility imagine him *inserting verses of his own composition* (the italics are his) among those which came to him from his (supernatural) source independent of his consciousness (as he believed)'. Now Dr. Watt claims to be writing as a historian; consequently the reader has the right to expect that when a statement of this kind is made all the relevant historical evidence should be set forth. For instance one of Muhammad's wives is reported to have said that the revelations he received were remarkably in accord with his own wishes. Again the reader has the right to be told more of the philological evidence of the foreign informant's influence of which the *Quraysh* complained. One can sympathize with the writer's desire to spare the feelings of Muslims but would it not have been better to set out the evidence without any discussion of Muhammad's sincerity? The fact that the chapter Joseph is practically identical with a jewish *midrash* was established beyond question by Geiger more than a century ago: it is also a historical fact that the *Khawarij* refused to admit that it was divine revelation. Again, one is entitled to ask why, if the verses of the Quran were not Muhammad's own composition, did he drop the use of *saj'*, the style of the *kahins* and *sha'irs,* as soon as he was accused of being one of them? Is it creditable that the change was made apart from his own volition? Of course it is plain that the Quran contains much that is of the essence of divine truth and there is good ground for believing that Muhammad did from time to time have psychic experiences which he afterwards put into the haunting cadences of the Quran."

These are a few examples of the venom, bias and enmity towards Islam. The examples can be multiplied beyond any stretch of imagination because most of the Western scholars indulged in this most irresponsible attack on Islam.

Distortion and Misrepresentation

The authors and scholars from the West also resorted to the distortions, misrepresentations of facts, and wrong information which on the one hand give rise to misapprehensions in the minds of the uninformed people and on the other breed, quite justifiably, dis-satisfaction, anger and fury in the Muslim world. A few examples are given below:

Sir William Muir writes:

> "In Islam the relation of Allah to the world is such that not only all free-will but all freedom in the exercise of the intellect is preposterous. God is so great and the character of His greatness is so pantheistically absolute that there is no room for the human. Hope perishes under the weight of His iron bondage and pessimism becomes the popular philosophy."

Professor Clark says:

> "Islam saw God but not man; saw the claims of Deity, but not the rights of humanity; saw authority but failed to see freedom, therefore, hardened into despotism, stiffened into formalism, sank into death."

Islamic history is the worst victim of this treatment. Dr. Joseph Sehacht, despite all his learning and scholarship writes:

> "The chieftains considered themselves bound only to Muhammad and after his death both the state and the religion were threatened with dissolution. Thereupon certain influential associates of the prophet succeeded in effecting the maintenance of the monarchical principle and under it one of them was chosen the first caliph; that is, the successor to Muhammad in all the latter's functions except the specifically prophetic. The political leaders succeeded in focussing the lust

> of the various tribes for booty upon a common goal, the holy war for the spread of Islam. The extensive development of the doctrine of the *Jihad* at an early period indicates that the spirit of battle was fostered at the expense of everything else."

Edward A. Ferman, in his *History and Conquest of the Saracens,* writes:

> "To the pagan Arab, he, the Apostle of God, the preacher of righteousness; to the Christian of the most corrupt church who still acknowledged Christ as his God and Saviour, he was of a truth the very Anti-Christ and his followers are justly branded by the new of infidels. The other point in which I said that Mahomet was blameworthy was in endeavouring to establish a system beyond the limits of his own country. We may feel certain that Mahomet began his career merely as the Prophet of Arabia and gradually persuaded himself that he was the Prophet of the whole world. The result has been that a religious system adapted only for one age and country has been pressed upon the necks of all ages and the countries in which its votaries have been dominant. Mohametanism is a national system which attempts to be universal and which most grievously fails in its attempt The creed of Islam showed in far greater points how ill-suited it was to be transplanted beyond the limits of its native soil"

Even the renowned historian Arnold Toynbee commits a grievous folly and says something which is nothing short of gross misrepresentation. Toynbee writes:

> "Islam, as an institution, has suffered throughout its history from the note of secularity which has been characteristic of it hitherto. Insofar as this note of secularity has been a social blemish in the history of Islam, it must also be regarded as having been a personal misfortune in the career of Muhammad. The movement of Muhammad's life-work might have been something more ethereal than Islam, as Islam has

> been and is, if only the Prophet's career had not taken this decisively political turn in its last chapter. The historic development of Islam is a consequence of the fact that Muhammad's career, in Muhammad's actual circumstances, developed quite differently. Instead of sealing his prophetic message with his blood by becoming Caesar's victim, it was Muhammad's ironic destiny to compromise and debase his prophetic message by becoming an Arabian Caesar himself. No doubt Muhammad reasoned with his conscience thus; and no doubt he was deceiving himself in yielding to his arguments; for, in the event, the temporal power with which the Arabian Prophet endowed—or encumbered —his Islam at this crucial point in his career has proved to be not a vehicle but a prison-house, which has cribbed and cabined and confined the spirit of Islam ever since."

The learned historian has failed to understand the real message of Islam and is looking upon the problem from bigotted Christian view and the result is the strange phenomenon which he has produced.

Professor A. J. Arberry's views on *Sunnah* do not correctly present the position of Islam. He writes:

> "To revert now to Muslim religious thought, we should expect to find these same qualities of imagination and literalism displayed in the development of the theological system and its social applications. We do, in fact, see it very clearly in the interpretation of Koran; but a simpler example will be found in the treatment of the person, acts, and sayings of Muhammad. Under the impulse of veneration for the Prophet and for his office, the religious imagination begins to elaborate its conception of what a prophet should be—sinless, for example, and endowed with miraculous powers; and it progressively raises its standards, literalism obediently toils up behind it, producing out of the stores of tradition and by interpretation of Koranic verses the evidences and proofs required to consolidate

> the concept as a theological dogma. The religious imagination, not content with accepting the inspiration of the Koran, insists that the inspiration of the prophet cannot end there; this would be to allow too much liability to err. In all that he said and did he must be, at least tacitly, inspired, and *every* action must be capable of serving as the model for human action in the same sphere. The scholars, intent on expanding the doctrinal and legal systems based on the Koran and needing for these purposes the additional materials supplied by the tradition, formally incorporate it in the theological structure as a second infallible source. Then they build up a vast and intricate science by which spurious traditions can be detected and rejected and the accepted traditions can be classified in categories of "good", "less good", and "weak"."

Dr. Wilfred C. Smith outdoes all others when he offers the following definitions of 'Muslim' and Islam' which are given after the moving sermon: "A scientific study of religion waits upon many things, of which one is a clear definition of its terms".

"Muslim: any peson who calls himself a Muslim." "Islam: the religion of the Muslims."

He further elucidates:

> "The definition of Islam' is more revolutionary than it sounds. For instance, it does not prejudice the question whether Islam is always identical. In fact, especially in an individualist society, one man's religion is hardly likely to be the replica of another man's. More broadly, as one group faces another set, differing perhaps radically in time, place, and social status, it is not unnatural and surprising that one 'Islam', the religion of the Muslims in the one case, should be different from another 'Islam', the religion of the other Muslims in the other case."

Professor Brockelmann, a leading German orientalist, writes in his *History of the Muslim People* that "Arabs are selfish and self-centered. This is admitted in the *Ahadith* and the Holy Prophet permitted them to pray in the following way:

> "O Lord; Shower the mercy upon me and upon Prophet Muhammad and bestow it not to anyone else."

This is a sheer distortion which has totally changed the meaning of the *hadith.* The event is about a *beduin* and not the Arab in general and then in the *Hadith,* it is narrated that a *beduin* was praying in this way. When the Holy Prophet (peace be upon him) listened to it he asked him not to say the last words (i.e. bestow it not to anyone else) and instructed the man not to limit and narrow down something that was very wide.

The *Encyclopaedia of Islam* also presents queer interpretations and distortions.

In the article on Hazrat Aisha it says:

> "*Almost every intrigue was inspired by her* and she doubtless had a hand in the insurrection against that Caliph (Othman). But when Othman was besieged in his palace Aisha was not at Medina but *had prudently gone on a pilgrimage* to Mecca."

The article calls Ali "her *mortal enemy*". About Caliph Omer the *Encyclopaedia* says:

> "The ingenious theory put forward by Lammens about the 'triumvirate Abu Bakr, Omer, Abu Obaida. Al-Djarrah', these three individuals united by a bond of intimate friendship are said to have dominated and so to speak monopolised the authority of the prophet, controlling him either by direct action or through his wives (Aisha *bint* Abu Bakr and Hafsa faint Omer) may be to some extent correct but should not be pushed too far."

It is further said:

> ".... and it is also to him that a series of ordinances goes back, religious as well as civil and penal —the era of *Hijra,* the *punishment of drunkenness and stoning as punishment for adultery, in connection with the last it looks as if he did not hesitate to interpolate a verse in the text of the Quran.*"

The *Encyclopaedia* speaks of the Holy Quran in this vein:

> "It is the weakest part of the Kuran in which Muhammad's imagination apparently became exhausted, and he was content with tiresome repetitions of his earlier tales and especially with the tale of the prophets."

In the article on "*Maawiah*" it is said:

> "Here, he gained insight into the workings of the new regime and learned to know the men with whom he was later to work or struggle: the autocratic Omer, presumptuous Ali, a whole crowd of ambitious people like Talha, Zubair and Aisha."

About Musab bin Al-Zubair it is written:

> "Handsome, chivalrous, generous to the most foolish prodigity, he resembled his elder brother Abad Allah and the family of the *Zubairids* only in his tyranny and in his fits of severity in exacting punishment which bordered on barbarity." In the article on Imam Hussain it is said that the events:

"Were to prove the existence in the son of the same indecision and the same lack of intelligence that had been the ruin of his father."

This is the tone and temper of some of the writings of the *Encyclopaedia of Islam.*

Professor Hitti's *History of Arabs* also abounds in such mistakes and distortions. He begins the chapter on Islam by this insinuation:

> "It (Islam) has such close affinities with both (Judaism and Christianity), however, that in the conception of many medieval European and oriental Christian it stood as a heretic Christian sect rather than a distinct religion. In his *Divine Comedy,* Dante consigns Muhammad to one of the lower hells with all those 'sowers of scandals and schism. Gradually, Islam developed into an independent and distinct system of belief. The *Kabah* and *Quraysh* were the determining factors in this new orientation."

About the right-guided caliphs he writes:

> "The first party triumphed. The aged and pious Abu-Bakr, a father-in-law of the prophet, and one of the first three or four to believe in him, received the oath of allegiance from the assembled chiefs, probably in accordance with a previously arranged scheme between himself, Umer ibn al-Khattab and Abu Ubaydah ibn al-Jarrah, the triumvirate who presided over the destinies of infant Islam."

The author alleges that the famous companion al-Zubair had a dispute on Caliphate with Ali. In the case of Ibne-al Muqaffa he writes:

> "A Zoroastrian convert to Islam whose suspect orthodoxy brought about his death by fire."

This insinuation has been made despite the fact known to all students of Islamic history that Ibne-Muqaffa was put to death for betraying the caliph by leaking out the contents of a treaty which was written by him. And our learned author does not even hesitate to say, while discussing the prevalence of the use of drinks and intoxicants that the prophet himself used *Nabidh*. Now what relation has the *Nabidh* which the Holy Prophet used to the intoxicants which were taken by the latter wealthy and corrupt people—only a leading orientalist can explain. Our learned historian also tells us that:

> "Prohibition, one of the distinctive features of Muslim religion, did no more prohibit then than did the eighteen amendment to the Constitution of the United States."

This is how he depicts the holy cities of the Muslims:

> "With this increased flow of wealth the two Holy Cities became less holy. They developed into a centre of worldly pleasure and gaity and a home of secular Arab music and song. In Makkah was established a club-house patronised by the guests. To al-Madinah Persian and Byzantine slave songstresses flocked in increasing numbers. Houses of ill-repute flourished in al-Madinah and were patronized by no less a poet

than al-Farazdaq of national fame. As these female slaves sang and played soft melodies for the entertainment of their wealthy masters and guests, the latter, attired in colourful robes, reclined on square mattresses or cushions while they inhaled the perfume of burning spices and sipped from silver goblets the ruddy wines of Syria."

And all this on what authority? On the authority of *Kitab-ul-Aghani* which is not a book of history nor a record of that what happened but a collection of folklores, stories, tell-tales and the like and about which even the author himself admits that:

> "Most of our information about the lighter side of the Caliph's lives comes from *Aghani,* primarily a literary work, and similar books, which should not be taken too literally. *Aghani,* Vol. I, p. 3 gives this criterion for the choice of date: "elegance that pleases the onlookers and entertainers the hearers."

Throughout the book—and not of this book alone, but most of the history books written by Western authors—this kind of irresponsible account which is not based on facts is presented without the least qualm of conscience. It is surprising as to why the Western scholars, who have established in different fields very high standards of criticism and authenticity, when they come to Islam, do not remain adhered to those standards. As a result of this they sometimes say things that are ridiculous and this pains those serious students who hold a good opinion about the labours and contributions of the leading orientalists. Look for instance to Professor Alfred Guillaume, leading and respectable orientalist, whose devotion and sincere efforts in the field of learning is beyond any shadow of doubt and whose services in the cause of promoting better understanding about Islam must be gratefully acknowledged. But it is most unfortunate that he too has not been very careful in checking the contents of his book *Islam* published in the Pelican Series. He writes:

> "A woman in Islam cannot sue for divorce on any grounds."

Can anything be more farther from truth? His observations in the chapter *"Islam Today"* are most unfortunate and quite baseless. He is of the view that modernist movement in Islam has gained momentum in the last century.

The New Line of Attack

J. M. Rodwell in his translation of the Quran suggested a new line of attack upon Islam. He wrote:

> "A line of argument to be adopted by a Christian missionary in dealing with a Muhammadan should be, not to attack Islam as a mass of error, but to show that it contains fragments of disjointed truth—that it is based upon Christianity and Judaism partially understood —especially upon the latter, without any appreciation of its typical character pointing to Christianity as a final dispensation."

This line of argumentation has become *very* popular with the Western scholars.

Professor A. S. Tritton writes:

> "The religion which Muhammad preached was electic but that does not hinder it from being a real religion. His debt to the Bible is obvious to anyone who has eyes to see; it may be that his religious life was started by suggestions received from outside the Arab circle of ideas. He took stories from both Testaments to illustrate and enforce his ideas about God, providence and the last judgement. Man being what he is no one can invent a new religion entirely unlike those which have gone before. The Koran often mentions prayers at night; they cannot be separated from the nocturnal services of the monasteries. One cannot escape the impression that Muhammad purposely made the observances of his religion different. The five daily prayers were in antithesis to the hours of the church. The fast was at first copied from the Jews but was later changed to something more like the Christian practice, again with a difference. Christians used the *naqus* to announce the time of public worship and the Jews used the ram's horn on the day of atonement and

the new year; the Muslims employed the human voice. Muhammad chose Friday as the day for public worship—again the difference —but he did not make it a day of rest, perhaps borrowing the idea from Zoroastrianism from which was taken also the bridge across hell along which all must pass. The pilgrimage came from pagan Arabia. It was maintained as part of the policy by which the inhabitants of Makkah were reconciled to Islam. After the conquest the new converts there received many gifts from Muhammad to the disgust of the people of Medina, both Helpers and Emigrants, who felt themselves slighted and wronged. Muhammad had to defend himself and did so on the ground that he was binding the hearts of the new Muslims more tightly to Islam. It is hard to resist the conclusion that the retention of the pilgrimage was to preserve the profits of it to Makkah and made it worth the citizens while to be Muslims. At the same time it was adapted to the religion of Abraham. He and Ishmael had built the Kaba, the course between Safa and Marwa was in memory of the Hagar's frantic search for water for her son, and the well *Zemzem* was the source which was given to her by a miracle."

Dr. Joseph Gaer writes:

> "As a camel driver, Muhammad had learned much of the teachings of Judaism and Christianity from the many Jews and Christians he had met and talked. When the New Testament was read to Muhammad, the story of Jesus convinced him that what his country needed was an inspired prophet. The teachings of the Testaments, New and Old, were now always in Muhammad's mind."

Joseph Schacht tries to prove that "the Muslim law does not have a Muslim (and still less a Koranic) basis. It is Roman, Byzantine, Persian, etc., law assimilated —never perfectly—to a 'revealed' system of moral requirements."

And Professor Hitti goes to the extent of discovering Zoroastrian influences in the famous Quranic verse:

> "Allah is the Light of heavens and the earth."

He writes:

> "The verses in this *surah* dealing with light betray Zoroastrian influence."

Liberalism vs. Modernism

Another painful fact is that the Western scholars, following the line of European powers, try to encourage all those elements who want to discard Islam or distort it and call them liberal and modern and progressive; and condemn and ridicule those who are working for the revival of Islam. This is the approach which orientalists have adopted about Islamic revival.

Manfred Helpern, in an article in the *Muslim World* remarks:

> "The neo-Islamic movements project into modern political life a more archaic approach to problems, deriving most of their emotional and conceptional characteristics from an age which long preceded the evolution of modern nationalism. "

The leading scholar Vera Michales Deen writes:

> "The Muslim countries are now engaged in a struggle that will determine whether the rigid authoritarianism of Islam can be adapted to modern life—and adapted without the bloodshed of revolution—or make the attempt, favoured by some Muslim leaders, to return to its glorious but now vanished past. Islam has never experienced a process of intellectual change comparable to the Reformation in Europe. It must go through such a reformation in our time if it is not to be rejected by the younger elements of Arab countries who want modernisation. On the contrary, the inherent authoritarianism of Islam may make it far more susceptible to the authoritarian idea of Communism."

This is how the Western scholars are looking upon the world of Islam. Notwithstanding an incontestably rational and balanced approach, honest divergences in viewpoints are likely to arise, as one is given to conceive and evaluate of other's attitudes, faith, philosophy of life and code of ethics, etc., in the light of one's own experience and through stages of one's own perception. The experience being alluded to is individual and collective, primal and recent, religious and secular. Perception is a function of interaction between previous experience the object of interest and the present inclination of mind. The degree of this inter-relationship can vary, but the nexus itself does not vanish. In accordance with Islam, the Muslims unilaterally consider the Christians as 'people of the Scripture' and regard Jesus Christ as a prophet, with feelings of profound reverence. The incorguity with the Christians is not over the 'religion of Jesus Christ', but over the altered form and features that it developed after the departure of Jesus. As Dr. Enslin observed: "It is today perfectly obvious that there is a vast difference between the nature of the messages of Jesus and Paul. But it is nonetheless certain that had there been no changes, there would have been no Christianity". Because of the attributes of these 'changes', many authorities on religion concur that the 'religion of Jesus' and Christianity are not precisely synonymous denotations. For these and similar other reasons, some of the fundamental doctrines of Christianity, e.g., the Trinity, the Divine Sonship of Jusus and the Original Sin, find points of departure from the Islamic religious principles.

From the perspective of Christianity, the points of divergence from Islam lie in the Islamic: (a) mode of spread, (b) punishment for crimes, (c) economics, and (d) the provisions on polygamy and divorce. Though there is discordancy on these points pertaining to diverse areas, a common denominator is shared by each religion. The role of a characteristic religio-historic experience in Europe furnishes a common background for these divergencies—the cleavage between Church and State which was effected in the fourteenth century and thereafter in the West. Contrarily, the inseparable interlocking of the spiritual and the secular in Islam poses some hindrance in the intellectual and emotional accommodation of some portions of the Islamic code by the Christian West with a contrasting religious experience. Factually, the preceding truism is not as vehemently applicable to Islam's mode of spread. For the sake of completion as also suggestd by Leonard, a comparison between the smallness of means available and the astounding results achieved during the initial course of Islamic history, will indicate the mode of spread — innate appropriateness of Islamic faith and its potential for appeal to human reason and conscience.

Islam is, par excellence, a religion of laws and a complete code of life. Being a composite and unified way of life, Islam demarcates a far wider perimeter of influence in the life of a believer, as in Islamic society, than is the case with any other universal religion. The totality of Islam pervades equally through sacred and secular, economic and political, cultural and social avenues of individual and societal aspects of life. The all encompassing nature of Islam combined with its universally admired features of simplicity, practicality and realism has immeasurably aided in retaining its religious vibrancy until today, despite the corrosive impact of a colonial past. This fact seems to acquire even larger dimension considering the present era of general religious decline. The presence of nominal theology and mythology, and the virtual absence of a religious hierarchy in Islam, unlike in other higher religions including Christianity, has helped in maintaining the internal cohesiveness of the Muslims. Through the two cardinal underpinnings of the Islamic ideology—the Quran and the *Hadith*—Islam has preserved the original purity of its revelations, as these sources remained free of any deformation. Commenting on the Quran about a century ago, William Muir (Sir) noted: "There is probably in the world no other work which has remained twelve centuries with so pure a text". This authenticity and approximation to the original which has been but not so much the good fortune of other universal religions, has maintained a continuing newness and preserved the vitality of Islam.

In the sphere of human credo, any attempts lightly undertaken to demonstrate the fortes of one and the vulnerabilities of another is an exercise, more often than not, in futility. Granting due cognisance to this fact, the effort here is not to draw comparisons merely to establish the superiority of one religion over the other, but to glean those points which have a direct bearing upon and pertinency to the present theme. The same outlook permeates through comparative histories. Often enough and lacking in precision, the term 'renaissance' is utilised, sometimes even interchangeably, to describe the present Islamic resurgence, and this is done in the context of European history.

After all, the chorus of reform in the renaissance period—14th and 15th centuries A. D. —had protested abuses in the church. The Humanists, the adherents of the New Devotion, the movements raised by Wycliff and Huss, had differed in detail but they had one voice against the clergy—its moral and financial corruption and the obstacles it erected between man and his God. The renaissance attitude was a re-evaluation because it departed in many respects from the medieval, or Christianity's viewpoint which attached overriding importance to the next world and dogmatised that the way to salvation lay in renouncement of life in this world.

With the recognition at last that Aristotle, Cicero and Seneca had not written to support the doctrine of the medieval church, an interest in the literature of Greece and Rome and a true perception of the meaning of Classical civilisation were 'reborn' —literal meaning of renaissance. Under the confluence of such drives, it had begun to be recognised also that ethics was not invented by Christianity. Acceptance of this idea subsequently evolved into a 'personal' concept of morality which still later was tranformed into a 'utilitarian' concept of morality in Western Europe. For one endowed with keen insight into history, it is easy to discover that the seeds of atheistic ideology were sown during this period and were to blossom on European soil in due course of time.

These combustibles of revolution bore manifest results, but not until the sixteenth century when the posting of Martin Luther's *Ninety-Five Thesis* caused an explosion. A revolution had begun that was to rend the universal Church into the greatest of all schisms: it was to plunge Western Europe into more than a century of religious and social conflicts, and it was to affect profoundly the course of European life in centuries to come. The future concept of nationalism in European mold lay dormant in the fold of events taking shape in the historic crucibles of the renaissance and subsequently the reformation.

Renaissance or Resurgence

To define the contemporary Islamic resurgence in a fashion as to claim unanimity is to simply state thus: attempts to conjoin efforts for energising the present by reclaiming the past. Interestingly, many pragmatic historians use similar expressions to describe the renaissance which "looked backward as the two centuries before 1300 A.D. had looked forward". "And, more than a few Islamic orientalists—the Oriental and the Western together—utilise the term renaissance while describing the Islamic resurgence. Perhaps a case of inadvertent usage, but in the literal and historical context of the term 'renaissance' it is an imprecise, if not improper, substitution for 'resurgence' in the Islamic context. As a matter of fact, these terms tend to describe two inherently dissimilar historical movements comprising of more religio-political features in contrast than in common.

For instance, if both historical movements attempted at 'reclaiming the past', then the renaissance looked to the past 'predating' the Christian era and into the classical (Greeco —Roman) period; while the resurgence is looking to the past 'coinciding' with the dawn of Islam and onward. The renaissance was basically a revolt against the tyranny of the medieval church; the resurgence is a revulsion against the acquired 'spiritual torpor'. The morally corrupt clergy in the renaissance was cast in the role of a villain; the morally sound men of religion *(ulema)* in the resurgence have carved out for themselves the role of a hero. The renaissance ultimately resulted in permanently cleaving religion from politics; the resurgence is striving to permanently reinforced politics with religion. Atheism was to be an inevitable by-product of the trends unleashed by the renaissance; close approximation of the sublime and the mundane will be a by-product of the resurgence. Nationalism in Western European mold was the political offspring of the renaissance who, time and again, violently rocked its own cradle and beyond, the resurgence aims at fostering a supranational entity with resultant elimination of the very cause of national conflicts.

With the afore-outlined differentiations in view, the notion that Islam needed to undergo its 'reformation' under a 'Muslim

Luther' appears absurdly irrelevant. And, no less irrelevancy is evident from the exhortation that the Muslims are 'to rethink Islam in modern terms'.

Islamic Contribution to Renaissance

Any serious student of history should be aware of the fact that no sharp breaks occur between one period of history and another, that we have only to be reminded that the elements of the new attitude were in fermentation a long time before a distinct trend is noticeable. Islamic preaching that 'there is no compulsion in religion' finds a wide applicability in the theory and practice of Islam and, from the Islamic viewpoint, is equally useful for other religions as well. (The Quran, 11 —256). Significantly, this Islamic belief might well have constituted the fibre, if not in content then certainly in context running through the whole texture of the renaissance. After all, new information and conceptions had been filtering into the West during the era of the Crusades. Knowledge of the Islamic civilisation being utterly devoid of religious hierarchy, and witnessing the practicality of the Islamic precept of no compulsion in religion must had been to the, and not so little, envy of those who were groaning under the oppression of the universal church.

As a mere historical fact of contributing Islamic ideas as such, it should only be of academic interest to the Islamic civilisation. After all, historically, cross-currents of ideas—cultural, religious, political, etc., be it of utility or to the detriment, have left indelible imprints on many a society and civilisation. But, as an historic incidence, inhibition of the Islamic belief of 'no compulsion in religion' proved remarkably eventful for both the Western and the Islamic civilisations. The revolutionising impact of the twin historic movements of the renaissance and the reformation on the Western civilisation, has already been briefly outlined. The Islamic civilisation through the vicissitudes of history, fell under the Western colonial domination and, thence, was fully exposed to the consequences of the renaissance. These influences carried in their wake mixed blessings—beneficial in the fields of natural sciences and mathematics: inimical in the arenas of religion, politics and culture.

Islam's original home base was located at the cross-roads of three continents. Beholden to a faith of all-embracing totality, possessing an unmatched dynamism and led by charismatic personalities, Islam enormously widened its sphere of influence. Today, the Islamic countries are spread over three continents, at one place forming a contiguous stretch from Pakistan to Morocco, which is briefly interrupted by a small geographical wedge of Israel. For its location, the Islamic landmass had to be constantly on guard against Europe; but having once been beset by a process of inner decay, it gradually fell under Western colonialism. Paradoxically, there was nothing to warn the collapse that came, beginning in the late eighteenth century when the Dutch took over the Indies, and running its course until the Anglo—Russian occupation of Iran. Islam in the beginning of its fourteenth century was confronted with diametrically opposite set of problems compared with the West in the Renaissance period. All but a few Islamic countries lay under colonial domination. This Western taking-over was so thorough that only four countries in the vast Islamic stretch—Afghanistan, Saudi Arabia, Yemen and Turkey—could retain their political independence for a variety of reasons and that also to a nominal extent. Islamic countries in the Far East were to share the same fate.

Ways and Effects

But only an abridgement of an otherwise vast and complex theme of the ways and the effects of colonialism on Islam—faith and polity combined —is appropriate here. An American scholar, Charles F. Callaghan, describes the colonial policy in sum and substance thus: "A methodical policy of deracination and destruction was followed" during the nineteenth century with the intention to "destroy the colonies by a complete denigration of their fundamental values". The Western colonial Powers though neglected of the traditional educational system in their Muslim territories, weakened the older set of values. As stated by G. H. Jansen: "A spiritual and cultural vacuum was created by allowing the traditional roots to wither away unnourished". Out of these so effected, only a small segment was allowed an alternative of Western system of education and, for a majority of such young Muslims even this turned out to be a semi-fulfilling affair through mental regiments which neither entirely satisfied nor amply educated the mind. The elite were educated into a state of alienation from their own cultural background, thereby creating a schism in the soul of the society. As Benda observed: "In the final analysis, Western education was the surest means of reducing and ultimately defeating the influence of Islam in Indonesia". A minuscule number of the Muslims only were able to receive the full benefits of higher Western education whereby they could, perhaps, attain a true understanding of the spiritual, cultural and other values of the West. It was no mere historical coincidence that a preponderant number of 'successful' freedom movements against the Western colonialism were led by the highly Western-educated personalities in Islamic countries, as in other colonies. For these and other reason, the highest echelons of Western education were available to few only from the colonial domains. The preferred medium of instruction was in European languages, and the language curricula put undue emphasis on the classical rather than colloquial aspects, with the result that after years of studying the language, the proficiency in it remained generally inadequate. Some of the colonial Powers achieved these results through policy designs, while others arrived at them by default.

The missionaries of civilisation were followed closely behind by the missionaries of religion; in some instances, however, a reversal of this pattern took place. It was missionary activity closely allied with the extension of imperial power that presented a significant challenge of Islam. Apparently holy men from these Western countries entered into a basically unholy alliance with 'Caesar'. That conversions would increase the number of 'loyal subjects' in the colonies was the motive, besides, of course, the evengelical urge and 'the yearning to pluck the brands from the burning pyres; The French occupation of Algeria was carried out under the advice that it would also be of 'the greatest benefit to Christendom'. The Dutch authorities in Indonesia, under the advice of Hurgronje, pursued a policy which even went so far as to reduce the number of Indonesians performing the *Haj*. For it was considered that in Makkah they were infected with the 'virus' of activist Islam. Active alliance between the pulpit and the British colonial Scepter brought forth an 'anti-Islamic' and Christian Bantustan in Southern Sudan. The much-professed Western adherence to the idea of secularism—separation of politics and religion and the neutrality of the State—provide no hindrance in the execution of official policies in the colonial territories. All these various missionary activities appear a mere fraction of the concept underlying the colonising endeavour that the lease of power to the State of Islam is a lease of life to her ideologies.

As to how far the missionary activities succeeded in their aims in Africa and the Near East, brief summing up may be borrowed from Latourette: "In proportion to the total population, Christians had become fewer than they had been since the second or third century". For factual accuracy, to cast a glance at the reverse side of the Western missionary undertakings in the occupied lands, the creditable humanitarian work accomplished stands out laudably.

The process of intellectual and cultural osmosis with the direction of exchange from the West towards the Islamic East and, more so during the past century, has partially succeeded in creating ambivalence in the minds of some Muslims about the role of religion in life. Western Islamic orientalists have made not an insignificant contribution towards this process, as until recently an overwhelming portion of Islamic literature was authored by Western scholars. No fair reason exists to blame them for this intellectual hold, however; the distortions produced concerning Islam is an altogether different matter. For the pettiness of this polemical material about Islam and the vulgarity of the inconsiderate remarks made against the Prophet of Islam, those are unworthy of mention and should be condemned in strongest terms not only by the world of Islam but also by the saner elements in the West. Nevertheless, the intellectuals of the enlightened West making some very unenlightened remarks against a universal religion, for its conspicuous oddity, requires some explanation more suitable than mere prejudice. As suggested by N. A. Daniels, "the polemical material corresponded to need. It made it possible to protect the minds of Christians against apostasy and it gave Christiandom self-respect in dealing with a civilisation in many ways its superior.

Mention, however, must be made of more than a few Western orientalists, including Gibb, who have often employed the disagreeable, if not offensive, term Muhammadanism: This may be a matter of single word, but a word whose use or non-use is most indicative of basic attitudes. Occasionally, some of the Islamic orientalists from the East also tend to share the same restricting experience with their Western counterparts. To mention one such instance, A. A. Fayzee —he recently expired —contends:

> "Since ethics are personal, attempts to enforce them through the *Shariah* are unnecessary."

Unmistakably reminiscent of the renaissance, this idea in its cultural milieu grew rapidly into outright atheism which has turned out to be a nemesis of the West, and yet may prove to be its undoing. On another occasion, Fayzee suggested that the observance in Islam, including "the fasting and prayers—retard inner spiritual development". For his failure to directly point out the ways to 'facilitate' inner spiritual development, he leaves, himself open to the charge of practising iconoclasm in Islam. Ironically, this type of imprudence betrays a lack in fine sense of history, notwithstanding the pretensions.

Reality of Militancy

As universally recognised, for Islam being a composite of the ideal and the real, it was inevitable that assertion to make Islam central to every aspect of life, including politics, in the Muslim countries be made. Not surprisingly the early period of Islam has been, historically, the most glorious period for the Islamic civilisation as well. The era of the 'right guided caliphs' is viewed nostaligically through the obscuring mists of time as the 'golden age' of Islam. A review of history manifests that spiritual, political and intellectual ascendency, or otherwise, in Islam have followed a common course. And herein may also lie the unmitigated clues for the Islamic Resurgence through utilisation of and reliance on the ideological self-sufficiency of Islam. Noteworthy is the fact that in contradistinction, the Christian civilisation began its historic ascent concomitant with the initiation of the split between the church and the State and, one may point out, several centuries after the advent of Christianity.

If Islam, being the consummate product of all the revealed religions, provides the ideological self-sufficiency, then the Muslims are the raw material for the potential convergence of belief and practice in Islam. A brief review of certain aspects of this equation in Islam today between past and present, between apprehension and confidence, between the stuff of events and the dictates of spirit reveals the essential differentiating factor. And this alterable factor is nothing but the gradually increasing repudiation of their 'spiritual torpor' by the Muslims. This in turn has resulted in increased efforts by the Muslims to energise their present by reclaiming the Islamic past. Occasionally though, because of the circumstances, eviction of imperialism by clues derived from its own nature, has been the prerequisite. This process is the essence of a somewhat teleological epithet of 'Militant Islam'. Conceivably, the subliminal fears of the West in tradition with the earliest reactions to Islam find expression in this erroneous term.

The sporadic struggle against colonial domination was waged in one part of the Islamic world or in another throughout this period, and the name of Jamaluddin Afghani (1839-97) stands out in this backdrop amongst the Islamic leaders of that period. At the time, the Muslims neither seemed to believe that the militant Europe could be effectively resisted nor was it known how to set about doing so. During his frequent visits to various Islamic countries this charismatic personality, blessed with eloquence, through the medium of fine oratory rejuvinated the spirit of Islamic resistance. Even more significantly, he envisioned Islam as a single historical entity and popularised the idea of Islamic federation under a 'just and strong ruler' guided by Divine law. In the scheme of things as envisaged by this great Islamic visionary, the Muslim nations were:

(1) to build their respective innate strength;

(2) to go on to achieve independence from Western colonialism;

(3) each state would then adopt Islamic constitutional order; and

(4) ultimately to join in an Islamic federation. Ever since *Afghani,* all Islamic nation States have acquired political independence through actual physical eviction of the occupying Powers or its mere threat. Now the efforts are underway and, in several of the Islamic countries

simultaneously to introduce an Islamic constitutional order. Contingent upon successful completion of this phase of the Islamic Resurgence, it will be a prelude to the Islamic federation as proposed by *Afghani.*

The Islamic Resurgence, proceeding at its current pace in countries with Muslim majority, presents a contrasting picture in the perspective of its inhibited, distracted and undynamic colonial variety from the adjoining past. Immediately prior to this and, for several centuries retrogradely, somewhat politically disoriented and spiritually debilitated variety of Islam comes into view. Although during these same nearly six centuries, the Muslims established the Ottoman Empire in the Near East and the Moghul Empire in India besides attaining some other lesser gains. And what had changed was not Islam per se; neither then, nor now.

Ever since the Islamic societies regained their political independence, the focus of major emphasis might have shifted, but the task remains essentially unfinished. "The real significance of Islam", as acutely remarked by Gibb, "is the inward reaction towards the Western cultural values which are seeking to find their place with Muslim society under cover of these borrowings". There is no arguing the fact that the fragments of another culture, when established in a new environment, are more often than not destructive in effect, especially if it happens to be an Islamic social environment. Even more significantly, the established cultural fragments pave way for and induct other fragments from the parent culture set into the new environment. Gibb lays out the alternatives for the Muslim society: "Everything depends on the capacity of Muslim society to defend and protect its values and cultural traditions against the Western invasion. If it fails in the task it is lost as a Muslim society, it will inevitably become a more or less faithful copy of Western society with secondary characteristics peculiar to the different countries and languages". And, it is also to 'defend and protect that a sincere attempt is being made by Islamic society in various countries simultaneous to remodel private and public life according to Islamic precepts. The *ulema,* it seems have finally come upon the course of will to reason and fact after years of vehement but often sterile debates the misery of disunity and the unity of strife. In turn this is inducing the Muslims in general to part with the tentativeness and stereotyped habits of mind acquired during an inglorious past. Consequently that Islam is the religious ideal, reality is being given a general recognition, and any discrepancy between the ideal and the actual is explained by the fact of decadent Muslims. Upon the completion of these stages hinges another vital issue — prospects of a wider unity, as envisaged by *Afghani.*

After all, the Muslims, with a tradition of internationalism, cannot afford to regress towards provincial loyalties while Western Europe and other parts of the world move toward supranational unification. The notion that nationalism and supranational Islamic unification are two mutually exclusive entities is utterly devoid of merit, at least according to the Islamic concept. As Islam was a source of inspiration for national independence during the colonial era so as compatibly can nationalism now contribute towards Islamic unification. Admittedly, the same can never be repeated in the context of European nationalism. As envisaged by the Islamic visionaries like *Afghani* and his disciple, Abduh, and in more recent times by Iqbal, Islam in alliance with national feeling is the basis of a supranational unification. Whether the spiritual nationality, which already exists so amply and uniquely in Islam, will suitably act as the matrix for overall Islamic unification, will be the cumulative decision of the Muslims. The issue of obstacles standing in the way of Islamic unification defy any circumvention. According to the Islamic ideology, the outcome of a monumental event emerges out of the struggle itself like a new creation and defying any prediction. And it would be remiss here not to quote Toynbee: "Pan Islamism is dormant—yet we have to reckon with the possibility that the sleeper may awake if ever the cosmopolitan proletariat of a Westernised world revolts against Western domination and cries out for anti-Western leadership". Here attention must be drawn towards 'proletariat' which, in this particular setting, connotes unpropertied middle and high-level governmental functionaries especially the latter. Is the expression 'Western domination' as well applicable on the Islamic countries of the post-colonial era? Did Toynbee ever mean if not necessarily here that the expression 'anti-Western' and 'Islamic' are synonymous? Accordingly, if the Westernised proletariat does not 'revolt', it stands guilty of perverting a wholly justifiable search for a dignified identity after centuries of decadence.

If the West could overcome its primordial fear of Islam which otherwise stands to cloud its judgement, no rational basis exists that Islamic unification may prove detrimental to Western interests. As far as one can assess, the real problem confronting the West is the spiritual void, both within and without. While the West should attempt to replanish its own spiritual reservoïr, it must, if not actually enhance, do nothing to retard the process of spiritual growth outside of it. This no mere hyperbole to suggest that in case otherwise happens, the West may cease to exist the way we know it. In this context, suffice it to mention that spiritual and political developments of Islam are interdependent.

The vain hope that the intermediate stages between the present misery of disunity and potential happiness of unification may be leap-frogged denies the necessity of realism. Irrespective of the unpredictability of future course reawakening of the Muslim to a heightened level of spiritual and political consciousness will remain a decisive factor. In this regard to describe the spiritual malady afflicting the Islamic people as 'spiritual torpor' may be a charitable view in all awareness. For the pathos of a tragic flaw which developed in the Muslims is self-evident from their slackening on the course laid out by the Chosen Messenger who incidentally, was ranked first amongst all great men in a recent book entitled, The *100: A Ranking of the* Most *Influential Persons in History'*.

An incomparable suggestion for accomplishing the task of Islamic Resurgence is given by Husayn Haykal: Muslims must renew themselves only from their own past and not be deceived by the material seductions of the West". Is it not that Islam, being a religion of divine values is not dissociable from any reality that is identified with it? The response will serve to highlight the axiom that Islam reformed is Islam no longer. The next logical derivation that ensues will be to regard Islam as the norm by which the world is to be judged: an enterprise which is intricately linked with the drive for and the achievements of the Islamic Resurgence.

Unlike Christianity, Islam is more than a religion. It is a complete way of life. The distinction between religion and state that exists in Western societies is foreign to Islam. It not only answers all recurrent questions of daily life, such a suffering, injustice, death, grief, fear, salvation in the hereafter, but also has institutions to deal with political, economic, social, educational and other public problems. It also has the unique concepts of *Ummah, Akhuwwah* and *Adl*.

Muslims have a long history of which they are very proud. When Christianity moved into the dark ages, Islam swelled in intellectual growth in centres like Baghdad, Damascus, Cairo, Toledo, Cordova, etc. It was the world's most vital civilisation up to the end of the 16th century, possessing greater part of the world's mineral, agricultural and industrial resources, financial power and technical and trading skill. The Hispano-Arab Spain produced great astronomers, mathematicians, philosophers and historians. To this great classical period of Islam, the West owes much of its inheritance of mathematics and astronomy.

But since then the Muslims have been in a chronic crisis—a crisis that began and reached its culmination during the Western dominance. The West, during its colonial control, aimed at, in the words of Arnold Toynbee, "nothing less than the incorporation of all mankind in a single great society and the control of everything on the earth, air and sea". He observes that "the struggling Muslims are once more facing the West with their back to the wall. But this time the odds are more heavily against them than they were even at the most critical moment of the Crusades, for the West is superior to them not only in arms but also in the techniques of economic life on which military science ultimately depends".

The imperial Powers set about this task of de-culturising the Muslims in a systematic manner to ensure that the latter should not be able to recover and reorganise themselves into a vital force. They introduced their political, social and economic ideas and produced a whole generation of Muslim elites who believed that the West provides the panacea for all the ills of the society. Unless they adopted Western culture as W. C. Smith remarks they were unlikely to survive.

The Western-educated elites, who took over power at the end of the Western dominance in most of the Muslim countries, introduced political, economic social and educational systems modelled on those of the West, but they failed to overcome the problems of their societies. Doubtless, economic expansion took place but the distribution of its benefits remained so patently unjust that the very fact of economic expansion became a source of widespread poverty and discontent. It has divided society into different classes pitted against one another. The wealth has concentrated in the hands of a few privileged people. For a vast majority of the population, the blessings of the 20th century are still denied.

It has dawned upon the Muslims that the blind following of the Western culture is the main cause of their degeneration. To put it more precisely, this degeneration is due to the fact that they have been kept too far from their glorious tradition. This has made the Muslim society rootless. Now a point has come when they are giving a second thought to the usefulness of reposing faith in those western institutions which have not only become a cause of their degeneration but are also a source of weakness to the West itself. To the masses, Islam is a fact, a goal, a commitment, and the only way to rise out the quagmire of ignorance and decay.

Muslims yearn for a decent life in the light of their own history and tradition. They call for a return to the simplicity of the generation of the Holy Prophet (peace be upon him). The movement is sweeping the Islamic world with varying degrees of force. The governments of Iran, Pakistan, Algeria, Kuwait, Syria, Saudi Arabia, Turkey, Iraq, Afghanistan, Yemen, Indonesia and Morocco are all receiving the echo of this call. Millions of Muslims of the former Soviet Union have also not been left untouched by this resurgence.

The impact of the call for the revival of Islam will probably not be seen in a correct perspective by general population in the West for a while yet. However, the Western governments have expressed their deep concern over the developments taking place in the Muslim world. They have invested billions of dollars in the region. Basides, they would like to have a certain degree of control over the warm-water ports and routes between the Suez Canal and the Bay of Bengal—not for trading purposes, of course, but for a regular and sure supply of the oil produced in the Muslim world.

Western intellectuals are not ready to ignore the current developments, and are observing the situation with great curiosity. Some Western commentators opine that these developments are retrograde, xenophobic, anti-Christian, anti-modernisation, uncompromising and pro-communist.

The West has atavistic fears. Its knowledge about Islam is unfortunately peripheral. Islam is a humanistic religion. It is a progressive, dynamic and forward-moving force. It is neither brutal nor retrogressive nor is it against science and technology. In order to have better perception and closer thinking, the Western intellectuals should study the Quran and the *Sunnah.* It is not the *Mullah* only who holds the Quran dear; rather it is the millions of Western-educated Muslims, having a first-hand knowledge of Western theories and institutions, who believe that it is the Quran alone that can lead out of the present degradation. Still the most important point of concensus all over the Muslim world, the Quran also sincerely preaches and promotes harmony and peace in the comity of nations. It threatens no one, and, on the contrary, enjoins that co-operation should be sought with all those who are willing to do so. Further, it is not a barrier in the say of achieving a comfortable modern life, provided the modernisation does not aim at fulfilling materialistic needs only. When modernisation disregards moral matters, it always ends up in the breakdown of social structure. And no ideology would, of course, permit this kind of progress.

No doubt the Muslims have been in a state of stagnation for the last five centuries. But how does one deduce from this that Islam is the cause of this stagnation or that Islam has nothing more to offer to mankind. The laws of the rise and fall of nations and their growth and decline cannot, in their application, be limited to a few centuries. Islam is still the only ideology available to man for his material and spiritual fulfilment. Capitalism, Socialism and Communism are not ideologies, they are at best strategies of economic growth. None of them professes to deal with the problems of creation, life after death, the mysteries of the soul, and mental contentment. To these systems all such considerations are irrelevant. They concentrate solely on the theories of development and on programmes for the material advancement of man in the context of the present.

It appears that the West is bent upon opposing and nullifying the resolve of the Muslim societies for moulding their lives according to the principles of Islam. This opposition should not be underestimated. The economic and political forces for the West have a tremendous power and potentials to thwart the Muslim revival. Peregrine Worsthorne in his article *"Islam: Exorcising* the *Western Gods"*, (originally published in The *Wall Street Journal'* on January 25, 1979) remarks that if the West chooses to use its economic strength, let alone its military might, it can break the Islamic resurgence movement without the slightest difficulty.

It is in the interest of the Muslims to tackle the tedious situation, and at least minimise the West's hostility. The Muslims should give serious thought to dispel the misunderstandings of the West. For this the following line of action is recommended:

(a) International Islamic institutions stationed in the major cities of the Western countries should be encouraged to counter the allegations which are being made in the Western news media.

(b) The Islamic Secretariat at Jeddah and Rabita al-Alam al-Islami should organise seminars in various Western cities, especially the centres of learning and opinion formation, to explain the motivating forces working in the Muslim world for Islamic resurgence with a special reference to its positive and progressive socio-economic contents.

(c) The governments of the Muslim countries, both individually and jointly, should make definite arrangements to present Islam to the non-Muslim world in a modern and scientific way, highlighting the emphasis that the Quran puts on knowledge and the need for promoting harmony and peace in the world.

(d) A panel of expert Islamists should be formed to project Islam as a progressive, enlightened, peaceful and forward-moving force, which threatens no one and, on the contrary, welcomes co-operation with all those willing to do so.

If the West appreciates the aspirations of the Muslim world instead of putting up resistance and blind opposition, it would be winning the goodwill and friendship of over 800 million people, and contributing to stability and peace in a very important region of the world. Let the Muslims choose their own way of life; this is their own business. The West should not be alarmed over the Islamic revivalist movements. Friendly relations between the Muslim world and the West can be maintained if the West, in its own interest, cares to handle the current renaissance fervour with understanding and tolerance.

6

Socialist Thought

Islam and Socialism are diametrically opposed to each other; they are not merely poles apart but are at loggerheads. There cannot be two opinions that Islam and Socialism are separated and distinct ideologies, both have definite doctrines in the social, political and economic areas, both have a way of life and behaviour pattern for the individual as well as for the community. It must, therefore, be borne in mind that both in their fundamental principles are contradictory to each other; and as such the expression Islamic Socialism, used lately by the people having vested interests, is self-contradictory, misleading and mischievous. It is in this context that an endeavour is made to bring out the incompatibility and the contradictions between Islam and Socialism so that the people are not confused in the matter of delivering their verdict and also those who are using the term Islamic Socialism may avoid it in the interest of conceptual clarity. In the world of Islam, lack of conceptual clarity on the very question of its ideology is fraught with grave dangers, as it may result in misdirecting its collective efforts.

Basic Concepts

Before initiating a discussion on the basic concepts and fundamentals of Islam and Socialism, let us take into consideration the fact that three systems—not that more don't exist in hibernation—are actively engaged in making a bid for the soul of man. The Western civilisation had held global sway for the last two centuries but has not given up. Although the former Soviet Union rose in great might and challenge and old colonial empires disappeared, yet the imprint of the Western democratic and secularist system on the emergent nations was deep. It has especially struck root in countries which either have no polity of their own or which pride in discarding their traditional mores in favour of Westernisation. There is no doubt that Communism made a phenomenal upsurge. It embraced as vast lands and populations as Russia and China and their immediate smaller neighbours contain. What is more, its magnetism has increased with the material power it has mustered and mastered.

Against the Christian West and the Socialist East—old and new—spheres of influence, the Islamic world was not until of late considered a factor of any pull and power. In the first place, the West had over run the almost entire world of Islam and laid it low politically and economically. Secondly, the influence of religion was anyhow dismissed as an anachronism in an era of materialism ushered in by Europe and reinforced by the Russian revolution. Surprisingly, however, Islam seemed to be staging a come-back. The Muslims in the Indian subcontinent forced the hands of the British rulers and the Hindu majority to the creation of Pakistan on the basis of a totally new concept of Muslim nationhood. The audacity and success of this assertion shook the foundation of contemporary milieu. The discovery of oil in the Muslim lands added a material dimension to the Islamic resurgence. The strategic significance of the Middle East puts the Muslim world in a decisive position of weight in the balance between the Christian West and the former Soviet East. Which of these three ways of life is ultimately destined to prevail? This is not only an absorbing academic question but also one which calls for active reflection.

Looking at things externally—and the externality of things is closely connected with their spiritual internality for as Iqbal said matter is but spirit in space and time reference—the decline of the West has long been set. Spengler argued it over six decades ago in his monumental *"Decline of the West"*. The British historian,

Arnold Toynbee, spent a lifetime in dispelling Spengler's pessimism through his volumes of *"Philosophy of History"*. He evolved the theory of "challenge and response", which was calculated to provide the West with an optimistic view of its survival. If a civilisation had the go and guts to face the challenge of rising powers, he averred, it could last forever. But the post-war West European decline was so steep that at the fag-end of his life, even the redoubtable Toynbee had had its day. Indeed his admission was pathetic. Said he—or to that effect—that although the decline of the West was predictable, it was not predictable—gauging the mounting strategic importance of the Arab Oil to the industrial West—that it would take place at the hand of oil-rich Muslim world.

Shrinking Power

The shrinking power of the West was patent. Its Asian and African empires were gone. And while half of Europe had fallen to Russia, the other half was paralysed by the dread of the awesome assemblage of Soviet forces and weaponry in the heart of the Continent. The United States certainly stoods intact but while its destructive nuclear power was matched—according to some Western estimates more than matched—by the former Soviet Union's, the defeatist psychology of its West European allies was a great blow to its competence to overwhelm its adversary. Again, Western Europe did not alone suffer from the psychological inhibition to stand up to Russia. America was also reluctant for a military showdown after its humiliating retreat from Vietnam. On the other hand, the events of recent years show that the former Soviet Union was on the offensive. It had captured many African, Asian—the latest being Afghanistan—countries without an adequate response from the United States. There was yet another factor which prevented a clear-cut confrontation. The West lacked a positive ideological motivation. Europe was the original breading ground of materialism and secularism which had been developed to perfection in the totalitarian order of the former Soviet Union. Therefore, so far as the basic philosophy of life is concerned, the two systems are only different in structure and contours. No wonder Mitterrand's Socialist Party could heap a crushing defeat on de Gaulle's Christian Democrats who had ruled France in one shape or form for the last three decades.

The Western weakness lay in its dualism. It split the affairs of the Church and the State taking cognisance of the historic background, the Lutheran deviation from the monolithical Church of Rome on moral grounds might have been well-justified. The territorial division of the Roman suzerainty was, however, forced on political grounds by racial and linguistic differentiation and particularism. And since the national State no longer owed allegiance to Rome, it had to provide for the spiritual sustenance of its people through national institutions and *ipso facto* the national Church had to be a subordinate department. The secularism which thus came into force put the premium on worldly matters without their subordination to moral values which were heretofore exclusively dispensed by the excluded Church of Rome. Logically, practical, day-to-day working life was divorced from moral compunctions. This paved the way for materialism. Freed from the shackles of Church control, no doubt the change brought about a resurgence in all fields of life. Scientific knowledge progressed and industry and trade prospered. Political systems flourished and territories were conquered. But the fact remained that the whole civilisation came to rest on an amoral foundation.

Again, the plurality of nationhood compounded the sins of materialism and secularism. Their competitive grab for territories led to bloody wars. Nationalism divided the human species into races and colours. The injection of the racial-national virus brought about the ultimate failure of Western civilisation. For when the communication revolution annihilated distance and turned the globe into a geographical entity, the West was without the spiritual and intellectual wherewithal to cope with the challenge of the times. It had not only divided the world into irreconcilable racial groups but itself presented the spectacle of a divided house. This bore two far-reaching results. One, the West could not contain the upsurge of the Communism which held aloft the banner of international fraternity. And two, it could not unite to meet the former Soviet expansionism. Narrow nationalism defeated all attempts at unification and the E.E.C. and European Parliament proved a force and facade. So actually Western civilisation had it good only so long as it was faced by an outside threat. It showed no capacity to face up to either the challenge of Communism which sought to invalidate its socio-economic system or the phenomenon of world unity which called for a genuinely international outlook. In other words, when it came to the crunch it collapsed.

The hall-mark of a civilisation is its horizon—what sights does it set for its people? Does it provide room for the ever-expanding frontiers of human progress? In this test, as we have seen, the Western civilisation has been found wanting in durability. The breach in the Church of Rome put Europe on a track which on one side led to secularism and materialism. Under materialism, capitalism clashed with Communism; under secularism, Parliamentarianism—anarchic or orderly—clashed with totalitarianism. Worst of all, the divisive racial nationalism defied the inexorable forces of global unity. The short-comings of the West only provided a backdrop for the ultimate failure of Communism because the former Soviet system presented in an aggravated form all the mortal ailments of Western civilisation. Not only was it based on undiluted materialism—albeit Marxian dialectical materialism—its atheism had set party bosses as infallible demi-gods who ruled the milling humanity from their regimentational throne. It has enslaved nations on a scale and in depth as no previous empire did in history. The Western moral weakness had no doubt made room for its expansion but the basis which failed in the case of Europe was not likely to sustain the former Soviet system. Already its much heralded world-order had cracked up in its foundations. The internationalism with which it initially made its bid against Western nationalism had proved a dream which vanished with the Sino-Soviet schism. The former Soviet leaders had so abysmally surrendered to nationalism that European Communist parties gave full latitude to develop as ultra-nationalist chauvinists because otherwise they had no chance to emerge as winners.

A civilisation and a system has to be judged by its roots. Even through a totally wrong and fallacious civilisation and system has prospered on the strength of sheer human initiative and energy, it has in the end to give way. The momentum is bound to expire. Their collapse showed that they did not answer basic human needs which they claimed to serve. What are those needs? Now first of all, a human being is an individual. He has his instincts and urges, aims and aspirations. He abides as much in a private world of his own as he lives in a society. His personal ego cannot be left out of account. Then he is circumscribed by his physical situation. His geographical location counts as much in his make-up as his station in life and the tempers of his times. His life-span is short as well as his ambit of activities. Occupying a given point of history, his vision is necessarily limited.

Yet his fulfilment demands a course of life which accords with external truth. While he must be at peace within himself, he should be able to pursue a career which would both harmonise with his society and bring out his potentialities. He may be living in a village but he must feel at once with mankind as a whole. Without these requisities, he remains unfulfilled. How can these multifarious demands be required? Obviously what he stands in need of is an insight into life which at once satisfies his essential individual spirituality, reveals a code of social and legal laws to organise his life and inculcate an outlook which covers a universal horizon. Again, equally obviously, by virtue of his circumstances, he is neither emotionally nor intellectually endowed with a capacity to conceive and evolve an all inclusive way of life on his own. These are the forbidding conditions which make revelation imperative and inevitable.

Position to Lead

Since a Muslim's life is so guided, he is in a position to lead a full life. He observes spiritual disciplines like prayer and fasting and follows a clear social and legal system. Above all, with a belief in a God who controls the universe, he believes in the unity of the human species as born of one breath. Thus his mental disposition is oriented by a polity which does not divide life between the spiritual and the mundane, the black and the white, the East and the West. The Islamic system is meant for the creation of a balanced society in which an individual can rise to the highest point of excellence. It induces an active and creative mode. It was in pursuit of that dynamic mode that the Muslims rose to be the masters of half the known world. Their decline set in only when their spark of faith dimmed. The nature of their decline was however different from the Western decline. The Western decline came about when on the exhaustion of animal energy in internecine national wars, the nemesis overlook them for following a defective philosophy which gave rise to secularism, materialism and dualism of life. On the contrary, were the Muslim faith in Islamic values revived, they could easily resume the thread of their onward march. And there are already signs that they are getting back in the race. Their resurgence is unmistakable. What kind of role awaits them? Since Islam stands for individual dignity and social equality, it needs must oppose both Communist totalitarianism and Western capitalism. And since Islam sets its face against racialism, it alone can meet the challenge of our age, namely, to preside over the destiny of a united humanity.

Muslims, therefore, should not feel at a loss for a system, for they always had a system of their own to operate and they should not behave like some forlorn caste-ridden societies which are compelled to adopt the Western system in desperation. The fact that Islam is for all times to come, necessarily involves movement of thought and change of moulds which *Ijtihad* provides. What shape an Islamic polity may assume in our times is a wholly different matter from seeking inspiration from a civilisation which has been proved rotten to the core. While the problem implies a challenging exercise the helpless choice bespeaks a loss of self confidence. Ironically enough, while Western capitalism is considered condemnable, the Western political system is held up for applause. The truth is that both fruit spring from the same worm-eaten tree. None of the so-called democratic variants can stand the test of scrutiny. For one thing, how can Western people practise racialism and profess equalitarianism? Islam is the wave of the future. How can one swim upstream? The issue clearly is one of conviction. So long as we have it what particular structure of polity is evolved does not matter. What matters are the basic fundamentals of (slam, which are forever and therefore do not undergo any change with the changing times as Allah the Creator Himself has promised in these words: "This day have I perfected your religion for you, completed My favour upon you and have chosen for you Islam as your religion." (The Holy Quran—*Al-Maidah* 5-3).

Islam is the meeting between God as such and man as such. God as such that is to say God envisaged not as He manifested

Himself in a particular way at a particular time, but independently of history and inasmuch as He is what He is and also by His nature He creates and reveals.

Intelligent and Capable

Man as such that is to say man envisaged not as a fallen being needing a miracle to save him, but as man, a theomorphic being endowed with an intelligence capable of conceiving of the absolute and with a *will* capable of choosing what leads to the absolute. To say, 'God' is to say also 'being' 'creating 'revealing' in other words it is to say 'Reality' 'Manifestation' 'Reintegration', to say 'man' is to say 'theomorphism', 'Transcendal intelligence' and 'free-will'. These are the premises of the Islamic perspective, those which explain its every application and must never be lost sight of by anyone wanting to understand any particular aspect of Islam.

While studying Islam in juxtaposition with Socialism, in order to bring out the incompatibility and the contradictions between Islam and Socialism, it is also essential to understand the latter in depth and details. The words Socialist and Socialism came into use first in England and France soon after 1825. Socialist seems to have been used in England in 1826 to describe the followers of Robert Owen and the word 'Socialiste' in France in 1832 with reference to the followers of Claude Henri de Rouvroy, Counte de Saint Simon. But all these earlier schools of Socialism were dismissed by Karl Marx and Engles as "Utopian Socialism". Both of them developed a consistent system of economic and political theory which they claimed amounted to an exact science. Their scientific socialism was based on the materialistic interpretation of history and was presented in crisp, popular form in the *Communist Manifesto* published in 1848. Later, Marx eleborated his views in his massive work *Das Kapital:* "Socialism, therefore, reduced to its simplest legal and practical expression means the complete discarding of the institution of private property by transforming it into public property and the division of the resultant public income equally and indiscriminately among the entire population".

"The Doctrine of Islam" says Schuon in his great book, *Understanding Islam,* "hangs on two statements: First' There is no Divinity (or reality, or absolute) outside the only Divinity (or reality, or absolute) *(La-ilaha illa Llah)* and Muhammad (the 'Glorified', the perfect) is the envoy (the mouth-piece, the intermediary, the manifestation, the symbol) of the Divinity *(Muhammadur Rasulu Llah)* these are the first and the second testimonies *(Shahadat)* of the faith. Here, we are in the presence of two assertions, two certitudes, two levels of reality: the Absolute and the relative cause and effect, God and the world. Islam is the religion of certitude and equilibrium." The Doctrine of Socialism on the other hand is totally based on Dialectical Materialism or Materialistic interpretation of history and flatly denounces and denies all metaphysical and eschatological truth.

The foregoing comparison clearly brings out the conceptual contradictions between Islam and Socialism, which in turn have resulted in differences in the consequential approach and outlook of man towards his environment.

Social Justice

Since the current scene in the world devolves round the subject of social justice and is confined to the economic field alone, it is necessary to point out that social justice cannot be achieved by attempting to segregate the economic life of man from his total existence. In doing so the danger lies in the evolution of a system that will not be in conformity with human nature and therefore will be either incapable of practical application or unsuccessful in achieving the objective or both Capitalism and Socialism bear eloquent testimony to this statement.

A Reaction

Socialism emerged as a reaction to the injustices and exploitation that came in the wake of Industrial Revolution based on the concepts of Capitalism. It was not the private ownership of the means of production that gave rise to injustices and exploitation but the concept of Capitalism based purely on materialism was the only cause of this phenomenon. Human behaviour in any walk of life is determined by the concepts in which one believes. A philosophy aiming purely at material well-being is taking care of only a partial need of man. Moreover, materialistic pursuits in the absence of a moral code of human conduct in various spheres of human activity must inevitably lead to selfishness and greed and injustices and exploitation are its natural concomitant. It is, therefore, observed that the Capitalistic States right from the end of the nineteenth century have continuously endeavoured to enlarge the scope of State intervention in the economic field which is not confined only to legislation governing planned development. All this has proved inadequate in eradicating injustice and exploitation both in the national and international plane.

Socialist thinkers moved by human misery and motivated by human welfare attempted "a complete transformation of the economic and moral basis of society by the substitution of social for individual control and of social for individualistic forces in the organisation of life and work". It was after a century of the birth of socialism or more precisely after exactly 69 years of the publication of the Communist Manifesto embodying the concept of scientific socialism that the first socialist State was established in Russia through a bloody revolution in 1917. None of the most celebrated thinkers and pioneers of Socialism were alive then but the most significant fact is that Russia at that time was not at all an Industrial State and the nature of the bloody revolution indicates the extent of human misery perpetrated by a despotic monarchy.

This was the time when Capitalistic Imperialism had spread far and wide throughout the world and their colonies consisting of over three-fourth of the human race were seething with poverty and misery as a result of colonial injustices and exploitation. A study of the works of great thinkers and political leaders of this age, in the non-white world, reveals a strong condemnation not of imperialism alone but also of the Whites and of Capitalism. Along with a universal wave of hatred in the colonial world against imperialism a disquieting pessimism also prevailed on account of bleak prospects of escape from this brutal tyranny of the Whites. In this background, it was but natural that Socialist Revolution in Russia kindled a ray of hope in the hearts and minds of this unfortunate mess of humanity. Socialism, thus, came to be regarded as the symbol of "Social Justice". This impression about Socialism more or less lasted throughout the Stalin era because of almost a complete lack of information about the happenings in Soviet Union very successfully managed through the iron curtain and massive propaganda about the establishment of a workers paradise behind it. The fall of Eastern Europe soon after World War II and the fall of China in 1949 to Socialism rather lent a support to this impression.

After the death of Stalin, a major break through, the iron curtain has been possible because of a host of events that took place since then in the Socialist World. The most important of these events are:

(a) Denunciation of the cult of personality by Khurshchev in 1955, revealing in detail the atrocities perpetrated by Stalin;

(b) Uprising in Hungary against Socialist order around the same time and the uprising in Poland in 1956 on the occasion of the Poznan International Fair;

(c) the manner in which these uprisings were quelled;

(d) the publication of the details of the Sino—Soviet ideological warfare;

(e) the ideological conflict between Mao Tse-tung and Liu Shao-chi;

(f) defection of people from the Socialist world, particularly of writers and thinkers who have written extensively about life behind the iron curtain; and

(g) the happenings in Czechoslovakia and the manner in which revolt against Socialist order has been curbed in this country.

All this has brought out and proved beyond any shadow of doubt that the dream of the Socialist thinkers is far from realisation and that the practical results of the operation of the Socialistic doctrine prove that:

(i) Evolution of a classless society and removal of class struggle is not possible through socialisation of the means of production, as classes exist not only because of the ownership of the means of production by private individuals and the existence of the working class but also because there will always be in existence classes based on colour, region, language, education, income, profession, health, intellect and the most important class of those who govern and that of those governed and a class struggle is inevitable between various classes.

(ii) It is not possible to remove inequality of income nor is it possible to distribute the social income equally among all the citizens.

(iii) The Socialist State cannot come into being without:

(a) denial to the individual of the right to form association, to publicly express one's views, to criticise the Government of the day, to choose a profession;

(b) enforcement of laws through force and intimidation; and

(c) ruthless and exemplary punishment of those who disagree or are suspected to be opposed to the views or policies of the Government.

Well Known Facts

The foregoing facts are now well-known and it is no longer possible to cover or conceal them by any means. These facts reveal that the Socialist Doctrine is one only incapable of practical application inasmuch as it does not provide anyone of its prime objectives but is also inconsistent with the concept of social justice. On the contrary, it inflicts a worst form of tyranny over the mind of man through denial of all individual freedoms, does not come into being without inflicting injustices and does not stay without force and intimidation.

There is little to choose, therefore, between Capitalism and Socialism. Both are not free from injustices and both are imperialistic in character and it is so because both are materialistic in concepts.

Islam stands for social justice and also for removal of class struggle. Islamic concept of social justice is not restricted to the economic field alone as is the case with Socialism and also with Capitalism. Social justice in Islam pervades the entire of human existence. It relates to all the relationships between man and man. Between the twin obligations of man determined by Islam *(Huquq-ul-Lah)* the obligations to God and *(Haquq-ul-lbad)* the obligations to man, a default in the former is a stated as pardonable while the latter is declared as unpardonable. A believer, therefore, whether in his capacity as a father, a mother or a child, a brother or a sister, a husband or a wife, a businessman or an employee, an industrialist or a worker, a student or a teacher, an orphan or a widow, poor or rich, landlord or peasant, the ruler and the ruled, in any capacity or in any walk of life whether social, political or economic can seek guidance and receive direction from Quran and *Sunnah.* Any peculiar situation where specific direction is unavailable through Quran and *Sunnah,* the remedy is provided through *'Ijma'* and *'Ijtehad'* but both *'Ijma'* and *'Ijtehad"* are subject to the condition that these are not repugnant to Quran and *Sunnah.* The Prophet (peace be upon him), therefore, declared in his last sermon that:

> "Verily, I have left amongst you the Book of Allah and the Sunnah of this Apostle which if you hold fast, you shall never go astray".

In Islam the principles governing economic life as embodied in the Quran and *Sunnah* are not compartmentalised that cover the total life of man. About the questions like inequality of income, concentration of wealth, ownership of the means of production, class struggle, economic exploitation and sovereignty, Islamic injunctions are as under:

> Equality of income has proved to be a mere catchword of a slogan. Inequality of income persists even in the Socialist states on account of differences and variations in abilities, education, work or profession. For instance, people with technical skills receive much more than unskilled workers. Quranic prescription on this subject is: "And that man hath only that for which he maketh effort" *An-Najm* 53-39.

Since it is impossible to remove variety of ability, education and profession from the human race, equity demands that returns must be related to effort. Those who have attempted to equalise incomes irrationally have, therefore, failed. An important question here would be the determination of an equitable return to the worker engaged in an employment. The answer would be that an Islamic state should not find it difficult to determine equitable return to the investor, the employee and the share of the state in any given situation and to enforce it by laws.

This is a characteristic of the Capitalistic Society and Socialism seeks to remedy the situation through nationalisation and prohibition of private ownership of the means of production of trade and of property.

Ownership Allowed

Islam does not prohibit private ownership of the means of production or trade or property but prohibits acquisition of wealth through immoral or illegal means and also does not favour hoarding of wealth. It seeks to remedy concentration of wealth in fewer hands through inheritance, *'Zakat'* and *'Sadaqat'* and *'Khairat'*. In practical application, therefore, Islamic injunctions preserve and protect the right of individual to own industry or trade or property, curb immorality, induce circulation and investment of wealth for the growth of the economy, prevent excessive concentration of wealth in fewer hands and provide for the welfare of the needy. Again a state in which Islamic order prevails can implement the Islamic directives in this behalf without any difficulty.

The Socialist concept in this respect and its practical application has already been explained. In Islam, man is not the owner of anything. Everything that he possesses belongs to God, including power and wealth. He merely acts as an Agent or a Trustee and, therefore, must use all that he possessed in accordance with the orders of the Real Owner. This is a very important aspect of a society based on Islam because it determines the very outlook, approach and behaviour of man in all spheres of his earthly existence.

It is appropriate to briefly discuss nationalization at this stage.

The concept of appropriation of all private property or nationalization of the means of production as well as the prohibition of the ownership of private property or the means of production is clearly against the injunctions of Islam. Islamic state, however, is not prevented from creating property or owning industry. The difference between the two must be clearly understood. Appropriation or nationalization means deprivation of the right of citizens and is, therefore, illegal and unjust. Creation of property or establishment of an industry by the state does not impinge on the rights of citizens. Similarly, the state in Islam is not prevented from interfering in the economic life of the people and regulating the operation of the private sector in the overall interest of the nation.

The entire Socialist theory and its practical application is based on the struggle between two classes: the owners of the means of production and the workers. By removal of the class of the owner of the means of production, Socialism seeks to establish a just order. In the eyes of Islam the Socialist theory is not only irrational but immoral and unjust. As it has been explained earlier, classes do not exist merely on account of ownership of the means of production and work but also on account of colour, region, language, education, skills, health, intellect, wealth, the government and the governed and therefore class struggle cannot be eliminated merely by state ownership of the means of production. State ownership of the means of production does not also remove the two classes because the managers of the means of production and the working class again become two classes where struggle is inevitable. Moreover, the lot of the worker does not improve merely on account of state ownership of the means of production, as is the case in both the Socialist states and non-Socialist states where the state owns some industry. The lot of the workers is invariably related to the state or National Economics whether the country is Socialist or otherwise. Denial of all freedoms and forcible appropriation of private property are unjust and immoral in Islam.

The Islamic view of the human race is not one *free* from classes as that is inconsistent with nature. Islam, therefore, does not attempt to remove natural classes but removes class consciousness. The Quran declares: "Lo ; the noblest of you in the sight of Allah is the best in conduct (pious)" *Al—Hujurat* 49— I 3.

Hard Facts

It is not, therefore, on account of wealth, colour, region, language, education or any other qualification that one is superior to the others except piety. In practical life too the rich and the poor, the white and the black, the educated and the illiterate, from one region or the other, all stand shoulder to shoulder with each other five times a day in submission to their Creator and once every year all participants in *Haj* belonging to various regions, speaking different languages consisting of various classes of people perform the same rites and wear the same dress without any distinction.

Those who speak of Islamic Masawat (equality) must know that Socialism is nowhere near Islam in this respect. Islamic concept of *Masawat* (equality) and brotherhood are incomparable to any other concept or philosophy of life on earth.

Yet, since classes do exist and class conflict or struggle is inevitable, the Islamic state, through legislation and rules and regulations, can resolve them on the basis of equity and justice. The Quran in this respect declares unequivocally: "And if two parties of believers fall to fighting, then make peace between them and if one party of them doth wrong to the other, fight ye that which doth wrong till it returns unto the Ordinance of Allah: then if it returns, make peace between them justly and act equitably. Lo; Allah loveth the equitable" *Al-Hujurat* 49-9.

A Phenomenon

This is again a phenomenon of the Capitalistic Society but the Socialist prescription does not provide the remedy. On the contrary, it is far more tyrannical and unjust because of its basic strategy of force and denial of the rights of individual freedom and of property. The Islamic order is based on equity and justice with the individual, with the classes and the communities and with nations in all the directions of life and all fields of activity.

This is a typical Socialistic slogan. Irrespective of the fact whether the people in the Socialist state are sovereign or not, Islam is basically and diametrically opposed to this view. The Quran declares on numerous occasions that sovereignty belongs to God and no one has the right to share it with Him. The following is one of such quotations: "Knowest thou not that it is Allah unto whom belongeth the sovereignty of the heavens and earth" *Al—Baqarah* 2-107.

Man, according to Quran, is a mere Agent *(Khalifa)* of God on earth and it is his duty to carry out His injunctions in all matters including the affairs of the State, it is incomprehensible that man with the best of intentions and all sincerity of purpose can evolve a code of life superior to the one given to man by his Creator. On numerous occasions in the Holy Quran it is stressed that "Allah is Knower and Wise". Who on earth could claim to be more knowledgeable and more wise than the Creator of man? Those, therefore, who proclaim that Islam is their faith and Socialism is their economy and they believe in sovereignty of the people, must analyse their proclamations to find out whether:

(a) Islam provides a complete code of life in all fields of human affairs including social, political and economic;

(b) or it deals with only certain aspects of human life;

(c) or is inadequate in dealing with economic or other fields of human activity; and whether;

(d) Islam's claim that sovereignty belongs to God is correct;

(e) *or* the sovereignty of the people runs concurrent with God.

(f) or people are sovereign.

If the answer to (a) is in the affirmative, then the answer to (b) is in the negative. In this case Islam is adequate in dealing with all the affairs of man on earth and there is no need for a *Momin* (believer) to seek guidance from any other philosophy or "ism" whatsoever. The answer to (a), (b) and (c) cannot be in the affirmative because Islam cannot be both adequate and inadequate at the same time. If the answer to (b) and (c) is in the affirmative, then to (a) it is in the negative. This is directly in conflict with Quran and Sunnah and it is impossible for a believer to hold this view.

Similarly if the answer to (d) is in the affirmative, then to (e) and (f) is in the negative because each is contradictory to the other. If the answer is in the affirmative either to (e), then it amounts to "*Shirk*" which is the gravest of all crimes in the eyes of Islam, or (f) which means denial of the sovereignty of God, a view which a believer cannot hold.

It is essential, therefore, for those who profess faith in Islam to publicly deny belief in Socialism or Capitalism or any other "ism" and to desist from declaring that Islam and Socialism are consistent or compatible with each other. Simultaneously it is necessary to declare that sovereignty belongs to God and not to the people. If, however, they persist in their slogan, then it is necessary for all Muslims to take serious note of their intentions. Every Muslim should submit himself to the Commandment that came fourteen centuries ago. At that time what the Creater in His benign mercy gave to mankind was the last Prophet (peace be upon him) and the Holy Quran. Both the Quran and the words and deeds of the Prophet (peace be upon him) contained directions for man whether he lived fourteen centuries ago or lives now in this modern age, as also for those who will live hereafter till the world is in existence. It is impossible for a *Momin* (believer) to deny the validity of Quran and *Sunnah* at any time and in any respect.

Imperfect Intellect

The human intellect, admittedly imperfect as it is, has often foundered in search of truth and reality about its environment not because of insincerity in the matter of the search but because of incapacity of the imperfect intellect which could not perceive Divine strategy in its entirety. In frustration the human mind has at times rejected the very existence of a perfect intellect. This is an acceptance of defeat not of achievement. For the believers, the Quran has clearly and unambiguously stated:

> "Allah! There is no God save Him, the alive, the eternal. Neither slumber nor sleep overtaketh Him. Unto Him belongeth whatsoever is in the heavens and whatsoever is in the earth. Who is he that intercedeth with Him save by His leave? He knoweth that which is in front of them and that which is behind them, while they encompass nothing of His knowledge save what He will. His throne includeth the heavens and the earth. He is never weary of preserving them. He is the sub-line, the tremendous" *Al-Baqarah* 2—225.

In order to avail of the opportunities of peace, progress and prosperity offered by Islam there is need for us to be Muslims and to be contended by merely calling ourselves Muslims. There is need to establish a society or an order based on Islam. We have seen enough and wandered enough in search of our objectives through propagation and even acceptance of several prescriptions, creeds and philosophies' and have at last been disillusioned. Let us, therefore, go along the path shown to us by the last Prophet Muhammad (peace be upon him).

7

Communist Thought

Communist attitudes toward religion are based largely on a militant atheism and an avowed antagonism toward any system of ethics not based on the "class struggle". To a Communist, ideas of right and wrong of a given act are determined by the value of the act to the Communist movement. Thus, it becomes quite "moral" for a Communist to kill, to steal, or to commit treason if, by doing so, he thinks he is helping international Communism. Naturally, he is basically opposed to any system of ethics in which people look to a higher source than the Communist Party for their ideas of right and wrong.

Communism that Failed

During the last quarter of the century, the various Communist governments have been carrying out an intensive propaganda campaign, particularly directed at the peoples of South Asia, in an attempt to convince them that Communists believe in religious freedom. Carefully staged "proof of religious tolerance in Communist countries has been shown to virtually every non-Communist visitor at some point during his well organized tour. The resulting favourable reports from these observers have then been used to support the claim that Communists actually practise a policy of tolerance toward religion. That this is a mistaken impression, however, as shown clearly by what actually happens at home.

The "religious freedom" campaign has been used as a smoke screen, behind which has been carried out, on the one hand, a campaign against all religions; and, on the other hand, a programme of creation of special politico-religious groups for political exploitation and propaganda purposes abroad. Meanwhile, continuous official pressure is applied to genuine religious organizations to lessen their effectiveness and their hold on their members.

An indication of the motives behind this propaganda approach is seen in remarks by V. Semenov, Soviet Communist Party theoretician, in an article in the official Soviet Party organ *Kommunist* No. 18 of December, 1956. Pointing out that "religious belief is widespread and closely linked with productive relations with the East", and that "progressive national movements" in many countries of the East take on the specific form of "religious nationalism", Semenov concluded that for this reason, "the activity and the platform of religious sects, reformation trends and religious leaders deserve special attention—i.e., with a view of Communist exploitation.

The Communist internal campaign against religion has been directed equally against all religions, but particularly affects Islam, Buddhism, arid Christianity. It is a campaign founded on Karl Marx's statement that "religion is the opium of the people" and on Lenin's characterization of it as "the kind of spiritual Vodka in which the slaves of capital drown their human life". That the "purge" of religious influence continues even while the communist propaganda mill makes claims of "religious freedom" is shown by the following statement taken from the Soviet magazine *Komsomolskays Pravada* (Young Communist Truth) of October 18, 1947. "The Communist Party cannot be neutral regarding religion and it conducts anti-religious propaganda against all religious prejudices.

"There are cases in which some of the members of the

Communist Party occasionally hinder the thorough development of anti-religious propaganda. If such members of the Party are expelled, this is very good .... It goes without saying that only the Komsomol (Young Communist) can correctly clarify the harm in superstition and religious prejudices, who is free of them himself. A young man cannot be a *Komsomal* unless he is free of religious convictions."

Redundant Ideas

Another example of Communist thinking concerning religions in general is the following statement made by Stalin: "The Party cannot be neutral toward religion, and it does conduct anti-religious propaganda against all and every religious prejudice .... Anti-religious propaganda is the means by which the complete liquidation of the reactionary clergy must be brought about." The official journal *Pravada* noted that "all party organizations are required to conduct constant, purposeful atheistic propaganda."

An article in the official Party newspaper, namely, *Turkmenskaya Iskra* (Spark of Turkmeniya) of one of the former Soviet Republics, a predominantly Muslim area, reveals that the Communists' attitudes and actions concerning Islam within the Soviet Union are at variance with the claim of "religious freedom," which they used in their propaganda directed toward South Asia. Direct quotations from this official Communist statement follow:

> "Under the Soviet regime, the overwhelming majority of the workers of the USSR had freed themselves from religious prejudices, but survivals of the past are very much alive, and in our Republic there are still many religious people who profess the Islamic faith.
>
> "Islam" in Arabic signifies 'submission'. This name alone indicates the tendency to cultivate humility, docility and passivity. Like other religions, Islam has always played a reactionary role and has been

> utilized by the exploiting classes and foreign colonizers for the spiritual subjugation of the peoples of the East."

In an effort to demonstrate the alleged ill-effects of Islamic religious observances, the official Communist pronouncement goes on:

> "The precepts of Islam require of believers the performance of a number of rites oftentimes offensive to human dignity and extremely injurious to health. The most painful of these rites is without doubt the fast of Ramadan. Like other religious festivals and rites, it has been utilized in the interests of the exploiting classes."

The Communist article further demonstrated the priority of production over religion in the Communist mind, saying that religion "belongs henceforth, and forever, to the past, but occasionally, in our towns and villages, religious customs are still held on to with tenacity. One still finds people who observe the 30-day fast of the Ramadan. But usages of former times which damage the health of the people, which disturb the rhythm of work in our enterprises and in our *kolkhozes* (collective farms) must disappear. For it is no secret to anyone that a man exhausted by a long fast cannot work with all his capacity. During the Ramadan it happens often that certain *kolkhoz* workers do not go to work, something which unquestionably is reflected in the production of the *kolkhoz.*

To insist on showing these people the injurious character of their errors is the first duty of Communist Party organizations.

"The Marxist concept of the world has been, and remains fundamentally irreconcilable with every anti-scientific and religious concept of the world, such as that represented by Islam." *(Turkmenskaya Iskra)* (Spark of Turkmeniya), 16 April, 1957; article entitled *The Reactionary Character of Ramadan.*

Soviet home service broadcasts made it clear that the *Turkmenskaya Iskra* (Spark of Turkmeniya) article was not an isolated case. Moscow Radio announced that the Central

Committee of the Komsomol (Young Communists) had made it compulsory for its organizations to improve atheist propaganda among youth, and a Moscow Radio commentary stressed that religion was "hostile to the entire structure of our life," and that Komsomol organizations had to apply their efforts in order to "hinder the spread of this ideology". The need to expand atheist propaganda was further emphasized by Moscow Radio, and this theme was stressed concurrently in regional broadcasts. A notable example was Voroshilovgrad Radio broadcast which is reproduced below:

> "Religion always has been a reactionary ideology .... we must fight against religion; this is the ABC of materialism and Marxism. One must fight against religion in a Bolshevik manner, with passion and without mercy.... It is the sacred duty of the Party organizations to create all conditions for making atheist propaganda effective and militant."

In Communist China also, the "pressure war" against religion is carried on against the Islamic minority, as well as other religious groups. Here, the actual forceful persecution has been small, after an initial campaign during which thousands of Sinkiang Muslims fled across the borders. Instead, the Communists have operated almost wholly behind the facade of the China Islamic Society, a religious front organization designed to deaden Islam within Communist China, while acting as a mechanism to aid propaganda abroad. This organization in which most Islamic Chinese are not represented, has not been as successful as some of the other Communist religious groups, and Muslim areas have been reported more than any other as having "incidents" of resistance to Communist domination.

The Soviet provincial newspaper *Sovetskaya Belorussiya* (Belorussian SSR) in its issue of November, 14, 1956, included the following statements: "Among the most viable and harmful vestiges of capitalism in the minds of the people are religious prejudices and superstition the Communist Party of the Soviet Union has always considered and still considered scientific atheistic propaganda as an inherent part of the education of working people every slackening in the struggle against religious ideology invariably leads to a revival of religious prejudices and superstitions the overcoming of religious superstitions is a component part of the Communist education of the working people and a prerequisite for the successful construction of Communism in our land."

From these statements, it can be seen that under Communist rule, the plan to undermine all religions goes on continually, and their propaganda about supposed "religious freedom under Communism" is a deception.

In Communist China, as in the former Soviet Union, extensive efforts are being made to lessen religious influence among the people. Buddhists have been organized since late 1952 under the China Buddhist Association. Like all other official religious and social organizations in Communist China, it is a political indoctrination group, and has been used in the propaganda campaigns sponsored by the Government, especially the so-called "Peace Campaign." This association comes under the Bureau of Religious Affairs, an office which, judging by the name, would presumably be interested in the maintenance of religious attitudes and views. The head of the association, however, once told a Western journalist:

> "When we teach science and general knowledge in the schools—biology for instance—we never lose an opportunity to expose religion as superstition."

Thus, the intention of the Bureau of Religious Affairs, which controls the China Buddhist Association, is clearly not to promote religious practices, but to act as a damper on religious enthusiasm internally, while providing a useful propaganda device externally. As a result of this group's work there has been a marked decline in religious observances. After only two years of Communist, "education," the New China News Agency reported that in 6,000 villages in Chekiang Kiangsu, and Anhwei, "disused temples and nunneries became places for political meetings and study groups political study is developing, and the peasants are giving up membership in superstitious organizations'.

A Polish correspondent, in a description of a visit to Peking published in the official journal, *Polityka,* said:

> "The Buddhist religion, together with all its varieties, is in China (except in Tibet) quite dead. The (Communist) Chinese speak about their Buddhism as we speak about Jove and Juno.... The number of believers in any positive religion does not exceed three per cent of the population of China."

During the period of the so-called "Land Reform" most of the properties of the Buddhist monasteries were seized, and the monks were listed as members of the landlord class. Frequently, temples were used as political meeting houses, and occasionally for the purpose of executions, where the "landlords" paid with their lives for the crime of owning properties.

In Tibet, where Buddhism has been more strongly organized, however, strong opposition from Buddhists forced the Tibetan Chapter of the China Buddhist Association—a political group formed in October, 1956 to introduce so-called "reforms" in religious practices to defer its changes for a time.

The Communist decision to delay the full introduction of the so-called "peoples' democracy" in Tibet was undoubtedly influenced by the Tibetans' resistance to the Communist campaign to destroy religion.

In attempting to exploit the religious solidarity of all Buddhists in favour of political association between Buddhist countries and the former Communist bloc, and to make the World Buddhist movement help their so-called "peace" propaganda, the Communists failed to appreciate both the moral and the intellectual bases of Buddhism, and its hold on its believers. In this "Peace" propaganda, the Communists attempted to propagate the false idea that it is possible to be simultaneously a good Buddhist and a Communist, so far at least, without any notable success.

Similarly, the recurrent pattern of repression of Christian influences in the Soviet Union—Orthodox, Protestant, and Roman Catholic—is well-known. From the time they assumed power in Russia in 1918, the Communists carried on a deliberate programme against the Christian Churches, in which tens of thousands were executed, imprisoned, exiled, or sent to concentration camps. Periodically, they have had times to seeming tolerance, when seeds of religious influence had been permitted to grow, only to be eliminated later. Only during the Second World War was there anything approximating real tolerance, and this was obviously influenced by a desire not to tamper with army morale. Even during the periods of relaxation, the only group to receive tolerant treatment was the Russian Orthodox Church. Other Christian groups had seldom been tolerated at all. Since the war, active atheist propaganda and open anti-religious activity had again been manifested.

Also fresh in the memory of the peoples of South-East Asia is the brutal treatment accorded to Catholic and Protestant groups under Communist domination in China. No aspect of the Christian Churches and their work has been spared. Arrests and public mass trials of Christian leaders and their congregations became common-place when the Communists took over. Torture and house arrests were also used, with the end result that virtually no missionaries now remain in Communist China except in prison. Roman Catholic groups have been particularly attacked as tools of imperialism and spies.

To replace the traditional religious groups, the Communists organized more of their puppet politico-religious organizations, including the National Christian Council, which was said to represent Chinese Protestants. To provide a front group supposedly representing Chinese Roman Catholics, the Progressive China Catholic Church was formed. This group had been frequently shown by free Catholic groups to be a puppet organization, and automatically carries the condemnation as immoral prescribed by the Pope for all Communist organizations. It was clearly not representative of true Catholic views nor of Chinese Catholics.

In mid-July, 1957, a new campaign, of vilification was launched against the Vatican for its continuing refusal to "recognize" the hierarchy of political "priests", allegedly "elected" by their religious constituents in Communist China.

The election laws proclaimed in early 1953 contained a provision under which all Christians and Buddhists were deprived of the vote unless their churches were members of the government-sponsored politico-religious groups, and their own behaviour not suspect.

Recent years have been an apparent lessening of violent action against Christian religious groups in China, as this now suits the Chinese communist propaganda line. However, continuous pressure against these groups is maintained and many signs of overt action in the Chinese Communist influenced areas on the borders are still to be seen. When Communist aggression dipped into North Vietnam, nearly a million Christians fled to the south to escape the certain persecution they knew would be carried on by the Communist forces. Here also, as in Communist China, religious organizations were formed for the ostensible purpose of promoting Christian religion, but actually for the purpose of subjecting religion to political ends.

A new drive against Christians, and particularly against Catholics, in North Vietnam was initiated. The anti-Catholic campaign was apparently signalled by a feature article in the official Communist organ *Nham Dan.* In this article, it was charged that "reactionaries" hiding under the cover of religion were trying to use "divine powers" to threaten so-called "patriotic priests" and others who were supporting the regimes' land reform programme.

"Reactionary priests", it was claimed, had interfered with Communist programmes and were threatening Catholics with religious punishment unless lands that had been taken away from the big landlords and the Church in the land reform programme were returned. Party cadres were told that all activities carried out under the name of religion, which were not in compliance with the police and laws of the regime, or which were "prejudicial" to the interests of the people, were illegal. The cadres were then instructed to denounce these priests, to explain their crimes to the masses, and to punish them "impartially".

The campaign against religion went on in every Communist country. Every means was used to prevent youth from adopting religious views and to strife the faith of the older people.

Because it knew no system of ethics save that which promoted its ends, Communism necessarily involved a denial of religious freedom. The only belief free to win adherents under Communism was and is the "religion" of atheism.

Old Story

However, it is an old story now. Soviet Union has died its own death. The communism, though still prevalent in China and a few countries, is on the verge of collapse. And new Islam has to cope with a new Communists west.

8

Modern Thoughts

Ideology, in fact, is a system of ideas that has the potential to direct and control multifarious activities of an individual or a society and put it on a particular path of action to fulfil certain ends. It should also have the capacity to work as an inner faith, motivating its followers to adopt a certain way of life as free agents and not as a blind horde of people being driven from outside by some unintelligible external authority.

Islam and Modern Ideologies

The term ideology became more popular in the twentieth century. Previously, the term more often and more properly used for such a system was philosophy. But philosophy, with the passage of time, came to be understood as an abstract way of thinking, detached from real life. It was no more capable of motivating people to action. It was said to provide guidance for life, but lacked the required force to change its course. It was described as an opium, drunken or ideal speculation and a no-man's land, in which no worldly-wise man or woman would be interested. Although Plato had given his verdict that philosophers to be the rulers throughout the recorded history. Rather, philosophy was often misused to perpetuate the rule of most un-philosophical and unreasonable sort of rulers. The poverty of philosophy lay in its inability to achieve its ideals in practical life. The ideals for which philosophy stood proved to be nothing more than a beggar's wishes and the beggars could never be the chosers. A philosopher was considered, even by a commoner, to be an unpractical unsuccessful rather a simple and foolish type of person.

The term ideology, one could say, was used to give philosophy an additional connotation, that is, to signify that it was not merely a detached system of ideas but a system that could motivate and guide its followers to action. Despite this, philosophy as a theoretical aspect was the most vital part of any ideology and as such it was not discarded. Rather, as a part of practical ideology, it emerged in its true colours, purified of all sorts of distortions and deviations, and could find a more respectable place in the life of people. Another term which was nearer to the meanings of ideology, and also included philosophy as an important theoretical aspect, was religion. But as religion is based on such a system of knowledge with which the modern ideologists did not see eye to eye, it was not used by them to connote the practical message. Rather, attempts were made to replace religion with modern ideologies.

The term ideology has been used more vocally by the Socialists and it is Socialism which claims, as an ideology, to be able to control and direct each and every aspect of human life and to serve people's collective interests. It claims to have given a most revolutionary ideological weapon in the hands of the most advanced class among the various classes that have emerged in history. Socialists also claim that they have the only correct philosophical system based on modern dialectical materialism. They condemn all other ideologies as bourgeois and idealistic. The bourgeois and idealist philosophers, on their part, are not as much interested in the use of the term ideology as the Socialists are, because the former do not find it possible—or do not think it profitable—to put their philosophers to practice. The bourgeois keep their philosophical thinking subservient to their class interests which would not allow philosophy to become an active force, because once it became active, it would fight against their vested interests.

But, whatever the practical role of modern philosophy, and whether it is socialistic or bourgeois, it is based on a modern scientific outlook. The theory of knowledge of every type of modern philosophy confines itself to the limits set by modern science. It finds its answers to various philosophical questions from modern scientific inquiries. As a Western author on modern philosophy writes; "In opposition both to antiquity and middle ages, the modern philosopher is scientific in his outlook. Values do not necessarily certify the truth of possible facts. Theology no longer sets limits to a philosopher's thinking, nor dictates the conclusions at which he must arrive. Ceasing to be the hand-maiden of theology, philosophy has instead become the interpreter of rapidly advancing sciences....

Various Conclusions

The modern philosopher seeks to organise the results of the various natural and social sciences in a picture of the world as a whole, in which room will be found for such values of art, morality and religion as can be shown to be consonant with the established results of scientific investigation".

As modern science is essentially materialistic, philosophy based on it has turned out to be more or less materialistic in outlook. Philosophy asked the question: What is Ultimate Reality? Science answered: It is Matter. Modern science, with its sense-oriented source of knowledge, could have known nothing else but matter. Socialists, being the staunch followers of modern science, have adopted materialism as their ideology and developed it to its logical end. Claiming to be true materialists they accuse the bourgeois ideologists of being idealists, although the latter's idealism, limited as it is by modern science, is hardly free from the materialism taught and supported by science. If at all the bourgeois thinkers give an importance to individual will *or* self of man, for which they are accused of being idealists, it is to the extent that modern science allows them. And for modern science, "man to man is (still) a wolf". The concept of man's self is confined by science to the selfish, animal—or materialistic—nature of man. While the socialists claim to have successfully built a social system to keep the animal nature of man within limits, giving society an edge on the individual, the bourgeois keep the individual self free for the fulfilment of its animal desires. The belief in the animal or material nature of man—that man is basically selfish—as taught by modern science is equally popular in both bourgeois and socialist societies. Even the socialistic structure of economy, which is said to be exploitation free, does not seem to have raised the consciousness of man above the animal level. That is why it is reverting to economic liberalism.

It cannot, therefore, be said that modern philosophy, in its dialectical materialists or idealist form, has achieved, or is capable of achieving lofty human goals. The basic flaw which has led to this situation is the narrow outlook of modern science on which modern philosophy solely depends and which denies religion as a genuine source of knowledge and practice. As pointed out by Al-lama Iqbal, the great modern philosopher of Islam, "Both nationalism (as taught by bourgeois ideologies) and atheistic socialism (as taught by dialectical materialism) must draw upon the psychological forces of hate, suspicion and resentment (all characteristics of the animal nature of man as taught by modern science) which tend to impoverish the soul of man and close up his hidden sources of spiritual energy (which come into action only through a religious awakening)". Allama Iqbal further writes:

> "Neither the technique of mediaeval mysticism (Iqbal suggests a new method that would suit the present-day conditions), nor nationalism, nor atheistic socialism can cure the ills of a despairing humanity. The modern world stands in need of biological renewal. It is only by rising to a fresh vision of his origin and future (as provided by religion), his whence and whither, that man will eventually triumph over a society motivated by an inhuman competition."

So, it is only a philosophy which recognises religion as a genuine source of knowledge and gets inspiration from it, in addition to the guidance and information it gets from modern science, that can provide a most comprehensive and truly human and progressive ideology to mankind. The scientific outlook needs to be widened to include not only the material phenomenon, which is the object of sensory knowledge, but also the religious level of human perception. Islam, being the most advanced of all religious systems, does provide such an outlook. Instead of negating or under-rating the material aspect of life, it affirms it as a reality. All previous religious systems, and the related idealistic philosophies, considered the material phenomena as mere illusion, appearance or a half-truth, and taught renunciation of material and worldly pursuits as necessary to attain salvation. In a striking contrast, Islam lays stress on the trial through material existence as a necessary condition for human salvation. In Islam, there is no dualism between matter and spirit. They belong ultimately to the same source which provides a common ground for human action and thought. Says the Holy Quran, "To Him belong *'Khalq'* (the material creation) and *'Amr'* (the spiritual direction)", both aspects being equally important.

In the sphere of knowledge also, Islam considers sense-perception and religious experience as equally important and natural sources of knowledge. Both are keen to achieve ultimate objectivity in their specific fields. As Allama Iqbal points out: "The truth is that the religious and scientific processes have identical aim. Both aim at reaching the most real. In fact, religion is far more anxious (than modern science claims) to reach the Ultimate Real. And to both the way to pure objectivity lies through what may be called the purification of experience. "Elaborating further, Allama Iqbal says that a religious student" passes from experience to experience, not as a mere spectator, but as a critical sifter of experience who, by the rules of a peculiar technique suited to his spheres of inquiry, endeavours to eliminate all subjective elements, psychological or physiological, in the content of his experience with a view finally to reaching what is absolutely objective."

No Dichotomy

There is no dichotomy in Islam between the temporal and the spiritual; the structure of Islam is essentially religio-political. Thus, Islam has always refused to recognise the artificial compartmentalisation of life into spiritual and temporal sectors. It has treated life as a totality and has considered no aspect of human life too profane to remain within its jurisdiction. It has sought to reform, ennoble, spiritualize and enrich human life and the whole of it. It is for this reason that Islam has always been not merely a religion in the commonly understood sense of the term, but also "an ethical ideal plus a certain kind of polity", that is, "a social structure regulated by a legal system and animated by a specific ethical deal". It is primarily for the same reason that according to Allama Iqbal, "Islam has furnished those basic emotions and loyalties which gradually unify scattered individuals and groups and finally transform them into a well-defined people". Hence, the maintenance of the solidarity and inner integration of the Muslim community has been one of the chief religious ideals of Islam throughout the ages. For it is thus alone that the *ummah* of the Holy Prophet (peace be upon him) can maintain its distinctive entity and fulfil the specific mission which constitutes its *raison d'*etre. In this system the State forms an integral part of the apex and, as Allama Iqbal points out, "is only an effort to realise the spiritual in a human organisation" (*Lectures on the Reconstruction of Religious Thoughts in Islam,* p. 155).

Part - III
Real Law

9

Readings of the Revelation

What is the consequence of abstracting the text and treating it symbolically? Our impression is that such an interpretative approach either becomes trivializing or fascist. The trivializing aspect comes about because truths are abstracted from their context and end up being recorded as bland statements, like 'Islam is peace', or 'Islam teaches us to be just', or 'Jihad means to struggle for peace'. In such a context, how important could careful adherence to the *ahkam* (legal properties) be? The fascist part comes about because the key interpreter gets to play games with symbols that are manipulated exclusively by him and his cohorts. In that context, external or outward or literal Islam, with its laws and regulations, is so much drivel for people not sufficiently elevated. (One could call the first approach *ibahiyyah* and the second *batiniyyah)*.

Holy Quran First

In contrast, the consequence of closer readings of the revelation, of more grammatically aware and precise readings, of increased attention to the tiniest details of the revelation in its original language is, ironically, a discovery of a polysemantic and multifaceted text. The broadest, most varied and dynamic, vibrant and living understanding of the revelation comes from the closest, most careful, detailed, linguistic, and literally based reading. It happens too that the closest fidelity to the *ahkam* (such as those related to placing one's hands while standing during the *salah,* for example) opens up a range of authentic and true positions. Instead of denigrating the truth of following normative practices by trivializing them, this interpretation invests great significance and relevance to multiple true positions; instead of in-group fascism, this interpretation affirms other true positions, without denying any one of them.

In one passage we saw Ibn al-Arabi incorporating the peculiar linguistic fact that in the Arab language the word *khafiya is* its own antonym, such that, for those of the perception, the Hidden is the Manifest, the exposed is the concealed. When I mentioned this to a colleague of mine, she said that the secrets of the Quran are safely hidden away—in the outside, literal text! As with Poe's purloined letter, the best place to hide something is in the most exposed place. The *haqqiqah* is the *shariah.*

Let us examine the depths, details, and particularities of one portion of a verse to show what kind of polysemanticism comes about with a close; literal reading of the revelation. This portion of a verse in the chapter *al-Maidah* sets down the description of *wudu*. The portion reads, *O you who believe. When you go to the salah, wash your faces and your hands to the elbows and wipe your heads and your feet to the ankles [5:6].* The two operative imperatives are wash (gh.s.l) and wipe (m.s.h.). The question is which imperative governs the phrase 'your feet'.

Wiping is where wet hands brush over the bodily part in question, whether head or foot. Wiping the feet entails a brisk movement similar to the wiping over the shoes, and Sunni scholars have generally believed this movement of wiping over the bare feet to be negated by the *hadith* evidence in which the Prophet Muhammad admonished a group of Muslims to pay attention to their heels in *wudu,* saying, 'Woe to the heels in hell-fire'.'

This particular line of argument unfolds as follows. The obvious and literal meaning of the verse in the Quranic Arabic indicates the feet, much as in English 'wipe your heads, and your feet', means 'wipe your heads, and wipe your feet'. But the *hadith* seems to indicate 'washing' the feet, so as to make sure the heels are covered in *wudu*. How should these two different indications be reconciled? We examine some of the major arguments which seek to do just that below, and then we examine Ibn alArabi's treatment of this issue.

Let us look first at three areas essential to this *fiqh* debate. First, the recitations involved for the verse; that is, the authentic, correct *(sahih)* recitations of the word 'your feet'. Second, the list of authorities and what method of *wudu* of the feet they practised, and why. Third, the arguments proffered by scholars over the ages to address this issue. The raw citations and data are to give the reader a glimpse of the intricacies and fine points of the classical scholarly discourse, where the direction one moves toward truth is not out towards abstraction and generalization, but in towards detail and specificity. As with fractal geometries, Escher's drawings, Borges and Eco's writings, the 'truth' of things lies in the patterns one perceives as one peers closely and with a narrower field of view. The weight of this massive debate should demonstrate the futility of the desire for conclusion and answers, and should begin to show us instead the value of searching for polysemanticism in randomness, complexities, and ambiguities.

Good Recitations

There are three recitations of 'your feet', namely *arjulakum* (with *nasb), arjulikum* (with *khafd),* and *arjulukum* (with *raft*) :

1. The first recitation is recited by Nafi ibn Abu Nuaym (169/785), Asim ibn Abu al-Nujud (127/744), and Ali ibn Hamzah al-Kasai (189/801).
2. The second recitation of *arjulikum* with *khafd* is that of Abd-Allah Ibn Kathir (120/737), Abu Amr ibn al-Ala (1455/771), and Hamzah ibn Habib (156/772).
3. For the third recitation, Nafi is reported, by Walid ibn Muslim, to have also recited *arjulukum* with *raft,* and it is the recitation of Hasan and al-Amash Sulayman?

Generally, but not necessarily, as we shall see, the recitation of *arjulakum* supports a reading that implies that the operative imperative here is 'wash'; the recitation of *arjulikum* supports a reading that implies that the operative imperative is the proximate verb 'wipe'; and the rare recitation *arjulukum* supports a reading that implies that either of the two imperatives are operative—wipe *and wash* your feet.

Effective Authorities

The following are authoritative positions of early Muslims.

Arjulakum : Washing

Urwah ibn Zubair *(nasb):* recorded in Ibn Mundhir.

Mujahid ibn Jabr *(nasb):* in Ibn Mundhir.

Nafi ibn Abd al-Rahman *(nasb):* reported from Abu Ubayd, in Ibn Mundhir.

Kisai *(nasb):* in Ibn Mundhir.

Abu Ubayd al-Qassim ibn Salam *(nasb):* in Ibn Mundhir.

Al-Shafii *(nasb):* in Ibn Mundhir.

Ali *(nasb):* al-Qurtubi records, 'Asim ibn Kalib reported from Abd al-Rahman that he said, Hasan and Hussayn, Allah's mercy on them, recited *wa arjulakum,* and Ali heard that, and was adjudicating between the people, and said *arjulakum.'* Ibn Mundhir confirms that Ali recited with *nasb.*

Arjulakum : Wiping

Ibn Masud : *(nasb* : wiping);

Ibn Abbas *(nasb* : wiping): al-Qurtubi records, 'It was reported from Ibn Abbas that he said *wudu* is two washings [arms and face] and two wipings [head and feet]'. Ibn Qudamah records, 'It is related from Ibn Abbas that he said, I do not find in the Book of Allah anything but two washings and two wipings."

Ibn Kathir records that Ibn Abbas wiped the feet. He says, 'Ibn Abu Hatim said, *haddathana* my father *haddathana* Abu Mamar al-Mungari *haddathana* Abd al-Wahhab *Haddathana* Ali ibn Zayd from Yusuf ibn Mahran from Ibn Abbas about this verse that it is a wiping. '

Ibn Majah records in his *Sunan, 'haddathana* Abu Bakr ibn Abi Shaybah *haddathana* Ibn Ulayyah, from Ruhi ibn al-Qasim from AbdAllah ibn Muhammad ibn Aqil from Rubayya, who said, Ibn Abbas came to me and he asked me about this *hadith,* that is, the *hadith* in which it was mentioned that the messenger of Allah *(sallallahu alayhi wa sallam)* did *wudu* and washed his feet. Ibn Abbas said, "The people insist on nothing but washing, but I do not find in the Book of Allah anything but wiping"."

Arjulikum : Wiping

Al-Hasan al-Basri : in Ibn Mundhir.

Sulayman ibn Mahran al-Amash : in Ibn Mundhir.

Abu Jafar : al-Razi records, 'The people disagree about wiping the feet and washing them', and Ibn Abbas, Anas ibn Malik, Ikrimah, Shubi, and Abu Jafar Muhammad ibn Ali obligate wiping, and it is the position of the Imamiyyah among the Shiah.'

Ikrimah ibn Abd-Allah: al-Qurtubi records, 'Ikrimah used to wipe his feet. He said there is no washing for the feet: The Quran was sent down with wiping them.' He also records that Ibn Jarir said, '*haddathana* Yaqub *haddathana* Ibn Uliyah *haddathana* Ayub who said, "I saw Ikrimah wiping his feet, and he argued for it".'

Abu Dharr: Ibn Hajar (852) in *Fath al-Bari* records that to the *hadith* 'woe to the heels in hell-fire', Abu Dharr added, 'And he did not wipe his feet."

Al-Qatadah : al-Qurtubi records that al-Qatadah ibn Daamah (117/ 735) said, 'Allah made required two washings and two wipings.'

Arjulikum : Washing

Amr ibn Sharhbil al-Shubah : in Ibn Mundhir. He is recorded as saying, 'The Quran came down with wiping but the Sunna is for washing.'

Al-Thalab : Ibn Manzur in *Lisan al-Arab* cites Abu al-Abbas al-Thalab (291/903) as saying, 'The Quran came down revealing wiping but the Sunna is for washing."

Anas : al-Qurtubi records that Al-Hajjaj ibn Yusuf al-Thaqafi (95/ 714), governor of the eastern provinces, 'gave a *khutbah* in Ahwaz and mentioned *wudu*. He said, "Wash your faces and hands and wipe your heads and feet because there is nothing of the sons of Adam closer to filth than his feet, so wash them, their bottoms and their tops, and their tendons." Anas ibn Malik heard that and said, "Allah spoke the truth and Hajjaj spoke a lie, because

Allah said, Wipe your heads *wa arjulikum.* When he wiped his feet, he (simply) moistened them".' Al-Qurtubi also records, 'It is also reported from Anas that he said the Quran was sent down with wiping but the Sunna is with washing.' Ibn Mundhir records the above from Ibn Umar and also records, '*haddathana* Ismail *haddathana* Abu Bakr *haddathana* Muhammad ibn Abi Adwi from his father that Anas used to wash his hands and feet until they dripped.'

Ibn Kathir records the same story about Hajjaj: 'Ibn Jarir said *haddathani* Yaqub ibn Ibrahim *haddathana* Ibn Uliyah *haddathana* Hamid who said Musa ibn Anas said to Anas, when we were with him, O Abu Hamzah, Hajjaj gave us a *khutbah* in Ahwaz, while we were with him and he mentioned purification. He said, "Wash your faces and wipe your heads and feet because there is nothing of the sons of Adam closer to filth than his feet, so wash them, their bottoms and their tops, and their tendons." Anas heard that and said, Hajjaj spoke a lie: Allah said, *Wipe your heads wa arjulikum.* When Anas wiped the feet, he moistened them. The chain is authentic.' Ibn Kathir also confirms: 'Ibn Jarir said *haddathana* Ali ibn Sahl *haddathana* Mumal *haddathana* Hammad *haddathana* Asim about the case of Anas, and he said. The Quran came down with wiping but the Sunna is for washing. This too has an authentic chain.'

Arjulukum : Wash and Wipe

Hasan (combine): al-Zamakhshari records that Hasan said, 'It is a combining of two matters.' He also records, 'Hasan recited *arjulukum* with *raf,* with the meaning *wa arjulukum,* washed or wiped to the ankles'.

Dawud (combine): al-Razi records that Dawud al-Isfahani al-Zahiri obligates combining the two; it is also the position of al-Nasir of the Zaydis.

Al-Nahhas (combine): al-Qurtubi records, 'al-Nahhas said one of the best things said about the issue is that wiping and the washing are both obligatory together, so the wiping is obligatory because of the recitation of one who recites *nasb,* and the two recitations have the status of two verses.'

Arjulikum or Arjulakum : Wash or Wipe

Al-Tabari (choice): al-Qurtubi records that 'Ibn Jarir al-Tabari (310/ 922) judged that required for the feet is to choose between the washing and the wiping.' Al-Razi adds that this was Hasan al-Basri's position too, recording, 'The position of Hasan al-Basri and Muhammad ibn Jarir al-Tabari is that the one responsible [for *wudu]* chooses between wiping and washing.'"

Ibn al-Arabi al-Maliki records that Muhammad ibn Jarir al-Tabari ,reasoned that the recitation *is arjulikum* with *khafd* in conjunction with the head, so the head and feet are wiped, and the recitation with *nasb is* in conjunction with the face and arms, so they are washed; so in that way it functions in accordance with both recitations."

Al-Nawawi adds, 'Jubbai, the head of the Mutazilahs, chose between wiping and washing.'"

Significant Arguments

Arguments from Sunna : The conclusive argument for the classical Sunni scholars for washing is based on Sunna. A terse argument for washing is that given by Ibn alArabi al-Maliki, who says, 'Our proof is the continuous practice *[amal al-mutassil,* that is, from the time of the Prophet (PBUH) to today, of washing the feet] and the multiple unbroken chains of transmitted text *[naql al-mutawatir]'*. Related to this argument for washing is the consensus of the scholars, described by Al-Qurtubi as his last proof, namely,

Consensus *[ijma]*. They agree that the one who washed his feet has in fact fulfilled his obligation, but they disagree about one who has wiped his feet. Certainty is with what they have agreed about and not with what they have disagreed about. The transmitted tradition of all the vast majority *[jamhur]* is from their Prophet (PBUH) that he washed his feet in his *wudu,* once, twice, and thrice, until he had cleaned them.

But while the Sunna is to wash, this was not always the case. Ibn Qudamah reports, 'Said *haddathana* Hashim that *akhbarana* [it was told us in the form of a report] Ibn Ata from his father that he said *akhbarani* [it was told me in a report] Aws ibn Aws Abi al-Thaqafi that he saw the Prophet come to a *kizamah* of the people of Taif, and he did *wudu* and wiped his feet. Hashim said this was in the initial period of Islam.' Interestingly, the Sunna of washing is so established that when Ibn Manzur cites this *hadith* in order to explain *kizamah* in his dictionary, he says this: 'The *kizamah* is a pipe under the ground and water flows through it. It is mentioned in the *hadith* that the Prophet came to a *kizamah* of the people and did *wudu* with its water and wiped over his *shoes.*"'

But besides the argument from Sunna, the classical Sunni scholars also provide numerous arguments for washing based on the Quran. Most of these arguments are linguistic, but some fall into other categories. Let us look at the other categories first.

Symbolic Arguments : Al-Zamakhshari (d.538) in his commentary *Kashshaf* records *wa arjulikum* and says, 'The majority recite *arjulakum* with *nasb,* thereby indicating that the feet are to be washed. If someone asked me why did you [O Zamakhshari] make it recite with *jarr* [that is, *khadf arjulikum]* and make the admission of a property of wiping [when you actually argue for washing the feet], I would say that the feet are among the three bodily parts washed with a pouring of water on them, so they are places of anticipated wastefulness—that is blameworthy, and actual wastefulness is forbidden—so the feet are placed in conjunction with the third part, which is wiped (i.e., the head), not so as to wipe them, but in order to remind one of the obligation of frugality in pouring water over them.'

So avoiding waste is a consideration which explains away the linguistic inclination toward wiping. This argument relies neither on the Sunna of *wudu* nor on other linguistic possibilities. This is al-Zamakhshari's major argument, and it is repeated by many of the great classical scholars.

Another argument which does not rely on the Sunna nor on linguistic evidence appeals to a sense of symmetry in *taharah.* The argument is recorded by Al-Qurtubi in this way:

Amr al-Shabi said Jibril sent down wiping: Do you not see that *tayammum* has wiping for what was washed [in *wudu*—hands and face] and eliminates what was wiped [in *wudu*—head and feet]?

Ibn Kathir uses this argument too, recording that

Ibn Jarir said *haddathana* Abu al-Sayb *haddathana* Ibn Idris from Dawud ibn Abu Hind from Shabi that he said, Jibril came down with wiping, then Shabi said, Do you not see that *tayammum* is wiping what was washed and it eliminates what was wiped?

Ibn Qudamah uses this argument as well.

Linguistic Arguments

Now let us turn to the linguistic arguments. I have collated six different linguistic arguments. These include attempts to show that it is possible in the Arab language (meaning the Arabs have used such a linguistic configuration in the period before and during the descent of the Quran) to have 'your feet' be governed by the initial verb 'wash'.

The first linguistic argument we consider is lexigraphic. Al-Qurtubi records, 'Abu Zayd al-Ansari [215 A. H./830 C. E.] said, wiping in the Arab language is washing and wiping. An example is that the Arab says about someone after *wudu* who has washed the limbs that *tamassaha* [he has wiped].' This argument accepts that 'your feet' is governed by the proximate verb 'wipe', but goes on to posit that `wipe' in effect means a light washing.

Al-Qurtubi also argues that the word 'wipe' may also apply to 'wash'. However, wipe is usually seen as a subset of wash. The argument of al-Qurtubi is that 'Abd al-Haqq ibn Atiyah (546 A. H./1151 C. E.) said, "There are people among those who recite with a *kasrah [khadf]* who judged that the wiping of the two feet is a washing. It is correct that the word wiping shares multiple meanings, applying to wiping and to washing".'

A second argument takes the instances of imperative verb plus a delineated or non-delineated object, as they occur in the verse for wudu and for *tayammum.* We have for *wudu* a clear 'wash the hands to the elbows'. When it comes to *tayammum,* we have a clear 'wipe your face and hands'. Based on these instances, the arguments goes, we see that objects governed by the imperative 'wipe' are not given delineations, and the object that is definitely governed by the imperative 'wash' is given delineation, that is, up to something. Therefore, when we come to 'your feet', and we note that they are delineated with 'up to the ankles', we can conclude that the governing verb must be 'wash'. Al-Qurtubi says, 'Allah bounded the area and said *to the ankles* as He said about the arms *to the elbows.* This proves the obligation of washing the feet, but Allah knows best.'

Ibn Hisham in his *Mughni al-Labib* and al-Zamakhshari in his commentary on 5:6 say, 'It was said *to the ankles,* so He mentioned the end-point, and that dismisses the supposition that the feet are wiped, because wiping is not given an end-point in the *shariah*.'

A third argument is based on the idea that the sequence of bodily parts purified in wudu-face, hands, head, feet-is given precedence over syntactical considerations. To illustrate this argument, suppose that the imperatives were given precedence. We would then have, 'Wash your face, hands, and feet, and wipe your head'. But because the head should be washed before the feet, we have, 'Wash face, hands, (but wipe) head, and feet', meaning 'and wash too your feet'.

Al-Qurtubi with this argument, juxtaposes the strong case for wiping based on the Quran and the strong case for washing based on the Surma. Given this tension he argues that there must be an overriding concern which motivates the inclination of the Quranic phrase towards wiping. That concern, he says, is the sequence.

Al-Qurtubi says,

And it is said, Allah has *wiped* what you have when He has *washed* and purified you from your sins. *So* if it *is* from Arab tradition that the wiping may mean washing, then the statement which preponderates is this statement: *if* the consequences of the recitation with *khadf is* washing. . . and the many *hadiths* fix washing, and there is the warning not to neglect the washing *of* the feet in the numerous reports published by the Imams, then the wiping for the head *is* rather inserted between the things which are washed [arms and feet] for the sake of sequence, that the head should be wiped before the feet are washed, according to this syntax: so wash your faces and your arms to the elbows, and your feet to the ankles, and wipe your heads. But as the head is done before the feet, it precedes them in the recitation—Allah knows best—not because they share with the head in being wiped, but because the head precedes the feet in the process of purification.

Abu Thawr (d. 240) also explains that there must be some overriding concern which interrupts the list of bodily parts and their imperative verbs. He says that the reason your 'feet is placed' after 'your head' is not because it should take the imperative 'wipe', but because the verse is rather establishing the sequence of *wudu*. He says, 'The munificent verse mentioned something wiped [the head] among the things washed. The custom of the Arab when he mentioned like things and unlike things [e.g., wiped and washed bodily parts] is to gather the like things and then to put the other thing in conjunction to them [last], and that custom is not opposed except for a bounty, and the bounty, here, is the [teaching of the] sequence [of *wudu].*" Ramli [d. 1004] uses this argument too in his commentary to the *Minhaj* called *Nahayat al-Muhtaj.*

A fourth argument is that in the Arab language before the descent of the Quran, there is a kind of poetic sentence which puts two objects into conjunction, but where the second object is not governed by the same verb as the first object. This would explain how the Quranic phrase puts 'your heads' into conjunction with 'your feet', while the first object is governed by 'wipe' and the second is governed by something else, in this case 'wash'.

Ibn Manzur argues this way in *Lisan al-Arab.* He says, 'So one who recites it *arjulakum* does so for two reasons. First, in this there are things anterior and things posterior, as if He said, 'Then wash your faces and arms to the elbows, and your feet to the ankles, and wipe your heads', thereby putting things first and putting things last so that *wudu* would be a succession of things one after another. Then, it is as if He meant, 'Wash your feet to the ankles' because His statement *to the ankles* has already proven that is just as we described it [that is, the argument of delineation], so 'your feet' is arranged with washing, as the poet said:

If only your husband had come tomorrow!
Armed with sword, and lance

meaning 'armed with sword, and carrying a lance', where the verb `carrying' is supplied, as 'armed' is an inappropriate verb for 'lance'. Ibn al-Arabi al-Maliki uses the same verse to show that the noun of `feet' may be in conjunction with the word 'head' but not in conjunction with its meaning (that is, 'wipe'), like the poet's verse:

I saw your husband, clamoring
Armed with sword, and lance.

Al-Qurtubi multiplies the examples of this use of language. He says, 'The Arab puts something in conjunction with something with an act which applies to only one of them. The Arab says, "I ate bread, and milk", meaning, "I ate bread and I drank milk".' Another example is the statement of the poet:

I fed them straw, and cold water.

Another example is [from Labid ibn Rabiah]:

The two used the leaves of the cabbage plant, Giving birth

On the banks to her gazelle, and her brood.

Another example is:

I drank milk, and dates and cheese.

'The *taqdir* [the meaning of sentences with ambiguous syntactical elements] is as follows: I fed them straw, and gave them water to drink; the one giving birth on the banks to her gazelle; and the other brooding her ostrich (the ostrich does not 'give birth to' but rather 'broods' the egg); and finally, I'drank the milk, and I ate the dates. So, His phrase *Wipe your heads, and your feet* could be in conjunction with washing in spite of the conjunction with wiping, carrying the meaning and purport of washing. But Allah knows best.'

Al-Jurjani (d. *816),* al-Zamakhshari's commentator, also uses the poet's verses:

Armed with sword, and lance

And feeding the animal straw, and cold water.

A fifth argument is based on the different instances of *jarr,* which means the vowel 'i' *(khafd)* given to a word because of proximity. Al-Qurtubi finds this in the Quran, where we have, *Sent down to you will be a flame of fire, and smoke (55:35),* where 'and smoke' *is muhasin* (in some recitations), which *is khafd* because of *jarr,* because 'the smoke' means 'fumes', so the meaning is 'sent down to you will be *smoke,* and a *flame* of fire', where *smoke* and *flame* are the direct objects of the sentence, even though *smoke* is in *khafd.*

Also, al-Qurtubi adds, 'He said, *No, it is a glorious Quran, in a tablet preserved' (85:21-2).* Here *preserved is mahfuz-in,* which *is khafd* because of *jarr.* In this sentence, *Quran-un, majid-un,* and preserved are all nominatives (raft so that one would say, 'It is a Quran, it is glorious, and it is preserved, in a tablet', but instead of *mahfuz-un,* we have *mahfuz-in,* which is explained as being from proximity to *fi lawh-in* (in a tablet).'

Al-Qurtubi also cites Imru al-Qays, who said: *kabir-u unas-in* fi *bijad-in muzammal-i* meaning, 'He is great among the people, in his striped garment, wrapped up.' AI-Qurtubi remarks, `*muzammal-i is* made *khafd* by proximity, because "wrapped up" refers to the man, not to the striped garment, sc that its inflected termination would otherwise be *raf*".'

He also says, 'It is like the Arabs say, *hadha juhr-u dabb-in kharib-in* [this hole of a lizard, deserted]. The word *kharib-in* [deserted] is made *jarr* even though it would be raf.' That is, the sentence reads, 'this deserted hole of a lizard.' He says, 'This is the position of Akhfash and Abu Abidah, but al-Nahhas rejected it and said this statement is a great error, because it cannot be that the proximate be brought into relationship with something in such a sentence, but it is really an error, like changing the vowel to achieve a rhyme.'

Ibn Kathir remarks that the recitation with *khafd is* 'produced because of proximity and the relationship [to wipe your heads] in the sentence, as in the Arab's sentence *juhr-u dabb-in kharib-in,* and as in His statement, *They will have on them clothes of silk, green, and brocade [76:21].* This is common in the language of the Arab.'

The grammarian Ibn Hisham says, 'A word gives governance to another word when it is in proximity to it, like the statement of some of them: *hadha juhr-u dabb-in kharib-in* with *jarr* but most of them make it *raf.*' That *is, kharib-un;* this is a hole *(juhr-u),* deserted *(kharib-un),* of a lizard *(dabb-in).* He also cites Imru al-Qays's verse:

ka-anna abanan fi *afanini wadqihi*
kabir-u unas-in fi *bijad-in muzammali.*

Ibn Hisham al-Ansari also argues from a passage in 56:11-22, which reads in part, 'These will be nearest to Allah, in gardens of bliss .... Circling them will be ever fresh youth, with goblets, glasses, and cups ... and fruits ... and flesh of fowl ... and black/ white eye'." One question in this passage is what governs the phrases. Ibn Hisham notes that some take 'black/white eye' as *jarr*, that *is, hur-in*, so that 'black/white eye' is governed by 'ever fresh youth'. The meaning is then 'ever fresh youth ... with black/white eye'. But the conjunction could go all the way back to 'gardens of bliss'. Then, we would have 'gardens of bliss', with 'many fruits', and 'flesh of fowl', and *hur-in ayn-in*, which is then read as a synecdoche, as in 'companions with *hur-in ayn-in*'. '*Cups*' would be in conjunction with 'ever fresh youth', so that it would be 'ever fresh youth, circling them with cups'. But Ibn Hisham ends his discussion with the comment, 'Actually, the *khafd* of proximity is rare.'

Ibn Qudamah quotes Imru al-Qays's verse which we saw and also:

fa-zalla tuhatu al-lahm min bayni mundij-in
safifa shiwa-in aw qidir-in mu ajjabi

The meat cooks erred between a well-cooked
grilled row and quick boil

where *qidir-an* (cooked in a pot) is made *jarr—qidir—in—by* being in conjunction with what is proximate, but referring back to *al-lahm* (the meat).

Ibn Qudamah also cites the Quran, where we have *inni akhafu alaykum adhaba yawm-in alim-in* (I fear for you the punishment of a grievous day) (11:26), saying that *alim-in is jarr* because of the proximity of 'day', while it is a description of the punishment, which is *nasb* (the direct object), because of its proximity to the proximate *yawm-in*.

But Ibn Manzur questions the occurrence of the *khafd* of proximity as proving 'washing' in this verse by citing Abu Ishaq, the grammarian, who said, 'Making a noun *khafd* because of proximity is not permitted in the Book of Allah, while it is permissible for poetical imagery.'

Al-Razi too, is doubtful about this argument. He says that the *jarr* of proximity means that the 'feet' are the conjunction with 'wipe your heads', and are governed by 'wipe'. He cites the arguments that this *jarr* is not conclusive, saying 'If it is said no, it is not possible to say that this vowel "i" is there just because of proximity [while "feet" is still in conjunction with "wash your faces"], as it is in the statement:

juhr-u dabb-in kharib-in

and the poet's verse:

kabir anas fi *bijad-in mazmal-i*

we say that is false.' Al-Razi says the above examples may be explained by poetical exigency.

Second, in the above examples, there is no question of ambiguity. In the statement *juhr-u dabb-in kharib-in* the word, 'deserted' cannot be describing the lizard but must be describing the hole. So, he concludes, 'in this verse certainty in the face of ambiguity is not produced.' For al-Razi, the linguistic argument of *jarr* is ultimately inconclusive.

Al-Shawkani cites the possibilities of an argument of *jarr*, but then acknowledges its weakness and sustains an argument from Sunna. He says,

The ones who argue that washing the feet is not obligatory, argue from a recitation of *jarr* in His statement *arjulikum* being in conjunction with His statement *your heads.* They say *arjulikum is* one of the [three of the] seven recitations which are authentic. There is an argument for the conjunction being with washing the faces, even though it is recited with the *jarr* of the proximate; this has been related by the majority of the Arab 21 Imams, like Sibawayh and Akhfash, but it certainly *is* very rare; it differs from the obvious meaning and it cannot sustain the contested position. We argue instead that obligatory is carrying the argument with *his (sallallahu alayhi wa sallam)* consistent practice of washing the feet.

Finally, there is an argument that there is an ambiguity in washing or wiping the feet precisely so that the verse can bear two contexts: wash the feet in one context, and wipe the feet when they are shod.

Al-Qurtubi says, 'It has been said that if the *khafd* of the feet rather mentions restrictively wiping them, it could be for when the feet have shoes on. We learn this restriction from the messenger of Allah, as it is not correct about him that he wiped his feet, except when they were shod. So thereby the messenger of Allah explained with his action the context for washing the feet and the context for wiping them. This is a fine argument.'

Ibn al-Arabi al-Maliki also gives this argument, saying 'Or, the meaning of "wiping" could be for the context of wearing shoes, so the two recitations could be for both contexts [bare feet and shod feet], once *nasb* for the bared feet and once *khafd* for the covered feet.'

Ibn al-Arabi's Position

Ibn al-Arabi alludes to this argument when he discusses the *fiqh* disagreement about what to do when wiping over the shoe when there is a tear in the shoe. He says, 'We argue for wiping what emerges, because we were commanded in the Book of Allah to wipe the feet, so when something of the foot emerges, we wipe it. Thus, there should be no obstacle in wiping the torn shoe where some of the foot sticks out, because the verse's imperative of 'wipe' fits both cases of shod/bare foot.

Ibn al-Arabi reviews the various positions of the ulema, saying, 'The ulema concurred that the feet belong to the bodily parts of *wudu*, but they disagreed about a format of their *taharah*, whether that is through washing, wiping, or choosing between the two.' As we saw, the position of washing is the position of the majority of the classical Sunni scholars; the position of wiping is the position of many companions and successors, including Ibn Abbas, Anas, and Ikrimah; the position of choosing between the two is that of al-Tabari, Hasan al-Basri, Jubbai, Nasir, and Dawud. It is appropriate here to emphasize that Ibn al-Arabi is neither part of the Zahiri school of jurisprudence associated with Dawud and Ibn Hazm, nor is he a part of the Shi'ite school.

Ibn al-Arabi says, 'Our position is choice' and goes on to say 'the combination is best'. This last phrase probably refers to al-Nahhas own position which is characterized by al-Nahhas as `one of the best things said about the issue'. We saw above that al-Qurtubi recorded, `al-Nahhas said one of the best things said about the issue is that the wiping and the washing are both obligatory together, so the wiping is obligatory because of the recitation of one who recites with *khafd* and the washing is obligatory because of the recitation of one who recites with *nasb*, and the two recitations have the status of two verses.'

There is an argument of Ibn Hisham found in his classical grammar *Mughni* which holds that the *wa* (and) could have the meaning of *aw (or)*. In this case there is a linguistic argument for choice. The argument goes as follows.

The meaning of the *wa* here could be 'choice'. One of (the poets) said,

They said, Go far away, choosing for her
patience *'wa'* crying
She said, Crying *is* healthier if I want revenge.

The meaning then is patience *or* crying if patience is not joined to crying (that is, patience *and* crying).

Ibn al-Arabi's position embraces two themes, ease and relief of difficulty, based on the verse *We did not make for you in the religion any constriction (22:78)*, a verse which begins with *jahidu fi Allahi* (exert for Allah) and suggests the *ijtihad* of effortful exertion to understand the determined properties *(ahkam)* and the many consequences of a polysemantic text.

Wiping and washing are related as two forms of purification, the one being subsumed' in the other. Ibn al-Arabi says, 'Know that washing contains wiping from one perspective, so the one who washed has already subsumed wiping in it, just as star light is subsumed in the sun's light.' He acknowledges too that it is possible to see wiping simply as a synonym for washing, as we saw above, saying, 'The one who has wiped did not wash, except in a position of the one who believes, and quotes the Arabs, that "wiping" is a word for "washing", so they are synonymous.'

In Ibn al-Arabi's *fiqh*, each command which is operative in the outwardness is also operative in the inwardness. The command of this verse, therefore, has an inward dimension. He says,

The correct meaning of the *hukm* for the inwardness is that wiping is used for whatever specific practices are necessitated and washing for whatever general practices are necessitated.

Because of this, we propounded choice commensurate with the moment, because perhaps you run to a philanthropist for a designated need, on behalf of an individual himself, then that is in a way station of wiping. And perhaps you run to the king for a need diffused over the entire population, or needs, so that that individual would be included in this general public, so this is in a way station of washing in which is subsumed wiping.

Now Ibn al-Arabi investigates the linguistic evidence of the verse. He notes, 'As for the reciting of His statement [Wash *your faces,* and *your hands to the elbows, wipe your head] wa arjulkum* [your feet] [5:6], with either *arjula,* or *arjuli*—on account of the letter *wa*—according to whether the *wa* is in conjunction with "wipe", through *khafd,* or in conjunction with "wash", with the vocalization *arjula.* Our position is that even the recitation *arjula* does not actually contraindicate wiping, because this wa may be the 'and of simultaneity', and the 'and of simultaneity' makes the word *arjula.*'

Even though the recitation of *arjulakum* which we noted above, was generally associated with the argument for taking the initial verb 'wash' as the operative imperative, the argument for wiping is still linguistically strong. Ibn al-Arabi then gives examples of the 'and of simultaneity'. He says:

You say, *qama Zayd wa Umar-an;* and *wa stiwa-al-mau* was *l-khashabat*an; and *wa ma anta wa qasat-an min tharid;* and *wa marrartu bi-Zayd wa Umar-an.* You mean, (I passed Zayd) with Umar. And likewise for the one who recites [with *nasb*] *Wipe your heads and your arjula, with a.*

So,

The argumentation of the one who argues for wiping, in this verse, is stronger, because his argumentation shares with the proponent for washing in giving expression to the recitation arjula. But one who argues for washing does not share with the proponent for wiping in giving expression to the recitation *arjuli.*

From the verse 'wiping' is stronger, and the proponent for 'wiping' can point to either vocalization for proof.

Among 'our colleagues', Ibn al-Arabi says, there are those who 'preponderate the specific over the general, and among them there are those who would preponderate the general over the specific: all of that absolutely.' Using the metaphor developed above, some of our colleagues always go to a specific philanthropist, and others always go to the king. They are not sensitive to the context, but instead go fixedly and rigidly to one place.

Ibn al-Arabi then says,

> But our position is other than that. We walk with the Real according to a determined property *[hukm]* of the circumstance, so we generalize where He generalized, and we make specific where He makes specific.
>
> We do not initiate a property, because one who initiated a property has already initiated in his self Lordship, and the one who has initiated in himself Lordship has already diminished his servanthood, to the extent of this issue. And if he has diminished his servanthood, to that extent, he shall diminish the divine self-disclosure of the Real in him. And if he has diminished the divine self-disclosure of the Real in him, he has diminished his knowledge through his Lord. And if he has diminished his knowledge through his Lord, he is ignorant about Him to the context he diminished it, because if there should appear to that one, the one who diminished it, a property in the world [the macrocosm] or in his world [the microcosm], he would not recognize it. Because of this, our position is that we do not initiate a property in one fell swoop.

Ibn al-Arabi is completely familiar with the range of arguments produced by the legal scholars of his time. Their arguments generally seek closure and finality—although without exception, the final theme among all the classical scholars is 'But Allah knows best.' That is, even though they desire closure and finality, the classical scholars leave the door open to continuing divine guidance.

The desire to achieve a single and monolithic understanding of Islam is a perennial problem. Every *qadi* who ever insisted on having the right to use *ijtihad* to settle cases, using any of the schools of jurisprudence which best applied for that particular case, was also fighting against the desire of the sultan and state to codify and impose a Procrustean vision of Islam.

So the sum consequence of the polysemantic text of washing/ wiping the feet is 'that or perhaps that', or 'this and that'. The more one knows about this verse, the more one is aware of not knowing. For Ibn al-Arabi, the response to 'not knowing' is not *qiyas* or *ray* but *taqwa,* becoming protected by Allah through doing acts which will protect oneself from His punishment (which is its Arabic definition).

Interestingly enough, the conclusion or last word of Ibn al-Arabi for every issue, then, *is taqwa,* and this is a conclusion which is valid for every level of knowledge. Ibn al-Arabi's treatment of this particular issue is to multiply its polysemantic nature, to increase the possibilities, to deconstruct false closures and *taqayyid,* and the smugness of 'knowing'. He seeks to convince his audience that for this and every issue we must void ourselves of Lordship and exaltedness, becoming instead humbly receptive and alert to divine command.

In the mater of purity *(taharah)* in the same verse we have been considering (5:6), Allah says that He does not wish for us any constriction *ma yuridu Allahu li-ajala alaykum min haraj,* but instead, *He wishes to make you pure.* Then, following this verse He tells us to remember our covenant with Him, when we said, 'We hear and obey'. One might gloss here we listen, we hear, and we obey. For Ibn al-Arabi, assumption of lordship on our part, whether openly or not, precludes our listening, hearing, and ultimately, obeying. And right after that, Allah says, *And have taqwa [fear] before Allah; Allah is aware of the bottom of the hearts! (5:8).*

10

God's Words

There is a great thirst for the direct word of Allah. Knowledge in the Qūran is linked with water; rain comes down from the heavens, the parched earth drinks it, and vegetation is produced. Muhammad received the rain, which comes 'freshly from its Lord'. Rain is the direct knowledge which Allah gives to make us whole. River water is indirect knowledge—knowledge from our intellects—which gets mixed up with impurities and is subject to pollution. I used to joke that now we have acid rain: but, now I think that is our situation indeed. We no longer have the direct, clean, pure rainwater which Allah provides because the medium above us is itself polluted.

Clearing the Air

We have tried here to clear the air of the irritants and obstacles which come in the way of hearing the word directly. What Ibn al-Arabi does, above all, is to prepare his audience for the encounter and then to become transparent before the encounter. His intellect, his genius, and his skill pale in comparison with this gift: a way to hear in clear and clarifying language, the divine word.

And as therefore neither conclusions nor resolutions are appropriate, we take up three passages from Ibn al-Arabi's *fiqh.*

Three Passages from Al-Arabi

The First Passage : In the first passage, we hear Ibn al-Arabi's discussion on *awrah.* This word is not translatable, but it is describable. Classically, *awrah* meant the part of the body, men's and women's, which had to be covered. The classical *fiqh* books spent most of their time discussing the man's *awrah* and the man's clothing. Today of course, *awrah* means the shameful part of women, including their voices, smell, and very presence. In fact, in Urdu, woman herself is called shameful—aurat. In order to recover the direct knowledge of the Quran, let us take up Ibn al-Arabi's discussion here; I have first translated Ibn Manzur's descriptions of key words needed for this passage from Ibn al-Arabi's *Futuhat al-Makkivvah.*

Awrah ('w.r.): Ibn Manzur says, 'The *awrah* of the man and the woman is their private parts.' And 'the *awrah* is everything that causes embarrassment if it is exposed.' Also, 'The *awar* ['w.r.] has only one eye'. He also says, 'Covering the *awrah* during the *salah* and other than the *salah* is obligatory; about covering it when secluded there is a disagreement'. And 'in the Quran we have, Our *houses* are *awrah* (33:13), that is, they are open to the thief because the houses have been cleared of the men, but Allah caught them in their lie, saying, *But they* were *not awrah, they only, wanted to desert* [33:13]. It is said its meaning is. Our houses are *awrah,* that is, our houses are near the enemy and we were stolen from them. But Allah knew that their intent was deserting the battle.'

Ibn al-Arabi says, 'The ulema agree that covering the awrah is obligatory, with no disagreement, and absolutely, that is, during the salah I shall mention its boundary of the man and the woman.'

Mayl (m.y.l.): Ibn Manzur says, '*Mayl* is inclining toward something.'

Ibn al-Arabi says, 'The crossover for that in the inwardness. It is obligatory on every intelligent person to cover the divine secret which, if it were disclosed, would lead someone, who was neither knowledgeable nor intelligent, to a lack of a sense of taboo toward the Side of the divine, Exalted, Forbidden, because the reality of *awrah* is *mayl*. Because of this that person said *Our houses are awrah* [33:13], that is, inclined, bent on destruction, when they sought to desert; then Allah caught them in their lie, before His Prophet, with His word, *But they were not awrah; they* only *meant* to desert [33:13], that is, to desert what you [Muhammad] called them to. There is also the *awar* [one-eyed man], because his view inclines [m.y.l.] to a single perspective.

'Like that it is appropriate that the knowledgeable one cover from the ignorant one the secrets of the Real; secrets like His word, *There* are *no whisperings of three except He is the fourth [58:7];* His word, *We are closer to one than the jugular vein [50:16];* and His word, *1 become his ear, and his eye, and his tongue,* because when the ignorant one hears that, it leads him to forbidden conceptualizations like divine incarnation or bounded divinity. Therefore, it is appropriate that with which the Real turns and inclines to the hearts of the knowledgeable ones—Exalted is He and Holy—with His address, be covered up with whatever His Majesty necessitates of Independence absolutely from the worlds; in addition to His word on the tongue of His messenger, *I was hungry and you fed me not, I was sick and you visited me not, I was thirsty and you did not give me to drink.*

'So he covers up the knowledge of this secret from the ignorant one and he does not add to what He said as a commentary to it [that is, I *was hungry]* at all. He covers up as the Real does with His word, *So and so was sick, and if you had visited him, you would have found Me with him.* This is more ambiguous than the first statement, but He gives in this commentary to the ones who know Allah, another knowledge about Him which they did not have. That is that in the first He made Himself the very same sick and hungry one but in His commentary He made Himself the Helper of the sick one, as He is *with him,* because whoever helps the sick one is with him. How far away is this from the One who made Himself the sick one himself! Each statement in that way is real, and to every real *[Haqq]* is a Reality *[Haqqiqah].'*

Ammi (' m.m.): (This is one of the most loaded classical words, usually full of the absolute class distinctions of the elite and the mass. Ibn al-Arabi's use of the word is, however, quite different and is tied into one of the descriptions used by Ibn Manzur). Ibn Manzur says, 'A *ummayy ['m.m.]* man and a *qusriyy [q.s.r.,* utmost] man. The *ummay* is the *amm* and the *qusriyy* is the *khass.* In the *hadith:* When he used to go home, he gave upon entrance three *juz'*: a *juz* to Allah, a *juz* for his family, and a *juz* for himself. Then he apportioned *juz* for him and the people and he correlated that portion to the *ammah* through the *khassah,* meaning that the *ammah* were not with him at that moment, so the *khassah* communicated to the *ammah* what they heard from him; it is as if the benefits were transferred to the *ammah* from the *khassah.'*

According to Ibn al-Arabi, 'As for the covering up of that before the *ammi,* it is that one say to him about His statement, You *would have found Me with him* that the condition of the sick one is certainly that of dependency and need of the one in whose hand is the cure—and that is no one but Allah, so mostly what we need is to remember *[dhikr]* Allah with each instant to repel what befell him, which is different from the healthy one: He said, I *Myself am seated with the one who remembers [dhikr] Me.* This is the healthy condition. The *ammi* is satisfied with it and the knowledgeable one stays with what He taught him about that upon his knowledge; this is the cover up of the divine *mayl* from the gaze of the *ammi.*

'The ulema then disagree about whether covering the *awrah* during the *salah* is a precondition for the validity of the *salah* or not. There is one who says that covering the *awrah* is one of the Sunnas [voluntary but customary practices] of the *salah,* and there is one who says that it is one of the obligations of the *salah.*

'As for the crossover for that spiritually, we have already taught you the concept of *awrah* above. About this issue, as it is established [by an authentic *hadith]* that the one praying is in intimate conversation with his Lord and that the *salah* has been divided in two between Allah and His worshipper, so the one who sees predominate [in this issue] that the Real is the One praying through the acts of His worshipper, that is, the outward practices of the worshipper in the *salah,* as it is established that *Verily Allah said on the tongue of His worshipper during the salah, Allah hears the one who praises Him [sami Allahu li-man hamidah],* when one rises after *ruku,* and the worshipper is the speaker, certainly; and He said, *Give him [asylum] so that he may hear the Word of Allah [9:6],* while it is the messenger (PBUH) of Allah, who is reciting, certainly; [that one who takes this position says] the covering of the *awrah* is one of the obligations of the *salah,* that is, the likes of this should not be made manifest before the *ammi,* meaning its supra-sensory meaning and its secret, which is known by the knowledgeable one; rather, the *ammi* should believe in it [without understanding it], as is mentioned, *Only the knowledgeable ones will understand it [29:43].*

'And the one who sees that there is no gradation in this issue between the knowledgeable one and the *ammi,* and that there is nothing but what the text relates, and if it causes to lead, before the hearer, towards what it leads to—if he does not go outside of what the language requires for that—even though their degrees are granted preference [one over another], then the covering of the *awrah* in his view is one of the Sunnas of the *salah,* not one of its obligations. *Allah says what is real, and He is the guide of the way [33:4].*

'About the boundary of the *awrah,* there is one who says that the *awrah,* for the man, is the two private parts and there is one who says that it is, for the man, from the navel to the knee. It is, according to us, only the private parts.

'The crossover for that spiritually: whatever is blameworthy, hated, and filthy of humankind is the *awrah* according to Reality. The two private parts are a place for what we mentioned. It is at the location of the unlawful; and in addition to the private parts is what encroaches on the private parts, the navel on the upper and the knee on the lower; the encroaching area is at the location of the Doubtful, and it is appropriate that one protect oneself [:.v.q.y., cf. *taqwa]* [from the Doubtful], because *The herder going around the enclosed precinct may almost get into it* [and so should stay well away from the boundary of the Unlawful].

'About the boundary of the *awrah* for the woman, there is one who says that all of her *is awrah* except the face and palms and there is one who argues for that and adds that her feet are not *awrah.* And there is one who says that all of her is *awrah.* As for our position, there is nothing *awrah* of the woman, in fact, except the private parts, just as He said, (*their sawah {two private parts) became visible to them, and they [Adam and Eve] started weaving for themselves the leaves of the Garden [7:22],* so He treated Adam and Eve the same in the covering of the private parts; they are the two *awrahs.* Even though the woman is commanded [in the last shariah, of Muhammad] to cover [more], and that is our position, yet this is not because of it being *awrah.* That [covering of the leaves of the private parts] is a legal property set down by shariah mentioning covering; but it is not necessary that anything else be covered as *awrah.'*

The Second Passage : To understand this second passage, we need to understand Ibn al-Arabi's Arabic conception of *sawm.* It will become immediately clear why this word can not be translated, either by 'fasting' or by any conventional Arabic phrase.

Ibn al-Arabi begins his large chapter on the *sawm* with its definition. He says, 'You should know—may Allah strengthen you!—that the *sawm is imsak* [abstention] and *rifah* [elevation].' As usual, we turn to the description of the word in *Lisan al-Arrab* and find the same: Ibn Manzur says, 'The word *sawm* in the language is *imsak* [abstention] from something and *tark* [leaving] it.' This is the first description. For the second, Ibn Manzur says, 'There is *sama* [from the same three letter root s.w.m. from which the word *sawm* is derived] the day when it draws up and rises to the zenith of mid-way. Imru al-Qays (one of the pre-Islamic poets whose Arabic usage is authoritative) said, *idha sama an-nahar wa hajjara* (the day rose up and became mid-way).'

To demonstrate the second description, lbn al-Arabi says, 'One says, *sama an-nahar* when the day elevates. Imru al-Qays said, *idha sama annahar wa hajjra,* that is, became elevated. Because the *sawm* has been elevated above the rest of the worships [the pillars of Islam, such as *salah* and *zakah]* by a degree, it is called *sawm.* He—Exalted beyond—elevated the *sawm by* refusing any similarity with it to the worships, as we shall explain. He takes the *sawm* away from His worshippers even though they are doing it as a worship and attaches it to *Himself-subhana-hu* [He is exalted beyond]-and gives with His hand the reward to the one with the attribute of *sawm* who does it. He links the *sawm* to Himself by refuşing any similarity [of it to the other worships].'

Ibn al-Arabi will explain below why the *sawm* is elevated above the other worships using the same evidence which Ibn Manzur uses. Ibn Manzur says, 'There is a *hadith* where the Prophet (PBUH) said, Allah said, *Every act of the offspring of Adam is theirs, except the sawm, because it is for Me.* Abu Ubayd said, Allah has made the *sawm* special with it being His and as being something which He rewards.'

In fact, the conception of elevation *(rifah)* and abstention *(tark)* both point to the particular description of *sawm*. Ibn al-Arabi says, 'The *sawm* is in reality a *tark,* not a practice, and the refusing of similarity is a negative attribute which intensifies the relationship of the *sawm* to Allah. He said about Himself, *Laysa ka mithlihi shayun* [There is nothing like Me] [42:11], so He refused that there should be to Him a *mithl* [similar], because *He—subhana-hu—has* no *mithl,* according to intellectual and *shariah* proofs. And al-Nasai [one of the authoritative collectors of *hadith]* published from Abu Umamah that he said, "I came to the messenger of Allah and I asked him, Command me with a command which I can take from you. He said, On you is the *sawm,* because it has no *mithl* [there is nothing like it]." Thus, he refused that any of the worships which are made *shariah* for the worshippers be made similar to it.'

In order to pursue this particular conception, Ibn al-Arabi continues with the usual evidence for this worship. He says, 'And Muslim published in his authentic collection from Abu Hurayrah that he said, The messenger of Allah said, *Every act of this offspring of Adam is theirs, except the sawm; I reward it.* And *siyam (sawm) is* a shield; when there is a *sawm* day for one of you, do, not be loud and noisy on that day. If someone insults you or fights you, say, I am one with the matter of *sawm [saim], I am a saim* [one fasting]. And by the one in whose Hand the soul of Muhammad is, the breath of the one with *sawm is* better, according to Allah, on the day of judgement, than the scent of musk. And the one with *sawm* has two joys which he enjoys: when he breaks [fast] with his *iftar* there is a joy and when he meets his Lord there is a joy in his *sawm.*'

The last phrase is awkward and not an expected turn of phrase. This should be a signal to us that something quite particular is happening. Indeed, taking the conception of *sawm* which Ibn al-Arabi has developed gives an explanation why we have this strange turn of phrase. He says, 'Know that as he refused any similarity with the *sawm,* as was established in what preceded with the *hadith* of al-Nasai and the reality that *Laysa ka mithlihi shayun* [there is nothing like h/Him, 42:11], the *saim* meets with his Lord by the attribute of *Laysa ka mithlihi shayun* and sees Him by it, so He is the Seer who is Seen. Because of this, he said, There is a joy in his *sawm,* and he did not say, There is a joy in meeting his Lord, because the joy is not a joy enjoyed by himself but is a joy enjoyed in *it.* And the one about whom the Real is his eyes with which he sees and witnesses, he himself does not see except by His seeing.'

This last phrase is the thematic *hadith qudsi* which is as follows: 'My *abd* draws near to Me by means of nothing dearer to Me than that which I have established as a duty for him. And My *abd* continues drawing nearer to Me through supererogatory acts until I love him; and when I love him, I become his ear with which he hears, his eye with which he sees, his hand with which he grasps, and his foot with which he walks.'

Concluding, he says, 'So the joy of the *saim* is his meeting at the degree of refusal of similarity. His joy in the *iftar* [breaking of the fast] is in the world, in respect to giving due to the physical self which needs nourishment for itself. As the *abd* is described in this *hadith* as having *sawm,* and deserving the name *saim* because of this description, so after the affirmation of his *sawm* the Real negates it and attaches it to Himself, saying, [Every act of the offspring of Adam is theirs] except the *sawm;* it is Mine [or, it is for Me], that is, an attribute of *samadani* [cf. *Allah ussamad] [* 112:2], which is being beyond needing nourishment. "It is Mine only; even though I may describe you with *sawm, I* so describe you by some delimiting metaphor of *tanzih* [being beyond an attribute], not by the absolute *tanzih* which is appropriate to My Majesty. So I say, And I reward it." So the Real rewards the *sawm* for the *saim* when he turns to his Lord and he is cast to his Lord by the attribute of "He has no *mithl"*—which is the *sawm,* as the one to Whom "Tnere is nothing like unto" cannot see anything but one whom "There is nothing like unto." Abu Talib al-Makki-he was one of the masters of the folk of tasting determined the text *jaza-u-hu man wujida fi rahl-ihi fa-huwa jaza-u-hu* [12:75]—for what this verse requires for this circumstance.'

Now we can turn to the passage in question. 'The most surplusing and balanced *sawm is* "fasting" one day for yourself and fasting one day for your Lord and between them a day breaking fast .... But when some of them saw that the right-claim of Allah is more right, they did not see treating equally the right of Allah and the right of the worshipper, so they fasted for two days and broke fast for one day. This was the fasting of Mary, because she saw that *men have a degree over women* [2:228], so she said, Perhaps I shall make this second day of fasting one to counter this degree. And that was how it was, because the Prophet *testified* that *she* was complete [perfect], just as he testified to the completion of the Men.' And when she saw that the testimony of two women was balanced with the testimony of one man, she said, "Two days fasting for me is at the level of one day fasting of the Man." Thus, she got the station of the Man for that, and she equalled David in surplus in the fast. So because of this, the one who overcomes in himself his *nafs* has overcome in himself his [tendency to] divinization; then it is appropriate that he treats his *nafs* as Mary treated her *nafs* in this context, lest her *nafs* overtake her *aql;* this is a fine allusion for the one who understands it.'

Dahr: Ibn Manzur says, *'dahr is* an extremely long time'. And 'there is the *hadith,* Do not revile *the dahr because Allah is dahr.'*

Qayyum (q.w.m.): Ibn Manzur says, 'The *Qayyum,* one of Allah's names; Allah is Standing up by Himself absolutely, not by [the help of] anyone.'

Ibn al-Arabi continues, 'When completion became hers, she caught up to the Men, and the most completion was hers in her catching up to her Lord. It was like Jesus son of Mary, her son, because he used to fast *dahr* and not break the fast, and he used to stay up (q.w.m.) at night and not sleep. Outwardly, in the world he was with the name *dahr* in the day and with the name Qayyum—the one whom *sleep does* not *seize,* nor *slumber* (2:225) at night. So divinity was claimed for him, and it was said, Allah is the Christ, son of Mary (5:72), and that was not said about any prophet before him, because the most that was said about Uzayr was that he was the son *of Allah* (9:30). It was not said, He is Allah.'

Kufr: Ibn Manzur says the word *kufr* is derived from *satr* (veil, cover). *Kanaf:* Ibn Manzur says, In the *hadith* of Ibn Umar, we have about salvation, The believer draws closer to his Lord on the day of judgement until He places over him His *kanaf.* Ibn Mubarak said, He meant, He covers (s.t.r.) him.

'So look at what effect this [divine] attribute had,' Ibn al-Arabi says, 'from behind the veil of the unseen, on the hearts of the veiled ones of the folk of disclosure such that they said, *Allah is the Christ, son of Mary* [5:72]; *kufr* is related to them for that, set up as an excuse for them, because they did not commit *shirk;* rather they said, He is Allah, and the one who commits *shirk* is the one who makes with Allah another god. So this is one doing *kufr,* not *shirk.* Therefore, He said, They have done *kufr* who say, Allah is the *Christ, son of Mary,* thereby attributing to them a sitr [a cover, that is, *kufr*]; they took the humanity of Jesus to be a locus of divine manifestation [*majalla*]. Jesus warned him [self] about this station, in what Allah reported, as a confirmation for them concerning what they said. Christ said, O *Bani Israil, worship Allah, my Lord and Your Lord.* They said, That is what we are doing! So they worshipped Allah through him. Then He said to them, *The one who commits shirk with Allah, Allah has made forbidden to him the Garden [5:72],* that is, Allah has made forbidden His *kanaf* with which He covers [s.t.r.] him; but Allah already described them with being covered [s.t.r.] in that He described them with *kufr.* This is a verse whose literal meaning gives exactly that which the matter itself gives of that. The *tawil* [allegorical interpretation] of the verse is caught up in blameworthiness; if you comprehend what we have mentioned about it, you will fall into the great ocean and you will not be saved from drowning in it at all, because it is the endless ocean. There is no deeper' word of Allah for the one who sees it and has eyes to see it and is from Allah concerning it *upon insight [12:108].'*

The Third Passage **:** Ibn al-Arabi says, 'Abu Ahmad mentioned in a *hadith* of Abd-Allah ibn Buayl ibn Waraqa al-Makki from Amr ibn Dinar from Ibn Umar from Umar that he vowed to sit ('k.f.) in the sacred mosque, and the messenger of Allah (PBUH) said to him, Sit in *itikaf* and do *sawm.'*

Awliya: Ibn Manzur says, 'The *waliy [* singular of *awliya]* of the right hand is the one who is in charge of one's command and executes his tasks.'

'Its connecting crossover: Rasululah, the messenger of Allah commanded the one desiring to stand [q.w.m.] with Allah that they should stand with him by the attribute which is Allah's, and that attribute is the *sawm,* so that one should be with Allah, by Allah, for Allah, so nothing of them would be seen except Allah. This is the circumstance of the folk of Allah. It was asked of the

Rasululah, Who are the *awliya* of Allah? He said, *Those who, when they are seen, Allah is remembered [dh.k.r,* cf. *dhikr],* that is, in order to be made real by Allah they disappear in him from them and from the eyes of creation, so when the people see them, they see nothing but Allah, so their remembering of Allah is their seeing the *awliya.* It is like the above-mentioned verses. This is the station which the Rasululah asked for in his prayer, *And make me nur [n.w.r.],* and Allah answered his prayer, as we were told that he was sent to people *as one of good tidings, warning, calling to Allah by His leave, and an illumined lamp [siraj munir, n.w.r.]* 33-45-6; so He made him *nur* as he asked.

'His word to his Lord, *And make me nur,* was, So that I would be in my essence the very divine name itself *al-nur,* and the one whom the Real is *his ear, his eye, his tongue, his hand, and his foot;* and one who *would not speak from caprice [53:3].* So he is not he, and nothing remains for the one who sees him, who sees him, except Allah, that being known by the one who sees or not; this is the way the folk of knowledge of Allah witness him.

'Among the believers there are the *khulafa [kh.l.f.,* ones representing someone behind them, singular *khalifah]* who manifest in the world and among the masses with the attributes of the one who is behind [kh.l.f.] them. Bilqis [the queen of Sheba] said about her throne, *ka'anna-hu huwa,"* but it was nothing but *huwa [it/Him]!* But her veil was the extreme distance [between her palace and Solomon's] and the force of convention [which says thrones do not transport themselves across large distances instantly], and she was unaware of Solomon's power with his Lord, so this veiled her from saying, *huwa huwa* [it is It; he is He; etc.]. So she said, *ka'anna-hu huwa.* And what distance could be greater than one to whom *there is no mithl* [like] compared to one whose *mithl is* things? The complete one [Muhammad] said, *Indeed I myself am a human being who is your mithl* [like yourselves]-this based on a command of Allah. It was said to him, *Say,* and he said, *Say: indeed I myself am a human being who is your mithl [41:7],* and by this we know that it is based on a command of Allah, because he conveyed the command to us just as he conveyed what was commanded.

'This statement is a remedy for the sickness which arose in the one who worshipped Jesus in his commentary; they said,

Indeed Allah is the Christ, son of Mary [5:72], missing a great knowledge in that they said *son of Mary* and they did not realize. Because of this, Allah said in raising proof against the one with this description [the *mushrik*], *Say: Name them* [that is, name the partners of Allah, 13:33], but they could not name him [e.g., *Allah, the Christ, son of Mary*] except by one of the names they knew him by, in order that he understand from them what they meant, because when they gave them [the partners] names, it became clear, in the name itself *[Allah, the Christ, son of Mary]*, that he was not one of the messengers who were sent demanded that they worship.

'But we rather said, *huwa huwa* [h/He is He] based on what sound disclosure gives the *khass* and what clear faith gives the *amm*, just as the prophetic report from the divine relates, that Allah, when He loves His worshipper, He becomes his ear, his eye; and He mentions his faculties and limbs. And humankind is nothing but these faculties and limbs which the Real makes his he-ness itself.' So if you are a believer, do you know what you believe in? And even if you are one with a sound vision, do you know what you saw? Most of this prophetic explanation about Allah is concerned with the human faculty so that the believer would be one with a state of seeing, so that one would know by that the One who is the entity itself of the things and the entities.'

11

Transmission of Law

Legal Literalism

Ibn Arabi is not specifically pointing to some outwardly 'reformable' defect in the teaching and transmission of the law in his time, nor to the fraudulent pretensions or normal defects of particular individuals. Rather, he is primary alluding here to the fundamental—and in our present circumstances, humanly inescapable—problem that the just, appropriate application and interpretation of the traditional sources concerning the divine commands and their historical application by the Prophet usually require a far deeper understanding of both their ultimate contexts and intentions and the relevant factors in each particular case than can be expected of any but the rarest individuals, thôse whose every action is divinely inspired and protected from error. As he remarks, more openly in section II-7 below, those truly qualified `authorities' (the true *wulat)* in any age, whether or not they outwardly rule, are none other than the divinely guided 'saints'—i.e., the *awliya* (a term drawn from the same Arabic root as the words translated as `authority' in these passages, and having explicit connotations of spiritual authority *[wilaya]* that are not readily conveyed by the term `saint' in Western languages). (James Winston Morris, in Michel Chodkiewicz (ed.) (1988). *Les Illuminations de La Mecque* (Paris: Sindbad).

Let us examine the methodological basis for Ibn al-Arabi's *fiqh,* and then two cases of that method in practice. Ibn al-Arabi describes his colleagues as *ummal,* those entrusted to act, among the ulema, those who know.' As with all the technical words used by Ibn al-Arabi, this finds sufficient description in the Arab language, which is not the growing and changing language of Arabic but the language of the Quran. Ibn Manzur says about the word *amil,* which is the singular of *ummal,* 'The *amil* is the one who is put in charge [w.l.y., *cf. wilayah* and *awliya*] *of* someone's affairs, his wealth, his property, and his works.' The actual self of the true *amil is* invisible, because the activity one sees is rather that of the one on whose behalf the *amil* negotiates or contracts or speaks. Hence, the description of the 'people put in charge', the *awliya: When they are seen, Allah is remembered.*'

Another word describing people who give a certain kind of command *is umara (amr, a.m.r.),* where when 'they' command, 'He' commands. The superimposition of commands comes about with literal transmission. They are, Ibn al-Arabi says, *umara* who hear the divine Word and give it back just as they heard it, word by word. He says.

This [reward] does not occur except to one who propagates the revelation from the Quran or Sunna with the words which it came in. And this does not happen except for the transmitters of the revelation, among the reciters and transmitters of *hadith,* and for the legal scholars; but not for the one who transmits the *hadith* according to meaning (that is, not literally), like Sufyan al-Thawri and others believed in doing.

The problem with such transmission is that what is being transmitted is one's own understanding of a particular *hadith.* Such a transmitter has, in fact, falsely claimed to be a messenger himself. In great contrast, the *amil* transmits the word directly, without intervention and without adding his own ideas or understandings. The ones who propagate the revelation as they heard it, and give back the message as they heard it, the reciters and transmitters of *hadith, 'they* will assemble at the row of the messengers, on them peace." Because it is easy to transmit literally and exactly, and because it is difficult to be a prophet and carry the burdens of caring for a community, Ibn al-Arabi links the *hadith, There will be a people on the day of judgement the prophets will be jealous of*' to this situation.'

Thus, the importance of literal transmission. Besides this literal transmission which allows one to assemble with the prophets, there is another prophet-like activity. That activity is *ijtihad,* which looks like the creation of Law, while we know and accept as a tenet that the creation of *shariah* ended with Muhammad. Given that the decision of the *mujtahid* (one who does *ijtihad)* is confirmed by the *shariah,* given that new law is impossible, and given that, *There is no messenger after me, nor prophet,* Ibn al-Arabi categorizes that act of the *mujtahid* as giving him the degree of the prophets but without giving them Law. He says,

Allah honoured His messenger by making his people witnesses to the nations of prophets as He made the prophets witnesses to their nations. Then He made this nation special, meaning its ulema, by making Law for them *ijtihad* of the legal properties *[ahkam,* singular *hukm],* and by determining as the *hukm* what their *ijtihad* leads them to.

Then,

Such a one in this nation would not be a prophet, as he is not a prophet through revelation sent down. But Allah made law for the ulema of this nation their *ijtihad,* just as He said to His Prophet, *So that you would judge [h.k.m.] among the people by what Allah showed you [4:105];* the *mujtahid* does not judge except by what Allah shows him in his *ijtihad.*

One characteristic of *ijtihad* is that the right determination gets extra reward and the wrong determination still gets one reward. The standard text for this situation is found in *Subul al-Salam,* from Amr Ibn al-As, that 'He heard the messenger of Allah (PBUH) saying, When the *hakim [h.k.m.]* determines the *hukm,* that is [interjects the author of *Subul al-Salam],* when he wants to determine the *hukm,* based on his word, let him do *ijtihad,* because *ijtihad* is done before the *hukm* [is determined], then if he hits the mark, he gets two rewards, and when he determines the *hukm* and does *ijtihad* and errs, that is, is not consistent with what the *hukm* is with Allah, then he gets one reward'.

There is also a lesser known *hadith.* In *Musnad* Ibn Hanbal 2:187, *haddathana* [it was told to us in the form of a *hadith* by] Abd-Allah *haddathani* [it was told to me in the form of a *hadith* by] my father [Ahmad ibn Hanbal] *haddathana* Hasan *haddathana* Ibn Lahiah *haddathana* Amr Ibn al-As who reported that he said, 'I he [...] and the messenger of Allah came and he said, When the *qadi* judges [q.d.y.] and does *ijtihad*, and hits the mark, he has ten rewards; and when he does *ijtihad* and errs, he has one or two rewards.'

One of the ways Ibn al-Arabi explains this characteristic is found in his *fiqh* discussion of the prayer during the eclipse. He crosses over from the outward legal positions to the inward truths to show that if 'the *mujtahid* errs, he is at the level of the one who is in the concealed area of the eclipsed area. There is no burden on him; he is given one reward.' But there are those who, in full daylight, still refuse the light. About them, he says,

> But if the revealed text appears to him, and he leaves it in favour of his own opinion *[ray]* of his *qiyas* [deduction], manifesting his false allegation, there is no excuse for him before Allah, and he has offended.

Continuing, he says,

> Most of this comes about with the legal scholars following those who said to them, 'Do not follow us blindly, but follow the *hadith* which comes to you, if it opposes what we have determined as *hukm* [legal property], because the *hadith is* our *madhhab* [way, school]. We do not determine anything except by the evidence which appears to us, and which appears to us to be evidence; we do not make requisite anything other than that. We have not made requisite on you all following us, but we have made requisite on you to be petitioners of us.

These eclipsed legal scholars refuse the text itself. They do not appreciate that as the moment changes, the situation changes, and the legal properties change accordingly. Ibn al-Arabi says,

> During every moment, during a single event, the *hukm* [legal property] alters according to the *mujtahid*. Because of this, [Imam] Malik used to say, when someone asked him [for a legal decision] about an event, 'Did it occur?' If he said, 'No', he would say 'I will not give a *fatwa* [legal opinion].' If he said, 'Yes', he would give a *fatwa* at that moment according to what his evidence gave him. The blind follower [q.l.d.] of the legal scholars of our times has decided that he has fulfilled the duty of his following his leader by following the *hadith* which his Imam commanded him, and his blind following of the *hukm*, despite finding something

which opposes. So he disobeys Allah, in His word, *So take what the messenger gives you, and adhere to it [59:7]*, and he disobeys the messenger, in his word, *So obey him*, because he [Muhammad] did not say anything except from a command of his Lord. And he disobeys his Imam, in his word, 'Take the *hadith* when it is sent to you, and scorn my word.'

They 'are in eclipse perpetually, endless for them until the day of judgement. They are not with Allah, nor are they with His messenger, nor with their Imam. Of them Allah and His messenger and their Imams have washed their hands and they have no proof in respect to Allah. So let them see who gathers with these!

First Case

Respect for the literal words and phrases of the revelation involves respect for the silences as well. Ibn al-Arabi condemns the silences of the revelation being filled in with arrogant noise, often justified as *qiyas* (analogical deduction). There are two kinds of *mujtahids*, he says at one point. One predominates declaring taboo and the other predominates lifting difficulties (where the word is *haraj*, about which Ibn Manzur says, 'You are in *haraj*, that is, in tightness and constriction', and based on the verse, *We did not make any haraj on you all in the religion [22:28], by adhering to the verses and by returning to the root [asl]."* The latter 'is according to Allah closer to Allah and greater in level than the one who predominates declaring taboo, as taboo is an accidental thing which occurs randomly on the *asl*.'

Given this, in the absence of taboo declared by the revealed text, one should return to the root. The first issue is about purification for the circumambulation of the Kaaba." Ibn al-Arabi's position is, 'The circumambulation is permitted without *wudu* [a form of purification] for the man and the woman, unless the woman is a menstruant, based on the mention of the revealed text about it."' The restriction is only on the menstruant, 'and not every worship makes as a precondition for it this outward purification [of *wudu*].' So, in the absence of a text for non-menstruants, men and women, Ibn al-Arabi's position is to return to the root; then, we find that everything in existence has a face towards Allah, and in this respect, it is pure.

There is not in existence, according to the real determination, anything but The Pure, because the name *al-quddus* [The Holy] *is* associated with existence, and this is confirmed by His statement, 'To Him returns the entirety of the affair, so worship Him and rely on Him; your Lord is not Unaware of what you are doing' [11:123].

Here, Ibn al-Arabi glosses the Quranic phrase 'what you are doing'. He says it refers to 'your interference between Allah and His creatures'. The word he uses, *tafriq (f.r.q.),* carries negative connotations, where Ibn Manzur says, *farraqa* (differentiation) for something good *is farq* (difference), and *farraqa* for something bad is *tafriq* (interference). Therefore, Ibn al-Arabi says, 'It is not appropriate to intervene between the creature .and his Master except to enter in between the creature and the Master for good *[khayr].'* The negative intervention he is talking about is our speaking unfavourably about creation; the only proper intervention is interference for the good. He tells the following anecdote to demonstrate this. Ibn al-Arabi says,

'I met one of the Itinerants on the seashore, between Murcia and Manarah [in Tunis], and he said to me, I met in this place some one of the Truthful Substitutes when he was walking along the edge of the ocean; I greeted him and he returned the greeting. In the country was a great oppressive tyrant. I said to him, O you, have you seen what oppression there *is* in the country? He looked at me very angrily, and said to me: Do not say anything but the Good.'

Ibn al-Arabi explains, 'Because of this, Allah has made intercession Law and accepts legal excuses'. This is then linked to impurity. 'Impurity is an accidental thing, designated with Law-property; but purity is an essential thing'. Therefore, if there is an accidental property which emerges at some moment, then every other moment remains in its root property, which is purity.

Unfortunately, 'the legal scholars have been heedless of this, flailing at it, but they do not get it. We have already explained that one does not get into a disobedience completely, if one is a believer'. Ibn al-Arabi explains that the situation of the believer who does something bad is described as, *One who mixed a wholesome act with another which was bad [9:102].* The bad is the bad but the wholesome act is the faith of the believer (the *iman* of the *mumin),* because there is no disobedience by the believer except faith that accompanies it, which tells the believer that it is something disobedient. Hence, the 'faith which knows it is a disobedience is actually an obedience to Allah'.

This conclusion combines with Ibn al-Arabi's *fiqh* position on praying behind a bad-doing leader, which focuses on the standard legal question which is based on the paradigmatic case of the Muslims praying behind al-Hajjaj and whether their prayers would be accepted. Ibn al-Arabi says that, of course, one cannot pray behind a bad-doing leader; but let us look at the legal facts. When al-Hajjaj does *wudu* for the *salah* and follows every condition for the validity of the *salah,* how can the name 'bad-doer' apply at that moment? Furthermore, al-Hajjaj and others in the context of their bad-doing are believers obeying their faith' that what bad they are doing is disobedience.

Ibn al-Arabi sums up the situation as follows.

The most amazing thing about this issue is that we are commanded to have a fine impression of people, forbidden to have a bad impression of people. We saw one whom we knew to be a bad-doer, who did *wudu,* and did the *salah,* so how could we apply to him the name of bad-doer during the moment of his worship? And how much more is the fine impression than the bad impression of him in doing it? We have no knowledge of the future for him, and we do not see what Allah did in the past with him, and the *hukm* [determinative property] belongs to the *waqt* [moment] of obedience which he is upon, being involved [right then] in obedience. So the fine impression is prior.

Then, Ibn al-Arabi tells a story which is a warning to smug piety. He mentioned that someone 'firm in his religion told me about a man who was a legal scholar and a theologian who was a profligate of *nafs* [self].' This is a clue to the audience that this man struggled with his self (cf. *mujahidah),* and it is the terms of the struggle, not the discreet outcomes, which is of significance.

He said to me, 'I came upon him in a gathering where wine was being circulated, and he was drinking with the rest. The drink was finished, and it was said to him, "Send someone to fetch us some drink". He said to them, "I shall not to do it! I have not decided upon disobedience completely. For me between the cups there is a turning for forgiveness, and I do not wait for the next cup, so when the cup gets in my hands, I wait and ask whether my Lord will give me success and I will leave it, or He will desert me and I will drink it".' Like this are the ulema, may Allah have mercy on them! This knowledgeable man died while there was in his heart a disappointment that he did not meet me, but he did meet me, but he did not recognize me, and he asked me about myself, and he had love for me, may Allah have mercy on him. That was in Murcia in the year 585.

Concluding this section, Ibn al-Arabi tells another anecdote about a spiritual encounter' he had. He says,

I witnessed the Real in my innermost being during a *waqiah* [spiritual encounter], and He said to me, 'Tell My worshippers what I designated as My generosity to the believer: the good rewarded with ten like it up to seven hundred as many, and the bad with only one like it. The bad act does not oppose faith in its being a bad act. So why would My worshipper despair of My mercy? *My mercy pervades everything* [7:156], and *I am according to the impression of My worshipper of Me, so let the impression of Me be Good!'*

Second Case

The particular spiritual position of the believer presents certain legal, *fiqh* consequences. One of them is examined in the issue of praying over a person who has committed suicide. 'Should the one who killed himself be prayed over or not? There is one who said he should be prayed over, and there is one who said he should not be prayed over. For the first I argue.'

To support this position, Ibn al-Arabi addresses the background situation of intercession. As usual, he finishes his enumeration of the ulema's outward legal positions with their inward complement, which he calls *itibar*, a crossover. He says here, 'A crossover for this section is that as Allah has permitted intercession in the *salah* over the dead, we know that Allah approves of that, and that the petition for him is accepted.' But we have the seemingly obvious *hadith* which at first glance seems to refute that background. It is reported that *The one who kills himself abides in the fire, abiding therein ever,* and that *The Garden is forbidden him.* People take that to mean that *salah* over the suicide should not be done, but Ibn al-Arabi works from another text which will challenge that first glance understanding.

One key text precedes the text above and has the phrase, *My worshipper rushes to me on his own,* where 'rushes', Ibn al-Arabi says, is an allusion to other texts, which are always taken positively. He says, 'The wisdom alluded to, here in this issue, is the word of Allah, *My worshipper [abd] rushes to Me by himself; I forbid him the Garden.* There is an allusion here and a reality, and the allusion is to *They race* [to the Good, 3:114] and *They are foremost* [in seeking forgiveness, 57:21] and *Who approaches Me an inch, I approach him a yard*—all positive images. The root word 'rushes' includes the concept of taking one's own initiative. This contrasts with the usual situation, where Allah 'makes for him a specific limit [of lifespan]. But [the suicide] tries to hasten the meeting and *rushes* to Him before having come to that limit'. Now, this entire text, with rushing and with being forbidden the Garden, is in a differentiated mode *(tafsil),* and for that reason, it is possible—in the *fiqh* sense—to return to the undifferentiated mode, which is the root, the *asl* or *usul* (plural, roots). It can, he says, 'be brought toward the face which is best for the believer, for helping him out, with the *usul,*' and that 'is a priority'."

When the text is differentiated, that is, made specific and detailed, such as, 'As for His statement about the one who killed himself by iron, or poison, or throwing himself from a mountain', then one can argue that,

[I]t is not said in the *hadith* whether they are believers or something else [and this leaves the way open for debate], so one may advance a likelihood; and if the likely is going to be introduced, we return to the usul [basic, general, undifferentiated] texts, where we see that faith has dominion of power which, because of it, the ever-abiding without end in the fire is not possible. So we know, certainly, that the revelation must be reporting that about those who associate partners with Allah *[mushriks],* is designated that they will be punished forever, so he said, *Who kills himself with iron, among the mushriks, his iron in his hand will take him to the innermost fire of Jahannam, everlastingly, abiding therein everlastingly.* That is, this type of punishment is his determination in the fire. Like that, *Who drinks poison, and kills himself, sips it in the fire of Jahannam everlastingly, abiding therein everlastingly,* that is, that is the kind of punishment he is punished with, this *kafir* [ingrate]. And it is reported that *Who kills himself with something is punished with it.*

Now, since we know that the believer's faith cannot be ultimately opposed, so we know that the text above must apply to the *mushrik,* 'even if the revelation did not specify, in this report, the sort [of person] itself, yet because the *shariah* proofs are taken from many different perspectives, one of them coming together with another, in order to strengthen one by another, as *the believer is to the believers like the brick* wall, so one strengthens another.'

Also differentiated is the vision of the divine. We know that 'the folk of the Garden see their Lord with a blessed vision, after they have entered the garden, as the report says about the calling to the garden—*When the people take their places in the Garden they are called to a vision.*'

Ibn al-Arabi is going to separate the two events, the taking of their places in the Garden and their being called to a vision. He argues, then that it is possible that,

Allah has specified that, for this one who rushes to Him himself by killing himself, His word *I have forbidden him the Garden* may be before meeting Him; the blessed vision preceded the suicide meeting of Allah, and *then* he would enter the Garden, because the suicide saw that Allah was more merciful than the situation he was in, the circumstances which were the cause for him of this rushing. Otherwise, he would not have imagined that the repose with Allah would be better than the punishment which he was in when he rushes *to Him.*

To back up this argument, Ibn al-Arabi recalls the *hadith* we just saw: *I am according to the impression of My worshipper of Me; so let the impression of Me be Good.*

Allah says, *ana inda zann abdi bi, fa-l-yazunna bi khayr [I am according to the impression of My worshipper of Me; so let the impression of Me be Good],* and the suicide, if he is a believer, has a Good impression of his Lord. It was the Good impression of his Lord that made him kill himself. This is more suitable, that one attribute to him the phrasing of this divine report. Well, there is no revealed text which clearly states a contradiction to this *tawil* [interpretation], even if it seems far-fetched; may the observer in his observation keep far away from the stipulated roots which would contradict this *tawil* with eternal wretchedness [for him]! So if he is present in it and balances it, he will recognize what we say about it. In the authentic report, there is *They will exit who have in their hearts the least, least of a grain of mustard of faith,* and nothing else remains except what we said about it. Allah did not say in this report anything but that he *forbade him the Garden,* only.

In effect, it is the job of the legal scholar (the observer above) to argue the best possible case, in this case, for the suicide. Ibn al-Arabi admits that his interpretation is far-fetched, but the argument is nevertheless logical and complies with the technical rules of the fiqh.

So if we argue for the chastisement, then the Garden is something forbidden to him that he enters without chastisement, like with the person of great sins. The report is a text for the suicide and others, among the people of great sins—they are upon the *hukm* [property] of [divine] volition, because *the man written down in the scrolls will not enter the fire,* even though he is one of the ones of great sins, if there was nothing with him but *la ilaha* in all his Islam in his period of life in the world.

The reason for the [extreme threat] is so that one would realize that the carrying out of the threat against the suicide is for before entering into the Garden, that he will not be forgiven suicide. But Allah is more Generous than that the carrying out the threat be imputed to Him; rather imputed to Him should be His volition and the preponderance of Generosity. It is as one of the Arabs (desert Arabs) described it:

inna idha awad-tu-hu (IV) aw wa d-tu-hu (I)
la-akhlifu iadi
wa unjizu mawidi
When I vow or swear
I may go against my threat
But I would carry out my promise.

There is no mention in the revealed text about the threat *[iad,* root w.d.], but there is a mention about the promise *[wad w.d.]: Never think that Allah would go against His promise [to His messengers] [14:47].* The *iad* is specifically used for bad [e.g., a threat], but *wad* may be either good or bad. This argument is entirely justified linguistically. Ibn Manzur says about the root *w.d.*

Al-Azhari said, In the *Arab* discourse, *wad-tu [I* promised] the man good, and *wada-tu (I* threatened) him bad. If they do not want to mention good, they say, *wad-tu* and do not insert the *a,* and when they do not want to mention bad, they say, *awad-tu* and do not omit the *a.* There is a verse from Amir ibn Tufayl:

inna in awad-tu-hu aw wad-tu-hu
la-akhlifu iadi
was unjizu mawidi.

There are many who may object to Ibn al-Arabi's legal discourse, but it is not because he is not literal or firmly grounded in the revealed texts or does not follow the rules of legal discourse. But instead there seems to be another reason. Ibn al-Arabi's extreme literalism in the first case served to restore the essential quality of creation-purity. In the second case, he pushed literalism to the extreme and forced interpretations which he admitted were far-fetched. Why? To intercede positively for the eternal soul of a believer. We have quite the opposite legal discourse (if one can even use this term) today: a number of Islamicists who will identify impurity and pollution as essential and general traits of creation. Far-fetched interpretations are used to serve that purpose, but none are profferred to help out the believers.

Perennial Situation

That such a situation is perennial is suggested by Ibn al-Arabi's discussion of the addition during the prayer call of the morning *salah,* 'The *salah* is better than sleeping!' Some legal scholars argued that it was something introduced by Umar, so it is not strictly speaking Sunna (normative prophetic practice). But Ibn al-Arabi says, 'as for our position, we ourselves argue for it as being shariah, even though it is an act of Umar, because the revelation determined it in his word, Who *practises a practice [Sunna] which is fine, [and it is practised after him, he gets its reward and the like of the reward of theirs, without diminishing their rewards at all],* and we have no doubt that it is a fine Sunna [practice], so it is appropriate to express it as the shariah'. And then, 'Anyone who dislikes it, dislikes it only from fanaticism *[taassub].* Who argues that, does not to do justice to it. We take refuge in Allah from the havoc of the egos!'

12

Codification of Law

Ibn al-Arabi and Ijtihad

Frank E. Vogel remarked that Western studies of Islamic law have 'often omitted, justifiably or not, any consideration of the law's application'. This has led to confusion about concepts such as the 'closed gates of *ijtihad'*, where, as Wael B. Hallaq noted, we get 'the oddity that scholars should declare *ijtihad* non-existent, while they at the very same time acclaim certain *fuqaha* of their own age as *mujtahids,* exercising *ijtihad.'* Although Vogel gives an intriguing outline of an approach which should be used to address this and other issues, I believe there is much more than what meets the historical eye.

Discussions about *ijtihad* are in fact indications of deeply held political positions. Solving the question of *ijtihad* is, therefore, beyond the scope of a narrowly conceived historicity.

Vogel lists three 'peculiar tenets associated with the theory of *qada'*, which make the application of law problematic, but which also more deeply evince a radical and uncompromising world-view. First is the tenet that the *qadi* be a *mujtahid,* one able to do *ijtihad.* Second is that 'nothing but the revealed texts and the concrete facts of the case ought to constrain the *qadi's* conscience.

And third that there can be no reversals or appeals of decisions based on *ijtihad* of the *qadi.* Vogel's notes that Ibn al-Muqaffa and others must have perceived that if 'this conception of *qada*—so idealistic, individualistic, multifarious, and unpredictable—were given full scope, Islamic legal systems would face great practical difficulty'. Vogel, and a great number of legal scholars over the centuries, favour an 'Islamic legal system' over idealizing conceptions. There are thinkers, however, who do not do so, particularly Ibn al-Arabi, and it is their concept of *ijtihad* which we examine here.

Vogel correctly links this idealizing conception of *qada* to an endemic tension between the sultan and the state, which wants a standardized, centralized, and codified system of law that can be practiced universally and then I would propagate it to every city of the cities of the Muslims, and I would command them to practice it, and they would not refer to anything else.' Imam Malik said, 'Do not do so, O Amir of the believers, because the people have had handed over to them positions, and they heard *hadith* and they examined reports, and each people takes what was handed over to them, and they yield to Allah with it, so leave the people alone and what they choose for themselves in every country.'

The desire of the ruler is to codify laws. The kind of application of *shariah* which Malik conceived is impossible for emerging states. The state is interested in one answer not multiplicity, in one mass not diversity, in efficiency and not variance. One tentative contact between those scholars who would aid the state in codification occurred within two centuries of the death of the Prophet. Vogel describes it as follows:

> [Ibn al-Muqaffa] recommended to the caliph that the latter examine all of the conflicting rulings on each issue, select among them, and then codify his choices into a written law. This proposal was defeated, and with it a bid that the ruler—wielding the authority *of siyasah* [political power] with its breadth, flexibility, responsiveness to utility, and, above all, powers of compulsion—should seize control of legislation and thereby replace the ulema and their rigorously individualistic and conscience-based *ijtihad.*

However, other contacts succeeded a thousand years ago and the superstructure of *fiqh* became autonomous and fixed. The contact was genuine compromise. The sultans wanted a codified law which would place all the authority and legitimacy of Islam at their disposal, creating a system of law which would be efficient and centralized, maximizing of utility and concentrating all discipline and punishment under the sultan's or state's hand. The ulema wanted a *fiqh* which could be responsive to the highly diverse cultures and situations the Muslims found themselves in; a system which would maintain a hierarchy of knowledge, not a hierarchy of property or be subjugated to demands of efficiency over appropriateness; and a place in a community which sought their knowledge, tradition, and authority. The compromise reached was the 'closed door of *ijtihad*'.

The ulema severely constricted their massive *fiqh* superstructure until it was reduced to 589 issues.' They agreed that for these 589 issues they will proffer one position, which would be the representative position of their *madhhab,* school of jurisprudence. No one would be able to switch from one school to another and no one would be able to reopen the legal discourse first set by the founding Imams, even on evidence. They got the door shut on flagrant abuse of legal power by the sultan, while the latter got a codified law and a large degree of *siyasah.*

But it is my argument that many of the ulema, and especially the Sufi scholars," were quite conscious of the sultan's and later the state's designs on Islamic law, and that they supported a conception of *qada* which, while causing great practical difficulty, was nevertheless essential to the meaningful life exhorted in Islam. They struggled explicitly to keep the authority of practising *ijtihad* located indigenously, and away from state power.

What is at stake in this debate? For Ibn al-Arabi, the denial of *ijtihad* amounts to nothing less than the denial of Allah's continuing, living solicitude and the mission of the Prophet as a mercy to the worlds. In one passage where Ibn al-Arabi talks about what we are calling the closed doors of *ijtihad,* he draws out in the starkest terms imaginable, the true location of *hukm,* which means property, ruling, and decision. The *hukm,* he says, belongs to Allah, not the intellect. When we do not know the property of a thing, we must rely on Allah. This act of relying on Allah is *ijtihad,* and entails becoming 'like the corpse in the hands of the washer', which is a definition of being an *abd* (a bondsman or slave) to Allah. When the *abd* achieves this radical passivity, it is as when Muhammad believed that he threw the sand, at the Battle of Badr, but it was Allah who throws—You *did not throw, when you threw, but Allah threw (8:17),* a verse which negates one thing, affirms one thing, and then affirms another thing.

Let us examine one of Ibn al-Arabi's discussions on this issue, found in his chapter on mysteries of *taharah* (purity), when he discusses wiping the shoes for *wudu,* when travelling, but with the added situation that there is a hole in the shoe. Ibn al-Arabi is going to use this particular *fiqh* issue (one of the *589)* to demonstrate, again thematically, that it is Allah who Acts, something which orthodox and conventional ulema would entirely endorse, but in a way, which if they perceive, they would find highly dangerous. In particular, Allah Acts; the *shariah* has confirmed the *hukm* of the one who does *ijtihad;* so h/He a/Acts.

As with all of Ibn al-Arabi's works, the original, fixed and transcendentalized Arab language is used; this is not the living language of Arabic. I use Ibn Manzur.'s (d. *711/1311) Lisan al-Arab* to access this language. The first word we need is *khuff.* Ibn Manzur says, 'A person's *khuff is* what touches the ground from the *batin* [bottom] of one's *qadam'.* About *khafa (kh.f.y.),* a word that will be crucial for this passage, Ibn Manzur says, 'The *khafa* of the lightning is its sparks. And to kh.f.y. something is to make it *zahir* [topside, outward, manifest], appear [z.h.r] and to bring it out. One says the downpour [kh.f.y.] the mice, when it brought them out from their burrows. Imru al-Qays said, describing horses [racing across the desert], *khafa-hunna [the horses] brought them out [the mice] from their burrows).'* And al-Lahyani said, 'If you keep the secret, we will not kh.f.y. it'. His word, *We will not kh.f.y. it* is, 'We will not make it *zahir'.* And the recitation of His word, *'Verily the Hour is coming, but I shall kh.f.y. it' (20:15),* means, 'I shall make it *zahir',* which al-Lahyani related from al-Kasai, Muhammad Ibn Sahl, and from Saiyd Ibn Jabir. And kh.f.y. something is to keep it concealed; kh.f.y. also means to make it *zahir,* and the two are opposites. And *akhfaytu* (kh.f.y. 'I concealed') something means *satartu-hu (s.t.r.,* 'I veiled it').

Ibn al-Arabi says,

As for the *hukm* in the *batin* [inwardness], we call shoes *khuff* because of *khafa,* as the shoes completely veils [s.t.r.] the foot. So when the shoe is torn, and something of the foot becomes *zahir* [exposed], then wipe that part of the foot which is *zahir,* and wipe the shoe. And that only as long as it can be called a shoe-inevitably with this condition. Here is a strange mystery for the one with sharp understanding. The *khafa is* also the *zahir!* Imru alQays says, *khafa-hunna out of their tunnels,* that is, they brought them out and they made them *zahir.*

So in this passage we have the shoe connected to the word *khafa,* which includes the meaning of veiling something, with its act of veiling being the same definition used by al-Layth in Ibn Manzur's dictionary. We then have some part of the foot emerging, with the verb here being *zahara,* which is related linguistically to *zahir,* which is the antonym of *batin,* meaning contextually top and bottom or outward and inward. Ibn al-Arabi then noted the mysterious—but linguistically-based—connection *of khafy* and *zahir.*

Continuing, we find this:

We argue for wiping what emerges, because we were commanded in the Book of Allah to wipe the feet, so when something of the foot emerges, we wipe it.

As for the inward realm, the outwardness of the shariah is a veil *[sitr]* over a reality of the *hukm* of unity *[tawhid],* in relating everything to Allah. So, if everything is related to Allah, who is then left to be charged with performing the *shariah*? Ibn al-Arabi has a series of answers to this question which he explores throughout the *Futuhat,* but the fact is that certain kinds of descriptions of *tawhid* (oneness of God) are offensive, requiring an *adab* (courtesy) which attributes all good to Allah and all bad to oneself.

Then, Ibn al-Arabi says:

So the *taharah* concerning the shariah is connected and it is that you associate the *tawhid* of it with the fact, that you see it as a *hukm* of Allah in His creation, not a *hukm* of the things which belong to creation, like administrative wisdom. We saw that the outwardness of the *shariah* veils the reality of *tawhid.* This reality of *tawhid* is related to the 'radical ambiguity of existence'. William

Chittick writes that, 'the Quranic verse that Ibn al-Arabi cites more often than any other to show the radical ambiguity of existence was revealed after the battle of Badr, which turned in favour of the Muslims when the Prophet picked up a handful of sand and threw it in the direction of the enemy. Concerning the Prophet's throwing of this sand, the Quran says *You did not throw when you threw, but God threw [8:17].'* What this means in this passage is that the *taharah* of wiping of the shoe proceeds whether the veil is purified, the shoes or the foot recalling the authentic *hadith* of Allah that *Verily I become the foot of the abd [worshipper] with which he walks."*

The word *abd* here is crucial, because it is the same station of *abd* which characterized Muhammad and which is recited in one version of the testimony: 'I testify that Muhammad is His *abd* and His messenger'. The station of this kind of *abd* is one which negates any semblance of independence and Lordship, and which consequently affirms that the speech *(kalam)* is Allah's, not Muhammad's.

Another instance of this is the *abd* in this verse: *So they found one of Our abds [abdan min ibadina] on whom We had bestowed a Mercy from Us, and We taught him knowledge from Our presence [ladunna], (18:66),* where the *abd* is characterized as having knowledge not acquired by his own efforts, but as having knowledge directly and immediately bestowed on him by Allah.

So, now we have a situation where the act of *taharah* on this shoe/foot discloses a radical ambiguity of existence. Now we come to *ijtihad.* So, the *shar* is a *hukm* of Allah, not a *hukm* of the *aql* [intellect], as some of them believe. Therefore, the vision [Cyj of *taharah* of the shariah is based on Allah, One, Real. Because of this, it is not appropriate to contest the *hukm* of the *mujtahid,* as the *shar* [Law], which is a *hukm* of Allah, has already affirmed that *hukm* of the *mujtahid:* it is the *shar* of Allah to affirm whomever. This *[ijtihad]* is an issue in which all the experts of the schools of jurisprudence are falling into the forbidding, without calling to mind what we have pointed out, despite their knowing it. But they have been heedless of calling it to mind, so they have offended proper courtesy toward Allah in that, while the courteous among the worshippers of Allah succeed. So the one who faulted the *mujtahid* himself has in fact faulted the Real in what He affirmed as *hukm*.

The tearing of the shoe, which is outward, corresponds to the tearing of the shariah, which is also outward. Hence;

If the *shar is* torn, it becomes *zahir* in some issue as one of the properties of unity which would remove a property of the *shar* completely, transferring the *hukm* to a *taharah* of that unity which is effecting a removal of a *hukm* of the *shariah*, just as one who relates all acts to Allah, from every perspective, does not concern himself with what becomes *zahir* as a consequence, whether contradictory or harmonious.

What is needed is purification from this problem; the *shariah* becomes torn and at some point ceases to be called shariah, as happens with torn shoes. But as long as the name 'shoe' does apply, wipe over the part which emerges. Ibn al-Arabi says,

[T]hat is explicated, for that unity designated for this issue, is the perspective made *shar*, and this is that one say, *But Allah has created you and what you know*. So the practices of the creation belong to Allah, despite the fact that they are related to us. But they are not related to Allah from every perspective, so they do not affect the wiping. The *hukm* about that would be as we have determined it.

In what preceded, the contours of Ibn al-Arabi's opposition to the use of *qiyas* (analogy)" also appear which we will consider briefly below. Simply stated, the interpretation and the application of the *shar* can never admit of purely human intervention, such as logic and analogy.

This is Ibn al-Arabi's discussion of *ijtihad*, and it is found even today. But one need not demand the entirety of this conception of *ijtihad* to still see a lively tradition of *ijtihad* in the face of the state of Islam. If we focus less on the state and the official proclamations of its ulema and more on the lived reality of Muslims, we see a different situation with *ijtihad*.

Jurisprudence

From one perspective of application of Law, the concept of there being closed gates of *ijtihad* is indeed odd. By relying on stultifying descriptions of a static legal discourse, Western scholars have missed the actual function of Islam in communities. The enumeration of the 'sources of legal injunctions' (usul *al-ahkam),* or 'sources of legal discourse' (usul *al fiqh)* was the conventional series of four: Quran, Sunna, scholarly consensus, and analogy *(qiyas).* The process of legal reasoning was the conventional one of searching the Quran for an explicit reading, then looking at the Sunna if there was nothing in the Quran, and then falling 'back on scholarly consensus, and if no consensus existed, then resorting to the extension of an explicit command by analogy.

This process is a methodology reached after the fact. In fact, the entire enterprise of the *usul al fiqh is* highly contentious. As with most *post hoc* histories, it is difficult to re-evaluate the early history of the development of *fiqh* without the received version colouring our views. There was, and still is, no clear and obvious hierarchy in the first two sources. The Sunna gives stoning for adultery, the Quran whipping. The Quran makes circumambulation of the Kaaba merely permissible, the Sunna seems to make it obligatory. The Quran seems to have the feet wiped for wudu, as we shall see, but the Sunna is for washing. The list goes on: it is simply not obvious how the Quran and Sunna are to be taken, harmonized, or ranked. Adding the next two sources, consensus (ijma)—(whose consensus? when and where?)—and analogy, only adds to the confusion.

This *post hoc* method, tortuous in its implications, was obviously in dire need of personal interpretations, but the gates of *ijtihad* had been closed centuries before, so the hapless Muslim is constrained. I was startled to realize that the same description of the process of Islamic law which I had learned and absorbed years ago, after four years of direct study of the books of *fiqh,* simply looked bizarre. But putting aside the received histories and the powerfully argued *al-Risalah* of the founding father Imam Shafii, and concentrating on the actual case by case debates, I was able to re-evaluate the history. It did take me a while to determine why that conventional description was so jarring: it is because the phenomenon being described is two-fold, but the description is one-sided. As Vogel pointed out, Western studies of Islam often omitted the law's application, possibly because of the linkages with the state of Islam and ulema, to the exclusion of the masses and unofficial, underground expressions of faith (such as Sufi shrine activity).

Islamic law has two sides. There is the *fiqh,* which is the superstructure of interpretation erected on the revealed text. This superstructure sorts and classifies the determinative properties *(ahkam,* singular *hukm)* of the revealed text into categories such as lawful/unlawful; obligatory, recommended, neutral, disliked, and forbidden; generally addressed and specifically addressed, abrogated and abrogating; and so on.

And then there *is qada,* the 'settling of affairs', as we saw described by Lawrence Rosen. The *fiqh* and *qada* are two separate activities. *Ijtihad* is done everywhere and always, despite talk of its closed gates. The establishment of the *qiblah,* the direction of the Kaaba in Makkah, is a process of *ijtihad,* as the legal scholars always said. Accepting the *qiblah* of a particular mosque without personally assessing the *qiblah* on one's own is following another's authority *(taqlid).* Many mosques have an old architectural *qiblah* which those doing the *salah* today may ignore, turning instead in a direction perceived by *ijtihad* to be more truly the *qiblah.* In this example, the requirement to establish the *qiblah is* absolute: there is no room for *ijtihad* here to determine whether or not you must establish a *qiblah.* But the actual process of establishing the *qiblah is ijtihad.* Put these two together—the *fiqh* of the *qiblah* and the *qada* of determining it—and one can see why statements about there being no *ijtihad,* or a need for more, sound strange. There are two sides to Islamic law, and there are two types of *ijtihad:* there is the *ijtihad* of the *fiqh,* which has been severely restricted, and there is the *ijtihad* of the *qada,* which is constant in practice (at least in healthy communities).

This misunderstanding arises from not recognizing *fiqh* and *qada as* two different things and stems from not appreciating the concept of *hukm,* (a thing's property). The way to see how Islamic law operates is to focus on *hukm.* This word means property, with related meanings of ruling, decision, judgement. But the value of seeing *hukm* as property, and not as ruling or judgement is this: the divine name *hakim is* the 'one who establishes the property' of something; and *Allah says al-haqq (33;4),* meaning the truth of a matter is what Allah says about it. So the key process of *fiqh* is understanding the *din*, religion, which recalls its Quranic derivation—*tafaqquh fil-din* (cf. 9:122)—and that is examining the entirety of novel things and issues and circumstances and assigning them their name," which means giving things their *hukm*.

Naming

What the *qadi*, who Rosen describes, does is help disputants put names and properties on to their concerns. He is helping them to create a 'metasystem which creates order in a universe that is often experienced in a more disorderly way.

'Knowledge in this scheme is knowing the *hukm* of a thing. And knowing the *hukm* first requires knowing names. In a preceding passage, Ibn al-Arabi said, 'And that only as long as it can be called a shoe inevitably with this condition.' *Shariah* refrains run throughout the *Futuhat*, with Ibn al-Arabi always insisting on careful definition of names. As long as you have a shoe, the *taharan* of wiping over them is possible. Ibn al-Arabi does not propound the more stringent rules relating to tattered shoes—whether the holes involved are one or three inches wide, and so on.

Ibn al-Arabi propounds the easiest position, which is as long as you can call the thing a shoe, it is possible to wipe it. When what is seen is not a shoe but tattered rags, for example, then the *hukm* of wiping it is no longer possible. The importance of names is described by Chodkiewicz in this way:

In the *Futuhat*, Ibn al-Arabi casually recounts an anecdote that might conceivably serve as an exergue to the remarks that follow. The hero of the anecdote is Malik, the Imam founder of one of the four principal schools of Sunni jurisprudence.

Malik b. Anas was asked: 'What is your opinion about the lawfulness of the flesh of the water pig *[khinzir al-ma:* an expression that refers to cetaceans in general, but dolphins in particular]?' He replied, '*[fa-afta:* a judicial consultation, not a simple exchange of words] that it was illegal'. An objection was made: 'Does this animal not belong to the family of marine animals [literally, 'fish', whose flesh is lawful]?' 'Certainly', he said, 'but you called it a pig *[khinzir]*.'

Some might be tempted to class this ambiguous cetacean among the taxonomic fantasies of a maniacal casuistry. But Ibn al-Arabi's mention of it on two different occasions shows it to be something completely different for him. What is in question here is the authority of the name *[hukm al-ism]* and the secret of naming *[tasmiya]*, which leads us to the very heart of Ibn al-Arabi's hermeneutics.

Most of the application of Law is getting definitions straight. As we saw above, the foundation of interpretation is language, and specifically the language of the Arab. Ironically enough, it is remarkable how liberating a literal reading of the textual tradition is. The *fiqh* approaches each issue with a thorough and exhaustive examination of every relevant piece of information. Was the command made specific for a particular audience, or a particular situation? Are there preconditions? What is the entire range of the key word in question? When did the command appear, and in what context? Debate and discussion fill pages upon pages for each detail. The liberating aspect is that the entire discursive system is designed to answer quite simply this question: What minimum does this command of Allah's require of us?

As we saw, the *hakim* is the one who determines the *hukm* or property of a thing. Today in South and Southeast Asia, the word *hakim* is used for a traditional doctor. The word still retains its meaning, however, where the *hakim* as doctor seeks to determine the property of a person, to identify the constitution *(mizaj)* and to prescribe the medicine/food needed to restore the balance *(mizan)*. That this is not a closed system is clear from the fact that historically, the *hakims* did not restrict themselves to the paucity of prophetic statements about explicitly health-related matters, described as 'Prophetic Medicine' *(tibb al-nabawi)*, but instead incorporated Greek *(Yunani)* medicine into an Islamic discourse on health and disease.

If we note that the word 'in-formation' may be glossed as `data put in-formation', we can see how the *hakim* operates. The data is data, but the information is the way that data is filed and put into forms, and it is that process that is 'Islamic'.' So the important part is identifying novel things, *(hukm);* the central practice is taking new people with new problems and identifying the *hukm* over them and prescribing accordingly. Once the *hukm* is discovered, the remedy is indicated. Once the *qiblah is* determined, the direction one faces is indicated.

The reason then why the ulema (at least some of them) resisted the sultan and state is precisely because the state wants to seize the identification process by codifying and standardizing highly diverse human behaviour into narrowly defined and static categories. The *qadi* who insists that each case is unique, is not efficient, and the state can have none of that. The entire project of the ulema does not fit ideas of progress and efficiency which pervade typical development and social change paradigms.

Also, as opposed to a precedent- and adversarial- based legal system, fairness and justice are not seen as predictable outcomes based on repeatable events nor as the result of a dialectical process, but rather as the process of arriving at a unique description of a situation which restores a universe of harmony for the disputants, the *qadi's* role being that of facilitator.

This is, too, a system which resists efficiency, as does the constant use of *shura* (consultation) for explicitly political affairs. No one could say that the Quaker or Amish systems of *shura* are efficient: but they are remarkably effective.

Another indication that the project of the ulema resists centralization and state power is found in its rejection of 'one-man Islam' which involves a denigration of the slow, gradual, and cumulative nature of the ulema project and its substitution with a single perspective of reform that will solve all problems. Noah Ha Mim Keller, the translator of *Umdat alSalik,* remarks that 'each school [of jurisprudence] does not merely comprise the work of a single Imam, but rather represents a large collectivity of scholars whose research in sacred Law and its ancillary disciplines has been characterized by considerable division of labour and specialization over a very long period of time. . . . The result of this division of labour has been a body of legal texts that are arguably superior in evidence, detail, range, and in sheer usefulness to virtually any recent attempt to present Islam as a unified system of human life.'

The basic methodology of Ibn al-Arabi and the non-state ulema stems from a concern with the literal, linguistic meaning of the text. Ibn alArabi goes further, being more literal and more keyed into linguistic possibilities than most of the ulema. Chodkiewicz notes Ibn al-Arabi's 'concern for considering each of God's words and silences', but understands that this 'is certainly not sufficient to convince his adversaries of his orthodoxy'. In fact, 'Nothing better illustrates the impossibility of satisfying the *ulama al-zahir* by rigorous fidelity to the *zahir* or Quranic text than the reading that Ibn al-Arabi does of the famous verse [42:11] *Laysa ka-mithlihi shay'un.*' This verse, which means 'There is nothing which is H/ his similar', has *ka* which must be explained. Chodkiewicz comments that Qushayri and al-Razi, among others, take the particle *ka* as *li-l-mubalagha* (having an intensifying function), something like, 'There is nothing at all which is His similar'.

But while Ibn al-Arabi takes this meaning throughout the *Futuhat,* he also reads another linguistic possibility of this verse. Chodkiewicz says, 'Ibn al-Arabi completes it by another one, which is its exact opposite. God does not speak to say nothing: the particle *ka* can thus also preserve all the force of its normal meaning. And the verse thus means: "There is nothing like His similar"—an interpretation that, for the *fuqaha, is* supremely blasphemous.'

In his commentary on this verse (42:11), al-Razi affirms the 'problem' of accepting the Quran literally. He says, 'The *zahir* [obvious, literal] meaning of this verse has different modes; one says the intent of verse is to reject something similar to Allah, but the *zahir* requires the affirmation of something similar to Allah, because the *zahir* necessitates rejecting something similar to His similar, not something similar to Him.' Al-Razi, Ibn Hisham in *Mughni al-Labib,* and Ibn Aqil respond to this problem by citing the Arab usage of *ka* in the statement *ka-mithlika la yabkhulu,* that is, the likes of you would not be miserly, so we deny miserliness by your similar, and the Arab means denying miserliness by you, as al-Razi says it. Ibn Manzur sums up the problem by saying, *Laysa ka-mithlihi shay'un* means *laysa mithlahu,* and it could mean nothing but that, because if it is not said like that, this verse would affirm that He has a similar.

The ulema who promoted particular meanings of this verse did so for well-documented reasons. Al-Razi, for example, was concerned with the Jahmiyyah or Jabriyyah school of theology which over-abstracted divine attributes and tailored his argument to refute them. But the intellectual rigour of the ulema is such that ideas, even ideas the author is utterly opposed to, are presented straightforwardly. For example, in the long discussion of the issue of washing or wiping the feet during *wudu* presented by al-Razi, one could not discern which of the many arguments he presents would be approved of and which would be disapproved of, until he inserts his own comments directly onto the argument.

Another example of this is with the issue of a woman leading the *salah* when there are men present. There are arguments for and against. Abu Thawr, for example, takes the positive argument that the revealed text, 'Let him lead who is best at reciting *[aqra]* the Quran' is general, not specific to men. Ibn al-Arabi, as another example, takes the positive argument that leading a *salah is imamah* (leadership) and that *imamah is* a sub-set of being *kamal* (complete) (such that all complete people can be Imams, but not all Imams are complete), and since we know from an authentic *hadith* that among the complete people are Maryam and Asiyah (the wife of Pharoah), we know that *imamah* of women is permitted.

The only against argument proffered is that the Prophet (PBUH) *is* supposed to have said, 'Woman shall not lead man'. Now the majority of legal scholars through the ages have not accepted the *imamah* of women over men. When they argue, they generally leave aside the for arguments for this case. As for the against argument, scholars like al-Nawawi, Ibn Hajar, and al-Bayhaqi admit the *hadith,* 'Woman shall not lead men', is weak (and therefore cannot be used as evidence), but then say, 'But we [still] do not permit the imamah of woman over men'.

Added to the for arguments is the case of Umm Waraqah, who was commanded by the Prophet himself to be the Imam of her household in which there were men. Al-Darqutni, in an effort to divert this argument, goes to great lengths to fabricate a scenario where the men run out to the mosque before Umm Waraqah starts leading the prayer. Al-Bayhaqi tries to divert the argument by saying that the best rows for women are the back ones; this is a non-argument, because the woman may as well lead from the back rows or between the men's and the women's rows.

Ibn al-Arabi's acceptance of the position of those ulema who permit the woman leading men is based on the literal, outward, *fiqh* evidence. This is the basis of accepting one or another position. He is also able to delve into the inward or spiritual explanations for the outward truth. The inward affirmation of the outward position is found in crossing over from the outward to the inward. This he does by crossing over Man to *aql* and Woman to *nafs*," explaining that it is permissible for the *nafs* to lead the *aql* (but that is not permissible for *hawan-caprice,* which is crossed over to the kafir—to lead the *salah*). In this context, gender is inwardly determined; a female gender inwardly may exist in a male sex outwardly. More accurately, genders operate in a yin-yang mode.

One wonders what Muslim communities would look like if they took some of the positions held over the ages by the ulema, especially those not linked into state power. One can imagine far-reaching corrections and readjustments which could be made without extensive *ijtihad.*

Logic and Analogy

One of the ways in which positions such as this one, which forbids the leadership of women over men, gain sway, is by a storming of culture (paternalistic) over the legal text. The flexibility of opinion and cultural input into the legal discourse meant that the strict textual approach to *fiqh* and contextual approach to *qada* succumbed to sultanic forces. The kind of legal reasoning that emerges, then, seeks to cut off what Allah pronounced *(mantuq)* and fill in what Allah was silent about (*maskut*). In his strict rejection of all *qiyas* which is not explicitly *ijtihad,* Ibn al-Arabi recognizes the dangers of extending, through analogy, explicit commands into realms of silence. There is a firm boundary separating the *mantuq* and the *maskut*, and to breach the line is to take Lordship on oneself. To silence what was spoken and to vocalize what was silent is to assume Lordship. The *abd*, in complete contrast, seeks to be utterly passive and receptive to Allah's command, like the corpse in the washer's hands.

One of Ibn al-Arabi's arguments against *qiyas* is found in his discussion of *tayammum* (preparing for *salah* by dusting the hands and face). To understand how *qiyas* is related to the issues surrounding *tayammum,* we need to understand how Ibn al-Arabi crosses over (cf. *itibar)* a *hukm* from the outwardness to the inwardness. The most felicitous folk, Ibn al-Arabi says, are those who follow the *hukm* of Allah in the outwardness and also in the inwardness. For Ibn al-Arabi, each *hukm* has an outer and one or more corresponding inner dimensions. First, the linguistic base. About *itibar* and *ibrah ('b.r.),* Ibn Manzur says, 'The *ibr* [crossing] of the arroyo.' And 'in the *hadith* of Abu Dharr there is, What were the *suhufu Musa* [books of Moses]? He said, They were all *ibarahs.* That is, they were like admonishments which people would heed and would put into practice.' Also `in the *hadith* of Ibn Sirin, he said, I do *[itibar]* of *hadith,* the meaning of which is that he crosses over ('b.r.) the perspective of the *hadith* as he crosses it over with the Quran by its interpretation; for example, "the crow" is crossed over to the *fasiq* [bad man], and the rib to the woman, because the Prophet called the crow *fasiq* and declared the woman like the rib. The likes of that is done with allusions and nouns.' (The word *itibar* is the thing crossed over, in the Greek sense of metaphor.)

Ibn al-Arabi says,

A taharah of sight for example, for the inwardness, is considering things through the eye of *itibar,* so one's eyes will not chase after distractions. The likes of this are not for any but the one who has realized the performance of the *taharah* set down by revelation in [different] places, each one of them. Allah said, *In this is an ibrah for the ones having sight [3:13].* He made the *ibrah* with 'sight' because it is the secondary cause that leads to the inward, which is that to which the eye of insight crosses over. It is like this for each of the bodily parts.

Receptivity to divine speech *and* silence are necessary. This makes most kinds of analogical deduction, *(qiyas)* illegitimate.

One of Ibn al-Arabi's discussions about *qiyas* is found in his justification for taking the position that *tayammum is* not a substitute for purification. In this case of *tayammum,* the key properties in his discussion are water, dust, earth, knowledge, and *taqlid.* Water is crossed over to knowledge for those with insight, and if one examines the Quran, the water which animates dry earth and causes plants to grow is fluidly crossed over to knowledge which inspires the hard heart and causes good fruit to be produced. Dust and earth are humble, reminding the one with insight that we are dust to dust, and that the earth was made humble. Then, the *hukm* of *tayammum* is crossed over to situations where water—knowledge—is not found, or cannot be used.

For Ibn al-Arabi, *tayammum* is not a substitute for *wudu* or *ghusl,* as the ulema believe, but a *taharah* set down in the shariah in its own right. For Ibn al-Arabi, the only way to approach Allah in the *munajah* with Him," which is the *salah,* is to do *taharah* with water or with dust. Because each is set down by the *shar* (Law-giver), there is no question of denigrating *taharah* with dust simply because dust is not a linguistic or rational form of purification.

Therefore, in the absence of knowledge, *taqlid* is required. For Ibnal-Arabi *taqlid* is certainly not following the authority of one of the experts of opinion, but of one of the 'people of remembrance' or *ahl dhikr,* which means the one who can tell the person without knowledge that this or that is indeed the *hukm* of Allah, or of His messenger. Ibn al-Arabi says this:

Our position is that *tayammum is* not a substitute but rather a *taharah* set down by *shar,* specified and designated for a specific state; the One who revealed it revealed the use of water for this specified worship, and it is Allah, and his Messenger, so it is not a substitute. Rather, it is based on an extraction of the property for this issue, from a revealed text mentioned in the Book or Sunna, encompassing the property for this issue in a synopsis of that discourse. It is the *fiqh* of the *din.* He said, *Let a contingent from every expedition remain behind to apply themselves* [cf. *tafaqquh] to the din and admonish the people when they return to them that thus they may learn to guard themselves[against evil]* 19:122]-and we do not need *qiyas* for that!

Taking a standard argument, that we have no revealed text regulating beating one's father with a stick, and that we need to extend the 'Say not *uff* to them' (17:23) to cover beating with a stick, Ibn al-Arabi says this:

We say that we do not have the exercise of declaring the property over the *shar* [Law-giver] concerning anything, even among the things it is permitted that we be responsible for—no declaring of the property, especially not in the likes of this. If there had not been mentioned explicitly in the revelation something other than this [saying of *uff] qiyas* would not have been made required of us, and we do not augment it by the saying of *uff.* Rather we make as *hukm* what He mentioned, and it is His statement, *treat with kindness your parents [17:23]—so* the address is undifferentiated; we extract from this synopsis the *hukm* about everything which is not a kindness. Beating with a stick is not one of the kindnesses which has been commanded by the revelation in our relationships with our parents. So we did not make as *hukm* anything but the revealed text, and we do not need *qiyas*.

The *din* is perfected, and it is not permitted to add to it, just as subtracting from it is not permitted. So the one who beat his father with a stick has not treated him kindly, and the one who did not treat kindly his parents has rejected what Allah commanded of him, that he practise kindness toward his parents. And the one who opposed the word of his parents, and did what his parents do not approve of, something which is permissible for him to leave off, has in fact been disrespectful to them both. And it has been established that disrespect to parents is one of the great sins. Because of this, we argued that the *taharah* with dust—and it *is tayammum*—is not a substitute. Rather it is set down by *shar*, just as *taharah* with water was made *shar*.

Besides the peril one places oneself in with breaching boundaries between what Allah has stated explicitly and what He has not stated, between the *mantuq* and the *maskut*, societies yield to pressures to make Islam a culture. Thus, the patriarchy and racism found in culture is extended analogically to Islam.

The contest over *ijtihad* revolves around the role the intellect will play in determining rulings. For Ibn al-Arabi, *ijtihad* requires an *abd* who is so effaced that in effect the *hukm* discovered is the *hukm* of Allah. Novelty does not faze the *abd*, because in fact 'Every moment He is upon some task' *(kulla yawmin huwa fi shanin, 55:29)*, nor the *qadi* who sees each case as novel and unique. Whether desire for standardization and codification is natural or state-induced, the fact remains that the complacency this produces is antithetical to the perpetual receptivity—even confusion—required by the radical ambiguity of existence.

13

Spiritual Aspects

The attack on the *fiqh* by modern movements, such as fundamentalism, includes an attack on spiritual things as well. Western scholarship on Islam is beginning to recognize that traditionally, the majority of the ulema participated in one or more *Sufi* paths.' For them, the concept of *ilm*, of sapiential knowledge, meant an integration between virtue, praxis, knowledge, and sanctity, just as it meant the integration of law and spirituality. One problem which disturbs contemporary Muslim life, is that of the separation of law from spirituality and vice versa. There are Muslims who elevate their spiritual life beyond the concerns of their daily lives and discard law as an essentially mundane, rigid, and trivializing discipline. Then there are Muslims who have reified the law, taking a static and arid lump of rulings as the last word on a dead revelation. I would like to explore here the world-view which maintained an integration of law and spirituality and offer encouragement to those who work for a reintegration of *shariah*, *fiqh*, and spirituality.

The world-view which sustained the traditional Sufi scholars posited the following scenario. The essence of Islam is the shariah. The messenger of Allah, Muhammad, was sent as a mercy to the worlds and a demonstrator of the *shariah*. The *fiqh* is the application of the *shariah* to different times and places based on deeply and vigorously debated rules and methodologies (e.g., *the usul al fiqh).* Spirituality is sought and expressed within the confines of the *shariah* boundaries. This world-view maintained Islamic communities through hundreds of years. It is my hope that by engaging the areas of law and spirituality, once again, in an integrated discursive system like the *fiqh* we may achieve some degree of integration, where our physical and worldly lives are perfected through our imaginal and spiritual lives; or to say it another way, our spiritual lives are perfected through our physical lives.

Divine Guidance

The classical ulema have a very clear idea of how divine guidance is to be applied and realized in communities. The importance of knowledge of language is seen in such works as the fourteenth century Ibn Manzur's *Lisan al-Arab,* where he creates, Noah-like, an ark to contain the words in circulation during the time of the Prophet and massive works identifying his Companions. In it, as many details of their lives as possible are assembled to enable the *hadith* scholar to evaluate chains of transmission which testify to a very particular structure of knowing—developed and maintained by an amorphous knowledge elite, the ulema. Their vision is by no means the only possible vision—its formal structure did not appear until three or more generations after the death of the Prophet. So while that vision is often either assumed as obvious, or rejected equally out of hand, I prefer to identify its implicit values and its normative force. Once we recognize its normative position, we immediately begin to identify its challengers. Three groups especially have been seen by the ulema as threatening and illegitimate.

The Khawarij, Batiniyyah, and Ibahiyyah Types : These three groups are present today, so one may speak of types. First is the Khawarij challenge. Historically, this is the group which sought a radical Islam, shorn of its cultural, linguistic, and human accoutrements. It is this group which could contemplate the murder of Uthman, draw a definition of 'Muslim' so tight as to wage war on slackers or Muslims not up to their standards. This group in its later incarnations could destroy the tombs of the Prophet and companions, as the Wahhabis did. Their orientation towards the future and their vision of movement and progress make this type peculiarly modern. Their ideology makes it desirable to erase centuries of learning and tradition (going directly to Quran and Sunna, they ignore and denigrate centuries of Muslim scholarship). This type, as it manifests itself in modern fundamentalism, creates clear lines of battle, quickly and surely defining its enemies (Jews, tradition-bound Muslims, Americans), seeks rapid development and success (throwing derision at the traditional responses of *sabr* [patience], and the other worldliness of Sufis), and mocks the sacred, whether in art, attire, housing, or occupation.

Ibn Manzur emphasizes their tendency to restrict and make the religion hard and harsh. Among the Khawarij, there is another group called Haruriyyah—a name based on their locale. Ibn Manzur says, 'al-Harura is a place outside of Kufah to which is related the Haruriyyah, belonging to the Khawarij, because al-Harura was the first place they founded their community, and the place where they declared their authority after they opposed Ali.' He then goes on to describe how the word is adjectivally used: 'The linguistic extension is, "Someone is Harurawi." ' He then quotes al-Jawhari, who said, 'al-Harura is a name of a village.' The word also appears in a *hadith* from Aishah when she was questioned about the menstruant making up the *salah*. Ibn Manzur says, 'She replied, "Are you a Haruriyyah?" They are the Haruriyyah belonging to the Khawarij who fought against Ali. On their part they used to make harsh that which in the religion was an easing, so when Aishah saw this woman making the affairs of menstruation harsher, she compared her to the Haruriyyah. They make their affairs harsher in many of their issues, and they torment themselves with them. It is said they want to oppose the Surma and leave the [local] community just as they left the [larger] community of the believers.'

Groups which make their religion more difficult and demanding in order to distinguish themselves from the larger body of Muslims fit this type.

A second group are the Batiniyyah, a word based on *batin*, the inward, who denigrate the body and the material. Ibn al-Arabi describes their error in this passage:

> Know that Allah addressed humankind in his totality and did not honour his outwardness over his inwardness, nor his inwardness over his outwardness. They are dedicated, the ones who invite people [to the religion], most of them, to knowledge of the *ahkam* [legal properties] of the *shar* (cf. *shariah*) in their outwardness, but are heedless of the *ahkam* set down by revelation in their inwardness, except for the few, and they are folk on Allah's path. They investigate that, outwardly and inwardly. There is no *hukm* [legal property] which they determine according to the revelation, for their outwardnesses, except they see that that *hukm* has a relationship to their inwardnesses. They take, in that way, the entirety of the *ahkam* of the revealed religions. They worship Allah with that which He made *shar* for them, outwardly and inwardly, and they succeed where the majority fail.

Continuing, Ibn al-Arabi says,

Three groups arose, one misled and another making others misled. One takes the *ahkam* of the *shariah* and discharges them for their inwardnesses, and they leave nothing of the *ahkam* of the *shariah* for their outwardnesses. They are called Batiniyyah, and they are, in that, in different schools. Imam Abu Hamid [al-Ghazali] indicated, in his book *Kitab al-Mustazhiri* refuting them, something of their schools and explained their errors therein.

Summing up, Ibn al-Arabi says,

Felicity is with outward folk. They are diametrically opposite inward folk. But felicity, all felicity, is with the group who combine the outward and inward; they are ulema (knowers) of Allah and His *ahkam.*'

Although there is a historical identification by Sunnis of the Ismailis as the Batiniyyahs, this tendency is found among many scholarly and progressive Muslims, who have intellectualized, abstracted, and made philosophical and symbolic, their approach to the sacred text.

A third group may be called the Ibahiyyah, the ones who make everything permissible, denying divine punishment, and relativizing all actions.

The Khawarij voice is the fundamentalist voice which commands a great audience, and not just because of the Western media. The secularist or liberal voice, which has elements of Batiniyyah and Ibahiyyah, gets its amplification from a cosy relationship with liberalist yearnings in the West and political power in the East.

Since one could hardly imagine a Muslim who claimed not to believe in the fundamentals of Islam, fundamentalist is not a very apt description. Let me introduce the term 'technist' for the Khawarij tendency as it appears today.

A technist is a Muslim who believes fervently that the historical decline of Muslims is due to a problem of technique: if only Muslims had correctly applied such and such a technique, they would not be suffering today in Bosnia, Somalia, Palestine, and elsewhere. And if only Muslims would apply another technique (e.g., 'be as brothers unto one another', or apply the *hijab,* or the *hudud* as in the Hudood Ordinances in Pakistan), we would be as successful as the Israelis or Americans or Japanese. The ultimate in technist thinking is the notion that the Quran is a constitution, reducing, as only technists can do, a sacred text into a tremendously unidimensional and flat document.

One consequence of the text produced by the technists is that they have in effect co-opted the revelation and the *fiqh,* Well-meaning Muslims, Sufis and spiritualists, lay and non-academically trained Muslims alike, tend to accept the technist arrogation of the texts without challenge. Believing themselves bereft of *hadith* and the Quran, they forsake the text and search elsewhere for solutions to the problems facing their communities.

The contemporary Batiniyyah and Ibahiyyah viewpoints have accepted the primacy of the modern world-view. Now, in order to live in this world, they must derive a means of handling the Islamic text. The means derived often revolve around a rejection of literal and narrow-minded interpretations and an emphasis on a moral and ethical Islam distanced from its historical roots.

Views of Technists

The views of technists concerning man and caliphate, for example, are utterly modern. For centuries the Quranic commentaries restricted the entire caliphate complex, described in the Quran, to Adam and the other prophets. Suddenly, due to the attractiveness of an all-powerful modern Western man, technists were saying that we are all supposed to assume caliphate. This ultra-modern sleight of hand allows technical Islamicists to paint an Islamic facade over newly industrializing countries' efforts to gain power and prestige, to treat nuclear weapons as a simple Islamic progression from swords and arrows, and to explain why modern Muslims are wielding such power over environments and peoples whereas traditional Muslims were wallowing in passive and unaggressive relationships with others and with nature.

Nation States

If their nation-states are caught in neo-colonial nets, then it must be because the leaders are not ideal. Logically, if you could install ideal leaders, you would avoid all problems. So the search for a caliph who will forcefully implement the *shariah*—whose politics must be absolute because they are linked to absolute religion—preoccupies the technists.

Ironically, the traditional view is that caliphate is preceded by absolute servanthood to the divine, such that the only person qualified to lead is the one who is so effaced that the divine rules through him as a marionette is led by the puppeteer. One recalls the admonishment to His messenger in the Quran, It is *not you who killed them: it was Allah who killed them; and you did not throw when you threw, but Allah threw (8:17).* Ibn alArabi's metaphor for this is the *hadith qudsi,* that is, a *hadith* of Allah's words, ' . . . I am his ear with which he hears . . .'

For centuries the scholars of commentary have interpreted (13:11) *Verily Allah does not change what is with a people until they change themselves* as meaning, 'Verily Allah does not change what is with a people [by way of good] [to bad] until they change themselves [by doing bad, and so become deserving of punishment]'. For example, al-Razi's commentary on this part of the verse is as follows.

As for His statement, may He be exalted, *Verily Allah does not change what is with a people until they change what is with themselves,* the word of all the commentators indicates that the meaning of *will not change is* what *is* with them by way of good fortune to the descent of vengenance, unless there are among them people of disobedience and wickedness. Al-Qadi said, there is no other possible meaning except this one ... since He, may He be exalted, begins with good fortune in *din* [religious matters] and *dunya* [worldly matters], and then blesses in that whom He will ... Al-Qadi [also] raises the issue that He does not visit punishment on the children of the polytheists due their fathers since they have yet not changed what is with themselves by way of good fortune.

Today, of course, the interpretation is quite the opposite, implying that if only we will change ourselves—become punctual, brotherly, and technically correct—God will make us successful, like the Americans or the Japanese.

These modern technical interpreters are not literal, nor do they have any special claims to authencity. They entirely dispense with the connecting chain *(silsilah)* which links ourselves to the prophetic period, seeking to tear out the revealed data onto their supposed *tabula rasa.* In fact, by claiming to consider only the Quran and Sunna—which they do not do literally nor very well—they ignore the inevitable cultural baggage they bring. And this baggage, quite clearly, was packed in the West. By sweeping away centuries of Islamic civilization, they claim to approach the texts literally. They reject previous scholarships, legal schools, and spiritual paths.

They claim to take just from the Quran and Sunna, effectively denying the interpretive process and so erect for themselves an unassailable stance. The way to challenge this stance is to demonstrate that they do indeed, bring with them their modern baggage, their televisions and computers, their ache for industrial power and prestige, and their frustration with female suffrage and universal education, thereby coming to conclusions utterly at odds with a thousand years and more of commentary on the Quran.

It is impossible to give credence to someone who takes a Quranic verse, especially in translation, and says 'so and so' is what it means. To be authentic, a discussion of a verse or a *hadith* must be prefaced by references to classical commentaries. This does not necessarily preclude novel interpretations, but it discourages the arrogance of believing that fourteen centuries of devoted Muslim scholarship missed something we only now see.

The answer of how Quranic verses have to be understood and interpreted is that it is all contextual and interpretive. It is the Muslims who are striving to respond to the divine commands, to live a life of sacred obedience, to produce on earth-as much as He wills—a just society. The way we accomplish what is good, is by engaging at every step our understanding of the divine revelation. *Fiqh,* then, is one of the means we have of following, of engaging, the guidance of the Quran and Sunna. The *fiqh* has its rules of engagement, its courtesies, and protocols for disagreement, its systems of logic and demonstration; it has its rules of citation and chains of authority which are evaluated intellectually, not charismatically.

The Islamic life is not a technique. Nor is it an abstract ethics, a vague desire to 'do good'. It is rather the manifestation of guidance, the strides we take for ourselves and in society to follow the straight path. One beauty of Islamic civilization is that so many scholars have expressed a number of positions and interpretations. While this dismays the technist, it emboldens those who wish to realize the general divine command for their particular situation.

One example of a *fiqh* discussion which rejects the reifying and reductionist machinations of technists can be found in the following case. For this issue, the imamah (prayer leadership) of a child, Ibn al-Arabi examines three different positions and gives a metaphor for each position.' There is quite clearly no one position which is absolutely better than the others. The issue is not one of the right answer, but one of delving more deeply into the case in order to find appreciation at the higher levels, instead of moving down to a least common denominator. In fact, in order to quiet inevitable conflicts in Muslim communities, some suggest we ignore the details of Islam and hold firmly to the bigger picture. Frithj of Schuon denounces this kind of exoteric ecumenism, writing that :

> When a man seeks to escape from 'dogmatic narrowness' it is essential that it should be 'upwards' and not 'downwards': dogmatic form is transcended by fathoming its depths and contemplating its

> universal content, and not by denying it in the name of a pretentious and iconoclastic 'ideal' of 'pure truth'.

Or worse, as James Cutsinger adds, 'in the name of a tolerance whose chief objective is of a strictly social or political sort'. Schuon's metaphor is the false ecumenism where, 'to reconcile two adversaries, one strangles them both, which is certainly the best way to make peace.'

Ibn al-Arabi's discussion follows :

> The [scholars of the *fiqh]* disagree about the leadership of the child, *sabiy [s.b.y.]* who is not mature, even though he is a reciter of the Quran. Some people permit that absolutely, and some people forbid that absolutely, and some people permit it for the supererogatory prayers, but not for the required *salah.*

The crossover [from the outward ritual to the inward truth, but not vice versa] of the matter for that is, that one says, 'So and so childishly tends [s.b.y.] to something' when he inclines to it, and since the child inclines toward the property of Nature, and is swayed by his individual desires, he is called a child; meaning, he is inclined to his cravings. He is without maturity in respect to intellect, which is required for the prescription of the Law. Nature, in its standing, is without the intellect, so it is not correct for Nature to have priority, nor for the one who inclines to Nature to have priority, even if he is inclining to Nature by rights, so in fact Nature has the position of the one behind, and indeed [the one who inclines to Nature] is behind, and the one who is behind shall not be a leader standing in front: it is the opposite of what the property of leadership is about.

So the one who considered *this* crossover did not permit the leadership of the child even if he is a reciter. And the one who considered the fact of his having memorized *hamil [h.m.l.]* the Quran, understood the leadership to be that of the Quran, not of the child-leadership to be subject to being followed on account of the Quran, so he permitted the leadership of the child. He said, 'We gave him jurisdiction as a child' [19:12]—i.e., jurisdiction of leadership—and They said" 'How shall we talk to one who is in the cradle, as a child'? [The newborn infant Jesus] said, 'I am a slave of Allah; He gave me the Book and made me a prophet [19:29-30]—and prophethood is the position of leadership, despite his being called a child.

And the one who saw the worship of the child to be a free—will worship in the absence of a prescription of the Law requiring him to do it—and who saw that the supererogatory prayers are a freely-willed act of worship, he permitted the *salah* of the child as the leader for the supererogatory prayers, but not the required prayer, due to the supererogatory prayers' relation to free-will.

Thus, without seeking to create a new position, Ibn al-Arabi instead examines previous decisions and describes what Allah had disclosed for him about the truths behind the different positions. In fact, in the thousands of pages of text expounding Ibn al-Arabi's special understanding of the *fiqh* positions, he enumerates the various positions held historically by the *ulema* but usually indicates which of those positions he himself prefers and then illuminates the 'crossover' (from outward ritual to inward truth) involved in each case. As a result, one gains from this kind of study of the *fiqh* a deep understanding of the physical manifestation of following the commands, and at the same time bridges the inward and outward aspects of the revelation, affirming at once the necessity and value of strict obedience to the outward realm of ritual while grounding and authenticating the inward spirituality of the believer.

Part - IV
The State

14

Organised Institution

The modern concept of state is, that it is an organised institution, which is run by the people through their elected representatives for the collective welfare of the people, residing in a specified territory. The ultimate power vests in the people, who are real sovereign and, therefore, masters of their destinies. They are free to legislate and enact any law, following their own desires. The constitution of the state is moulded according to the history, belief, customs and ideology of its people. All the secular states of the world, whether Democratic or Socialistic are administrated by man-made laws, and institutions, and are based on the theory of material advancement, and utilitarianism.

Concept of State

The concept of state in Islam is altogether different from the present-day concept of state. In modern times when territorial nationalism is the order of the day and material and economic considerations almost wholly shape peoples' outlook and policies, the making of an Islamic State stands out as the triumph of an ethical concept. But the Western observers may question: firstly, what the character of Islamic State is and, secondly, as to how an Islamic State can be realised in a democracy in the twentieth century. In this context it becomes necessary for us to ascertain as to what the true form, character and nature of an Islamic State is and how far it can be realised in the structural pattern of a modern society.

In this context, it should be kept uppermost in the mind that Islam is not merely a religion in its narrow import. It is not a set of dogmas, mythological beliefs or mere rituals. It does not divide life into water tight compartments. There is no dichotomy in Islam between the temporal and spiritual; the structure of Islam is essentially religio-political. In this system the state forms an integral part at the apex and as Dr. Muhammad Iqbal points out "is only an effort to realise the spiritual in human organisation". *(Lectures on Reconstruction of Religious Thoughts in Islam,* page 155). Thus, Islam presents the whole of reality to man and wants to give him guidance in every walk of life. It requires him to discriminate between the right and wrong and to accept a path because it is right and not because it is secular or non-secular. It attempts to bring the realities of this world in harmony with the ideals that provide security for this world and the Hereafter. It is a complete code of conduct. It is a way of life and a philosophy of life. It is a social, economic and political system. Hence, it is a statecraft.

It is in this context that the whole outlook and effort for raising the edifice of the state has to be different from the lines on which people ordinarily pursue the task of state building. Thus spiritual and ethical values of Islam have played a decisive role in this regard. This has been embodied in the concept of Islamic State—a state patterned on the socio-moral, religio-political principles of Islam. It is not torn by the dualism of state and church whose separation has been deemed an absolute dogma in Western Political Science. The church is not recognized in the genuine Islamic State as an exclusive institution representing religion. The concept of state religion or the Papacy or theocracy cannot give a correct picture of the character of the Islamic State. In a theocracy, the Pope assumes a special intimacy with God and nobody can reach God except his intermediary. This concept is alien to Islam. The criterion of an Islamic State is not union of the ruler and the government, but the principle of justice and religion combined with social action. Thus, in order to understand the concept of state in Islam, let us examine the essentials of the state.

To constitute a state four elements are essential: (i) territory; (ii) population; (iii) organization; and (iv) sovereignty. In regard to the fourth element, the Islamic State differs fundamentally from all other states, and in that occupies a unique position.

No state can be termed independent unless it enjoys sovereign power i. e. the absolute right to make laws for people within its jurisdiction. This gives rise to the question, who should possess such right? In ancient times, when *might is right* was the rule the most powerful individual, through sheer brute force, used to conquer certain territories and instal himself as the ruler of the people. He called himself king and arrogated to himself the absolute right of law making and the right to set up any form of government that suited his convenience. Being himself the chief law-giver for his people, he was considered above law, and, as such, not bound by any law, not even his own. And in consequence of the enjoyment of this and other exclusive rights and privileges, he regarded himself as God incornate. As an obvious corollary of this belief, he had full control over the life and death of his subjects who are required to give him unquestioning and unconditional obedience and to serve him blindly. The people were, thus, reduced to the position of mere serfs and chatties: they enjoyed no fundamental rights, nor could they claim, freedom of expression or liberty of conscience.

Later in history, when feudalism became the order of the day, a few feudal lords joined the monarch in claiming the right to make laws for the country, but the people remained where they were earlier so far as their rights and privileges were concerned. The monarchs along with those few lords enjoyed innumerable exclusive privileges and all that at the cost of those whom they ruled by virtue of being the law-givers for the land.

During the mediaeval period, the ecclesiastical authorities in Christian Europe tried to set up theocracy i.e. the rule based upon divine laws; but as the few Commandments which were regarded as infallible could not cover all aspects of human activities, the priests found an excuse to arrogate to themselves the right of making additional laws for the people. They also put themselves above the law, and as such enjoyed exclusive privileges, depriving the people of their just and inalienable rights.

Following the pattern of theocracy and in order to assert their so-called inalienable hereditary rights and infallibility, the mediaeval English monarchs claimed the 'Divine Right of Kings' the traces of which theory are still to be found in England, the most democratic country in the world. For that matter, the maxim "The King can do no wrong" still holds as good in England today as it was during the mediaeval and post-mediaeval period.

Even in Greek democracy, which is regarded by some as an ideal institution, the people were divided into two classes: the free (men) and the slaves. The latter, in the opinion of Aristotle, were not fit to participate in government. Their position was like that of animals whose only duty was to serve their free masters who owned them. They had none of the rights of citizens. Nor were women given any right and, so much so that Aristotle would confine to more domestic duties. The philosophers who called the Greek democracy into existence because the sole law-makers for the country and their antipathy towards women and healots resulted in social inequality. In other words, Greek democracy assured freedom only for the free, male Greeks, and was confined to Greece.

Rousseau, the well-known French philosopher, was, however, the first to enunciate the idea of popular sovereignty, and it was after the French Revolution that attempts were made to found state on this basis in Europe.

First State

The Islamic State, as is well-known, was founded by the Holy Prophet in the seventh century of Christian era; and continued with full vigour during the period of first four Caliphs *(Khulfa-i-Rashidin)*. But soon enough, its complexion changed owing to certain variations in its ideals. However, certain basic ideals like equality, liberty, justice and even toleration remained in force to a certain degree in the post-Rashidin period.

But owing to the existence of institutions like monarchy and feudalism, the fundamentals of Islamic State, could not find a foothold in European countries, although a very energetic, glorious Islamic State was in existence in Spain for several centuries. The abolition of the institutions of monarchy and feudalism in the wake of French Revolution, however, paved the way for the reception of these ideals into Europe.

Even in modern democracies which are based upon popular sovereignty, equality, liberty, justice and toleration are rarely to be found. Strange though it may sound, this contention is nevertheless based on facts. No doubt, in modern state laws are made by the representatives of the people, yet they are made in such a way as to suit the interests of either a class or a party at the cost of the opposition or they remain so defective that different interpretations are put for different sections of the people. They are so nicely twisted that they always favour the "sovereign" class. In all modern democracies, from the President or the King down to the legislature, they are all allowed, in the first instance, to enjoy some sort of exclusive privileges, for instance, exemption from taxation, exemption from appearance in the court or immunity of arrest (while performing their official duties), reservation of seats in trains or planes, or other priorities in several other respects. Secondly, the ruling party makes such laws which could suit and advance its own interest, although it may adversely affect the opposition e. g., if the Labour Government is in power, it will promulgate laws suiting the labourer and normally at the cost of the capitalists and *vice versa.*

The most flagrant example of discrimination in this respect can be found in South Africa where the original, native inhabitants were deprived of their inalienable right to franchise by the foreign ruling class. This racial discrimination was also to be found on another level in one of the most democrative countries of the world viz., the U.S.A.

Even in the most democratic country of the world, viz., England, one finds the same phenomena of inequality although little in conparison to above mentioned countries in operation: For instance, one does find discrimination, though in a lesser degree, so far as the interpretation of law and dispensation of justice are concerned.

Even in the eastwhile communist states which are regarded more advanced in this respect than their capitalist counterparts, the same phenomena of inequality, injustice and intoleration prevails on account of the same defect. The heads of communist states along with their lesser party bosses, were all above the law; nay, they imposed themselves on the people through the force of an election. As there is no check on the sovereign powers of the legislators, they deprived the people even of their liberty of conscience; and by putting an end to private enterprise and initiative, they reduced human beings to the position of an inconsequential part of a huge machine.

This defective system of law-making is primarily due to the fact that the right of sovereignty has been entrusted to human agency without any divine restriction. And it is because of basic human weakness that men when they are entrusted with the law-making power, more often than not misuse it in their own favour or in favour of the party or class which they represent. In other words, unrestricted sovereign powers have been assumed by human beings, in all the states from time immemorial resulting in exclusive privileges for the ruling authorities and deprivation of inalienable human rights of the people as a whole.

In an Islamic State, on the other hand, sovereignty belongs to God, the Almighty Allah. This does not, however, mean that in an Islamic State, all the laws are to be made by God Himself or that the Quran provides all possible positive laws and that people have nothing to do with sovereign functions. On the other hand, the laws, enacted in an Islamic State are, to be made by the people of the state, but in the light of the Quranic fundamentals. Thus, in an Islamic State, the people enjoy a partial and restricted right of law-making. They cannot, of course, make any law which runs contrary to the Quranic instructions, meant for universal application. In this sense, the people who make the laws, are not really law-makers. Nor are they above the law; they are only the executors of law and they stand at par with ordinary citizens.

First Source

There are two kinds of verses in the Holy Quran, namely decisive and allegorical, the latter being those which are capable of different interpretations. The decisive verses are the basis of the Book, and contain the fundamental principles of religion. So that whatever may be the differences of interpretation over allegorical verses, the fundamentals of religion are not affected by them.

Second Source

The *Sunnah* or *Hadith* (the tradition of the Prophet) is the second, and undoubtedly a secondary, source from which the Islamic laws are drawn. *Sunnah* literally means a way, rule or manner of acting. In its original sense, therefore, *Sunnah* indicates the doings, and *Hadith* the sayings of the Holy Prophet, but in effect both cover the same ground and are applicable to his actions, practices and sayings; *Hadith* being the narration and record of the *Sunnah,* but containing, in addition, various Prophetical and historical elements of Islam. As the Holy Quran generally deals with the broad principles or essentials of Islam the details are generally to be supplied by the *Sunnah* of the Holy Prophet. Even for the two important religious institutions of Islam, viz., prayer and *Zakat,* no details are to be found in the Quran. The details about these injunctions were only supplied by the practice of the Holy Prophet. These are but two examples: but since Islam covered the whole sphere of human activities, hundreds of points had to be explained by the Holy Prophet by his example in word and deed, while the moral side, his was the pattern which every Muslim was required to follow. The persons, who embraced Islam, thus, stood in need of both the Holy Quran and the *Sunnah.* And it was because the *Sunnah* occupied such a tremendous though a secondary place in the super-structure of Islam that the early Muslims devoted themselves so assiduously and so energetically to collecting all traditions with every possible care that was humanly possible. In judging whether a certain *Hadith* was spurious or genuine, the collectors not only made a thorough investigation regarding the trustworthiness of the transmitters but also applied other tests for its acceptance. No *Hadith* was to be accepted, if it was opposed to or was against the plain teachings of the Quran. Being the secondary source of law, *Hadith,* is, however, to be judged by the Quran. If it agrees with the Quran, it should be accepted; if it runs counter to the spirit of a Quranic injunction, it should be rejected.

Third Source

Ijtihad is the third source from which the laws are drawn. The word itself is derived from the root *"jehad"*, which means exerting oneself to the utmost or to the best of one's ability, and *Ijtihad*, which literally conveys the same significance, is technically applicable to a lawyer's exerting his mental faculties to the utmost for purposes of solving difficult problems. Reasoning or the exercise of judgement, in the theological as well as in legal matters, plays a very important part in Islam. The Quran does recognise revelation as a source of knowledge higher than reason. But it also admits that the truth of the principles established by revelation may be judged by reason, and in doing so, it repeatedly appeals to reason and denounces those who do not use their reasoning faculty. It also recognizes the necessity of the exercise of judgement in the formulation of a decision. *Ijtihad* or the exercise of judgement is expressly recognised in the *Hadith* as the means by which a decision may be arrived at when there is no direction in the Holy Quran or the *Hadith.* The following *Hadith* is regarded as the basis of *Ijtihad* in Islam:

On being appointed Governor of Yemen, Muadh Bin Jabal was asked by the Holy Prophet as to the rule by which he would adjudicate. He replied "by the law of the Quran". "But if you do not find any direction in the Quran, how would you decide", asked the prophet. He replied, "I will apply the *Hadith* and Sunnah". "But if you don't find any guidance in the *Hadith* as well?" He was again asked. "I will then exercise my judgement and act on that," came the reply. The prophet raised his hands and said, "Praise be to Allah who guides His Messenger as He pleases".

This *Hadith* shows not only that the Holy Prophet approved of the exercise of judgement but also that his companions were well aware of the principles, and that *Ijtihad* was freely resorted to by his followers, when necessary, even in the Prophet's lifetime.

Fourth Source

The fourth source of Islamic law is *Ijma.* The word *Ijma* is derived from *jams* which means collecting or gathering together, and *Ijma* carries the double significance of composing and settling a thing which has been unsettled and hence determining and resolving upon an affair, and of agreeing or uniting in opinion. In the terminology of the Muslim jurists, *Ijma,* means a consensus of opinion of the Mujtahids, or an agreement of the Muslim jurists, of a particular age on a point of law. *Ijma,* however, is not an independent source of law; it is only *Ijtihad* on a wider basis and like *Ijtihad,* it is always open to revision.

In the second century of the *Hejira* arose the famous schools of the great jurists who codified the Islamic law according to the needs of the time; and this codification became, the chief basis of Islamic law at that time. However, owing to the degeneration that presently set in the Muslim society (in consequence of which it could not produce jurists of the calibre of the famous four *Imams),* the community as a whole began to believe that the codification, as done by those great *Imams,* was final; and that there was no scope for further *Ijtihad* in *Shariat.* Whatever may be the justification, this belief was nevertheless contrary to the very teachings of Islam. Since the Islamic laws are to be derived from the Quran which is regarded as a universal guide for all time, it is inevitable that *Ijtihad* should continue to be exercised. It is, therefore, a mistake to suppose that the door of *Ijtihad* was closed after the four *Imams.* It has already been shown that the Quran and the *Hadith* have both directions to the effect that the Muslim world should continue to exercise its judgement in making laws itself. Since the ultimate test of the correctness of *Hadith* is the Quran itself, the conclusion is evident that Islam allows independence of thought, subject only to one thing—that the principles laid down in the Quran are not contravened.

It will thus be seen that the Muslim community possesses the partial and restricted right of law-making. It is this restriction imposed upon the framers of law in an Islamic State which has created a world of difference between this state and all other states. The beauty of the Quranic principles is that they, being of divine in origin, are equally applicable to the whole mankind, irrespective of a person's status, position, colour, race, sex, language or nationality. If a thing is declared legal, it is legal for all in any shape or form. There are to be no exceptions; and even if they are allowed, they are allowed for all under certain conditions and circumstances. We can, therefore, conclude that owing to the restricted right of legislation entrusted to the most learned scholars among the Muslim community, nobody is regarded as a legislator (in the modern sense of the word) in an Islamic State. The authority or authorities in such a state can only be regarded as the executor.

The Fraternity

In accordance with the famous verse of the Holy Quran "The believers are but a single brotherhood". The first characteristic of the Islamic state is fraternity. This verse asserts that Muslims, whatever, be their country, race, colour, or language, are members of a single brotherhood. Among the believers white and black, rich and poor, master and servant, Arab and non-Arab, stand together and enjoy equal rights and bear equal responsibilities in running the state. Such is the force of Islamic brotherhood that even blood relationship counts for nothing. An unbeliever, even if connected with a believer by blood ties, falls into a totally different category of citizenship. As regards the division of the Believers into nations and tribes, the Holy Quran says, "We made you into nations and tribes so that you may recognize each other. Verily the most honoured of you with Allah is he who is the most righteous of you" (XLIX). This verse emphasises that all regional and tribal distinctions are merely for the sake of convenience. Neither can they form the basis for the classification of rights of status of human beings nor should the separation or fusion of nationalities depend upon them. Among the Believers if any distinction is to be made at all, it should be on the basis of *Tuqwa* or piety. The flowering of Islamic fraternity perhaps, reached its climax on the occasion of *Hijrat* when the prophet knitted one *Mohajir* and one *Ansar* together in the brotherhood of Islam and they both lived under the same roof as brothers.

The Sovereignty

Since sovereignty in an Islamic State is restricted to the four corners of the *Shariah,* whose principles are universal and equally applicable to all, the obvious resultant characteristic of such a state is equality. It is, however, a mistaken notion that Islam sanctions absolute equality among its votaries. Absolute equality is denied by nature, as no two persons are equal in every respect. Any amount of effort on the part of a state to equalise the mental faculties or even physical gifts of different persons will prove fruitless. Consequently, a well-known verse of the Quran says: "Verily, We have given preference to some over others". However, the question arises, "What is the concept of equality in Islam"? It means equality before law and in matters of civic rights and obligations to the state. Above all, it means affording of equal opportunities to all, irrespective of caste, colour, race or birth; it also connotes social equality, a principle which even some of the most progressive and democratic states in the world have not been able to enthrone even in the present age. Only merit, character and devotion to the cause of Islam should enable a person to occupy the highest position in the state. A person's worth should not be judged by birth, but by efficiency, character and services to the cause of Islam.

The Liberty

The third characteristic of an Islamic State is liberty, which in its true perspective was, for the first time, presented by Islam to humanity. The greatest character of individual liberty is involved in that very *'Kalimah'*. "There is no god but one God" excluded all other authority but that of God. A Muslim is free as he is not required to obey any other authority, but that of God. In other words, this would mean that he is only free within the limits, prescribd by the *Shariah*. None can encroach upon the rights of others, but at the same time can feel free within his or her own rights. Freedom of expression and liberty of conscience are the two cornerstones of Islamic polity. Even an ordinary citizen of the state can criticise the highest in the state and call him to account. However, licence in the name of liberty is not allowed; none enjoys the right of slandering people or to make fun of the authorities. It is, however, the obligation of the Islamic State not to deprive any citizen of the liberty Islam confers upon him without proving his crime in the court of law and without giving him full opportunity and facilities for his defence.

The Justice

The fourth characteristic of an Islamic State is justice. Justice in an Islamic State, should be impartial and no respector of persons, whether high or low, prince or peasant, white or black, Muslim or non-Muslim. The Quran enjoins upon Muslims to decide a case on the basis of equality, justice and upright testimony. As such, the entire Muslim community is to be held responsible for the administration of justice. The following verses of the Holy Quran sum up the conception of justice in an Islamic State: "O ye who believe be (firm) maintainers of justice, bearers of witness for Allah's sake, even though it be against your own selves, or your parents or your kins and whether it be against rich or poor; for Allah can best protect both. Follow not the lusts (of your hearts), lest ye swerve; and if ye distort (justice) or decline to do justice, verily Allah is well-acquainted with all that ye do". (IV: 135). "If (O Muhammad;) thou judges concerning the affairs of non-Muslims, judge in equity between them (however hostile may be the attitude towards thee). For Allah loveth those who judge in equity", (V: 45). Thus the Holy Quran has emphasised again and again that however hostile, mischievous or cruel may be the person with whom the authorities have to deal, it is not permissible for them to deviate even slightly from the path of justice. In the light of the above Quranic injunctions, it becomes incumbent upon the head of the state to provide free impartial justice to all irrespective of caste, creed, colour, nationality, race, status or sex.

According to Islamic notions, the head of the Islamic State has a two-fold judicial function, one positive and the other negative. His positive functions related to the establishment of peace in the state, maintenance of concord among the various sections of the people and the protection of the weak against the strong. His negative functions concern punishment of the evil-doer and the restitution of the rights of the injured. For the dispensation of justice, the head of the state has to appoint *Qadis,* well versed in *Shariah law.* God-fearing and of irreproachable character and sterling piety. The *Qadis* who apply divine law, consider themselves responsible not only to the head of the state but also to God Almighty and, as such, dispense justice equitably and speedily. Since the *Qadis'* court is regarded as God's court, no preferential treatment is to be given even to the highest in the state. "The King can do no wrong", does not hold good in an Islamic State so far as the dispensation of justice is concerned. No one can claim exemption from appearance in the court or even a preferential seat in the court. Recording of deposition of influential persons through commission is not allowed by Islamic law. The Islamic law lays down easy procedure for the conduct of cases and cheap and speedy justice is to be meted out to rich and poor alike free of cost. However, Islamic State lays greater emphasis on the prevention of crimes than on punishing the culprits after the offences are committed. Seeking legal opinion from well-known scholars has been in vogue since the very inception of Islam. The authorities allowed learned scholars to give free and legal advice to all and sundry. This institution enabled the state to assume that every citizen know the law, for it gives an equal opportunity to every person to know such legal details which he or she did not already know. Often *Qadis* who were not quite sure about some legal point, referred the case to *Mufti* and took a *Fatwa* from him.

Dual Responsibility

The fifth characteristic feature of the Islamic State is that everyone from the Caliph to an ordinary citizen is doubly reponsible, viz., to God and to some sort of earthly authority. The fear of God and the punishment in the hereafter being common to all, the people are responsible to the head of the state, who, in turn, is himself responsible to the former. Hence, there is a double check upon the actions of all the citizens in an Islamic State. In public, they do not commit any act of omission or commission for the fear of the state officials, in private, they also abstain from committing any wrong as they are conscious of the presence of Almighty. Thus, the dichotomy of distinction between the public and private life of a citizen in an Islamic State disappears altogether. The absence of the fear of God is the weakest point in all modern states, particularly in a communist state, where people, devoid of moral conscience, as they are, can commit any wrong, unnoticed by the state officials; whereas people in an Islamic State dare not do any such act of omission or commission as they are conscious of the fact that their God is having a vigilant eye over them and they shall not escape punishment.

In accordance with a verse of the Quran "We created believers" and unbelievers, the population in an Islamic State is divided between believers and unbelievers. Among the believers, there are two kinds: first those who believe in all the revealed religions and their prophets and also in Islam as the last religion and Prophet Muhammad (peace be upon him); and, secondly, those who believe in their own revealed books and prophets, but not in Islam or its Prophet Muhammad (peace be upon him). Since the Islamic State is an ideological state, it is but natural that its administration should primarily be entrusted to those who believe in its ideology and agree to sacrifice their all in running the state and making it a success. In order to defend the frontiers of the Islamic State and to promote the cause of its ideology, military service is made compulsory upon all the able-bodied Muslims without any exception; in return, they are guaranteed maintenance allowance from the state. The second group of believers, viz., the followers of the revealed books who believe in the existence of the God but do not believe in Islam or its ideology when such people agree to live within the jurisdiction of an Islamic State, their relations are guided in accordance with the famous verse of the Quran, "No compulsion in matters of faith". The Islamic State regards them as *Zimmis* or its own responsibility; and guarantees them full liberty of conscience protection of property, life and freedom of religious belief. Nay, it goes one step further and provides full scope for the growth of their culture and traditions and the administration of their civil affairs in accordance with their own religious laws. An Islamic State does not believe in forcing its own culture and traditions on others or in adopting coercive measures to get the culture of the *Zimmis* submerged into that of the Muslim, as it is usually seen under a nationalist disposition. As the *Zimmis* are not obliged to defend the Islamic State, they are required to pay a small tax in return, known as *Jazia:* in case they offer themselves for military service, they are exempted from the tax too. No distinction is made between the Muslims and the followers of other revealed books in matters of the civic rights and the latter could qualify themselves for all offices of the state except the religious ones. Thirdly, the unbelievers are those who either do not believe in the existence of God Almighty and in the Hereafter or associate other partners with God. The followers of this Godless cult are fundamentally opposed to all the believers of God; and are at the perpetual warfare with them. Islam which believes in the establishment of peace by liberating mankind from all shackles of slavery is the worst enemy of the Godless cult. So long as this cult survives, Islam cannot flourish and will not be able to achieve its ideals; and, therefore, as a moral force, it is directly opposed to this evil force. As such, this Godless cult has been described in the Holy Quran as *fitna* (mischief) which must be rooted out from the Universe so that the faith of God may flourish.

Guiding Principles

As all the guiding principles of the Islamic State are derived from the Quran which, according to Muslim belief, is a divinely revealed book, some people assert that it (the Islamic State) is a religious institution. In reality, the Islamic State is not a religious institution in the sense of medieval Christian theocracy in which certain ecclesiastical authorities claimed for themselves the right of law-making. Others assert that the Islamic State is temporal as it is required to administer affairs which are temporal in character and not spiritual. It is, however, not temporal in the modern sense of the term, since the modern state is not guided by religion, and it usually lacks moral conscience and a moral basis for administration and application of its laws. Since the fundamental ingredients of an Islamic State are derived from the Quran, it becomes a little difficult to separate religion from temporal function. And since its chief function is to protect Islam and to promote its cause, both within and without and to administer both religious and temporal affairs. In accordance with the Quran and the *Sunnah,* this state may be regarded as both religious as well as temporal. It should, however, be made clear that the state religion of Islamic State must be Islam for whose protection and maintenance, it is called into existence and continues to exist.

It will be a falacy to compare the Islamic State with any modern state, as it fundamentally differs from all of them and stands as a class by itself. Since it is based on Quranic principles and has a definite mission to perform, it may be regarded as an ideological state. It may, however, be termed as theo-democracy, for, in such a state, under the sovereignty and paramountcy of God, a limited popular sovereignty has been conferred on the believers.

Since the Islamic State encompasses both the religious and the temporal spheres, and come into existence through a contract between the (elected) *Ameer* and the general *Ummah* (community), it is nothing if not a devise to fulfil the aspirations of the individuals themselves collectively and, to a certain extent, individually. The state is thus not marked by any suicidal controversy between the state and the individual. According to the Islamic polity, the state, the *Ameer* and the *Millat* are all animated by an ethical ideal, and it is the duty of each one of them to strive after and towards this ideal. Accordingly, the personal liberty of the individual is guaranteed to a very large extent under this system; and political power is not concentrated in the hands of one person.

Yet another feature of the Islamic State is to carry on the administration through mutual consultation. The Quran says, "those who (conduct) their affairs by mutual consultation" *(Amr a him Shura Beina Hum)*; and "(O Muhammad) consult these (i.e. in the affair. Then when thou hast taken a decision put the trust in (Him)" (Ill: 150). Thus, there should exist in an Islamic State a Majlis-i-Shura or Council consisting of representatives of the people, reflecting the total legal wisdom of the entire country. The appointment of this council is made by the *Ameer* himself from among various sections of the people; the only criteria for appointment being their intimate knowledge of the *Shariah*, their character. The Ameer-in-Council is to legislate in consultation with the *Majlis* and administer the state with their consent. Since the final authority is the Quran and the *Sunnah*, pleas should be based on, and in accordance with them. The decision is to be unanimous and the *Shura* feels collective responsibility.

The Islamic State is noted for separation of powers. Although the *Qadis* are to be appointed by the *Ameer*, the highest executive head in the state, in consultation with Shura, yet judiciary is completely independent of the Executive. The fact that *Qadi* can accept a suit against the very person of the *Ameer* without any previous permission and can try him in an open court—this feature of Islamic judiciary is an index to the independence of judiciary in an Islamic State. Nor is the *Ameer* exempted from personal appearance or to be given any preferential seat, in the court. The question of taking deposition of great and prominent personalities by means of commission does not arise in an Islamic State.

The Centralization

Another feature of the Islamic State is centralization in matters of legislation. The nature of the Islamic state which is based on

Quranic principles, demands that there should be uniformity in legislation. It is only the Central Legislative Assembly which could legislate in connection with matter touching the religious aspects of life or the common problems of the state for instance, foreign policy, taxation, justice and constitution. However, in matters of temporal administration, much can be left with the provincial authorities. In case of provincial revenues and expenditure, the provincial treasuries can work as independent units; the Provincial *Baitul Mal* is to receive and disburse the amounts realized. In early Islam too, *Zakat* realized from a certain place was used to be spent on the needs of the local people; balance, if any, in the Provincial Treasury used to be deposited with the Central Treasury, whereas deficit, if any, in the Provincial Treasury met from the Central *Baitul Mal*. The whole empire is to be divided into provincial units. The Governors, appointed by the Caliph in consultation with the *Shura* and the local people, could be transferred and dismissed from their posts.

The economic policy of the Islamic State is to be based on some positive injunctions in the Quran. It lays down, "So that the wealth should not circulate only among the rich from among you". Hence, the distribution of wealth among all classes of believers has been emphasised by the institution of property tax, known as *Zakat*, to the extent of 2½ per cent on surplus property, each hoard as well as commercial capital; and restrictions on the process of testamentary disposition, laws of inheritance and the prohibition of usuary. The Islamic State believes in the imposition of minimum taxation and the provision of maximum comforts for the people. The believers who are supposed to pay less than the *Zimnis* could, however, be required to pay all their surplus wealth to the state in case of emergency. Since the believers have to stake their lives and property for the defence and the maintenance of the state, they are secured due provision for their food, shelter and other necessities of life. Islamic State does not believe in class war nor does it undertake a complete socialization or democrative management of the basic instruments of production and distribution. It does allow the individuals to acquire private property so that their incentive may not be lost; but, on the other hand, it does not allow the concentration of wealth into few hands in order to perpetuate capitalism in its naked form. The economic system in an Islamic State thus stands midway between the two antagonistic systems in the present world capitalism and communism.

The objective of the Islamic State is to "establish prayer and pay *Zakat;* and enjoin good upon the people and to restrain them from committing wrong "(XXII: 41). The Quran also refers to Muslims as the best people sent down to Universe in order to do good and prevent others from committing wrong. These verses are very significant and sum up the chief objectives of the Islamic State regarding the duties of the Muslims. The first part of the first verse relates to prayers and *Zakat* which enable Muslims to practice in actual life the principle of equality, liberty, fraternity, justice and obedience to the *Imam.* The first part of the second verse regard the Muslims as the best people and as such incapable of doing wrong. They are, therefore, required to persuade others to do good as also restrain them from committing wrong. This express Quranic injunction entails enormous responsibilities upon the head of the state as well as its people. This obligates the state not only to carry out these orders within its own jurisdiction but also beyond it if occasion arose.

It is, thus, that the Islamic State is to be at perpetual war with forces of tyranny, wickedness, and godlessness. In order to emancipate mankind from bondage, whether physical or intellectual, the Islamic State is required to wage *Jihad.* But *Jihad* or holy war is not to be fought for personal aggrandisement or national glorification. It is to be waged only for the establishment of the rule of God and for ending man's tyranny over man and man's injustice to, and man's inhumanity to man.

The first Islamic State was set up by the Holy Prophet (peace be upon him) in the city of Yathrib, later named Medina-tun-Nabi, which ultimately became shortened into Medina. This should be our model, because it is our belief that whatever the Holy Prophet (peace be upon him) did was perfect as he was not only a living embodiment of the Holy Quran but also acted under Divine guidance through revelations.

The State came into existence after the *Hijrah* from Makkah, but before that the Holy Prophet had entered into a compact with the leaders of *Banu Aws* and *Banu Khazraj,* two leading tribes of

Yathrib who had embraced Islam and invited him to shift to their town. This pact was made at a place called Aqaba and was in the nature of a bilateral treaty under which the Medinites on their part, accepted the Holy Prophet (peace be upon him) as their religious and political leader and undertook to protect him from all his enemies, and in particularly the *Quraish*, and the Holy Prophet (peace be upon him), on his part, bound himself never to forsake them or to return to Makkah. The words used translated into English read:

> "Nay in life and death I am with you and you are with me. I will fight whom you fight and I will make peace with whom you make peace."

The formula adopted for the oath of allegiance taken by the Medinites at the hands of the Holy Prophet (peace be upon him) was to the following effect:

> "We pledge that we will hear and obey you, in times of our distress and in times of our plenty and shall stand by you whatever may befall us of happiness and of anguish, and that we will speak the truth wherever we be not fearing the censure of the censurers in the path of Allah." *(Bayat-i-Aqaba Thani).*

City of the Prophet

The conditions prevailing at Medina at that time were one of utter chaos. Not only was there no administrative machinery to bind the tribes together but they were actually weary of their traditions of unending tribal wars. *Banu Aws* and *Banu Khazraj* were divided into twelve clans and the Jews into ten and each clan was fully autonomous. The first task, therefore, was to teach the new converts the principles of the new faith. Hence, the first thing undertaken was to construct a mosque where the community could be collected and taught the practical lessons of fraternity, equality, liberty and justice. Thus, the new community was welded into a disciplined group with a common ideology.

Having got the followers together, the Holy Prophet (peace be upon him) gave practical shape to the injunction of the Holy Quran that "the believers are but a single brotherhood, so make peace and reconciliation between your (contending) brothers and fear God that ye may receive mercy" (XLIX: 10) by obliterating the distinction between *Quraish, Aws* and *Khazraj* and pairing them together as brothers in Islam. Each of the 150 *Muhajirs* adopted by an *Ansar* as a brother with whom he was even agreeable to share his wealth but, the *Muhajirs,* not wishing to be a burden on their hosts, were content to engage themselves in various trades with the help of their *Ansar* brothers and this brought prosperity to them and really integrated themselves with the *Ansars.*

After organising his followers into a social polity the Holy Prophet (peace be upon him) applied his mind to the essential task of providing protection to the newly formed community from the *Quraish* who were still bent upon destroying the Muslims. To meet this external threat it was found necessary first to consolidate the position of the community within Medina itself which was then in habited by a large number of Jews also. The hand of friendship was extended to them and treaties of mutual security and defence were entered into guaranteeing them equal civil rights, freedom of religion and mutual protection against external aggression in return for their recognition of the Holy Prophet (peace be upon him) as the paramount executive, military and judicial authority. The Jews willingly accepted this condition and became as a body the allies of the Muslims and thus the city state of Medina came into existence as a political entity.

The Holy Prophet (peace be upon him) was not content to leave all this in a nebulous state; so a charter was drawn up meticulously recording the terms of agreement and the rights and obligations of the respective contracting parties. This became the constitution of Medina and is, perhaps, the first written constitution to be drawn up in the world. It was drawn up in two parts. The first part consisted of 23 articles dealing with matters concerning the *Muhajirs* and *Ansars* and those who were "attached to them and crusaded with them", while the second part dealt with the relationship between the Muslims and the Jews.

The basic concept of this charter was that all would accept the Holy Prophet (peace be upon him) as the Paramount Authority in all matters administrative, judicial and military, and obey his lawful orders. He was to be the commander of the combined army, the executive head of the state and the final court of appeal but not a ruler in any sense of the term as the sovereignty over the universe, according to Islam, vests in Allah alone and all without any exception are subject to His laws.

The next main concept was that the Muslims were to form a single unit of this political community, separate and distinct from the rest, and the Jews as a body were to constitute the other unit. The two together were to form a federation for the purposes of war and peace and the defence of Medina. In all other matters each federating unit was to be completely autonomous but subject to the paramountcy of the Holy Prophet (peace be upon him). Each unit was to enjoy complete freedom of religion and governed by its own laws, customs and traditions except that the practice of blood-revenge and counter-revenge was to be totally banned and no interference on the basis of kinship or tribal affinity was to be permitted in the affairs of the state, and particularly, in the administration of justice.

This compact did not extend to purely religious wars *(jehad)* but the Jews expressly undertook that they would not in any event grant protection to the *Quraish* or their allies.

So far as the Muslims were concerned the number of *Ansar* tribes was fixed at ten and the *Muhajirs* were declared to be one tribe. Each tribe was to be treated on a par with the other in respect of their rights and duties. War and peace and the administration of justice were to be matters of common or federal concern and were to be the concern of the clan, tribe or individual. This put an end to tribal anarchy and gave birth to a sense of collective responsibility. Henceforth, everyone was to be a party to peace and war and, therefore military service was compulsory for all. In the same way, all were collectively responsible to see that no one dared harm or encroach upon the rights of others and that everyone, according to the teachings of the Holy Quran, acted with absolute fairness, free from any bias or partiality, fear and favour, even though it be against one's own interest or the interest of one's parents, kinsmen or tribesmen (IV: I 35). Tribal affiliation was recognised only to the extent that the tribe was saddled with the responsibility of ransoming its own captives from the enemy and the payment of a debt was made obligatory on the debtors' kinsmen as well.

The Protection

The right to grant protection was to be enjoyed by everyone, high or low, and the pledge given even by the lowliest was to be binding on the entire community but no Muslim was entitled to grant protection to a *Quraish* to Makkah or to prevent anyone from taking revenge from such a *Quraish* for the cruelties perpetrated by them upon the Muslims in Makkah.

If to these we add that the entire Muslim community was already firmly pledged to believe in one God, accept His sovereignty over the universe, follow His Commandments as revealed to the Holy Prophet (peace be upon him) and to obey the latter's lawful commands, then the pattern that emerges is of a community organised on the basis of the cherished principles of equality, liberty and fraternity in the real sense.

The main characteristics of this state that can be gathered from the above are:

— That it was an institution established through a democratic process namely, the free will and accord of the people desiring to form the same and to accept the Holy Prophet (peace be upon him) as the paramount authority (Pledge of Aqaba Thani and Agreement with the Jews).

— That it was a constitutional organisation set up under a written charter (Charter of Medina).

— That it was a federal structure comprising two communities, the Muslims and non-Muslims, and not two territories.

— That it was an ideological state based on the concepts and fundamental principles embodied in the Holy Quran.

What these fundamental principles are is well-known not only to every Muslim but also to the entire world, for the simple reason that Islam is a living force and a world order. Although the fundamental principles of Islam are universally known, yet it would not be out of place to recount them here.

Concept of Sovereignty: The concept of human sovereignty is completely absent from the political philosophy of Islam. The Holy Quran proclaims: "It is only for Allah to command" (XII: 40) and "to Allah belongeth the dominion of the heavens and the earth (II: 107). This has been repeated often in the Holy Quran: "To Allah alone belongeth the dominion of the heavens and the earth and all lies between" (V: 17); Knowest thou not that Allah hath power over all things" (II: 106). Next to Allah sovereign power resides in the people, as in respect of Adam. Allah announced to the angles that He is going to create a *Kholifa* on the earth (II: 30). Again Allah said: "Oh David, We did indeed make thee a *Khalifa* on earth—so judge thou between men in truth and justice" (XXXVIII: 27). This introduces the concept of *'Niabat-i-Ilahi'* and from this flow the following consequences:

- That next to Allah the sovereign power resides in the people. As Sir Abdur Rahim put it in his book on *'Islamic Jurisprudence'* (p. 62), Islamic law does not admit of "the sovereign power being dissociated from the people howsoever they might choose to exercise it".
- That all are equal before the law.
- That the exercise of power is a trust.
- That power has to be exercised in accordance with the Commandments of Allah and in His name.
- That everyone vested with power is accountable for his actions.
- That no one is above the law; none not even the *Khalifa,* enjoys any immunity.

This puts an end to the concept of divine origin of kings hithertofore adopted by the Hindus, the Pharoahs of Egypt, the Sassanians of Iran and the Christians of Europe. Under this concept, the sovereign was the source of law and it was religious duty to obey his commands; but under the Islamic system, the king was not the source of law and, therefore, not above the law.

Fundamental Principles

Liberty : The Principle of *Tauhid* is the fundamental principle of Islam and the *Kalima-i-Tauhid* is the greatest charter of individual liberty. When a Muslim declares that "there is no god but one God", he at once excludes all other authority but that of God, because this demands "loyalty to God and not to thrones" as

Allama Iqbal puts it *'Lectures on the Reconstruction of Religious Thoughts'* (p. 147). This also implies that in Islam there is no room for kingship or dictatorship. There is no ruler and no ruled. Everyone is *free* within the limits of the divine law. Freedom of expression and liberty of conscience are the cornerstones of Islamic polity and even an ordinary citizen could differ from the opinion of the Holy Prophet (peace be upon him) himself and voice his own views. Liberty did not, however, mean anarchy, for one could encroach upon the rights of others or refuse to obey those in authority or revolt if those in authority were acting within the limits of the divine law. Allah ordains:

> "Oh ye who believe: Obey Allah and obey the Apostle and those charged with authority from amongst you. If ye differ in anything among yourselves, refer it to Allah and His Apostle." (IV: 59).

Justice: Islam seeks to set up a just society and, therefore, attaches the highest importance to justice, equity and fair dealing. The Holy Quran says:

> "Oh ye who believe; stand out firmly for justice, as witnesses to Allah, even as against yourselves or your parents or your kin and whether it be against the rich, or poor; for Allah can best protect both. Follow not the lusts of your heart lest ye swerve. If ye distort justice or decline to do justice, verily Allah is well acquainted with all that ye do." (IV: I 35).

Justice is placed next to piety (V: 9). God is also the fountainhead of justice and the doing of justice is a religious duty. The entire community is also made responsible for seeing that none dares harm or encroach upon the rights of others. The entire community was, therefore, involved in the administration of justice. There was no immunity from the law for anyone. The Holy Prophet (peace be upon him) himself never claimed any such immunity. Indeed in his last *Khutba* at the *Hajja-tul-Wida* he publicly declared that if he owed anything to anyone or had deprived anyone of his property or had done any harm to anyone's life or reputation, he was present there to pay his legal dues or recompense any such claimant as he was bound to do under the law. It is reported that of the whole assembly only one person stood up and claimed a few *dirhems* which were promptly paid.

Two important constitutional principles are founded on this:

(i) that everyone is equal before the law and enjoys equal opportunities; and

(ii) that in an Islamic State even the head of the state can be sued not only as a private individual but also in respect of his public acts. The rule of law was a reality under such a system and this is what led German historian Von Hammer to say that under the Islamic system the "law rules through the utterance of justice and the power of the governor carries out the utterance of it" quoted by Syed Ameer Ali in *"A Short History of the Saracens"* (p. 62).

Another consequence of such strict adherence to justice was that all appointments to state offices were made only on the basis of merit and the seeking of office was considered to be a disqualification.

The Holy Prophet (peace be upon him) was always recognised as a truthful, honest and absolutely impartial person, so much so that even non-Muslims used to bring their disputes to him for decision, yet he himself never claimed infallibility. He did not hesitate to point out that he decided the cases brought him on the evidence adduced and that, like any other human being, he was liable to *err* in forming his judgement. Error on his part was, however, unthinkable, because whenever he was in doubt he received a revelation giving him the solution of his doubts. The classical instances of such revelations are the verses of *Surah Nisa* dealing with the inheritance of female heirs and a *Kalalah* (issueless person), and the verse of *Surah Nur* dealing with the punishment for adultery and false imputation of unchastity against a female.

The Charter

Under the Charter of Medina, the prophet was the court of final appeal but the services of the savants of Medina, chosen from amongst the senior companions, were also utilised for acting as a court of first instance. In the provinces, however, the judicial power was at first vested in the governors but later the practice grew up of appointing, in addition, a separate *Qazi* as an independent functionary.

The Holy Prophet (peace be upon him) had in his lifetime also introduced a department of *'Al-Mazalim'*, which had a wide and general jurisdiction both correctional and remedial in nature. Under this, persons doing wrong to each other could be compelled to do mutual justice and even litigants could be restrained from falsely refuting just claims by inspiring awe into them. This was the basis on which the criminal jurisdiction later developed.

The procedure was naturally simple but even at that early stage the rules had been laid down that parties must be present at the time of the hearing of the disputes, that the burden of proof lay upon the party asserting a claim and the defendant had to deny the claim on oath. If he did so, then the plaintiff was called upon to adduce his evidence; but if the defendant refused to take the oath, the case could be decreed against him straightaway. The number of witnesses required was usually more than one. In certain cases, however, the number was prescribed in the Holy Quran as in the case of marriage, divorce, theft, imputation of unchastity and adultery.

Concept of Fraternity: Fraternity was the fourth fundamental principle embodied in the Holy Quran on which was based the ideological State of Medina set up by the Holy Prophet (peace be upon him). "The believers are but a single brotherhood" (XLIX:10), declares the Holy Quran and then describes them as "friends and protectors of one another" (VIII: 72), with the warning that unless they protect each other there will be "tumult and oppression on earth" (VIII: 73).

The Holy Prophet (peace be upon him) has explained this concept thus: "The *Ummat* (Community) is a single fold in which each is a shepherd unto the other". This, at once, eliminates all differences and distinctions on the basis of caste, colour, creed, race or birth. All—whether black or white, master or slave, rich or poor, Arab or non-Arab—stand on the same footing and equally share the responsibility of running the affairs of the state. The Holy Prophet (peace be upon him) himself removed any possibility of doubt or misconception with regard to this when he declared in his last Sermon at the *Hajja-tul-Wida:*

> "Oh people, listen and obey, even though a mangled Abyssinian slave is appointed your *Amir* provided he executes the Book of Allah among you."

This principle of egalitarianism is not only the foundation of the body-politic of Islam but also its greatest strength. It is on this principle that the *Muhajirs* and the *Ansars* were united together in a bond that was stronger than blood relationship and enabled the Muslims to grow from strength to strength.

Another political consequence which flows from this principle is that in an Islamic State the non-believers form a separate category but not necessarily an inferior one. They were guaranteed protection of property, life and honour, granted freedom of religion and liberty of conscience and assured of non-interference with their culture and traditions or their religious laws. Religious tolerance is inbuilt in the teachings of the Holy Quran and the traditions of Islam. Had it been otherwise, there would have been no Jews left in Asia Minor or Hindus in India or Christians in Spain.

The non-Muslim citizens were called *'zimmis'*. They enjoyed the same rights as the Muslim citizens except that they were exempt from participation in any religious war *(jehad)* and the payment of poor tax *(Zakat)* but they paid a special tax called *jaztyah,* for the protection given to them. Their constitutional position can be best gathered from the following declaration made by Hazrat Ali:

> "Their life is my life, their blood is my blood and their honour is my honour. See that none ill-treats them, for they are your *'zimma'*, your responsibility from God."

The Democracy

Democracy comes next. The affairs of the state were not only required to be regulated in accordance with the laws of the Holy Quran but had also to be decided by mutual consent. The Holy Prophet (peace be upon him) himself was advised by Allah to "consult them (the believers) in all matters of administration and when thou art resolved, then put thy trust in Allah" (III: 159). This verse and verse 38 of *Surah Al-Shoora* lay down the basic principle which should guide the Muslims in the transaction of their national affairs. This principle was followed by the Holy Prophet (peace be upon him) in all matters not covered by a revelation and he never sought to impose his will upon anyone. It is reported in the *'Fatuhul Bari'* (Vol. 7) that on the occasion of making preparations for the Battle of Ohud there was a difference of opinion between the Muslims on the strategy to be adopted. The Holy Prophet (peace be upon him) accepted to follow the majority view that the Muslims should go out and give battle instead of defending Medina from within.

The Accountability

Last but not least, comes the concept of accountability. Authority or power to rule, according to Islam, is a trust—*'Amanat'*—of the people and not the birth right of anyone. The Quran says: "Verily Allah commands you to give over the trusts to those entitled to them and that when you judge between men, you judge with justice" (IV: 58). The nature of this trust is later indicated thus: "Establish regular prayer, pay *Zakat,* enjoin good upon the people and restrain them from doing wrong" (XXII: 41). These are the objectives of an Islamic State, to achieve which those placed in power or authority must strive. This concept of trust automatically brings in that of accountability, because a trustee is in law liable to account. Under the Islamic system this liability extends to rendering account not only to the people who appoint him but also to God as it is also a Quranic injunction.

In the light of these principles, therefore, the final picture that emerges of this first Islamic State is that it is an ideological state set up by the free will of the people in a constitutional manner and following the democrative principle of decision-making in which every citizen has an equal right to participate. Governance in this state is a trust which has to be discharged with due regard to the principles of justice, equality, liberty and fraternity for the welfare of the entire community and in such a manner that the basic needs of all are satisfied and everyone enjoys equality of opportunity without distinction of race, caste, creed, colour, faith, birth or rank.

This was a unique welfare state for which no parallel can be found in the history of the world. In this state, the Government was really a social service designed for evolving a polity based on social justice under which there was no difference between even the head of the state and an ordinary citizen. They observed same laws, had the same obligations and shared the same simple and frugal life. It would be futile to compare this state with the modern states because it differs fundamentally from all of them. The people in it are not confined to any territory nor is sovereignty vested in any human agency. "Islam is non-territorial in its character," says Allama Iqbal, "and its aim is to furnish a model for the final combination of humanity". The entire *Ummat* is a nation no matter where located and that is why as the *Ummat* increased territorial limits of the state also expanded. The state was divided into provinces for administrative reasons but Medina remained the capital. The concept of state sovereignty is non-existent as sovereignty in Islam vests in Allah. Similarly, the concept of government is also different because government is a trust from the people and has to be exercised in accordance with law and justice for the welfare of the people. Above all, in this ideological state the bifurcation of the unity of man into temporal and spiritual is done away with. The Christian doctrine of "give unto Caesar what is Caesar's and unto God what is God's" is replaced by the thesis propounded by the Holy Prophet (peace be upon him) that "the whole earth is a Mosque". In Islam, the Church and the state constitute one indissoluble whole and, until the very essence of Islam passes away, this unity cannot be relaxed. The state, according to Islam, is only an effort to realise the spiritual in a human organisation, as Allama Iqbal maintains and it is not an end in itself but only a means to an end.

This was the model given us by the Holy Prophet (peace be upon him) himself and after him the next model for us is the structure of the state prevailing during the period of the *Khulafa-i-Rashi*-deen. The basic structure, of course, remained the same but certain changes had to be introduced to meet the changed circumstances as a result of the expansion of the state for beyond the sandy dunes of Arabia to Palestine, Syria, Iraq, Egypt and even further. The first elated to the selection of a *Khalifa*. According to a *Hadith* (confirmed by both *Bokhari* and *Muslim),* the Holy Prophet reported to have said:

> "The affairs of the state of the Bani Israel used to be in the hands of their prophets and when one prophet died another succeeded him; but since after me there is no other prophet so in the near future there will be *Khalifas* after me and many of them". When asked if he would like to give any instructions about them, he said: "Take the oath of allegiance at the hands of him who is chosen as the first (the most fit), by the *Jamhoor* (People)."

The method suggested by the Holy Prophet (peace be upon him) was, thus, the democrative method of election by the people. But since the *Khalifa* had to be a person of undisputably high qualifications, the method adopted for the selection of the first *Khalifa* was first to get the approval of the council of senior Companions of the Holy Prophet (peace be upon him) and then to put him up for election by the entire community. In the council, the *Ansars* wanted the *Khalifa* to be chosen from amongst them but after Hazrat Umar pointed out that the community was one and the fittest person is that community was Abu Bakr (the senior most and most venerated among the Companions of the Holy Prophet whom he himself had in his lifetime during his last illness, assigned the task of leading the congregational prayers), the proposal of the *Ansars* was withdrawn. Thereafter, Hazrat Umar was the first to take the oath of allegiance at the hands of Hazrat Abu Bakr. He was followed by Abdu Obaidah, the *Ansar* nominee, and the rest of the council. On the next day, the entire community assembled in the mosque at Medina, and unanimously approved the selection with acclamation and took the oath of allegiance. It should be noticed that the method very closely approximates to the modern method of nomination and election, with a salutary variation of nomination by a high-powered select committee of elders. Since the seeking of office was a disqualification, it was necessary that knowledgeable persons should select a man of unimpeachable character and unquestionable capability.

Hazrat Abu Bakr, in turn, during his last illness, proposed the name of Hazrat Umar before the council of prominent Companions.

When he found that they unanimously agreed, he convened a general assembly of the people and made known the unanimous view of the prominent Companions. This, too, was accepted with acclamation and all the people present took the oath of allegiance.

Hazrat Umar was stabbed by a slave of Mughaira bin Sha'aba and it was felt that he might not survive; he was accordingly approached by the prominent Companions to nominate his successor. He, however, refused to do so. It was actually suggested that he may consider his son, who was duly qualified, as his successor. He replied that he had no power to do so but if he had the power he would have nominated Salim, a manumitted slave, who was no longer alive. He, however, set up a council of regency consisting of the six most important Companions (including his son) and asked them to select one from amongst themselves (but not his son) within three days of his death. The choice fell upon Hazrat Usman and the people again accepted him unanimously. By this time, the state had spread beyond Arabia and so the oath of allegiance was also taken in each province in the presence of governors.

Hazrat Usman was murdered by a rebel group and Hazrat Ali was selected as *Khalifa* by the people of Medina, including the rebel group, but the principle of unanimity was unfortunately lacking in his case. There was difference of opinion even among the prominent Companions. The provinces of Syria and Iraq, which were governed by Muawiah, did not accept his *Khilafat.* This led to war with the Iraqis and opened the floodgates of dissension. The Iraqis were defeated and forced to accept the *Khilafat.* Some well-meaning Companions then attempted to bring about a reconciliation but their attempts were thwarted by the assassination of Hazrat Ali. On his death-bed Hazrat Ali refused to nominate his son, Hasan, as the next *Khalifa* but, unlike Hazrat Umar, he did not debar him from being elected. The result was that Imam Hasan was, in fact, elected by the people. Muawiah, who had earlier refused to take the oath of allegiance to Hazrat Ali, did not accept the *Khilafat* of Hasan as well and proclaimed himself the *Khalifa.* After a brief tussle Hasan abdicated in the interest of general peace, but was soon poisoned to death. Muawiah, thereupon became the undisputed ruler of the entire Muslim empire. By nominating his son, Yazid, as the next *Khalifa* during his lifetime he laid the foundations of the Umayyed dynasty. Yazid succeeded his father and imposed his *Khilafat* by force. His armies sacked Medina, laid sieze to Makkah and brutally murdered Imam Husain, the second son of Hazrat Ali, who had been invited by the treacherous Kufans to deliver them from unjust rule of Yazid. The Umayyed dynasty ruled from Damascus till A.D. 749 when they were supplanted by the Abbasids.

It will be futile to delve any further into the tragic history of the succeeding periods as the republican era of Islam ended with Hazrat Ali, except to point that the rulers of the Umayyed and Abbasid periods did not adopt the title of King nor was the hereditary principle of kingship ever fully accepted. Although each nominated his successor from amongst the members of his family the rule of primogeiture was not strictly adhered to. Of the fourteen rulers of the Umayyed dynasty only four had their sons as successors. The practice was to nominate the eldest and fittest member of the royal family.

The principle of election of the *Khalifa* was adhered to right up to the days of the Ottomans even though it had been reduced to mere formality. The Ottomans, even though they had adopted the title of *Sultan,* preserved the idea of free election. Each new Sultan was solemnly elected by the *Ulema* and divines of Constantinople, who claimed to act in the capacity of representatives of the *Ummat.* Thus theoretically, at least, the broad characteristics of free election were all along maintained till the Turks, after the First World War, abolished the institution *of Khilafat.*

The conclusion that emerges from the above is that election of the head of the state is the recognised principle but since he has to be a person of high qualifications the election is preceded by a preliminary selection and nomination by a recognised body of knowledgeable persons. It is for this reason that in the early period only the prominent Companions of the Holy Prophet (peace be upon him) were considered suitable. But this was not an essential condition; had that been so Hazrat Umar would not have mentioned the name of Salim, a liberated slave in connection with this high office.

Muslim jurists like Al-Mawardi, Qazi Baidhawi and Al-Ghazali have laid down elaborately the qualifications necessary for being eligible for election to the office of *Khalifa.* He was expected to be free from physical infirmities, profoundly knowledgeable both in theology and statecraft, capable not only of leading congregational prayers but also in the field of battle, courageous and, above all, indisputably pious and dedicated to the service of the *Ummat* according to the injunctions of the Holy Quran and the *Sunnah* of the Holy Prophet (peace be upon him).

Al-Mawardi also prescribes qualifications for the electors. He suggests that they must at least be adults, literate, intelligent and of known integrity, because Islam enjoins upon them to exercise their franchise honestly, freely and intelligently in favour of the right person regardless of kinship, tribal affiliation or any other consideration. This is in no way opposed to the practice of general *Baiyat* (allegiance) on the hand of the elected *Khalifa* as the *Baiyat* follows their decision and is its manifestation. If one did not agree to accept a nominated person, he could refuse to take the oath of allegiance as Muawiah did in the case of Hazrat Ali.

After the choice of the *Khalifa,* the next important variation introduced in the model state left by the Holy Prophet (peace be upon him) was the establishment of a *Majlis-i-Shoora,* or Advisory Council for meeting the Quranic injunction to act only after consultation. Although the members of the *Shoora* were chosen by the *Khalifa* from amongst both the *Muhajirin* and *Ansars* they did not change with the *Khalifa* as the selection was based on no other consideration but merit. This made the *Shoora* a very important body, more or less of a permanent nature, which was in no way subordinate or subservient to the *Khalifa.*

The *Shoora,* it appears, could initiate proceedings for the impeachment of the *Khalifa.* S. Khuda Buksh, however, in his book 'The *Orient under the Khalifas"* (p. 268) says that "for deposing a Sovereign the people generally met in the chief mosque. Some men of position addressed the assembly when charges were formulated and made against the ruling *Khalifa* and his deposition was declared in the interest of Islam. "History does not record any account of the deposition of any *Khalifa* but the very fact that Muslim jurists unanimously accept that a *Khalifa* could be deposed again affirms the principle that the only and exclusive source of sovereignty and power in Islam was election by the assembled community".

All matters of administration had to be placed before the *Shoora* which decided by a majority of votes after full discussion. The voting was not on any party basis but each member tried to convince the others by his arguments supported by Quranic injunctions and *Hadith.* The endeavour was always to attain unanimity which was more often than not obtained because all acted with a sense of collective responsibility and with an open mind.

The *Shoora* was in effect also the legislature of Islam. No law could, of course, be made which was opposed to the Quran and the *Sunnah* or not in conformity with the principles that could be deduced therefrom but even within this limit no law-making was possible unless approved by the *Shoora* in coming to a decision the *Shoora* followed the democratic method of majority voting which was based on two *Ahadith* to the following effect: "It is incumbent on you to follow the most numerous body"; and "My followers will never agree upon what is not right". This is the principle that later developed into the doctrine of Ijma'a which is now unanimously accepted as one of the source of Islamic law. Originally, it was in fact a referendum of the entire Muslim polity; subsequently it came to be confined to the concensus of the juris-consults or *'Faqihs'* after the end of the republican era on the pretext that since the limits of the state had spread far and wide the referendum of the entire polity had become an impossibility. The learned jurists claimed to act as the representatives of the Muslim world.

Maulana Shibli Nomani maintains that under the *Majlis-i-Shoora* there was another body which discussed problems of day-to-day administration while the Shoora deliberated upon policy matters or rather dictated the policy of the *Khalifa.* Be that as it may, the importance attached to it was so great that Hazrat Umar used to say that "the institution of the *Khilafat* is void without the deliberative council (the *Shoora)*".

The third important change introduced was the complete separation of the judiciary by Hazrat Umar. Having regard to the importance Islam attached to the principle of equality before law and its insistence on absolute fairness in the administration of justice this separation of powers was considered essential. He felt this to be necessary from the very nature of things so that power should be a check to power and all power should not be concentrated in one hand. Thus, it was not Montesqueu or Hallam who conceived of the doctrine of separation of powers and the theory of checks and balances in the distribution of the powers of the state considered so necessary by present day political theorists.

In addition to the above, Hazrat Umar also set up the institution of jurisconsults called *Ifta* to advise the executive and assist the judges as well as the lay public. This body consisted of capable and trustworthy scholars of law *(Muftis)* who could give legal opinions *(Fatwas).* They were not only legal advisors of the state but also a body which gave legal aid to the lay public on the salutary principle that no one should suffer due to ignorance of law. This principle has only in the twentieth century been recognised in the Western World.

Under the *Umayyads* the *Muftis* were permitted to charge a fee for the services rendered by them. They were also permitted to represent lay clients before the judges by filing a *Tawakel Nama* and from this developed the institution of *vakils* or advocates.

Under the Ottoman Sultans the *Ifta* became a department of state with the *Mufti-i-Azam* as its head. Some idea of the importance of this official can be gathered from the fact that during the days of the Crusades, Sultan Salahuddin Ayubi sought a *Fatwa* from him permitting the killing of a non-Muslim wherever found but the *Mufti-i-Azam* refused to issue such a *Fatwa* as it was opposed to the injunctions of the Quran to the following effect:

> "And fight in the way of Allah against those who fight against you but begin no hostilities. Surely Allah loves not aggressors" (11-91).
>
> "So if they keep aloof and fight you not, and make you an offer of peace, then Allah has allowed you no way of aggression against them" (IV: 91).

Hazrat Umar also divided the administrative functions of the state into the following departments, each under a Companion of the Holy Prophet (peace be upon him) whose position could be likened to that of a Minister of State under the American system:

(i) *Bait-ul-Mal* or Treasury;

(ii) *Mahasil* or Board of Taxes and Revenue;

(iii) *Jund* or Military Department;

(iv) Educational and Religious Instructions Department;

(v) *Dar-ul-Qaza* or Judicial Department;

(vi) *Ahdas* or Police Department;

(vii) *Mazalim* or the Board of Inspection; and

(viii) *Ihtisab* or the Department of Public Censor.

The state, as already mentioned, was divided into Provinces, each headed by a Governor and a *Qazi*. The administrative set-up in the Provinces followed the same republican pattern as in the Centre and enjoyed a considerable amount of autonomy subject to the superintendence of the Centre. Hazrat Umar even gave to the Provinces the power to elect their own governors subject to confirmation by the *Khalifa*.

The sources of revenue at that time were (i) *Zakat*, (ii) *Ghanimat*, (iii) *Jaziyah*—payable by non-Muslims, (iv) *Khiraj*—share of produce of land left with non-Muslims in conquered territories, (v) *Fey*—income of state lands and (iv) *Sadaqat*—contributions in times of need. To these Hazrat Umar added (vii) *Ushr* or *Zakat* out of agricultural produce payable by Muslims. In addition to the above, there was a levy called *ju'l* or compensation for not being able to participate in *jehad*. It was the duty of every Muslim to provide his own equipment and weapons when taking part in *jehad* and as such if he was unable to do so and had the means to provide the same he had to pay for equipping a substitute.

Lastly, to overcome the difficulty felt for meeting new situations arising out of growing problems now covered by Quranic injunctions or *Hadith*. Hazrat Umar developed the practice of *Ijtihad* or analogical deduction. This became necessary due to the extremely limited legislative powers of the Islamic State. Like *Ijma'a* the doctrine of *Ijtihad* is also based on Quranic texts and traditions of the Holy Prophet (peace be upon him) particularly, the one who to his conversation with Mu'az bin Jabal approving of the latter's proposal to decide cases on the basis of *Qiyas* where neither the Quran nor the *Hadith* provided any direct solution. This *Hadith* is reported both in Abu Dawood and Tirmizy. It is on this basis that Hazrat Umar introduced the institution of imprisonment and transportation, banned the sale of a slave girl who had given birth to a child from her master, suspended the *Hadd* punishment for theft in times of scarcity of food, stopped the practice of distribution of lands of non-Muslims in conquered territories, and granted maintenance allowance to an irrevocably divorced woman.

This is comparable to the modern judge-made law. The judges never claim to make law but only to interpret it, yet that interpretation sometimes alters the law itself. The same principle is followed in *Ijtihad* but its importance cannot be minimised if the Islamic law is not to become static. Instances are not wanting of attempts to creatively interpret the Quranic teachings and the *Sunnah* of the Holy Prophet (peace be upon him) to meet the new impacts on the growing Muslim society. But, unfortunately, the introduction of the condition by the *Faqihs* of later periods that *Ijtihad* was only permissible by *Mujtahids* possessing special qualifications led to the misconception that the doors of *Ijtihad* had been closed. Be that as it may, the fact remains that it has not been restored to for more than 700 years now. This is what led Allama Iqbal to lament that the decadence of Islam was largely due to the discontinuance of the practice of *Ijtihad,* which seems to have dulled the capacity of original thinking among the Muslims.

Notwithstanding the separation of the judiciary, the distribution of executive power and the grant of a measure of autonomy to the Provinces, the *Khalifa* retained in his hand the power of superintendence and revision of the work of all authorities through the *Mazalim* jurisdiction. At first during the *Hajj* gathering which was attended by all functionaries, anyone could complain before the *Khalifa* against any authority and the complaint was immediately dealt with in the presence of the person concerned; later such a complaint could be filed at any time. This was a very important jurisdiction which made accountability really effective so far as officials of the state were concerned. This can well be compared to the Writ Jurisdiction of the present times except that it was wider and free from the restrictions with which the modern system is circumscribed.

Under the Islamic system, even the *Khalifa* was responsible to each and every citizen no matter where located and held, himself also equally accountable and open to correction. Two every interesting stories about the first two *Khalifas,* credited to be authentically reported, may give some idea of how these two treated their responsibilities. The first is about a blind widow who had no one to look after her. Seeing her plight, Hazrat Umar thought of helping her by doing her household chores but when he got there the next morning he found her place tidy and done up. The same thing happened the next day and the day after. So he sat watching throughout the next night to find who the mysterious helper was. At break of dawn he saw a person enter the widow's house and clean it up. He waited outside for the person to come out and lo! who should he find coming out? None other than Hazrat Abu Bakr the *Khalifa* himself. On another occasion Hazrat Umar coming to know that a man was dying in one of the bye-lanes of Medina rushed there to find a crowd already collected and an old woman roundly abusing the Khalifa. Finding that he had not been recognised, he tried to plead for the *Khalifa* (himself) and to point out how difficult it was for the *Khalifa,* who was but an individual, to keep information about everyone. The woman replied that if he could not do so, then he should not have become the *Khalifa.* Hazrat Umar admitted his lapse and ordered the man to be removed to the mosque for proper treatment.

Remarkable indeed is the relationship between the nation and the *Khalifa.* The latter never considered himself to be the master but always the servant of everyone in the state and carried on the governance under what Al-Mawardi calls a Bilateral Contract and Rousseau, the modern propounder of the constitutional theory of the state, Contract Sociale. It will be worth reproducing here the words of the Khutba given by the first *Khalifa* immediately after his election. He declared:

> "O people, I swear by Allah that I never coveted the office either by day or night nor had I any inclination towards it. I never prayed to God openly or in secrecy

> to confer the same on me. But I certainly feared that some mischief might arise. In fact, a tremendous amount of work has been assigned to me which is beyond my power to fulfil except with the help and guidance of Almighty Allah. I wished to see the strongest of men in my place. Now, it is beyond doubt that I have been elected your *Amir*, although I am not better than you. Help me if I am right. Set me right if I am in the wrong. Truth is a trust, falsehood a treason. The weak among you shall be strong with me till his rights have been vindicated and the strong among you shall be weak with me till, if God will, I have taken what is due from him. Obey me as long as I obey Allah and his Prophet. When I disobey Him and His Prophet then obey me not."

This is the social contract par excellence to which, authorities maintain, no parallel can be found in the history of the world. It defines the relationship between the *Khalifa* and the people who elect him, lays down the limits of his authority, and gives the people the right to remove him if he departs from the right path. Every subsequent *Khalifa* adopted the same formula in his first *Khutba* after election. Even after the end of the republican period of Islam the formula was adhered to, because it was in accord with the essence of the nature of an Islamic State which in theory never changed.

The concept of Islamic State, as discussed above, reveals that most of the modern theories of constitutional government—like social contract, separation of powers, checks and balances, rule of law, natural justice, equality before law, government as a trust, sovereignty of the people next to God, and welfare of the people—were known to Muslims from the earliest times. It is, therefore, considered that there can be no great difficulty in setting up an Islamic State within the framework of a modern democracy based on political theories of the present-day statecraft. But the difficulties that arise are with regard to the institutions similar to those set up by the Holy Prophet (peace be upon him) and the *Khulafa-i-Rashidin*. Let us now consider how, in what manner and to what extent those institutions can be reconstituted in the present day conditions.

The political theorists will pose the question: Can they be re-introduced in the present changed conditions? Take, for instance, the institution of the *Khilafat*. The unity of the state and the *Ummat* has now, of course, disappeared along with the concept of the *Khilafat* and the Universal State. The Muslim world is now divided into several independent states each claiming separate identity. This happened several hundred years ago when at one and the same time there were three Muslim *Khalifas* in three different regions and each was equally great. During the time of the *Abbasids* there were actually three *Khilafats*, one in Asia *(Abbasid)*, another in Africa *(Fatimid)* and a third in Europe *(Umayyads* in Spain). Thereafter, the Ottomans, after the conquest of Egypt, obtained the surrender of the *Khilafat* in their favour from the Fatimid Khalifa Salim and retained it till it was abolished by the Turks after the First World War. Even during this later period, other independent Muslim States existed in the subcontinent, Malaya and Indonesia. The idea of a Universal *Khilafat* having eased to be operative and found unworkable as a living factor in the organisation of modern Islam. Allama Iqbal thought that "for the present every Muslim nation must sink into her own deeper self, temporarily focus her vision on herself alone, until all are strong and powerful to form a living family of republics (Lectures *on Reconstruction of Religious Thoughts in Islam*, p. 159).

If the republican form of government is not inconsistent with the spirit of Islam and the *Khilafat* forms the Islamic system of government, then is it not possible to institutionalise the *Khilafat* by vesting it in a body of persons or even an elected body? This was the view of the Turkish Grand National Assembly after the deposition of Sultan Abdul Hamid, the last *Khalifa*. The Turks argued that after the Holy Prophet (peace be upon him), who was the last Prophet, the concept of *Niabat-i-llahi* had ceased to be operative and, therefore, keeping the *Khilafat* indivisible thereafter was purely a matter of expediency. It worked as long as the Empire of Islam was intact, but after the break-up of the Empire its utility had not only disappeared but it had in fact become a hindrance in the way of reunification of independent Muslim States. The fallacy in this reasoning lay in equating the *Khilafat* with *Niabat-i-llahi*. The *Khalifas* themselves never claimed this right; they only claimed to act as *Khalifa-i-Rasool*. Indeed, Hazrat Umar considered it presumptuous to even assume this title. He, therefore, introduced the title of *Amir-ul-Momineen* and this was the title adopted by subsequent *Khalifas* right up to the time when the Ottomans adopted the title of *Sultan* and considered themselves to be the Shadow of God on Earth—*Zill-i-llahi*—a concept totally opposed to the spirit of Islam.

Notwithstanding the innovations it seems that if we return to the pristine form of Islamic republicanism and institutionalise the concept of Universal *Khilafat* there can be no serious objection, Allama Iqbal also took such a view when he said:

> "It seems to me that God is slowly bringing home to us the truth that Islam is neither nationalism nor imperialism but a league of nations which recognises artificial boundaries and social distinctions for facility of reference only and not for restricting the social horizon of its members". (*Lectures* on the *Reconstruction of Religious Thoughts*, p. 159).

However, even if it is not possible to have a Universal *Khilafat* or to vest the *Khilafat* in a Council of an Islamic League of Nations, there can be no serious objection to the head of each independent Muslim State being vested with the attributes of *a Khalifa* provided he fulfils the qualifications required for the post. The important thing is not whether we call the head of a modern Islamic State a *Khalifa* or not but whether he can act like Abu Bakr or Umar.

So far as his election is concerned, the Islamic polity can well adopt the procedure laid down by Hazrat Umar, namely, initial selection or nomination, if the legislators wish to use the modern terminology, by an electoral college or council or regency consisting of highly qualified persons, to be followed by a general election. The qualifications can be prescribed by the Constitution to ensure that only capable persons are elected and the Electoral College itself should consist of both elected and ex-officio members so that all shades of public opinion are represented and, in order to be successfully nominated, the candidate should obtain a majority of votes from each section, namely, elected and ex-officio members.

Let us now discuss the legislature. *Majlis-i-Shoora* can easily be expanded and adopted to become a modern legislature. Of course, it will have no power to legislate in a field or in respect of a subject already occupied by or provided for in the Quran and Sunnah, but it should be capable of exercising the powers of *Ijma's* and *Ijtihad*. It is, therefore, necessary that they should also be persons possessing special qualifications needed for this task and these should also be carefully laid down in the Constitution. Once elected, they should function as independent members and not be tied to any political party or its programme. They should vote on the questions laid before them on the basis of their own honest conviction. No other consideration ought to be allowed to prevail.

The *Shoora* once elected should not be at the mercy of either the Head of the State or the Prime Minister. Once elected, its members should hold office for their full term unless earlier impeached by the *Shoora* by a special majority. The Council of Ministers should be appointed by the Head of the State and be removable by him. They should be members of the *Shoora* but should be appointed purely on the basis of merit. The Head of the State himself should also be removable by impeachment by the *Shoora* and that too only if a special majority of votes is cast in favour of such impeachment. Alternatively, impeachment should be by a vote of censure passed at a joint sitting of the Electoral college and the *Shoora* by a special majority of both.

It will, thus, be observed that there is no scope for the Anglo-Saxon type of democracy or the parliamentary form of government in the Islamic system. The presidential system appears to be more akin to it. For the successful operation of the parliamentary system it is necessary that there should be only two major political parties opposing each other. Whenever this is not so and there are a number of small parties in the field, the parliamentary system has not worked satisfactorily. Even in the United Kingdom, with the emergence of the Liberal Party as the one which can effectively tilt the balance, the British are themselves having a second look at their system. Indeed if we look around we shall find that the parliamentary system has not proved successful in any Muslim country, the main reason being that it is entirely foreign to our concepts.

So far as the judiciary is concerned, there is no difficulty at all in adopting the Islamic pattern because the concept of an independent judiciary, even though appointed by the executive, is our special contribution to the world. It has in fact been prevailing from the very infancy of Islamic State. Our system of administration of justice is far superior to that of any other system. Delay and dilatoriness in the process of administration of justice now prevailing are due largely to the importation of British concepts into it which have resulted in encouraging the giving of false evidence and the adoption of dilatory tactics in litigation. These should be removed and the power should be given, at least to the superior courts to strike down laws repugnant to the Quran and the *Sunnah.* Muslims have from the earliest of times established very high traditions of complete impartiality and equality in the administration of justice and there is no doubt that given the proper facilities the judges in the present-day Islamic State can acquit themselves equally well.

It is, however, suggested that an *Ulema* Council should also be set up in modern times to bring back the old *Ifta* jurisdiction and to assist the judges in solving complicated questions of *Fiqah.* It should be obligatory for judges to consult them before striking down any existing law on the ground of repugnancy to the Quran and the *Sunnah.* The legislature should also have the right to consult them whenever any question arises regarding the validity of law proposed to be passed by it.

Revisional Jurisdiction

The re-introduction of the revisional or correctional jurisdiction of the Head of the State on the pattern of the *Mazalim* jurisdiction on the executive side is also suggested. A Board or *Nazir-ul-Mazalim* can be set up to advice the Head of the State who should be the Chairman of this Board having a number of Ombudsmen under it. The Ombudsmen should act as courts of first instance from whose decisions there should be an appeal to the Board, whose decision should be final. It is only in this way that principle of accountability of the executive can be made meaningful and effective.

Some machinery like that of the *Muhtasib* should also be devised for enforcing religious duties and obligations and preventing encroachments on the rights of others, which come under the category of *Haquq-ul-lbad.* This will prevent unnecessary litigation by making the people respect each other's rights.

Nothing has been said about sovereignty, because the concept of state in Islam is unique in this respect as the sovereignty over the universe vests in Allah Almighty.

To put it in a nutshell, what has been discussed above is a bare outline of the pattern that it may be possible to adopt in the light of modern conditions to bring the system of government into line, as far as practicable, with the essential characteristics of the Islamic pattern. It should be pointed out that unless we accept the unity of the *Ummat* as a cardinal principle of our faith, the superimposition of a pattern based on this foundation will not be of much use. We must eschew the notions of nationalities within the nation and false concepts of the state as a federation of several nationalities. The Islamic State is a unitary state wherein brothers-in-faith reside and enjoy equal rights without any distinction of caste, colour, creed or race. In unity lies the strength of the Islamic State and in the pursuit of the welfare of the people its greatness. Its aim is to create dynamic social order based on the principle of justice cooperation, brotherhood and self-sacrifice for the welfare of all. In such a society there should be no scope for disharmony or discord and the changes of conflict would be reduced to the minimum, for if everyone behaves in this spirit no one should have any grievance against the other.

15

The Polity

The ulema, over the centuries, have developed a structure for determining the entire set of rules and regulations arising from the Quran and the Surma (normative practice) of His messenger, Muhammad (PBUH).' This structure is called *fiqh* and is a legal discourse. But this legal discourse has been marginalized and attacked from many quarters, and for that reason few people are aware of the political ideas which the ulema hold. This chapter attempts to convey certain traditionally held political ideas of the ulema which will challenge conventional political notions held by some political scientists and students of Islamic civilization.

The ulema and the Islamic legal discourse *(fiqh)* have been continually and ferociously attacked, even from within the Muslim world, from many quarters from secularists to modernists, reformists to fundamentalists. If these groups have one thing in common, it is a desire for power, and more specifically for state-centred schemes for Muslim progress.

Simply stated, the ulema stand in their way as modern state centralization has historically been shunned by the ulema. In fact, the very essence of the ulema project that edifice erected to determine rules and regulations from the revelation is its decentralization, slow accumulation of positions and argumentation, local dominion, and diffusion. No one person can define and represent the Islamic experience, so the ulema resist Islam being centralized in the person of the nation-state leader, or in any university or institute. And as for state-centred schemes for progress, in accord with traditional religions, the ulema do not see progress as a virtue. As Norbert Wiener remarks.

Most of us are too close to the idea of progress to take cognizance either of the fact that this belief belongs only to a small part of recorded history, or of the other fact, that it represents a sharp break with our own religious professions and traditions.

The importance of the nation-state and the concept of progress to the dominant voice of politics in and about the Muslim world, helps explain why the ulema are portrayed as the enemy or at least as the obstacle, to necessary 'change' and 'development'. But they are not unique in this respect.

Jerry Mander in his book *In the Absence of the Sacred,* quotes Oren Lyons, describing legal procedures of the Iroquois Nation: 'We meet and just keep talking until there's nothing left but the obvious truth, and both (disputing) families agree on the solution'. I was struck by the similarity between this description and that of Lawrence Rosen of a *qadi* (judge) in a Moroccan town.

For rather than being aimed simply at the invocation of state or religious power, rather than being devoted mainly to the creation of a logically consistent body of legal doctrine, the aim of the *qadi is* to put people back in the position of being able to negotiate their own permissible relationships without pre-determining just what the outcome of those negotiations ought to be.

What the ulema share with other traditional knowledge-elites is a desire to preserve a social realm where law is played out in the communal arena with language (or other discursive formats), where not only contention is resolved, but also societal definition and direction is nurtured. This definition and direction comes from the community itself, and not from a media dominated by huge corporations or the government, or from a priestly class of lawyers who design and prosecute laws. In fact, there seems to be no place in their vision for the totalitarian, corporate, legal fiction called the State which we take for granted.

The word *qadi* recalls the Arabic word's meaning of one who settles the affair *(qada),* and Rosen shows how the discretion given to the *gadi*a discretion typically criticized by Western observers as laxity allows him to make law a 'metasystem which creates order in a universe that is often experienced in a more disorderly way'.' The disputants are facilitated by the *qadi* to continue defining the situation until the solution is obvious to all. Consensus developed over time and not coercion, is the central product of this legal activity.

Great Chasm

There is a great chasm between a 'traditional' society, which will mean here a society which organizes itself around divine guidance, and a 'modern' society, which means a society with a state. As we shall see, the concept of state which has fully emerged in the last hundred years or so, and which saturates our field of vision, is alien to many traditional societies and to central activities of Islamic civilization. Yet when we want to investigate politics in Islam, we tend to look for states and at monarchical rulers like caliphs, sultans, and amirs; and when fundamentalists dream, they dream of a powerful, Utopian Islamic State. The fact remains that politics in Islamic civilization is located predominately in quite a different arena, and the ulema, including Ibn Taymiyyah, traditionally resisted all kinds of forces which might have potentially led to the kind of state powers which we have seen recently.

The dream of an Islamic State seems to include visions of sticks taken to rebellious Muslims, timorous non-Muslims citizens, and autocratic rulers on white horses solving all the prevailing problems. But the preoccupation with caliphate seems entirely modern, arising especially in the face of the humiliation suffered at the hands of nineteenth and twentieth century imperialist powers. Historically, Muslim communities throughout the world established the *shariah* by themselves, not *ex cathedra,* as the central focus of their community. Glimpses into daily life, chosen from hagiographic accounts of Sufis and their travels, popular poetry, inscriptions, and accounts of peasant revolts, reveal Muslim communities implementing the *shariah* themselves, striving thereby for a just society. In fact, the very word government *(hukumat)* in Arabic,' as recorded by the lexicographer Ibn Manzur below conveys a negative role for government, not a positive one.

The Arab says *hakam-tu,* I prevented someone and *hakam-tu,*

I averted someone with the meaning of I prevented someone and I averted someone. In this category, one says about the *hakim* among people that he is *hakim* because he prevents the oppressor from oppression. Al-Mundhiri reported from Abu Talib that he said about their statement *hakama* Allah among us, that al-Asma'i said the root of *hukumat* (government) is averting the oppressor from oppression.'

Here the government's role is simply to prevent oppression, because positive political benefits arise directly from practising the *shariah*. There is no place in this Arab conception of *hukumah* for massive bureaucracies, governmental spending and taxing, standing armies and governments. This conception suggests that government is quite an incidental affair, necessary only to stop the oppressor, and that the real political activity of the community is to be found elsewhere and I suggest that place is the communal arena of the *fiqh*.

The Fiqh in the Political Realm : The ulema traditionally exercised a distancing from encroaching state power. Indeed, we find great animosity among the ulema, including fundamentalist favourites like Ibn Taymiyyah, for emerging state power." According to Rosen, the law 'provides a context for the peaceable formation by individuals of their own ties,' so in the classical Islamic theory of the state, law and government were kept largely separate from one another ... By remaining resolutely focused on the individual, the legal establishment forsook the politicization of the law; by avoiding inclusion of the law as an instrument of state policy, the political authorities passed up the opportunity to use law as a vehicle of political centralization.

As with primitive people, Muslims traditionally refused state power over their lives. The kind of distinctions we find between 'then' and 'now', between the largely hidden and suppressed alternative political configurations and our contemporary situations, suggest a fundamental dichotomy. This can be variously characterized as the pre-Columbus era, the last five hundred years (for those concentrating on the civilizations of native peoples) and tradition and modernity (for those emphasizing the sacred, such as the perennialists and traditionalists).

But state power is almost invisible, as often is modernity, and so the fundamental dichotomy between anything today (government, media, religion) and then is not always perceived. One way to call attention to modern and state contexts is to draw on analyses which trace the radical changes influencing daily life. Writers like Mumford, Berman, Illich, Feyerabend, and Ellul show us a world where everything is called into question, where the questions of 'why do we do this' and 'why do we think this is normal' assume a particularly poignant note. The popular anti-hero Travis McGee meditates:

> I get this crazy feeling. Every once in a while I get it. I get the feeling that this is the last time in history when the offbeats like me will have a chance to live free in the nooks and crannies of the huge and rigid structure of an increasingly codified society. Fifty years from now I would be hunted down in the street. They would drill little holes in my skull and make me sensible and reliable and adjusted."

In Foucault's lecture 'The Political Technology of Individuals'," a fundamental change in politics is seen with the process of defining the 'police' in the seventeenth and eighteenth centuries. He locates a book written in 1779 which is the 'first great systematic program of public health for the modern state'." At the same moment, 'the French Revolution gives the signal for the great national wars of our days.... meeting their conclusion or their climax in huge mass slaughters'.

While for Saint Thomas, the king should imitate God to lead men to the good life, and for Machiavelli, the art of politics is to increase the power of the prince, the aim of the modern state is to 'reinforce the state itself'." This gives rise to a political arithmetic, a statistics which creates a calculus of power, where 'the individual exists insofar as what he does is able to introduce even a minimal change in the strength of the state, either in a positive or in a negative direction ... And sometimes what he has to do for the state is to live, to work, to produce, to consume; and sometimes what he has to do is to die."

Without a calculus of demography, a statistics of population, what we now call politics—state, power, or government—had little to do with the daily life of traditional societies. With the calculus, the individual becomes the business of the state. From before his birth to after his death, the state is concerned with any increase or decrease the individual might confer on its aggregate power. The state has an interest in monitoring and deciding the fate of infants, educating children, intervening to protect them from parental abuse, immunizing them, and so on. What rational opposition can there be, where one must argue today for 'freedom from state interrogation' over 'health' and 'saving lives'?

The desire of the modern state, which is to endlessly interrogate and govern the subject interminably, with forms that need to be filled out, credit card records, and social security numbers, is contrasted with the reticent 'primitive'. Resistance to development is a resistance to this interrogation.

The very idea of 'naked' truth, and truth 'laid bare' rests in a worldview quite opposite to that of the classical Muslim scholars. Now, the truth of someone is that person's failing, sins, and frailties. In the Islamic world, one did not broadcast shortcomings. In his discussion of the metaphor of rinsing the mouth and sniffing water in the process of *taharah* (ritual purity), Ibn al-Arabi reveals the typical emphasis given to this civilizational value. 'Even if his recompense (for speaking of evil),' Ibn al-Arabi comments, 'is in His statement, *[Allah loves not that evil should be noised abroad in public speech, except where injustice has been done]*, [4:148], nevertheless silence about it is most excellent."

The resistance of the primitive is well-illustrated in a passage in Munif's novel about the advent of oil exploration in what is now Saudi Arabia, where the bureaucrats say, 'The information we need is simple and necessary, and it is confidential too.' To their long series of questions about his parents, Ibrahim blurts out 'What do you want with my mothers?' And then after even more questions, 'What's wrong with you—can't you talk about anything but my father and mother?' Finally, he cries out, 'God help me—leave me alone!"'

Communities who refuse statehood and states are found throughout the world, from the Penans in Malaysia to the Aborigines in Australia, from Indian nations throughout North, Central, and South America to Kurds and Pathans in South and Southwest Asia. *Cultural Survival Quarterly* reports that three-fourths of the 120 military conflicts in the world in 1987 were native nations defending themselves against nation-state. The ultimate supremacy of the nation-state is not yet established and many communities throughout the world are struggling against it till death. In a world dominated by state powers, and at least—if not more—as influentially by corporations, it is no wonder that the voice of the ulema is seldom heard.

Caliphal Politics

The classical discussions of caliphate are sparse, overly abstract, and full of hidden agendas. They are not very helpful while questioning how authority is configured in Islamic societies. The voluminous discussions of who is best suited for leadership *(imamah)* during the prayer *(salah)*, in contrast, is very helpful.

Should it not then be possible to extrapolate from the discussion of the *salah*, ideas about a larger universe? Is not the ideal leader for the *salah*, the ideal leader for the larger society? Is not the discussion of the criteria for a good leader for the *salah* at the same time a discussion of the good leader of society? If indeed we can examine the *salah* as a microcosm of the Muslim universe, a number of propitious consequences ensue.

What I am proposing here is nothing short of an entire re-evaluation of politics in Islam. The entire fundamentalist discourse on the Islamic state in fact arises from the invisible concealment of a traditional world view having its own kind of politics, by a modern world-view of the sovereign state. Let us therefore delve into this matter of politics, because one of the main reasons of examining the *fiqh* discussion of the *salah* as a microcosm for the larger discourse of Islamic communities, which is so propitious, stems from the reassessment of politics which it occasions.

Historically, there is a noticeable absence of sustained and direct discussion on Islamic leadership. The subject matter of kingship or caliphate tended to create treatises at once highly abstract and overly specific. The works of Mawardi, Nizam al-hulk, al-Ghazali, and Ibn Khaldun, for example, when addressing kingship or caliphate, have quite definite agendas to pursue; attacking amid abstract and idealistic verbiage, a powerful woman behind a would-be leader, or simultaneous caliphates, or justifying pinning one's hopes on converting a ravaging Hun. Arkoun lists what Mawardi overlooks:

Al-Mawardi talks neither of the Shi'ite theory of the designation of the caliph based on a text, nor of the great conflict *(al-fitna)* between Ali and Muawiya, nor of Yazid who, according to the

Shi'ite version, had Hussein assassinated at Karbala, nor of the conditions of civil war which initiated the fall of the Umayyeds and the ascendance of theAbbasides, nor of the politics of Mamun toward the Mutazilites and to Shi'ism, nor that of Mutawakkil for installing Sunnism, nor of the conquest of power by the Buyides.

The actual caliphate was formally abolished by Ataturk in 1925, and even though it was obvious that the caliphate had been an extremely ineffective system for decades, even centuries, the loss of the caliphate had a tremendous impact on Muslims throughout the world. Muslims in India, for example, spontaneously arose and began walking to Turkey to recover their world. Ali Abd al-Raziq's short treatise, published in Egypt in 1933 on government in Islam, arguing that the caliphate is not essential to the Islamic community, quickly brought him major troubles and seemed to many to be salt thrown on their wounds. To this day, many Muslims have put their hopes in a revived caliphate. We have a situation here where there is a dearth of material on Islamic government, together with an inchoate understanding that, against Abd al-Raziq, politics is essential to Islam.

The problem, as I see it, is that there is no state in Islam-state being understood in the Western sense of a sovereign, corporate institution with a reality across time and space, independent of its human constituents or components. When people talk of the 'Islamic theory of state', Ayubi notes,

> They are addressing themselves specifically to the problem of government and especially to the conduct of the ruler, and not to the state as a generic category or to the body-politic as a social reality and a legal abstraction ... Even when the Islamic bureaucracy developed and became quite complex, officials and other 'public' personnel appointed to certain jobs or dismissed from them, never signed a contract with the 'State' or any other 'moral personality', but simply with a certain individual employer (al-muwalli).

The issue is not one merely of definition. The concept of a sovereign, corporate nation-state entails absolutism and totalitarianism—no matter how much people in liberal democracies want to believe that their freedom and rights are protected. Traditional scholars spoke of this kind of politics as Thoreau did, where the best government is the least government, or none at all. Ayubi writes that neo-fundamentalists 'invoke the text and quote the source, but in doing so they are highly selective and remarkably innovative. Political precedence is of practically no interest to them; neither is the main body of official jurisprudence, apart from a few exceptions such as Ibn Taimiya.

We tend to equate politics with state and government, and thus when we ask about politics in Islam, we are actually asking about states and governments. At that point, we gather the fairly small series of works, like al-Mawardi's, discussing the caliphate and the sultanate, which digress into discussions about intact testicles and other criteria for leadership, and end up with Abd al-Raziq's ultimate destruction of the whole thing, with his persuasive argument that the Prophet left no system of government and Muslim scholarship never actually addressed the entire issue of how people should be governed.

The moment we disengage 'politics' from 'state', an entirely new situation arises. The many Muslims who were appalled at Abd al-Raziq's position, and at all subsequent liberal positions on government, were right but they were inarticulate (the actual official rebuttal to his work seems to have zeroed in on his use of 'Bolshevik' in a long list of possible governmental systems which could be seen as Islamic). If we ask, 'What governmental system did the prophet leave his community?' the answer is 'the *fiqh* of the *shariah*'. If the *shariah* is the politics of the Islamic community, then its entire legal discussion—the *fiqh—is* the expression of politics in Islam. And whereas we have a few hundred pages on the subject matter of caliphate and sultanate, we have perhaps a million pages on the subject matter of *fiqh*.

So if we want to examine Muslim views on leadership, power, relations with the other, differences in communities, structures, and institutions, we would do well to pass over the official statements on caliphates and sultanates and turn instead to the actual arena of political contention and discussion—the *fiqh*. Taking the selection of a leader for the *salah* to be a microcosm of political leadership in Islam unleashes a torrent of positions, arguments, ideas, and terminologies which begin to reflect the historical realities of politics in Islam. At the same time, it offers Muslims an authentic discursive format which allows for an Islamic assessment of politics today. The basic need, then, is to re-evaluate this *fiqh*, both for historical understandings as well as for contemporary problems.

The Jurisprudence

What exactly is the *fiqh?* It is perhaps the most concrete and voluminous monument of Islamic civilization, one format of Muslim understanding *(tafaqquh,* f.q.h.) of the *shariah,* the rules and regulations of Islam. Although the *fiqh* can become atrophied and reified, static and full of the weight of authority, it is traditionally the living expression of the Muslim community's commitment to realize the guidance of the *shariah.* For the Muslim, 'right life' is a consequence of right action, and the criterion for right belief is right conduct. Hence the importance of *fiqh.*

The *fiqh* combines concern with both the spiritual and the quotidian, and serves as the arena for political-economic life, regulating activity in the markets, mediating disputes, and determining David Easton's authoritative allocation of value' as well as administering rites of passage (birth, puberty, marriage, death). Its tendency for accumulation means that it preserves centuries of deliberations, discussions, decisions, and debates.

Therefore, the extension of the *fiqh,* and specifically the *fiqh* of *salah,* to the macrocosm allows us to reconstruct a political discourse. The fiqh surrounding the issue of privacy and windows, for example, tells us something about the priorities of Muslim scholars. We can reconstruct that when someone created a window, the neighbour's right of privacy prevailed: the existence of filled-in windows in traditional Muslim cities is the physical sign of the following event. Someone opens up a window to improve his house, and a neighbour begins to worry that the window looks into his house, disturbing his privacy; they take their case to the *qadi* (from the Arabic root q.d.y. as we saw, meaning to settle or resolve). The *qadi* seeks *sulh,* harmony among disputants, and so he brings along a builder to the site. If indeed the window 'harms'—from the axiomatic *hadith* `There shall be no harming, nor being harmed', *la darar wa la darar*—the window is boarded up. I suggest that in this process, the traditional politics for Muslim societies is seen.

In this process, obedience to the revelation is manifested within community relationships. This is why a break between spirituality, as expressed in obedience to the revelation, and politics, as depicted in interactions in communities, is inconceivable in traditional Islam. Let us look now explicitly at spirituality and politics.

16

Foundation of State

The arrival of the Prophet (PBUH) at Medina in A.D. 622, marked the first step towards the establishment of an Islamic state. Considering that Medina was still inhabited by non-Muslims, atheist Arabs, and Jews, the Prophet (PBUH) in his first legislative act drew the lines, in a convention, that would regulate relations between the different factions of the citizens of Medina.

In the first part of his ten years of leadership in Medina, Prophet Muhammed (PBUH) laid down the foundation of a city-state, that would grow within a few years to encompass the whole Arabian Peninsula. He started with the construction of a mosque that would serve as a school, a centre for consultations and information, a court for receiving envoys and delegations, as well as a place for worship and prayers. He constructed a market place for the Muslims to counter that of the Jews. He then directed his efforts to building a Muslim army. In the latter part of his stay in Medina, he assigned to his governors and representatives the different parts of Arabia.

Laying down the basis for the subsequent rules guiding relations of the Islamic state with other countries, Prophet Muhammed (PBUH) set good examples in his diplomatic correspondence with foreign royalty, in the dispatch of envoys to neighbouring districts, in the establishment of new rules, or the implementation of old ones. These were related to the laws of peace and war, and the modalities and contents of the agreements that, he concluded with the opposing parties. He was thus paving new roads and giving a new meaning to the concept of international diplomacy.

During the succeeding periods of the four Orthodox Caliphs and the Umayyad rule (A.D. 631-750), the Islamic state witnessed an era of expansion that brought it into direct contact and interaction with the Byzantine, the Persian and the Chinese Empires and peoples. The experience and sophistication of these civilizations enriched Islamic culture and concept. It was during the Abbaside period (A.D. 750-900) that the Islamic state, reaching its peak in political influence, cultural maturity and economic prosperity, represented the universal state.

Medina Convention

When the Prophet (PBUH) and his Meccan disciples reached Medina, it was inhabited by two major tribes, the Aus and the Khazraj, which had long been feuding with each other. In addition, there were several Jewish communities in Medina. Besides the Aus and the Khazraj, not all of whom were Muslims yet, the Medina society consisted of the Muslim exiles from Mecca, the Muslim helpers from Medina and the non-Muslim Arabs and Jews. In these circumstances, Prophet Muhammed (PBUH) became the teacher, arbitrator and the centre of all powers. In this capacity he applied himself first to the task of introducing order in Medina and organizing relations among different factions on a proper basis. With this objective in mind he issued a charter, by which blood feud was abolished and lawlessness repressed. Equal rights were granted to the Jews, who committed themselves to helping the Muslims in defending the city.

In this convention, to which all the communities adhered, the Prophet (PBUH) considered the Muslims, whether exiles from Mecca (Muhajeroun) or helpers from Medina (Ansar), as one community (Ummah), while addressing each one of the Jewish communities as a separate entity. Those who allied themselves with the Muslims would have their support and be on an equal footing.

The parties to the Charter of Medina would conduct war or peace collectively. No party would unilaterally conclude peace with a belligerent adversary or wage war against a third party by itself. No one among the non-believers (Mushrikin) was to grant protection (Aman) to a Qurayshite or to his property, nor would he prevent a faithful from acting against a Qurayshite.

The Jews would share the expenses with the faithful. As long as they were fighting, the Jews of Bani Auf were an Ummah (a community) with the faithfuls. They had their own faith just as the Muslims had theirs. The Jews of Bani-Al-Hareth, the Jews of Bani Saedah, the Jews of Bani Jusham, the Jews of Bani Al-Aus, of Bani Thalabah, had the same (rights) as those of the Jews of Bani-Auf.

No one from the Quraysh or from those who supported it would be granted the protection of the parties to the convention. They (the parties to the convention) would support each other against any other party that would attack Medina. Anyone leaving Medina or staying in it would be safe, except for those committing injustice or misdeed.

Thus, the main political features of the convention were:

- For the first time in the history of Hijaz, a political unity was formed of the different factions and tribes of Medina under the leadership of the Prophet (PBUH).
- The influence of the Jews, which prevailed in the past due to their manipulation of the hostilities among the Medina tribes, was to be countered and minimized.
- The Prophet (PBUH) then secured not only a fortified front against any possible attack from his declared enemies, the Qurayshites, but also formed the first ring in the chain that would besiege Mecca and contribute to its weakening. From there he could divert his attention to the most immediate business of organizing the state affairs, internally and externally.

Formation of the State

In establishing the structure of the new state, Prophet Muhammed (PBUH) built a mosque that would serve as a headquarter, as well as a place of prayers. He then designated a new commercial centre for the Muslims, apart from the old one which was controlled by the Jews. By such an undertaking he laid the foundation for an economic structure of the state that would function on the basis of Islamic principles, free from the influence of the Medina Jews.

From the first day of his arrival in Medina, the Prophet (PBUH) concerned himself with the formation of a military force, well organized and trained, that would be capable of defending the state and safeguarding its interests. The Islamic army was assigned military expeditions, that would serve the ultimate political and diplomatic ends. The frequent attacks on the trade caravans, going to and coming from Mecca, were intended to weaken the Qurayshite economic power. At the same time these expeditions served as training experiments as well as a show of strength to other Arab tribes in the region.

On the international front, the Prophet (PBUH) dispatched a number of envoys with messages to monarchs and leaders of the neighbouring states and tribes, acquainting them with the new faith and inviting them to embrace it. He sent a messenger to the Emperor of Persia and another to the Byzantine Emperor. The former tore the message and banished the envoy from his presence, whilst the Byzantine Emperor received the ambassador with considerable courtesy. A third envoy, sent to a prince subordinated to the Byzantine, in the Damascus region, was cruelly murdered.

Islamic Era

At the age of forty, Prophet Muhammed (PBUH) received his Commission and started to preach the new faith of Islam. The name 'Islam' came from an Arabic expression which implied complete 'surrender' to Allah, the one and only God. He, therefore, called for abandoning the old beliefs, repudiating paganism and discarding many inherited traditions and superstitions. Beginning with his immediate family and close relatives from Quraysh, the Prophet (PBUH) gradually widened his circle of activities to include all the inhabitants of Mecca and those groups who came to visit it during the seasonal pilgrimage.

Although the new religion adopted many of the traditions and values prevailing in that society, it was a potent blow to the dominant social structure and its basic values. It is comprehensible, then, that the initial mild rejection of the Meccan leaders to the new faith became a fierce resistance as it spread. Prophet Muhammed's (PBUH) adversaries pursued an escalating opposition that started with dialogue and negotiations. It was stepped up with the application of different kinds of pressure and culminated with the torture of those professing adherence to the new faith.

The heads of the Quraysh clans percieved Prophet Muhammed (PBUH) 'as the head of the community, however small, like a state within a state.' The relations between the two communities and their leaders, in many aspects, followed a course similar to that, which existed between two states. In conducting these relations, the methodology used was not far from diplomatic practices prevailing nowadays. In resolving their differences, both sides resorted to dialogue and negotiations, employing 'intelligence' and 'tact' and implied promises or threats. They applied these skills in their direct contacts or through their envoys and delegations. Both parties suggested compromises, and at certain stages accepted them.

Prophet Muhammed (PBUH), in his discourses resorted to persuasive arguments and discreet preaching: 'Call unto the way of thy Lord with wisdom and fair exhortation, and reason with them in a way that is best and most gracious.' On the other hand, the leaders of Quraysh, who could not use force or inflict on Prophet Muhammed (PBUH) the same mischief they had inflicted on his followers—as he belonged to a strong and respected family of Quraysh—had to opt for the diplomatic practice available to them. They sent delegations to his uncle and protector, Abu Taleb, on three occassions, and each time they used a different approach. Failing to find a solution, they decided to negotiate directly with Prophet Muhammed (PBUH). On these three occasions they tried again either to strike a deal or to challenge his prophetic missions, or to reach a compromise. Both parties sent delegations outside of Mecca and both met with representatives coming to Mecca in their endeavours to win alliances or to obstruct the other party's manoeuvers to do so.

Delegations within Mecca

The Quraysh tribe, fearing the spread of Islam among the people of Mecca and its repercussions on their prestige, values and beliefs, decided to send a delegation to Abu Taleb, the Prophet's (PBUH) uncle and protector, demanding that either he prevent his nephew from pursuing his discourse or denounce him. The delegation which consisted of some dignitaries explained to Abu Taleb the harm that Prophet Muhammed (PBUH) was causing to their beliefs and traditions. They pointed out that Abu Taleb, who did not embrace the new faith himself, was in disagreement with Prophet Muhammed (PBUH), as they were. However, Abu Taleb apparently mollified them before they left.

On the second occasion, the Quraysh delegation came to Abu Taleb and used a threatening tone, asking him to prevent his nephew from opposing their beliefs. They told him that if he continued to do nothing about it they would fight him.

Abu Taleb conveyed this to his nephew and requested him not to burden him with a load that could prove to be too heavy for him to shoulder. The Prophet (PBUH) replied that even if the sun were placed in his right hand and the moon in his left, he would never relinquish his mission.

The third delegation from the Quraysh came to Abu Taleb with a third option. They suggested that he deliver Prophet Muhammed (PBUH) to them and they give him in exchange Amarah bin al-Walid, who was a wise and presentable young man from the family of Quraysh. Abu Taleb condemned this sort of bargaining where he 'was to deliver his adopted son to be killed', as he put it, 'while accepting their son to be fed and protected.'

In the three encounters, it is to be noted that both sides had observed the prevailing social (tribal) norms when they pursued their patterns of negotiations, namely, the obligation to stand on the side of the family and to help and defend even those members whose point of view they did not share. The Quraysh recognized Abu Taleb's family obligations and the latter accepted this burden despite the fact that he did not share Prophet Muhammed's (PBUH) belief. It is worth mentioning that both sides resorted to their verbal skills and persuasive arguments throughout their talks. Also both sides implied latent power in supporting their respective positions. The Quraysh delegations implied the unanimity of the Quraysh clans and their firm resolution. Abu Taleb reckoned on his family prestige and the fact that it could not be easily challenged.

Prophet Muhammed (PBUH) expressed his steadfastness and confidence in the support of God who would help His faith to ultimately prevail.

In the second phase of these encounters, the Quraysh leaders decided to contact Prophet Muhammed (PBUH) directly and to talk him out of his discourse. In the first attempt they agreed on sending one of their dignitaries known for his knowledge of soothsaying and poetry. They selected Utbeh bin Rabiah, who met Prophet Muhammed (PBUH) and started his negotiation by referring to the damage the Prophet (PBUH) was inflicting on his peoples' beliefs and idols. Then, questioning his motives for rejecting the creed of his kinsmen they offered to reward him if he abandoned his mission. Utbeh conveyed to him their readiness to make him the richest man, if he sought wealth, or to concede to his leadership if he sought honour and prestige. In reply, Prophet Muhammed (PBUH) read to him a passage of the Quran related to the questions in the mind of the delegate about the Prophet (PBUH), the Quran, and the core of the new faith.

When Utbeh returned to his people he advised them to leave him to what he was striving to accomplish, assuming that if he prevailed, then his rule over the Arabs 'would be your rule and his glory would be yours' and that if he were killed by the Arabs, then 'they would have saved you the effort.'

This argument did not convince the Quraysh. Their leaders decided to launch another attempt. This time they invited Prophet Muhammed (PBUH) to meet them by the Kaaba. They started the negotiations by repeating their previous complaints and offers. Then they stepped up the offensive. They challenged his God's power, requesting him to move the mountain or to bring the rivers into their land or to resurrect their ancestors, so they could testify to his authenticity. Prophet Muhammed (PBUH) based his argument on the rationality and logic of his mission rather than on miraculous proofs or supernatural manifestations. He kept telling them after every request that it was not for that, that he was commissioned, but that God had sent him as His Apostle to deliver His message.

In their third attempt, the Quraysh leaders sought to reach a compromise. They sent a delegation of four dignitaries, who proposed to Prophet Muhammed (PBUH) that they worship his God and he worship their gods. If either party was the true one, then both parties would benefit from their common practice. The Prophet's (PBUH) response was a firm rejection of this bid and it was expressed in the Quran as 'Say: O ye that reject the faith! I worship not that which ye worship. Nor will ye worship that which I worship... to you be your religion and to me my religion.' One can interpret this encounter and the aim of the negotiations conducted through it as endeavours to reach a compromise over the disputed matter.

Negotiations generally imply the attempt to reach a compromise, based on concessions made by both parties. The extent of the concessions made by either side may reflect inversely the power it possesses to support its argument. Often negotiations are conducted for purposes other than reaching a settlement. They may be launched by one party with the intention of exploring the status of the adversary. In some other instances, negotiations may be conducted for the mere purpose of gaining time, in preparation for another course of conflictual encounter.

The Soviet Field Marshal Shoposnikov might have meant that when he said, 'If war may be said to be the continuation of politics by other means, then peace, in its turn, is no more than the continuation of conflict by other means.'

Through the interactions the Quraysh leaders had with Prophet Muhammed (PBUH), they sought either to explore his plans, or to reach a kind of negotiated settlement, or to challenge him in order to expose his weak points in preparation for 'the continuation of the conflict by other means.'

Delegation Dispatched Abroad

After failing to reach a settlement with Prophet Muhammed (PBUH), the Quraysh notables resorted to other means, aiming" at obstructing him and containing his successes. On the personal front, they intensified their pressure on his followers and his immediate family, the Banu Hashim. In order to expose what they expected to be his weaknesses, they sent a delegation to Medina to meet the Jewish rabbis there. Since Prophet Muhammed (PBUH) declared that the Islamic faith is the continuation and the completion of Christianity and Judaism, the Jewish rabbis of Medina could help in refuting this claim. It is mentioned that the rabbis of Medina advised the delegates to put three questions to Prophet Muhammed (PBUH). TWO of the questions were related to stories recorded in the Old Testament. If he failed to answer any of these questions, then he would prove ignorant of the Jewish faith and that would negate any connection claimed between the two religions.

When repression against the followers of Islam intensified, the Prophet (PBUH) advised those who could not secure protection to migrate to Abyssinia. This choice was based on two circumstances. The first one was that the Abyssinian Negus was the nearest Christian leader, who could offer asylum to the Muslims. The second was that the Arab pagans had connections with South Arabia which belonged at that time to Persia, an ancient enemy of the Christian power of Byzantium. The number of followers, who migrated to Abyssinia, in the fifth year of the Prophetic Mission, was eighty two. After the immigrants settled in Abyssinia, the Quraysh tribe schemed to pursue them in their asylum and sent two delegates to the Abyssinian Negus. One of them was Amr bin-al-Aas, a very shrewd person, whose name appeared in a later period as a remarkable negotiator and warrior. The mission of the Quraysh delegation was to convince the Abyssinian Negus to disclaim the Muslim refugees and if possible, to extradite them.

At the same time the Quraysh notables decided to move farther in their sanctions against Prophet Muhammed (PBUH) and his protectors, Abu Taleb and the families of Banu Hashem and Banu Al-Muttaleb; (Hashem and Al-Muttaleb were two brothers. Prophet Muhammed (PBUH) and his uncle Abu Taleb descended from the first one). The Quraysh leaders met and concluded a written agreement, which they deposited at the Kaaba and by which they vowed to boycott Banu Hashim and Bani Al-Muttaleb. It was agreed that none of the Quraysh would deal with anyone of the two families in trade, marriage or social contacts. It is noteworthy that this boycott agreement was not directed against individuals, who followed the new faith, but included everybody in the two families (Hashim and Al Muttaleb) whether they were believers or non-believers of Islam. The reaction of Banu Hashim and Bani

Al-Muttaleb families was the same and the non-believers showed solidarity with the believers." The boycott agreement was an example of an inter-tribe or inter-state conduct of relations.

During the tenth year of the Prophetic Mission, Abu Taleb, the Prophet's (PBUH) uncle and protector passed away and he became more vulnerable to the hostility of the Quraysh. He left Mecca for Al-Taif to call its people to embrace Islam and to seek their support and alliance. There, he was met with defiance and rebuke. He returned to Mecca vowing not to submit, as long as God, Lord of the weak and helpless, was his support.

Migration to Abyssinia

In the fifth year of the Prophetic Mission, many of the Muslims migrated to Abyssinia to escape the repression of the Quraysh. They left in two groups totalling eighty two persons. Ruqayeh, the Prophet's daughter and her husband Othman (RA) (who was to be the third Caliph) were in the first group. The second group included Ja'far bin Abu Taleb, Abu Taleb's son and Prophet Muhammed's (PBUH) cousin. The Muslims believed that they would be given refuge by the Abyssinian Negus, who was a Christian and believer in one God. After they were accepted in Abyssinia, the Quraysh leaders dispatched a delegation of two persons to the Negus in order to convince him to extradite those who were offered asylum and to deliver them to their people in Mecca. The delegates, keen to succeed in their diplomatic mission, planned their approach carefully. They carried gifts to the monarch and his aides. First, they met with the patriarchs individually, and explained to them that they had sheltered some of their people, who had relinquished their fathers' religion, but who had not embraced the patriarchs' faith. Contrary to both religions, they had invented, as the delegates put it, a religion of their own, which was acceptable to neither party. They appealed to each patriarch to send these defectors back and to advise the king not to summon the muslim immigrants for a hearing. When the two delegates were received by the Negus, they presented their gifts to him and repeated the claims that they had put to the patriarchs. The latter attested to the delegates' claim and proposed to the monarch to disown the immigrants and to deliver them to their people, who knew them better and were aware of their mischief. The Negus refused to disavow those who sought asylum in his country and he declined to entertain the petition of the delegates without first verifying the charges against the immigrants.' When the Muslim group was brought before the king, they were asked what made them differ with their people and abandon their religion without embracing Christianity or any other beliefs.

On behalf of the Muslim group, Ja'far bin Abu Taleb took the stand to answer these questions. He addressed the Negus, and said that, 'Before Islam, we were people of ignorance, worshipping idols, committing atrocities and disrupting family relations until God raised up an apostle from amongst us; we know his ancestry, his truthfulness and his credibility. This apostle called on us to believe in one God and to worship Him and commanded us to tell the truth, to keep family ties, to protect whoever sought refuge among us...we believed in him and followed his teachings, while our people, oppressed us and endeavoured to impose their faith back on us. This is why we migrated to your country and solicited you and not anyone else, seeking your protection and hoping not to be mistreated by you.' The Abyssinian Negus requested Ja'far to read verses of his book and Ja'far read a passage, i.e. the *Sura XIX* entitled Mariam. The Sura tells the story of Zakaria, having a son Yahia (John) at a late age and of Mariam (Mary the Virgin), who although a virgin, by the will of God had a son Isa (Jesus).

The Negus was pleased with what was said and commented that what the Prophet (PBUH) was preaching and that which Jesus proclaimed, 'both were emanating from the same source.' He told the delegation from Qurayash 'You may both leave, these people I will never deliver to you.'

When the Quraysh delegation left the court, Amr ibn-al-Aas thought of another approach. He decided to inform the Negus that the Muslims believed that Jesus Christ was just a man—no better than a slave. He returned the next day and proposed to the Negus to summon the Muslims and to ask them what they thought of Jesus. The Negus put the question to them. Again Ja'far bin Abu Taleb spoke and said that they thought of Jesus what their Prophet (PBUH) had conveyed to them and that Jesus was a slave of God, His apostle and His spirit. He was the word of God delivered to

Mariam the Chaste. This argument did not satisfy the patriarchs, but it did satisfy the Negus, and the report goes on to say that he dismissed the two Quraysh delegates, rejecting their gifts and rebuking their mission.

Quraysh Boycott

Realizing that the Abyssinian Negus had extended his protection to the Muslim immigrants, and that the Muslims in Mecca were increasing in number, the Quraysh notables held a meeting where they decided to boycott Bani Abdul-Muttaleb. They recorded this agreement in a written document which they deposited at the Kaaba. Such an action provoked the Bani Hashim and Bani-Al-Muttaleb to ally themselves with Abu Taleb and Prophet Muhammed's (PBUH) followers. This alliance included the Muslims and non-Muslims within the two clans.

The boycott continued for a period of two to three years, during which the people, besieged in their quarter in the ravine of Abu Taleb, suffered from lack of food supply except for what was secretly infiltrated. One of the Quraysh notables, Hisham bin Amr, who was related on his mother's side to Bani Hashem, used to load a camel with food stuff and lead it to the opening of the ravine in the darkness of the night and release it to the people in the besieged quarter. He convinced another figure of the Quraysh, Zuhayr bin Abi Umayah, to raise the boycott, Zuhayr expressed his consent and reservation as they were alone in this matter, and both agreed to seek the support of other notables. After that Hisham went to a third and a fourth person and reached the same agreement with them. The group of five met together and drew a plan for abrogating the agreement.

The next day they went to the Kaaba and after the sermons Zuhayr called for the people of Mecca and addressed them, asking how they could eat their food and wear their clothes at a time when Banu Hashim were suffering and were denied the right to trade with them. He then vowed not to rest until this unjust and disruptive document was destroyed. When Abu-Jahl, one of the main adversaries of the Prophet (PBUH) interrupted his speech and insisted that the agreement be preserved, another one from the group of five came to the help of Zuhayr, then the third one came, followed by the fourth in the group. All expressed their concurrence with him. After them, Hisham bin Amr stepped forward to state that he too had never consented to the agreement from the beginning and that he would repudiate its contents. Although the number of people who condemned the agreement was not big—only five—the manner in which they spoke, one after the other, gave the impression that this was the feeling of the majority. When, in the end, one of them went to tear up the document, he found that it had already been destroyed.

Delegations to Mecca

Prophet Muhammed (PBUH) and his companions spared no opportunity to explain their religion to those, who came to Mecca and to call on them to accept the faith. He met groups of Arabs, who came to Mecca for pilgrimage and for trade. He received envoys and delegations, who arrived to inquire about the new religion and to acquaint themselves with its Prophet (PBUH).

In the ninth year of the Prophetic mission (A.D. 619), a delegation of Christians from Najran (a region south of Mecca) came to meet the Prophet (PBUH). After they had put their questions to him and listened to passages from the Quran, they left and were confronted by Abu-Jahl and a number of Quraysh men, who tried their best to counter whatever impression the Prophet (PBUH) had left on the delegation.

During the same period, an envoy from Hamadan (a tribe living in the northern part of Yemen) called Qays bin Amr came to meet Prophet Muhammed (PBUH) and to report back to his people. After discussing his mission with the Prophet (PBUH) and declaring his conversion to Islam, Qays expressed his own and his peoples' readiness to support the Apostle. He was requested to return to his people and to find out, if Hamadan was ready to take Prophet Muhammed (PBUH) in their midst and to support and defend him. Qays left for Hamadan and later returned alone to announce his peoples' adherence to Islam and their readiness to host him. Though, Prophet Muhammed (PBUH) expressed his appreciation for the positive response, he found it short of a firm commitment. His agreement with the Medina delegation later on proved to be based on something more concrete.

Prophet Muhammed (PBUH) maintained his contacts with people visiting Mecca. During the pilgrimage season he met the different tribes coming to Mecca, calling on them and convincing them to accept Islam. At one of these seasonal gatherings in Mecca, a delegation from Medina, representing the Aus tribe, came seeking alliance with the Quraysh against the Khazraj, the other major tribe in Medina. Medina, which was known as Yathreb, was inhabited mainly by two Arab pagan tribes (Aus and Khazraj) and an influential Jewish community. The continuing hostilities between the two tribes gave rise to the dominance of the Jewish community. The delegation from Yathreb was headed by Abul Hayser Anas bin Rafie and included Iyas bin Muadh. Prophet Muhammed (PBUH), hearing of the arrival of the delegates, and their purpose, came to meet them and said: 'Would you have what is better than what you have come for?' When they asked what that was, he said: 'I am the Apostle of Allah. He has sent me for all humankind; to call upon them to worship God and to ascribe no partner to Him. And He revealed to me the book.' Then he called on the delegation to embrace Islam and read before them verses from Quran.

Iyas, influenced by what he heard, expressed his sympathy and preference for what was presented, but he was rebuffed by his superior, who told him that he was there for a different purpose. It appears that, despite the fact that Prophet Muhammed (PBUH) did not convert the group, his message was delivered and it was to be conveyed to the people of Yathreb. So when he met other delegations from that city, his views were already known to them.

First Aqaba Delegation

During the pilgrimage season to Mecca in March, A.D. 620, Prophet Muhammed (PBUH) met a group of the Khazraj tribe, who came to Mecca for the same purpose as the other Yathreb delegation had come the previous season, that is, to seek an alliance among the Quraysh, against their opponents, the Aus and Jews. When Prophet Muhammed (PBUH) talked to them and explained to them the faith of Islam, it seemed as though they were not surprised with the basic idea, as they had often heard from the Jews about the awaited Messiah. They looked at each other and said, 'By God! He is the new Prophet the Jews had always threatened us with. Why should we not be ahead of them to join him?' They declared their faith in Islam and told him that, they had left their people divided in feuds and hostilities and that, they would return to them and call on them to accept the faith. They promised that if they were united around this faith, then no one among them, would have a more honourable position than the Prophet (PBUH).

They returned to Yathreb (Medina) and started propagating Masab bin Umair the new faith, aided by a Muslim who had previously emigrated to Abyssinia. The next year, five of them came back again to Mecca together with seven new converts and met the Prophet (PBUH) at Aqaba, the pass between Mina and Mecca. Here, he heard their plight and enjoined upon them the basic laws of Islam and sent one of his companions to teach them the religion and to lead their prayers.

This emissary of the Prophet (PBUH) followed the wise approach and sagacious advice of the Prophet (PBUH) in preaching Islam to those voicing their opposition to it in Medina. Once, one of the Medina notables came to him and in a threatening manner ordered him to leave them alone. The emissary prudently asked him to sit and listen to what he had to say. If he found it satisfactory, he might then accept it, otherwise he could point out what he disliked. The Medina notable Osayd bin Hudhayr accepted the proposal as a fair one. He listened to what the emissary read from the Quran and declared his acceptance of the faith. He then advised the emissary to go and meet Saad bin Muadh, the man, who would be followed by all his people, if he accepted the faith.

It is worth pointing out here that throughout all the meetings between Prophet Muhammed (PBUH) and those delegations and individuals whom he strived to bring to the new faith, the Prophet (PBUH) always invoked rational argument and discreet presentation and each and every time read to them, passages of the Quran. While all the other prophets had performed miracles as proofs of their divine missions, the only proof put out by Prophet Muhammed (PBUH) was the words he voiced. The value of a word to an Arab lies in its meaning, its rhythm, its music, and its logic and its eloquence. To the Arabs, the spoken word is a covenant, that commits them to the most serious obligations. The Quran described Jesus Christ, as being the word of God descended to Mary. The first word of the Quran that was delivered to Prophet Muhammed (PBUH) when receiving his commission was 'Iqraa', which means 'read'.

Those who specialize in Islamic history and literature, would appreciate the impact and deep effect the language of the Quran had on a people, who appreciate the value of the word. For them it is understandable that the only sign of Prophet Muhammed's (PBUH) divine inspiration was the Quran itself, its contents and its wordings. The first delegate from the Quraysh came to meet Prophet Muhammed (PBUH) to verify that is he a poet or a soothsayer. He heard him recite the Quran and went back to his people to assert that, what he heard was not the word of a poet, or that of a soothsayer. It is said that the only miraculous proof of the new religion Islam, was the language and the content of the Quran.

Second Aqaba Agreement

During the pilgrimage season of the thirteenth year of the Prophetic Mission (A.D. 622), a group of seventy three men and two women from Medina came to Mecca and met with the Prophet (PBUH) at Aqaba. It was in the darkness of night that Prophet Muhammed (PBUH) came to meet them accompanied by his uncle Abbas, who had kept his pagan belief. Abbas addressed the Medinese, telling them of the position Prophet Muhammed (PBUH) occupied among his people and within his family and that he had been defended even by those, who did not adhere to his faith. He went on to say that despite that, Prophet Muhammed (PBUH) had chosen to join them and to ally himself with them, if they believed that they would defend him. Abbas warned them that if they could not pledge this support to him, they must leave him, where he was protected and esteemed. The group from Medina gave their assurance and offered to take an oath of allegiance to Prophet Muhammed (PBUH).

Before the Medina party committed themselves to Prophet Muhammed (PBUH), they made it clear that their forthcoming agreement would sever ties, they had with another party, meaning the Medina Jews. They asked if he would give them up once his cause prevailed. Giving them the assurance of his constant allegiance to them, Prophet Muhammed (PBUH) had them swear their fealty to him in defending him, as they defended their women and children. Having sworn this mutual oath of allegiance, Prophet Muhammed (PBUH) requested them to solicit twelve captains from among themselves as representatives. Then, he addressed the twelve persons named by the group and stated to them that they would be the guarantors to what their people were committed to, as the Disciples were to Jesus. He would be the guarantor for his people. The twelve captains expressed their consent in confirmation of the pledge covenanted with their people.

On the basis of the second Aqaba agreement, Prophet Muhammed (PBUH) gave permission to his followers to immigrate to Medina. The migration to Medina of the Mecca Muslims was effected in successive waves. The last three to leave Mecca were Prophet Muhammed (PBUH), his close companion Abu Bakr (RA) and his cousin Ali bin Abu Taleb. On 25 September 622, Prophet Muhammed (PBUH) accompanied by Abu-Bakr (RA) arrived in Medina to start a new phase in the history of Islam, which marked the beginning of the Muslim calendar year. The arrival of the Prophet (PBUH) in Medina, where Islam had spread among all the Aus and Khazraj tribes, laid the basis for the establishment of the first Islamic state.

The Manifestations

Throughout this period one discerns manifestations of diplomatic practices, which formed the basis for the more sophisticated practices observed in the succeeding period. Relations and contacts between communities and tribes resembled relations and contacts among states now-a-days. The methods, manners and means of conducting diplomacy might have been quantitatively and qualitatively limited. There have been instances where pacts, agreements or pledges were conducted and concluded verbally or in writing, after negotiations and exchange of delegations.

Nevertheless, the examples mentioned indicate a degree of maturity in diplomacy. The norms and traditions known to the Arabs of that period were the background for such practices.

These were accepted and used by both communities, the Muslims and the pagans, but certain features reflected the new culture of Islam. For instance, when the two delegates from the Quraysh went to the Abyssinian Negus to explain the contradictions between Islam and Christianity in terms of Jesus Christ, the Muslims debated among themselves as to what they should tell the Negus. They concluded that they should be truthful about what they believed. The debate that would ensue eleven centuries later as to whether, diplomacy could revert to deception or should be based on truthfulness, was settled in the incident mentioned above. The Muslims believed that credibility does not only pay off, but also reflects their faith, which could be translated into modern terminology as reflecting their constant policy.

Another aspect of diplomacy in that era was that when negotiations were concluded, the argument of either party would reflect the power that backed the party's position. In the case of negotiations between the Quraysh and the Muslims, the Quraysh delegations always backed their argument with the support and unanimity of their clans, while the only power the Muslims relied on was the strength of their argument and their belief.

The third feature of this type of diplomacy was that it represented a way of life rather than a professional activity, that simply served the purpose of the mission. The Quran enjoined them to adopt a certain manner in their discourse or when effecting their responsibility. 'It is part of the mercy of God that thou dost deal gently with them. Wert thou severe or harsh-hearted, they would have broken away from about thee.' That thou have averted evil with good.' 'Call unto the way of thy Lord with wisdom and fair exhortation and reason with them in the better way.'

17

The Pious Caliphs

The Prophet Muhammed (PBUH) died on the 12 of Rabi I, A.H. 11 (8 June A.D. 632). Before he died, he had the satisfaction of seeing his message spread all over the Arabian Peninsula. If he had to use force in a number of military encounters, mainly against the Qurayshites and their allies in the neighborhood of Mecca and Medina, these were retaliatory in nature. His main conquest, that is the entry into Mecca, was achieved without bloodshed. The great majority of the Arab tribes and communities within the confines of the Peninsula came into the fold of the Islamic Ummah through peaceful contacts, and negotiations.

From the first days of his mission, the Prophet (PBUH) made it clear that it was not meant exclusively for one community or a certain race. Acting on the basis of the universality of the faith, Prophet Muhammed (PBUH) sent his envoys to the sovereigns of the two great powers, at a time when his authority was still limited to one city, and when he could not reach Mecca to perform the Umrah. In fact, it was the murder of one of his envoys by the Ghassanid governor, who was subordinate to the Byzantine Emperor, in Mutah (south of Jordan), that invoked the first military encounter with the Byzantines. From the composition of the force that was dispatched in the year A.H. 8 (A.D. 630) to penetrate the Byzantine borders, it seemed that the intention was to express a challenge and determination rather than to achieve conquest and occupation. The Prophet (PBUH), designated for the first time three leaders to take the lead in succession, if the first or the second were injured. He enjoined them before their departure not to cause any harm to the monks in their monasteries, whom they may meet on their way, and not to kill any women, children or aged persons, and not to flood a date-palm, or to cut a tree or demolish a house. The martyrdom of all three leaders in the Battle of Mutah and the retreat of the Muslim army that followed, were a further incentive for the preparation of a new round.

The Prophet (PBUH), during his last days of leadership, took the responsibility of assembling an army under the leadership of the seventeen year old Usamah, the son of Zeid, who had led the Battle of Mutah and was martyred there. The departure of Usamah was postponed only because of the illness and then the demise of the Prophet (PBUH). The first task his successor, the Caliph Abu Bakr (RA), took up to implement, was to dispatch the army where the Prophet (PBUH) intended it to go, with the same formation, i.e., the enlistment of all the close companions of the Prophet (PBUH), excluding Omer bin al-Khattab. The Caliph had to take permission of the leader, Usamah, for exempting Omer from this mission in order to stay in his company.

While the northern confines of the Peninsula bordered the Byzantine Empire and its subordinate Arab state of the Ghassanids, the north-eastern frontiers bordered the Persian Empire and its Arab vassal state of the Lakhmids. The relations between the Lakhmids and the Persians, were not smooth. In A.D. 610 the Lakhmids revolted against the Persians and defeated their army in the Battle of Dhi Qar. Within the confines of the Arabian Peninsula, no sooner was it known that the Prophet (PBUH) was dead, that the loyalty and order disintegrated. Some of the tribes, who had only recently abandoned idolatry, reverted at once to their old ways. Other tribes renounced loyalty to the central government in Medina. Within a short time, the city of Medina had again to contend with the apostates all around the Peninsula.

The Holy Successors

The successor of the Prophet in the capacity of the ruler of the state was called the Caliph (Khalifah) which literally means the successor. The first four Caliphs were called Al-Khulafaa Al-Rashidoun, which means the Righteous Caliphs. They were also known as the Orthodox Caliphs because they sought earnestly to follow the traditions of the Prophet (PBUH).

Abu Bakr (RA), the first Caliph, when asked about the fate of the assembled army of Usamah, responded by stating that he would not lower a banner that was raised by the order of the Prophet (PBUH). He did not attempt to reconsider the formation or the leadership of the army that had already been formed. He gave its leader the same instructions as those which the Prophet (PBUH) had given him. Abu Bakr (RA) addressing Usamah said 'See that you avoid treachery. Depart not in any way from the right. You shall mutilate none, neither shall you kill any child or an aged man, nor any woman. Injure not the date-palm, neither burn it with fire, and cut not any tree wherein is food for man or beast. Slay not the flocks or herds or camels, save for needful sustenance... And the monks with shaven heads, if they submit, leave them unmolested'.

When bidding them farewell, Abu Bakr Marched along with the Muslim army on foot, while Yazid bin Abu Sufian, the leader of the army, was on horse-back. In his last recommendations to Yazid he said: ...if you come to meet with men fighting with you, treat them well, and promise them of the good rewards,...and if you receive envoys of your enemies, be hospitable to them, and make short their stay, so that they leave you with the least information regarding your disposition. Let not the people about you converse with them, so that you, alone, conduct the discussion. Let not your secrets be disclosed, that may confuse your plans. If you consulted the others, be truthful to them, so you may get from them the true counsel.

Omer bin al Khattab (RA) (the second Caliph) was as strict in seeking to apply the traditions as Abu Bakr (RA) was. When Abu Obeidah, the leader of an army directed to Syria, wrote informing him of the victories he had achieved and inquiring about how to deal with the spoils he had collected and the lands he had conquered, Omer (RA).wrote a letter which said:

> I have looked into what you mentioned, in your letter, regarding the spoils that God had offered, and the agreement that you concluded with the inhabitants of those cities and districts. I have consulted, too, the companions of the Prophet (PBUH), who, each one of them has voiced his opinion. What I view stems from the Holy Book, where God says (...what God has bestowed on His Apostle from them, for this you made no expedition with either cavalry or camelry, but God gives power to His apostles over any He pleases, and God has power over all things. What God has bestowed on His Apostle—and taken away from the people of the townships, belongs to God, to His Apostle and to kindred and orphans, the needy and the wayfares; in order that it may not merely make a circuit between the wealthy among you; so take what the Apostle assigns to you, and deny yourselves that which he withholds from you and fear God, for God is strict in punishment...). (and those who came after them) those are the descendants of Adam (whether) they are red or black. God has given a share to those who come after, until the Day of Judgement. Leave, then, what God bestowed on you in the hands of its owners, and set djizyeh on them according to their capabilities, and distribute the djizyeh among the Muslims. That would enable the inhabitants to grow their land to prosperity, that they are better oriented with their land and more capable to do so. You have no way on them nor have the Muslims in your company. You may (only) have the djizyeh from them, according to what they can afford, since God makes it evident to us and to you where He says in his Book (Fight against such of those, who have been given the scripture as believe not in God nor the Last Day, nor hold that forbidden which had been forbidden by God and His Apostle, nor acknowledge the religion of truth, until they pay djizyeh with willing submission and feel themselves subdued). If you collect the djizyeh from them, then

> you have no way against them... and forbid the Muslims from suppressing or harassing them, or usurping their properties, except for what is their right. Fulfill your commitments to them in accordance with the provisions you set in the agreement you concluded with them. As to their demonstration with the cross on their feast days, do not prevent them from demonstration out of the city, without flags or banners, provided that they had pre-consent for celebrating that day. The cross should not be demonstrated in the midst of the Muslim community nor within their mosques.

The Conquests

The Muslim leaders, who had succeeded in conquering all the territory that stretched from Egypt in the west, to Persian provinces in the east, under the rule of the first two Caliphs, had come to achieve most of their victories through peaceful agreements. According to the instructions they had, they were to offer their counterpart the option to:

A. accept Islam and adhere to the faith, thus becoming a part of the Muslim Ummah, having the same rights and duties as all other Muslims,

B. keep their faith, under the safeguard of the Islamic State, and to pay the djizyeh (poll tax) and the kharaj (property tax), or

C. resort to the third alternative of fighting.

It was significant that the major military encounters in Syria and Iraq were basically against the Byzantine and Persian armies. The indigenous inhabitants of these countries had neither the urge nor any strong motive to fight their kin, the Arabs, in defence of foreign domination. Sir Thomas Arnold in his book *The Call for Islam* quotes the Jacobite Archbishop of Antioch, Michael the Elder, who wrote in the second half of the twelfth century, i.e. after five centuries of Arab rule, seeing in the Arab conquest the hand of God. After he relates the oppression the Catholic Church suffered under the Byzantine rule, he states that 'when the cities submitted to the Arabs, the latter allocated to each community the church, that was in its domain. In spite of that', he continues, 'it was not easy to get rid of the Byzantines, of their injustice, their hatred and their antagonism against us, and then to find ourselves in peace and security.' Sir Thomas Arnold also records that when Abu Obeidah reached Fahl (in Jordan) with his forces, the Christians in that territory wrote to him 'You Muslims are more favourable to us than the Byzantine, even if they are of our faith'. Abu Obeidah, after accepting the djizyeh from the inhabitants of Emmesa (in Syria) gave them back the tributes that he had collected, when he found that he had to face the great army, that Heraclius had amassed at Yarmouk River (in Jordan) since he might not be capable of ensuring the safety of the city. Nevertheless, the people of Emmesa expressed their support for the Arabs and pledged to close their city and to defend it against the Byzantine armies.

Though the Muslims had declared, since the ninth year of Hijri, that they would not accept polytheism within the confines of the Peninsula, they recognized Christianity and Judaism, and acknowledged their rights to keep their faith and perform their religious duties. During the rule of the four orthodox Caliphs, the same principle was applied to the believers of the two religions. As citizens of the state, they were free to apply their religious codes in social matters. They were exempted from being recruited or from participating in the efforts or expenses of the military activities of the state in the case of war. They were not required to pay the financial duties imposed on Muslims like the tithe or alms. Their contribution, as citizens of the state, were limited to two categories of taxation—the djizyeh which was imposed on adult men. Women, children, monks, aged men and invalids were exempted from being taxed. Those who were incapable financially were also exempted. The principle of accepting the djizyeh was decreed in a Quranic text (Sura IX; 29). The amount was defined in the Hadith, the range of which was between 1-4 Dinars per person per annum. Although the Quranic text specifies that djizyeh could be accepted from the people of the Holy Book, the traditions extended this provision to include peoples of other faiths. The Prophet (PBUH) accepted djizyeh from the Magians of Hadjer. Then both Abu Bakr (RA) and Omer (RA) followed the same rule with the Magians of Bahrain and Persia.

The other category of taxation (Kharaj) was that imposed on the land owned by the Kitabis. The rates of Kharaj varied according to the area of land, its productivity, the cost involved, and the value of its products.

18

Umayyad and Abbaside Caliphs

Ali bin Abu Taleb (RA), the fourth Orthodox Caliph, was assassinated on 27 January 661 (17 Ramazan A.H. 40). The assassin was one of the group that split from among his supporters and who formed the political and sectarian group known as Khawarij (the dissidents). The sect is presently known in different parts of the Arab countries as Abazi. Ali's (RA) eldest son Al-Hasan was then elected to the Caliphate by the people of Kufa. He had hardly been in office when Muawiyah invaded Iraq. The feeble support Al-Hasan could secure compelled him to withdraw and to accept the treaty proposed by Muawiyah. According to the treaty, Muawiyah was recognized as the undisputed Caliph, with the pledge to have Al-Hussein, the second son of Ali (RA), as the successor to Muawiyah. Muawiyah later on ignored his pledge and arranged to secure the oath of fealty for his son Yazid, as his heir. By this act, Muawiyah had created a precedent in establishing the system of hereditary Caliphate. Thus the power of the Islamic Caliphate was kept in the hands of the descendants of Umayyah (clan of Quraysh) for over ninety years. Through this period, the contenders from the other

Qurayshite clan, Banu Hashem, kept striving and never laid down their arms. The two branches of Banu Hashem's clan, the Alids (descendants of Ali) and the Abbaside (descendants of Al-Abbas, the uncle of both the Prophet (PBUH) and Ali (RA), had unified their efforts in a covert and then an overt struggle against the Umayyad. This struggle lasted until the second branch of Banu Hashem (the Abbaside) succeeded in overthrowing the last Umayyad Caliph. The Abbasides then followed the same pattern in bequeathing the seat of Caliphate to members of their family. The Abbaside dynasty in Iraq lasted for over five centuries, until Baghdad was conquered and sacked by the Mongols in A.H. 656 (A.D. 1258). However, the Abbaside Caliphate survived in Cairo as a spiritual office up to the sixteenth century. Then the Ottoman ruler, Sultan Selim, obtained a renunciation of the office in his favour from the last Abbaside Caliph, Al-Mutawakkil.

Golden Age

The Umayyad period and the first part of the Abbaside Caliphate was an era that could be described as the golden age of the Islamic State. It was during this period that State institutions were established, and relations with foreign states took a new course. After a period of conquests and expansion during the time of the Prophet (PBUH) and the Orthodox Caliphs, the Islamic Empire was more or less established as to its territory and to the pattern of government. Except for the first period of the Umayyad Caliphate, when military engagements continued in the far west of Africa and far east of Asia, the center of the State witnessed a peaceful and prosperous life. Past the peak of its strength, with its self-sufficiency diminishing, giving way to dependence on the luxuries of life, the Muslim Empire proceeded to have greater international intercourse, commercial, cultural, as well as political. Diplomacy, therefore, gained increasing significance especially in matters of international trade. Muslim envoys were sent to the courts of several monarchs for various political, commercial, cultural and social reasons, for the exchange of gifts and for other purposes.

It is significant to observe that in the Abbaside period, a branch of Islamic studies was devoted to questions regarding relations with other nations. This branch of studies within the Islamic jurisprudence (Al-Fiqh) became known as Siyar. Two known scholars in this field were contemporaries of the famous Abbaside Caliph, Harun Al-Rashid (A.H. 170-193 A.D. 786-809).

Muawiyah bin Abu Sufian : Muawiyah, son of Abu Sufian, ruled Syria as governor for twenty years. He was acclaimed Caliph in A.H. 41 (A.D. 661) when he was sixty years of age. His caliphate lasted for twenty years, until he died in April A.D. 680 at the age of eighty. The long undisputed rule of Muawiyah and that of his dynasty after him was attributed to his diplomatic conduct and skilled manoeuvres. He succeeded in wiping out the last traces of the long preceding crisis in the Muslim community. A typical feature in his character was *hilm*, an expression signifying leniency towards opponents, the smiling indifference that disarmed his adversaries, and his intelligent generosity, which bound his enemies to him with golden chains. To one, who criticized his lavishness, he said that war cost far more. He was conspicuous for his cunning, eloquence and keenness of mind. He described his preference for diplomatic methods saying; 'I apply not my lash where my tongue suffices, nor my sword where my whip is enough, and if there be one hair binding me to my fellowmen, I let it not break. If they pull, I loosen, and if they loosen, I pull.'

He once wrote to the Governor of Iraq, Ziyad bin Abih, advising him that, it was not the best approach for them both, that they administer people in the same manner. If they were both lenient, the people would be emboldened to show disobedience, and if they were both too tough, that would inevitably drive people to despair and recklessness. He then suggested that the Governor could represent the tough administrator, and leave to him the role of leniency and mercy.

Muawiyah was the first Caliph, who preached to the people while seated. He was also the first to have an enclosure inside the mosque, where he prayed protected, and where he received complaints of all, who desired to approach him. Inside the enclosure (maqsoura) he would be seated on a chair guarded by special guards. After the midday prayer he would return to his palace and give audience to the grandees of the state and the envoys of neighbouring princes. Muawiyah was also, the first to establish the department of mail correspondence. It was Muawiyah, too, who established a chancery—department which bore the name of the board of the signet (Diwan ul-Khatim). The chief of this department kept the seal of the Caliph, by which all correspondence made on his behalf was signed and sealed, and a copy of which was preserved. The seal was inscribed with the motto 'Every good deed has its reward.'

As to the conduct of foreign relations, Muawiyah established more than one precedent in Islamic diplomacy. During his engagement with Ali (RA) at Siffin, Muawiyah being pressured by the Byzantine, came to an agreement with them according to which he would pay them a certain amount of money as a tribute to Constans II.

According to the traditions practiced by the Byzantines of having hostages from the other party as guarantors of execution of the terms of the treaty, Muawiyah was holding hostages from the Byzantines. It is recorded that when the Byzantines violated their treaty with Umayyad, instead of punishing the hostages, Muawiyah chose to release them and said 'It is better to meet treachery with fidelity rather than treachery.' It was taken to be an implementation of the Prophet's Hadith 'Fulfil what you are entrusted with and never meet treachery with the same'. These two precedents became fixed rules in the Islamic principles governing relations of the Islamic State with foreign powers.

The treaty Muawiyah concluded with the Armenians in A.D. 653 was another significant event. The terms of the treaty stipulated that:

> For three years no djizyeh will be set on you (the Armenians). After that period you will pay, according to your pledge, that which you can afford.,.I pledge

> not to dispatch a governor to be within your fortresses, nor will I delegate an Arab officer, or a single cavalier or a judge. If the Byzantines march against you, I shall support you with all the enforcement that you need. To that I give the oath of God and my pledge.

This treaty by which the Armenians gave their autonomy was implemented in a manner favourable to their interest. After a long period of subjugation to the Byzantine sovereignty, the Armenians enjoyed the right of self-rule similar to those of Muslim governorates. The Caliph gave the same investiture to a new Armenian prince, as the ceremony establishing a Muslim Amir in his new office. In the presence of dignitaries, military and civilians, he would confer on the prince being crowned, the magnificent garments, the banner, which henceforth would accompany him, a sword and an elegant mount, all marked with the insignia of his function. After that, he would inspect a troop in stately appearance, while the band played a chant, proclaiming him to the office of princeship.

Harun Al-Rashid **:** Harun Al-Rashid the fifth Abbaside Caliph ascended to the seat of the Caliphate at the age of twenty-three and reigned for twenty three years from A.H. 170 to 193 (A.D. 786-809). When he died at the age of forty six, he left a glorious image of the Islamic State and society, owing partly to his great character and partly to the era which he represented.

It is history and legend together, which place Baghdad in the most brilliant period during his Caliphate. Though less than fifty years old, Baghdad had by that time grown to become a world center of prodigious wealth and international significance. Its splendour kept pace with the prosperity of the empire of which it was the capital. It was then that Baghdad became a city with no peer throughout the whole world. The munificence of Harun and his successors attracted to the capital, poets, wits, musicians and others, who could amuse and entertain. The luxurious scale of living made this period popular in history and in fiction, but what has rendered this age especially illustrious in world annals is the fact that, it witnessed the most momentous intellectual awakening in the history of Islam and one of the most significant in the whole history of thought and culture.'

It was in Harun's reign that the four schools of jurisprudence of the Sunni sect were established. He enlarged the department founded by nis grandfather Al-Mansur for the translation of scientific work into Arabic and increased its staff. Baghdad, as a shipping center, was in an advantageous position that made all parts of the world accessible to it. Into its bazaars came porcelain, silk, and musk from China; spices, minerals, and dyes from India; rubies, fabrics, and slaves from Central Asia; honey, wax, and furs from Scandinavia; ivory, gold dust, and slaves from Africa. From Baghdad and other export centers, Arab merchants shipped fabrics, jewelry, metal mirrors, glass beads, spices, and other items of merchandise to the Far East, Europe and Africa. The adventures of Sinbad the Sailor, which form one of the best known tales in the stories of *The Thousand and One Nights,* have long been recognized as based upon actual reports of voyages made by Muslim merchants. The tales of *A Thousand and One Nights* themselves draw a fanciful image of this age, where the name of Harun Al-Rashid is frequently mentioned.

The palaces of Baghdad were symbolic representations of the age. The buildings, made of marble, were usually several storeys high, lavishly gilded and decorated. The imperial Kasr (palace) was resplendent with inlaid jewels, and the halls bore distinctive names according to their ornamentation. The special feature of one was a tree, made entirely of gold, with birds perched on its branches made also of gold and studded with gems. These palaces would display courtly wealth and magnificence, especially on ceremonial occasions such as the reception for foreign envoys.

Such was the age in which lived the fifth Abbaside Caliph. As for the character of Harun Al-Rashid, he was described as 'one of the most powerful princes reigning at this period.' In his person was combined a character of numerous facets. He was known to be faithful in observing his religious duties, abstemious in his life, pious and charitable, and yet he was fond of surrounding himself with the pomp and insignia of grandeur. As a patron of arts and literature, Rashid was surpassed only by his equally brilliant and gifted son, Al-Mamun, but in strength of character and grandeur of intellect he had no superior. He was the only known Caliph, who travelled in search of knowledge. Himself a poet, he surrounded himself with poets and men of literature. Also, Haroun Al-Rashid was a leader of distinguished military qualification, who took on himself the duty of commanding his army in the many encounters, which he led against the Byzantines. He was known to perform the pilgrimage one year and to lead an expedition another year. In the year A.D. 190 (A.D. 806), he led an expedition against the Byzantine Emperor, wearing a headdress (Qalansuweh) on which was inscribed 'the pilgrim, the invader.' Al-Rashid was the first Caliph to have played and encouraged chess. He is supposed to have included among his presents to Charlemagne a chessboard. As an example of the lavish life he enjoyed, Al-Masoudi relates that his brother, Ibrahim, had given a dinner in his honour, where the Caliph was served with a dish of fish in which the slices looked exceedingly small. In explanation, the host remarked that the slices were fish tongues. The Caliph wanted to know the cost of the dish, and refrained from eating the slices, and ordered his brother to pay an equal amount in charity. One of the best known gems Al-Rashid acquired was a big ruby—one owned previously by several Persian monarchs—on which he inscribed his name. The ruby that cost him 40,000 Dinars, was so large and brilliant that it would shine in the darkness of the night. His sister wore jewels on her headdress and his wife had them on her shoes.

As an administrator, Al-Rashid initiated a system, by which he appointed a governor in Northern Africa, Ibrahim bin al-Aghlab, granting him the privilege of handing down the power to his descendants. The Caliph then, reserved the right to confirm the appointment of governors and to exact the payment of tribute. In his testament to the members of the Abbaside family before he died, he directed them: to observe faithfully their engagements, to be faithful to their Imams (Caliphs), and to be united among themselves. He was the first Caliph to name his first aide as a wazir (minister). He appointed Yahia bin Khalid as wazir and handed him his seal.

Foreign Relations

In his conduct of foreign relations, the Caliph was a soldier and a diplomat. His reign was marked by frequent military confrontations with the Byzantines, as well as with broken peace agreements. Arab historians tell of a letter addressed by him to the Emperor of Constantinople, which reveal the character of a diplomat of that period. The letter which was over fifty pages long, discussed in its major part the values of Islam, and invited the Emperor to adhere to it. After forty pages of his argument, the Caliph advised the Emperor that if he refused to accept the faith, he should pay the tribute and avoid war and its consequences. The letter enumerated to the Emperor, the advantages of peace and cited verses from the Bible to this effect. The letter was sent in response to the breach of a treaty which the Byzantines had concluded with his father Al-Mahdi.

Other Arab annalists record that in A.H. 187 (A.D. 803), after the Byzantine Empress Irene (A.D. 797-802) was deposed, her successor Nicephorus repudiated her treaty with the Arabs, according to which she was to pay an annual tribute. Nicephorus wrote to the Caliph an insulting letter which said:

From Nicephorus the Roman Emperor, to Harun, Sovereign of the Arabs: verily the Empress who preceded me gave you the rank of a rook and put herself in that of a pawn (in reference to the chess game) and conveyed to you many loads of her wealth, and this through the weakness of women and their folly. Now when you have read my letter, return what you have received of her substance, otherwise the sword shall decide between you and me.

When the Caliph read the letter, he became so enraged that no one dared to look upon his face, or to speak to him. He, then, wrote on the back of the Emperor's letter the following:

> From Harun, the Commander of the Faithful, to Nicephorus the dog of a Roman: verily I have read

> your letter, the answer shall be for your eyes to see, not for your ears to hear.

True to his word, Al-Rashid at once started a campaign directed against the Byzantine monarch. Sustaining heavy defeat, the latter called for a settlement according to which he agreed to pay increased tribute. No sooner had Al-Rashid returned to his headquarters, than Nicephorus, deeming it impossible for the Caliph to resume fighting in that harsh season, violated his agreement. But he miscalculated his adversary's will. Again he was confronted with military defeat, and again he negotiated for peace to which request the Caliph responded. The acts concluding a peace treaty and violating it were frequently repeated by the Byzantine Emperor. Every time, the request for peace was granted with heavier tributes imposed on him. In A.H. 190 (A.D. 806), the Byzantine Emperor agreed to pay the *djizyeh* on himself and his own family members, in addition to the tribute *(kharaj)* he was to pay on behalf of the state. He had to pay four Dinars for his son, and two Dinars for each member of the bishopric.

Al-Tabari relates that in the same year, Nicephorus wrote to the Caliph a message which read:

> To Abdullah (slave of God) Harun, the Commander of the Faithful, from Nicephorus, Monarch of the Romans, I would put to you a request that would entail no harm to your faith and to your interests, that is to grant me a maid from the inhabitants of Heraclius (which recently was conquered by the Arabs), to whom my son had been engaged. That you may do, if you see fir to do me a favour.

The Caliph ordered that the girl be sent to Nicephorus, together with valuable presents. The Caliph's envoy likewise received from Nicephorus on his return from his mission a load of Islamic coins carried on a horse, which amounted to 50,000 Dirhams, and garments of silk and embroideries in addition to four hunting dogs and three other mounts.

The Caliph often exchanged envoys with the Byzantine Emperor mainly for the purpose of exchanging prisoners or releasing them in exchange for ransom. In the year A.H. 181 (A.D. 797), the Caliph's third son Al Qasem was charged with the mission of exchanging and ransoming prisoners that was the first act of its kind in the reign of the Abbasides. The Muslim prisoners, freed in exchange for the Romans, numbered three thousand, seven hundred. Six years later, Al Qasem, after besieging a Byzantine fortress, came to an agreement according to which he would retreat provided that the Byzantines released 320 Muslim prisoners. In the year A.H. 186 (A.D. 802), there was a general exchange and payment of ransom whereby all Muslim prisoners held by the Byzantines were freed.

The ninth century opened with diplomatic contacts between the two imperial figures, Al Rashid and Charlemagne. It is reported that Al Rashid received an emissary from the Frankish monarch, who was treated warmly and returned with valuable gifts. The mutual friendly relations into which these two contemporaries entered were prompted by self-interest. Charlemagne viewed Al Rashid as a possible ally against the hostile Byzantium, while Al Rashid desired to use Charlemagne against his rivals and foes, the Umayyads of Spain, who had succeeded in establishing a powerful state there. Hitti, quoting the *Annals Royales,* described the gifts that Charlemagne received, including fabrics, aromatics and an elephant. Other historians include among the gifts sent by Al Rashid a clock which was described as a work of art. The clock would indicate the hour by means of balls falling on a plate of brass; as the hour struck, a number of horsemen (according to the hour) emerged from a door, and then re-entered as soon as the sound subsided. Similar emissaries were received for the first time from the Chinese Emperor and from India, who brought the Caliph rich presents and who were sent back with similar effects.

As to the mechanism and style of conducting foreign relations, the Caliph benefitted from the existing departments and developed some more to suit the new requirements. Although the appointment of wazir (minister) was known before the Abbaside Caliphate, it was Harun Al Rashid who delegated all his power to his lieutenant, Yahia bin Khalid, and named him wazir. He entrusted him with his seal which had descended to him from his grandfather, Al Mansur, and on which was inscribed 'In God I trust, in Him I believe'. Among the existing state departments, relevant to the function of conducting foreign relations were, Diwan ul-Aziz (the Office of the Government), Diwan al Kharaj (Central Office of Taxes), Diwan al Barid (the Post Office), Diwan al Rasael (Board of Correspondence) and the post of Chamberlain. Diwan al Rasael was an office, the president of which also undertook the duties of a Secretary of State. It was his responsibility to draw up the imperial mandates, diplomas and political correspondence. After these documents were approved by the Caliph or his wazir, they were sealed in red wax with the seal of the Caliph imprinted on it. Diwan al Barid served, in addition to despatching and bringing the mail, as a source of information. On the information coming from the different provinces of the state and the foreign countries, the Caliph formed his plans or administered his state. Upon Al Rashid's request, the known scholar and jurist Abu Yousuf, the disciple of Abu Hanifah, authored a book on land taxes *(Kitab Al Kharaj)* which became one of the first references discussing the conduct of foreign relations by a Muslim state. The book, addressed and dedicated to Al Rashid, who advised the Caliph on the Islamic principles and laws that should guide him in many aspects of conducting relations with non-Muslim individuals and communities.

The Protocol

Rules of protocol and ceremonies were meticulous and expressive of grandeur and magnificence. On the occasion of a reception, the Caliph would be seated on a throne, while a hundred men in splendid uniforms and with drawn swords stood around him, and dignitaries of the empire ranged to the right and left of the royal seat. As each dignitary made his entrance, the Chamberlain called his name. After presenting himself and making his obeisance, the guest would take his place by the side of those already in the room. His priority would be decided in accordance with his descent or his office. Once the discharge of the duties of protocol cost a Chamberlain his life. During the reign of Al Mahdi, father of Al Rashid, the latter was accompanying his elder brother Al Hadi, who happened to be the heir designate. At the point of crossing a small bridge on horseback, a lieutenant of Al Hadi told Al Rashid to wait and to let the heir designate pass first. Al Rashid complied, though with indignation. Later on, the first act he undertook, after being proclaimed a Caliph, was to punish that lieutenant for his remark. At the head of the social register stood the Caliph and his family, then the government officials according to their ranks and the scions of the Hashemite clan. Following them, came the satellites of these groups. In this last class were the soldiers and bodyguards, the friends and boon companions, as well as the clients and servants. Embroideries, brocades and robes of honor were manufactured for the use of royalty. Such products were known as tiraz and bore the name or cipher of the Caliph embroidered on them.

19

Contemporary Politics

What is so unique about Islamic polity? There must be something quite unique about the Islamic polity to deserve so distinctive an importance. Before we begin to recount the substantive merits of the Islamic polity, let us take into consideration the concept of divine being which is, in fact, the cornerstone of the faith. What is the most striking feature of Islam to a student of world religions is the clear, unclouded concept of the Supreme Worshipful Being— Allah—as contained in the Quran. There is nothing mythical, mysterious and mystifying about the Divine Being. The Holy Book of Islam describes Allah right in the opening Sura, *Al-Fatiha,* meaning "Preface":

> "Praise and glory belong to God, the Sustainer of all the worlds, the most Beneficent and the most Merciful, the Lord of the day of Judgement. It is Thee that we worship and of Thee we seek help and succour..."

Main Plank

The concept of God constitutes the main plank of any religious infrastructure; and, if one were to make an objective study of Islam from this perspective alone, one will have to admit its distinctive character. It is in this context that the Holy Prophet Muhammad (peace be upon him), blessed by and chosen of God, is the greatest benefactor mankind has known. His was a divine mission, one of lifting humanity from the depths of moral and spiritual degeneration and guiding its steps towards a new destiny, a new life of peace, equality and brotherhood. All world historians are agreed that there has been no revolution greater than the one the Holy Prophet (peace be upon him) brought about. If there has ever been a total revolution it was this. Unlike so many incomplete ideologies of later ages, it at once gave its followers moral elevation, economic emancipation and political freedom. It brought peace; it brought equality; it banished racism; it ended exploitation; and it founded a society which by its orderliness, discipline and progress dazzled the entire world.

In the present world, peace, unity and brotherhood are the crying need of the suffering humanity. The rich and the poor, the high and the low, the black and the white are all feeling the pangs and afflictions of privation and depravity; and advocating the cause of rights, equality and justice for all.

But does the present-day materialist world realise that centuries before the birth of United Nations and other international organisations, in the desert of Arabia a most comprehensive, profound and thought-provoking Book of God was revealed which exercised most remarkable influence on the concept of world unity and human brotherhood enshrined in the transcendent idea of *Tauhid* (Monotheism or Unity of God). This concept encompasses all the fundamental domains of human faith and action. It is, therefore, imperative to comprehend its vastness in order to fully understand the rational approach of the Quran in relation to diverse human problems.

The Quranic view of life is based on the purest Monotheism—the doctrine of Unity of God. God is one, and there is nothing like Him. He is Absolute, Indivisible Sovereign, Supreme, Dominant, Mighty. Belief in Him demands loyalty and devotion, and elevates human beings to lofty positions. He is the Creator and there is the law of nature with physical and moral order. There is cosmos in the universe which is essential for the meaningful life of human beings. It is this order which has evolved and developed various physical and social sciences for the broadening of human mind and understanding.

The Prophet of Islam was directly taught and clearly inspired by God. His complete life, actions and words were fully devoted to the teaching and dissemination of *Tauhid* (Monotheism). He was the Prophet of Divine Unity and God made him torch bearer of this message to rewaken this Truth in order to rejuvenate and revivify the dormant and slumbering nations. This sublime truth is the combination of the preceding revelations which Allah desired to be confirmed and established so that they could penetrate in the minds and souls of mankind.

The Quran has laid great emphasis on the Unity of God *(Tauhid)* and all the social and moral rules are the outcome of this concept. The belief in one God, Invisible and Almighty removes all superstitions, fetish and dogmas and stresses the possibility of clear understanding of good and evil. The idea of Divine mercy and justice *(Adl)*, clearly indicates the understanding of brotherhood and equality among men of their reconciliation in a common ideal. God ordained that His teachings through the Holy Prophet (peace be upon him) should not be confined to any race, community or nation, but to all humanity. It should be universal. God is not exclusively an Islamic God, but God of every human being and of the whole universe. He is All-Comprehensible, not limited to space or time.

Eternal Truth

The Holy Prophet (peace be upon him) had given the message of eternal Truth, which is crystal clear and positive than other doctrines. He had not employed any mysterious or supernatural means to explain His message. The Quranic stories and tales symbolically reflect the majesty and transcendence of the message of Allah. The idea of Monotheism preached by the Prophet of Islam attained the peak of its glory and is undoubtedly best suited to the spiritual conditions and scientific environment of our age. Rationally speaking the teachings of the Prophet Muhammad (peace be upon him) are as fresh and alive today as it was at the early stage of Islam. The manifestation of Divine Will reached its culmination in the belief of one God (Monotheism) in the world-at-large. The comprehension of this idea has reached its climax in the enlightened circles of the modern world.

It is futile to attempt at probing the mysteries of the Unknowable for the exact knowledge of God is beyond our reach. We fully understand His Laws and His Will, and realise His Universality and Almightiness through the creation of the Universe and the constellation of stars, moon, the sun, oceans and mountains and billions of living things in the world, all moving and working with scientific precision. Who is there to deny the forces working in unison, with unity in diversity? It is this universality and expansiveness that finds its way in every corner of the world. It is not only Islam that progresses. It is really Monotheism that has blown its trumpets and exercised a far-reaching influence on the minds and thoughts of the people endowed with reason and intellect. It is this aspect of Quranic teachings that great thinkers like Rousseau, Goethe, Carlyle, and even Napoleon were considerably influenced. Napoleon Bonaparte expressed his idea thus:

> "Arabia was idolatrous when, six centuries after Jesus, Muhammad introduced the worship of God of Abraham, of Ishmael, of Moses and of Jesus: The Aryan and some other sects had disturbed the tranquillity of the East by agitating the question of the nature of the Father, the son and the Holy Ghost. Muhammad declared that there was none but one God who had no father, no son and that the Trinity imported the idea of idolatory" *(Cherfils, Bonaparte* et *L' Islam,* Paris, pp. 105-25).

The Islamic deity is not merely 'god' *(Ilah)* but the God (Allah). He is not merely an object of ritualistic worship, but the possessor of all the dimensions of Highest Excellence,—indeed, of Absolute Perfection. He is the Fountainhead *(Samad)* of all the Values and Ideals. He is the Omnipotent, the Omniscient, the Omnipresent, the Infinite, the Absolute, the One *(Ahad)* and the indivisible God, who neither incarnates nor has any Partner or Son or compeer. He is Transcendent in His Being and Immanent in the cosmos through His love, knowledge and power. He is the Creator, the Sustainer, the Nourisher and the Evolver of everything that constitutes the cosmos, equally: He is the Righteous God who bestows no special favour on any individual or community on the basis of such distinctions as those of race or colour on creed.

Islam gives the integrating principle in the one true God, Allah. Bentham and Mill and the recent Pragmatic philosophies give it in the concept of utilitarianism, which is based on the principle of pure expediency. Hegal and Hegelians give it in the state deified. The protagonists of nationalism and racialism give it in the Nation deified and Race deified. Karl Marx and Marxists give it in the Economic Force deified.

The basic concept which the Glorious Quran envisages is the adoration of one True God (Allah). This has to be performed as the noblest creature and Vicegerent of God—as a fully-integrated being committed to cosmic mission. He should have complete faith that God's personality enshrines the Perfect Ideal of Integration and man is his viceroy. His adoration, should therefore be dynamic and comprehensive. It should be vast and expansive, not confined to worship only. It should encompass the development of whole personality, launching of societies for the welfare and amelioration of the individual and community, raising their socio-economic, cultural, educational, scientific and technological level to a state where they could ponder, reflect and observe and unravel the vast impregnable mysteries and knowledge hidden in Nature. This would also give man a chance in the pursuit of physical sciences and make him active crusader for the spiritual and moral emancipation of humanity and the establishment of social, economic and political justice as ordained by the Quran.

The basic concept which the Quran inculcates in human mind is the concept of the Unity of God, on which is based another concurred idea of the Unity of man which has to be nourished and developed vigorously by man. A great writer and thinker C. F. Andrews in his booklet *"The Genuine Islam"* remarks: "One of the greatest blessings which Islam has brought to East and West alike has been the emphasis which, at a critical period in human history, it placed upon the Divine Unity. For during those Dark Ages both in East and West, from 600 to 1000 A.D., this doctrine was in danger of being overlaid and obscured in Hinduism and in Christianity, owing to the immense accretions of subsidiary worships of countless demi-gods and heroes. Islam has been, both to Europe and India, in their darkest hour of aberration from the sovereign truth of God's Unity, an invaluable corrective and deterrent. Indeed, without the final emphasis on this truth which Islam gave from its central position facing both India and Europe. It is doubtful whether this idea of God as one could have obtained that establish place in human thought which is uncontested in the intellectual world today" (Vol. 1, No. 8, 1936).

Kingdom of Allah

The basis of Islamic polity, no doubt, is the kingdom of Allah. Although sovereignty of Allah is fundamental to the concept of state in Islam, statehood *(mulk)*, writes Ibn Khaldun, exists by nature in man and is necessary for his existence.

Islam created a community of believers on the basis of Unity of God, and bound them by the concept of brotherhood, socially integrated in equality and dignity. Political power and authority is inherent in the idea of community because society cannot exist without it. Although power in Islamic political history is not an end in itself but a means to an end, viz., the realisation of the good Iife envisaged in Islam: the acquisition of political power should be deemed natural and normal.

Islam stands for certain ethical and spiritual values which may collectively be called the ideology of Islam. For the purpose of translating this ideology into practice, the setting up of a well-organised political system is indispensable.

Islamic polity aims not merely to establish a state but to organise a society of the Muslims and convert it to a society endowed with an ideology. The Holy Quran, the source of eternal guidance, has not laid down any cut and dried pattern of Government to be followed by all Islamic States. It does, however, indicate the broad fundamental principles on which Islamic polity should be based.

The religious polity of Islam, according to Allama Abdullah Yusuf Ali, is not committed to any particular form of sovereignty such as kingship, aristocracy, or democracy. It defines certain great principles and lays down certain conditions for a righteous state. The principle of liberty is insisted upon. The supremacy of law is one of the fundamental tenets of Islamic polity. It is supreme not only over the subjects but over the rulers as well. This supreme law has its source in divine guidance. The Holy Quran does not interfere in matters political, nor does it lay down specific rules of conduct in state matters. But as already mentioned above, it has provided a set of principles which can *very* well form the basis of Islamic polity. Islam is a dynamic force, a concept of life, a guidance for the springs of thought and action and not a static code of action. That was why the Holy Prophet (peace be upon him) did not lay down any definitive form of government for his people, nor any hard and fast rules for organising governmental or administrative machinery.

Islamic political theory is normative in character and is concerned with a specific ethical ideal—the raising of humanity to the highest well-being both materially and morally, by means of an extensive commonwealth built on belief in One God whose authority is supreme.

Islam builds its polity on the foundation of the sovereignty of God and the vicegerency of man. All power emanates from Him: Islamic polity may well be called the 'kingdom of God on earth', administered in accordance with the Commands of God and the teachings of the Holy Prophet (peace be upon him). The basic principles mentioned in the Holy Quran are that the Muslims should obey God, His Prophet (peace be upon him), and those who from amongst them are put in authority over them. The other important constitutional principles are that Muslims should cooperate in righteousness and justice: these are important constitutional principles that form the basic principles of good government.

Allah says: "Oh you faithful; Obey God and obey His Apostle and those in authority from among you" (4:59).

The First Duty of a Muslim is to God: He should not at any cost compromise his allegiance to the clear injunctions of the Holy Quran and the teachings of the Holy Prophet (peace be upon him) by obeying or following an order which is un-Islamic, or in clear contravention of the tenets of Islam. The basis of human action should be moral and not political: there should be no divorce between fundamental morality and political activity. The only enduring polity which can ensure justice and fairplay to all and can contribute to the welfare of humanity can be the one based on the principles of Islam.

Government in an Islamic State should be organised on the basis which makes it possible that all decisions should be the result of mutual consultation, the fundamental principle that has been clearly defined in the Holy Quran—that Muslims are expected to order their affairs by mutual consultations which is the basis of democracy. It is inherent in the idea of consultation that the majority view should prevail and the personal opinions subordinated to discipline and requirement of unity.

The foundations of polity in Islam are laid in the Holy Quran and the teachings of the Holy Prophet (peace be upon him). The sacred law of Islam, the *Shariah,* is the final legal authority in all Muslim countries. The *Shariah* is a Divine Law and all its ordinance are so formulated that one of them conflicts with the real nature of man and the genuine requirements of human society at any time.

Says Allah: "For everyone of you We have ordained a Divine Law and an open road" (5:48).

Scholars define *Shariah* as the sum total of the Islamic guidance revealed to the Holy Prophet (peace be upon him) by God and transmitted by him to humanity as enshrined in the Holy Quran and the authentically recorded words and deeds of the Holy Prophet (peace be upon him). The original meaning of the word '*Shariah*' is a stream of water. As much as water is the source of life so is *Shariah* of Islam the course of orderly and harmonious social life.

The *Shariah,* says an eminent scholar, contains all the principles necessary "to correct and cure" the social diseases of the Islamic world. Properly understood *Shariah* derives its principles from the Holy Quran from "What is true and valid for the *Sunnah* (including the *Hadith),* from the consensus of the community represented by its scholars and learned men. "Viewed as such the *Shariah* is a binding authority on every Muslim".

In Islam, the *Shariah* is a positively ordained Divine Law to which man and society must conform. Polity in Islam is rule by *Shariah,* the Divine Law. It is "the key to Islam in politics, the instruments to which Islam affects the mundane lives of its adherents".

"Islamic law in its fullest sense regulates the cult it is the embodiment of the true Islamic spirit, the most decisive expression of Islamic thought and the essential kernal of Islam generally."

Islam is a religion of law in the full meaning of the word. "The *Shariah* is more than a set of rules, it entails a whole mentality and a way of life, the core and kernal of Islam itself", says Professor Joseph Schacht. "Islam is a polity and a method of governance", say G.H. Jansen in *Militant Islam.*

Its polity and method of governance are based on Divine Law. In an Islamic State, the Government draws its inspiration of its constitution from the Holy Quran and the teachings of the Holy Prophet (peace be upon him) and obtains from the *Shoora,* the Council of State, the advice and help of the representatives of the Muslim community. Its legislation assures to the individuals perfect equality of rights and justice. The supremacy of the *Shariah* is held as essential to the efficacy of the Government. The flexibility and adaptability of law admits of development and progress.

The state is a natural result of human life which requires association and organisation. Human association is necessary as 'man is a citizen by nature', as philosophers say.

Pristine Islam, as preached and acted upon by the last Prophet (peace be upon him) was a clarion call for a fundamental and radical break with the age of ignorance, with its irrational, superstitious and inhuman usages, traditions, customs and conventions, a call which was summed up by the Holy Prophet (peace be upon him) in the following declaration at his farewell pilgrimage:

> "Behold everything of ignorance is put down under my two feet. The blood-revenges of the Dark Age are remitted."

The last and lasting message of the last Prophet (peace be upon him) heralded the end of the ancient world of paganism, oppression, inequalities and injustices, of pride and privilege based upon distinctions of tribe, family, race and colour; and the beginning of the new age of reason and light, of human dignity and equality, of human rights and duties. All idols and icons, whether made of stone or wood or flesh, were smashed.

Allama Iqbal had grasped the essential 'modernity' of Islam in his observation:

> "The spirit of modern times ... is wholly in keeping with the spirit of Islam."

Dr. Samuel Johnson, with his typical Johnsonian perspicacity, affiliated the Prophet (peace be upon him) with the modern world.

Divine Government

"His (Muhammad's) thoroughly democratic conception of the Divine Government, the universality of his religious ideal, his simple humanity.... all affiliated him with the modern world."

Islam is the most misunderstood religion. It has been misunderstood not only by its historical rival religions such as Judaism and Christianity, but, ironically, by its own adherents. Self-seeking *Muftis* and *Qazis*, at the behest of their royal masters, and under the influence of Muslim feudal classes misrepresented and misinterpreted Islam as a dogmatic, conservative and obscurantist creed, deviating from the simple, rational democratic and humanist spirit of pristine Islam.

While, on the one hand, Jews and Christians have represented and painted Islam as a militant religion carrying Quran in one hand and sword in the other, orthodox and fundamentalist Muslims, on the other hand, have identified and equated Islam with the medieval tradition and outlook with orthodoxy and obscurantism, with oriental passivity and inaction. If, on the one hand, Islam does not glorify aggression and war, on the other, it is not an ascetic and passive religion.

Islam is a positive, activist and radical religion which sought to establish a society on the foundations of unity, justice, human dignity and equality, and which gave a conception of religion different from the ancient and the medieval. As against Buddhist and Christian view of life and the word Islam gave a new meaning and dimension to religious and spiritual life, showing to man and guiding him on the path not only of eternal peace and bliss in the Hereafter but also to peace and order through justice here and now on earth. Islam enjoins on man to change the order of the world, to enforce Good and prevent Evil.

Gautama Buddha and Jesus Christ, though concerned with man's spiritual and moral transformation, did not adopt any practical and militant means to change the social, economic and political order of the world." It was no more the purpose of Gautama than Jesus to establish order in the world. Nothing could have been further from his thoughts than the redress of social justice", writes a very distinguished scholar of Buddhism. Buddhism and Christianity never formulated any ideal of a social, economic and political order, their spiritual and ethical ideal and outlook were other-worldly and aimed at personal salvation.

In the Islamic scheme of things there was no Church, no Pope, and no Emperor. The Holy Prophet (peace be upon him) and the first four Heads of the early Islamic Republic did not establish any ecclesiastical and clerical order and hierarchy like the Church, or like Buddhist Sangha, nor did they establish any hereditary imperial dynasty. However, the early and pristine Islamic order, based upon Justice, Equality and Brotherhood, was later replaced by despotic kings and their suppliant obscurantist juris-consults, who through casuistry distorted and changed the simple, rational and democratic order of the early days.

Iqbal's Attempt

The main burden of Allama Iqbal's attempt to reconstruct Islamic thought was the removal from Islam "the hard crust which has immobilised an essentially dynamic outlook on life, and to rediscover the original varieties of freedom, equality and solidarity with a view to rebuild (ing) our moral, social and political ideals out of their original simplicity and universality". The Islamic polity and state as conceived by Allama Iqbal was "a contractual organism long before Rousseau ever thought of such a thing".

The rationality and liberality of Islam and of its Prophet (peace be upon him) has been acknowledged and accepted by all truth-seeking and truth-loving scholars, historians and thinkers. "The Prophet of Makkah", writes Edward Gibbon, "rejected the worship of idols and men, of stars and planets, on the rational principle that whatever rises must set, that whatever is born must die, that whatever is corruptible must decay and perish. In the *Author of the Universe,* his rational enthusiasm confessed and adored an

Infinite and Eternal Being, without form or place, without issue or similitude.

A philosophic theist might subscribe to the popular creed of Muhammadans: a creed too sublime perhaps for our present faculties. The first principle of reasons and revelation was confirmed by the voice of Muhammad .... More pure than the system of Zoroaster, more liberal than the Law of Moses, the religion of Muhammad might seem less inconsistent with reason than the creed of mystery and superstition which, in the seventh century, disgraced the simplicity of the Gospel".

Islam's natural and rational conception of religion, its reliance on reason and argument as against blind tradition, is admitted by impartial Western historians. "Islam stands alone", writes Guizot, author of *The History of Civilization in Europe*, "among religions in discountenancing the reliance on tradition without argument".

Professor A. G. Widgery, in his book *Living Religions and Modern Thought*, writes about Islam: "There is a simplicity about this religion, and when Muslims, have allied themselves definitely with modern culture, Islam may make a bid for the allegiance of the modern world. It has much of the character of Occidental Unitarianism, and is in the main free from the kinds of dogmas which are being neglected or definitely discarded by the Christian world".

Allama Iqbal, in his brochure, *Islam and Ahmadism*, has made observations about the nature and functions of Islamic State which identify it with the modern, democratic, civil and non-theocratic state: "The Islamic idea of the division of the religious and political functions of the state must not be confounded with the European idea of the separation of Church and state. The former is only a division of functions, the latter is based on the metaphysical dualism of spirit and matter. Christianity began as an order of Monks having nothing to do with the affairs of the world; Islam was from the very beginning, a civil society with laws civil in their nature though believed to be revelational in origin".

Islam has played a pioneering role in the evolution of human civilisation in the sense that it was the first to rise above the considerations of race, colour, language and nationality—problems that still afflict humanity—and did not just give a call but actually established a world brotherhood, based on its lofty ideals.

Part - V
Diplomacy

20

Centuries Old Institution

The Arabs came into contact with the rest of the world during the seventh to ninth centuries, carrying a message that embodied rules and principles and directives on relations between individuals and nations. They accepted some prevailing principles, modified others and introduced new rules and principles. In either case, these accepted, modified, or introduced rules were codified and established in the form of law and faith. Their observance by Muslims was assured because of its status as law and their origin as religious beliefs.

A large proportion of the presently accepted rules of international relations were already established and recognized by the Arabs of that period. They respected their commitment to treaties and conventions and they gave priority to peaceful settlement through mediation and arbitration. They recognized immunities and privileges of diplomats, granted the right of asylum through the institution of Aman, and observed the rules concerning aliens, neutrality, and good-neighbourly relations.

Certain Rules

One can point with confidence to certain rules of international relations, practised at present, that were established by the Muslim Arabs of that period. Equality among men and nations, brotherly relations and the principles of universality in the legal sense, were the contribution of Arabs to the world. When Islam was teaching that, men were brothers and people were created to live together, being descendants of the same father and mother and that no Arab had advantage over a non-Arab, or a race over another race, the Romans and Byzantines were classifying the peoples of the world into three categories—the civilized, the barbarians and the savages. It took Europe eleven to twelve centuries more to acknowledge these principles through the motto of the French Revolution. Yet, their applicability to other nations remain questionable.

While the Muslim State was prevented, according to the teaching of the Quran, from intervening in the internal affairs of another state with which it was bound by a treaty, even in order to aid the Muslim minority there, the present practice of the big powers interfering in the affairs of smaller states is often justified as providing support to certain minorities in those states.

The Arabs observed certain principles regarding the conduct of war, i.e. the inviolability of peaceful individuals who did not participate in the acts of hostilities (children, women, invalids and monks); the protection of religious places and vital resources the sacredness of death and dead bodies; the fair treatment of people under occupation; the prisoners of war and hostages; and many other situations which were codified in the Geneva Convention fifty years ago.

The contributions of the Arabs to international law and to diplomacy rules continued to be made by the successive Islamic States until the fall of the Ottoman Empire.

It is true that the Muslim States did not follow strictly at all times the rules and principles of Islam, in the same way as it is true that big powers, at present, who laid down prevailing rules of international relations adhere to these rules upon convenience.

Interaction between Muslim values and those of the other nations, and the Arab contribution to the formation of the principles of international relations, ceased to continue into modern history. Not only did they not participate in the legislation of international rules at times such as that when the victorious nations negotiated them in the framework of the League of Nations, but they were also subjected to rules imposed upon them under the mandated regime—a regime which differentiated between European countries liberated from the Ottoman rule and Arab countries. Of these, the League of Nations recognized the independence of the first, but put the latter under the mandate of big power. The only standards were European values and traditions.

In present diplomatic practice, the Anglo-Saxon traits are being challenged frequently. The evolvement of the United Nations with more than 180 member states may allow the majority to have its say. In the struggle among powers the stronger may prevail, but in the confrontation among civilizations, interaction could be the only solution.

Early Arab States

Arabia or 'the Arab Island' is that geographical area which includes the Arabian Peninsula and the region which lies between the Tigris River and the Mediterranean Sea. It extends over 2.5 million square kilometers. The desert occupies the biggest part of the land.

From the first century A.D. up to the period under study, Arabia was surrounded by great powers. The Roman Empire in the west, which was succeeded by the Byzantine Empire in the north, was competing with the Persian Empire in the east. All these powers were struggling for the extension of their influence in the area. The beginning of the second century A.D. witnessed the absorption of an independent Arab state by the Romans. This was the Nabatian Arab state with its capital in Petra. It had emerged in the Hellenistic period, and controlled the tradeways from the south of Arabia to the north. It had succeeded in safeguarding its independence during the earlier part of the Roman era, but was conquered in A.D. 106. On the other hand, Palmyra, which was situated in the eastern part of Syria, between the two feuding powers of Rome and Persia, managed to maintain its independence through its policy of alternating between neutrality and alliance. Its king, Odena, was acknowledged by the Roman emperor, Gallienus as co-emperor of the Orient. After his death, his wife Zenobia maintained his power until Aurelianus destroyed Palmyra in A.D. 273.

After the destruction of the two independent states and until the emergence of the Islamic State in Medina, the other Arab states that existed in the northern parts of Arabia were vassal states. In the sixth century, the Ghassanid dynasty ruled over Damascus. Its kings were designated by the Byzantines and the Lakhmids in Babylonia who were themselves under the influence of Persians. In A.D. 610 Arab Lakhmids, revolting against the manipulation of the Persians, they attacked the Euphrates and decisively defeated the Persian Army at Dhi-Qar. During the same period South Arabia was occupied by the Abyssinians.

Different Arab tribes ruled over the other parts of Arabia, particularly the area around the Arabian Desert. These tribes, far from being subjected to any external influence, ruled these territories as independent states. In spite of the fact that the territorial boundaries among these tribal states were not clearly fixed, and although they were independent from each other, they had many characteristics in common. The population of each tribe-state consisted of two categories of peoples, the stationary city and village dwellers, whose livelihood depended on farming and trade, and the wandering bedouins who traded cattle and moved seasonally in search of water and pastures. Their culture and social norms, all revolved around a common language and similarity of basic religious thought.

The common spiritual and cultural ties, that bound the Arab population were vividly expressed by their unique language and an appreciation of the rhythmic word. Brockelmann attests to this by saying that, 'the Arabs owed their awareness of constituting a people, in spite of all tribal contradictions, principally to their most important common spiritual possession, their poetry.' Among the Arabs of that period there were some Christians and Jews, but the majority were polytheistic. Each tribe had its own gods and goddesses and its own places of worship, but they all revered the Kaaba and would go on pilgrimage to Mecca. In addition to all the gods and goddesses they worshipped, the Arabs believed in one greater God, 'Allah' who was the creator of the world and contrary to popular belief, the Arabs did not borrow the concept of 'Allah' from the Jews or the Christians.' It is this God that

Abdul-Muttaleb, the grandfather of Prophet Muhammed (PBUH), referred to during the Abyssinian attack on Mecca (A.D. 570) when he said, 'the Kaaba has its God who will protect it.' Abdul-Muttaleb named one of his sons Abdullah (the slave of Allah) after the same God. It happened that Abdullah was destined to become the father of Prophet Muhammed (PBUH). The other gods and goddesses were inferior to Allah and worshipping them, as some people believed, was just an expression of reverence to the greater God: 'We worship them only that they may bring us near to Allah.' On the eve of the advent of Islam, this polytheistic cult, according to Brockelmann, 'no longer filled the entire religious consciousness of the Arabs.'

One of these tribal states was that of the Quraysh tribe in the city of Mecca, which lies in the Hijaz region in the northwestern part of the Peninsula. In the center of Mecca stood the Kaaba, a four cornered structure, which is believed to have been originally built by Prophet Abraham. The Kaaba and the surrounding area was regarded as *Haram,* a sacred inviolable place not only for the Quraysh but also for the other Arab tribes. In fact, the city derived its relative wealth from the seasonal trade between South Arabia and Syria and from the influx of pilgrims to the Kaaba and the nearby mountain of Arafat. Prophet Muhammed (PBUH) descended from the family of the Quraysh. He was born in A.D. 570, in a year known as the Year of the Elephant. That is, in that year the Abyssinians attacked Mecca with an army supported by elephants in order to destroy the Kaaba and eliminate this center of power. It is interesting to note that the recognized leader of the Quraysh, Abdul-Muttaleb, the grandfather of Muhammed (PBUH) had negotiated with Abraha, the Abyssinian leader, and had decided to withdraw from Mecca, together with his people and their belongings, thus leaving the assailants to face an empty land. Eventually, the invaders were defeated.

Concept of Modern Diplomacy

To qualify certain incidents or manifestations during this period of history as incidents of diplomatic conduct, one must briefly study the different interpretations of the expression 'diplomacy' and delineate a concept that can be taken as a basis for further evaluation of what would be considered diplomatic conduct.

The word 'diplomacy' is an expression that has been used in English for no more than two centuries. It is derived from the word 'diplome', which originally meant a folded document. A diploma is understood to be a document by which a privilege is conferred, a state paper or a charter. In the nineteenth century this expression came to mean 'the science of foreign relations, for which, as a base, diplomas were issued by monarchs.'

In other terms diplomacy was defined as 'the science and art of negotiation' and 'the art of reconciling the peoples' interests among states.

William Macomber defines the modern concept of diplomacy as:

- the art and practice of conducting relations between nations, as in arranging treaties....the business or art of conducting international intercourse;
- the ordered conduct of relations between one group of human beings and another group alien to themselves;
- the management of international relations by negotiations, the method by which these relations are adjusted and managed by ambassadors and envoys. The business or art of the diplomats;
- the application of intelligence and tact to the conduct of official relations between the governments and independent states;
- the art of resolving international difficulties peacefully. It is also the technique or skill, which, reigns over the development, in a harmonious manner, of international relations.

In contemporary practice, diplomacy has a wider scope of conduct due to the growth of relations between states and the availability of diverse means and methods of communication. In essence, diplomacy 'is concerned with the management of relations between states and between states and other sectors.' It is concerned with advising, shaping and implementing foreign policy. As such it is the means, by which states, through their formal representatives, articulate, coordinate and secure specific or wider interests. Correspondence, private talks, exchange of views, lobbying, visits, threats and other related activities are used. Besides being concerned with peaceful activity, diplomacy may be employed during war, armed conflict or while preparing for an act of violence over another territory such as seeking flight clearance for an air strike. Thus diplomacy may involve the entire ambit of foreign relations, policy formation as well as execution. In this broad sense, a nation's diplomacy and foreign policy are the same. In the narrower, more traditional sense, diplomacy involves means and mechanisms, whereas foreign policy implies ends and objectives.

Evolution of Diplomacy

Diplomacy has existed since nation-states began. The concept of a diplomat is, however, rather new. Diplomacy in its initial stages did not employ permanent personnel. Envoys were recruited for a particular mission, and when their work was done, they returned to their original duties. In the early stages they were usually selected from among the clergy, later on, nations dispatched orators to deal with issues due to their skills of persuasion.

The practice of employing envoys to reside in the host country began in the fifteenth century through the Italian city-states. This pattern was later copied by the French. At the Congress of Vienna (1815), and in subsequent agreements of the Congress of Aix-La-Chapele, the pattern of permanent diplomacy was codified."

Up to the beginning of World War II, very little change took place in the manner and means of formulating foreign policies. After the establishment of the United Nations and advances in the means of communication, two major phenomena have occured. The first is represented in the increasingly important role of multilateral diplomacy. The second is observed in the number of parties who are involved in the process of implementing the foreign policy, and in the increasing possibilities of decision making from the center. In other words, the role played by heads of states and ministers in conducting foreign relations, and direct instructions from the government have decreased the role and influence of ambassadors in shaping and conducting foreign relations. On the other hand, widening relations and diversity of interests have expanded the duties of ambassadors, both in the fields of bilateral and multilateral relations.

Diversity of Diplomatic Manifestations

Conducting foreign relations through diplomacy, could be manifested in different ways under different titles, depending on the diversity of targets, methods, tools and manners of practice. Diplomacy, open or secret, bilateral or multilateral, varies with the states, the situation, the political environment, and the interests involved. However, aided by supportive elements, it remains an art rather than a science and supplies the indispensable element of personal contact in the relationship between states.

Recognition of a state by another is an essential element in establishing relations between the two. Recognition of a state could be *de facto*, which is a provisional acceptance of the authority of a state over a territory—the legitimacy of that however, is questionable—or it could be *de jure*, which implies a complete unqualified recognition of that state.

Methods of conducting foreign relations can be through parliamentary or summit meetings, through dialogues, usually carried out by ambassadors for exchange of information without involving definite commitments, or by an act which is imposed on the other state as *fait accompli*, and which forms the basis of a negotiated settlement.

The goals of diplomacy, like maintaining peaceful relations, settling a dispute, imposing hegemony, developing relations or evading a situation, may decide the shape and tools of diplomacy used in each case. Comity, *rapprochement*, appeasement, *detente* or treaty, are different tools used in attaining diplomatic goals.

Application of Diplomacy in the Pre-Islamic State Period : There are significant manifestations of established diplomatic conduct in the period that preceded the establishment of the Islamic State. To facilitate the study of these, one would divide this period into two phases. The first one began in A.D. 570, the birth year of Prophet Muhammed (PBUH), and lasted until A.D. 610, the date of his first revelation; and the second phase which was marked by the endeavours of the Prophet (PBUH) to spread the new religion among his people and outside Mecca. This phase lasted until A.D. 622 when Prophet Muhammed (PBUH) immigrated to Medina, thus starting a new era with the establishment of an Islamic society and state.

During the first phase, it is possible to identify three cases that could represent the outcome of diplomatic conduct. The first one was the success of Abdul-Muttaleb in regaining his camels, that were confiscated by the invading army of Abraha. He achieved this by meeting the latter and negotiating their release. The other example was the consensus throughout North Arabia to consider four months of every year as months of peace and non-aggression, so that the caravans could go through and pilgrimages could take place in safety. These months were the seventh month at one interval and the three months that end and begin the lunar calendar.

Needless to say, such an agreement in itself is not diplomacy, but the process of reaching such an agreement and the constant observance of its rules were good indications of the diplomatic conduct of that period. Unfortunately, no clearly recorded documents are available to testify these two cases.

The third example is one known as the Fudhul Pact. There was an agreement among the different clans of the Quraysh in Mecca to come to the aid of any inhabitant of Mecca (or of those visiting it), if subjected to injustice, and to support him against the oppressor until his rights were restored. The story as rendered by Ibn Hisham is that the heads of the Quraysh clans held a meeting (around A.D. 590) in the house of the senior most among them, Abdullah bin Judaan, and reached this agreement. The meeting took place after one trader of Zabid voiced a complaint against Al-Aas bin Wael a known figure in Mecca, to whom he had sold some merchandise, but who had failed to pay him back. It is recorded that this pact was invoked again, during the rule of Muawiyah (the first Umayyad Caliph A.D. 661-680) when his governor in Medina, Al-Walid bin Utbeh had a dispute with Al-Hussein bin Ali (son of the fourth Caliph) over some property. The latter declared that if he were denied fair treatment, he would go to the Apostle's Mosque and would call for the invocation of the Fudhul Pact. Abdullah bin Al-Zubair who was attending the meeting announced right there, that he would lend him his support and would fight for him. Two other Medina citizens vowed to take the same stand. When the Governor became aware of this collective support, he yielded to the opposition and conceded to Al-Hussein.

21

Basic Principles

In conducting their diplomatic relations, the Arabs observed certain rules that were, and still are, considered as necessary to facilitate these activities. These are the immunities and privileges extended to diplomatic envoys and the manner of dealing with diplomatic missions, which now comes under protocol.

Some of these rules were known and observed by the Arabs before Islam and some other rules were traditions, recognized in international contacts. Regarding the previously mentioned rules, Islam had accepted them, modified them, or presented new ones. In all cases, the most significant modification of these rules was that they were basically codified in religious and legal terms.

Diplomatic Immunity

In Arab traditions, before Islam, certain rules of immunity were observed on the basis of place, time or circumstances. The pilgrims to Kaaba were immune, their safety being secured during the four forbidden months and both, envoys and those who requested Aman, were to be protected. Islam recognized these traditions and further legislated them.

The right of Aman was extended to anyone including envoys. The latter were entitled to the protection of Muslims not only under the institution of Aman, but also for the nature of their mission. While Aman could be granted or denied, an envoy was to be received with no obstacles to mar his visit. The only limitation on his freedom was the checks that were applied to the act of spying. If an envoy acquired military information, that would be prejudicial to the Muslim army, it was permissible to retain him until this problem had been taken care of. This constraint did not imply ill-treatment or imprisonment of the envoy, even if he reacted unfavourably.

When Prophet Muhammed (PBUH) received two envoys from Musailemah bin Khabib (who claimed prophethood and suggested partitioning the land between them) he asked the envoys what they had to say to that. They attested to what Musailemah had claimed. Prophet Muhammed (PBUH) responded by saying 'By God, if it were not (the fact) that envoys could not be killed I would have severed your heads.'

As an evidence of the modification Islam made on the rule of immunities granted to diplomatic envoys, two examples can be cited. In presenting the Arab concept in comparison to the then prevailing traditions, Joinville in his book *Origines du Droits International* says that, in the nineteenth century, the right of inviolability granted to ambassadors was not based on a principle of law, but only on the value of a word given. If the king who gave his protection to an envoy died while the latter was still in the country, the authorities would take the ambassador and his companions as prisoners and slaves, whether they were Muslims or Christians. On the other hand, the principle of Aman was binding not only on the one who extended his protection, but also on the Muslim community as a whole. When a Venetian delegation came to the Prince of Padova, Francesco Carrara, a few centuries later, the Prince cut off the noses and ears of the delegates. Even at the beginning of this century, the Rules of the Hague (1907) stipulated in Article 13 that an envoy would lose the right of inviolability if he committed an act of treachery. On a contrasting plane is the example of diplomatic forbearance set by the Umayyad Wazir of Andalusia, Al-Mansur. He was receiving a delegation dispatched by the King of Leon when the head of the delegation, who had come to request a three-day truce, uttered some insulting remarks to him. It is related that Al-Mansur smiled and requested the envoy to proceed and present his request, which was then courteously accorded.

Diplomatic Privileges

Foreign envoys were received by a Muslim ruler with courtesy and honour. Nizam ul-Mulk stresses that ambassadors are the representatives of their monarchs and they should be treated as such. From the early days of Islam instances were recorded to this effect. In the year A.H. 9 or A.D. 631, a delegation from the Thaqif tribe came to Medina to meet the Prophet (PBUH). They were received and accommodated in a simple but dignified manner. Before meeting the Prophet (PBUH), they were informed of the Muslim way of salutation; they ignored it and insisted on their own traditional salutation. When offered food, they would insist that the host should try it first.

It has been already cited that Abu-Bakr, when instructing the first army that was directed to Syria, ordered the leader Yazid, that in case he received envoys coming from the side of his enemy, he should treat them well. Muawiyah was known for his affable treatment of visitors that 'made him seem more like a Sayyid of an Arab tribe than a sovereign.'

Diplomatic envoys were exempted from taxes imposed on the inhabitants of the Islamic State. Only goods carried by the envoy for commercial purposes were subjected to taxation. Abu Yousuf, the well known Islamic legislator in the Abbaside period, stated that an envoy who brought material for trading would pay one-tenth tax after conducting the sale. In a comparable modern instance, the Vienna Convention of 1961 enumerates cases of exempting a diplomatic agent from duties and taxes, but Article 34 excludes from exemption taxes imposed on personal income earned by a diplomat through commercial activities which take place in the host country. It further excludes from exemptions, taxes due on private real estate owned by a diplomat and the indirect taxes included in prices and tariffs.

An envoy to a Muslim state was not allowed, on his way back to an antagonistic country, to carry with him arms, horses or captured slaves. If he had bought them, they would be returned to the seller and his money would be refunded. The measure was taken on the premise that these would add to the power of the enemy.

Ceremonies and Protocol

Ceremonies and protocol are tributaries to the mainstream of diplomatic activities. They help in organizing such activities, with the intention of giving the right impression of power and greatness. They also are meant to avoid any unfavourable reaction resulting from an unintended error or lapse.

In the early Arab history, one finds that measures of protocol evolved along with the course of development and growth of the Islamic States. In early Islamic history, rules of protocol were simple and rudimentary. They became more complex and refined in the later period of the Umayyad and Abbaside reigns. At the peak of that period, ceremonies and rules of protocol that were observed in the three capitals of Andalusia, Byzantium and the Abbaside Empire were, in many ways, so similar that it was difficult to make out which one of them was imitating the other.

The main principles of these activities could be found in the early days of Islam. The Quran laid down certain rules for proper conduct which were certainly applicable in the case of diplomatic behaviour. At that time, delegations coming to meet the Prophet (PBUH) were taught to observe the rules of precedence and how to address him. 'Ye, who believe, put not yourselves forward before God and His Apostle...' 'Ye, who believe, raise not your voices above the voice of the Prophet (PBUH), do not speak aloud to him in talk, as ye may speak aloud to one another...'

When the delegation from the Thaqif tribe came to meet Prophet Muhammed (PBUH), they were instructed in greeting him with the Islamic salutation. When Abu-Bakr (RA) went to bid farewell to the Muslim army that was dispatched to Syria, he went on foot while the army leader, Yazid bin Abu Sufian was riding.

The latter addressed the Caliph asking him either to ride or to let him dismount. The Caliph refused either proposal saying that he was making this 'gesture' for the sake of God. When Omer bin al-Khattab (RA) entered Jerusalem dressed simply and met Bishop Sofronius, the Greek historian Theophanes claims that the bishop exclaimed 'truly, this is the abomination of desolation spoken of in Daniel the Prophet (11:31) as standing in the holy place.' This indicates that during the first phase of Islamic history, heads of states and their district governors were modest in their appearance and simple in their manner of contact with the others, being first among equals, distinguished only by their responsibility. At a later stage, Caliphs were separating themselves from the population, whether in the mosque or inside their palace. In the court of the Abbaside Caliph, a post for the Chamberlain was created under the name of Hajib. His duty was to introduce the 'accredited envoys and distinguished visitors into the Caliph's presence.' Priorities, ranks and titles of honour became known from the beginning of the Umayyad Dynasty rule. Muawiyah used to sit in the audience chamber within the mosque on a square seat, covered with richly embroidered cushions, which formed the Caliphal throne. On the right stood his paternal relatives in a row according to seniority and on his left stood his maternal relatives, in the same order. During the Umayyad and Abbaside rule, the Caliph's viceroy in the province was addressed as Amir. In the districts the governor appointed by the Caliph or by the Amir of a province was known as Aamil. During the Abbaside rule, the highest official in rank, assisting the Caliph, was called Wazir. On the other side of the borders, the Byzantine Emperor had among his high officials and the most important, the *Magister Officiorum,* who administered among other things the ceremonies of the royal court and introduced foreign envoys. His function was apparently not much different from that of the Hajib. The Emperor was liberal in distributing titles to his subordinates. The high officials belonged to the classes of *illustres, spectacles* and *clarissimi.* Some of these titles like 'Magnificence' and 'Excellence' survive to the present day. Such liberality in granting titles of honour was not limited to the high officials of the Byzantine government. In the first half of the tenth century, the patriarch of Constantinople writing to the

Arab Amir of Crete, addressed him as 'Most Illustrious and Most Honorable and Beloved.' In the later stages of the Islamic State such pompous titles could be traced to the practices of the Byzantine Empire.

The ceremonies performed in the Abbaside period displayed the wealth and glory of the Islamic State. In A.D. 917, the Caliph Al-Muqtadir received the envoys of Constantine VII in his palace with great ceremony. Their mission involved the exchange and ransom of the prisoners. The array that greeted the guests included 1,60,000 cavalry and footmen 7,000 eunuchs and 700 chamberlains. A hundred lions marched in the parade and 38,000 curtains of which 12,500 were gilded, hung in the Caliph's palace. The envoys were especially impressed with the Hall of the Tree which housed an artificial tree of gold and silver weighing 50,000 dram, in the branches of which lodged birds of the same precious metals so constructed that they chirped by automatic devices. In the garden they marvelled at the artificially dwarfed trees which by skilled cultivation yielded dates of rare varieties.

Detailed Descriptions

Arab historians reported detailed descriptions of the glorious ceremonies performed in the ninth century, particularly during the reign of Harun Al-Rashid and his two sons, Al-Amin and Al-Mamun. Al-Nasser, the Umayyad Caliph in Andalusia and a contemporary of Al-Muqtadir in Baghdad, received around the year A.D. 948 (366 H) a delegation from Constantinople, dispatched by Emperor Constantine. The Caliph arranged troops with full arms and decorated uniforms for the reception of the envoys. The palace was decorated with curtains and rugs. The Caliph's associates and members of the royal family were in the receiving line according to their seniority. The ceremony was so magnificent that it impressed not only the envoys, but also many of the notable hosts. These dignitaries were so dazzled by the splendour of the occasion that when the time came for them to receive the envoys with speeches of welcome, they were struck dumb.

Reciprocally, the Arab ambassadors were received in Constantinople with brilliant court ceremonies, diplomatic courtesies and astute display of military strength. At the imperial table the Arab envoys occupied higher places than the Western ones.

The foreign envoy was usually led into a magnificent hall in the palace through a crowd of richly clothed dignitaries and through rows of bodyguards with glittering arms. Finally a curtain was drawn back and he gazed on the emperor clad in his robes of state and seated on his throne. On each side of the throne roared golden lions, mechanical birds sang on a gilded pomegranate tree and while the visitor prostrated himself, the throne was raised aloft so as to make it unapproachable.

These glorious receptions of envoys were often accompanied by presentations of gifts on both sides. A Frankish historian relates that Charlemagne's envoys returned home from a mission at the court of Harun Al-Rashid with gifts that included fabrics, aromatics, an elephant and a clock. Arab historians report that the delegations from India brought Harun Al-Rashid valuable presents, and that his son Al-Mamun received similar rich gifts from the Byzantine Emperor.

With regard to the etiquette that was observed during that period, one may quote a ninth to tenth century Arab author who describes a gentleman of that period Al-Washsha, in his book *Kitab Al'Muwashsha* as: the one who is in possession of polite behaviour, culture (Adab), manly virtue and elegant manners, who abstains from joking, holds fellowship with the right comrades, has high standards of veracity, is scrupulous in the fulfillment of his promises, keeps a secret, wears presentable clothes and at the table takes small mouthfuls, converses or laughs, but little chews his food, licks not his fingers, avoids garlic and onions and refrains from using the toothpicks in public meetings and on the streets.

During the ceremonies organized at a Byzantine court on the occasion of receiving Arab ambassadors, a requirement of etiquette was to inquire about the Caliph and his officers, their news and their health, but never to inquire about their wives, a formula which resembled that offered to Western ambassadors.

Relations with Other States

Relations with Byzantium : Relations of the Islamic State with Byzantium, during the Umayyad and Abbaside Caliphate, were marked by hostilities. Between A.D. 650 and A.D. 711, the Arabs conquered parts of the Byzantine provinces in North Africa upto the shores of the Iberian Peninsula, and in Asia Minor their conquests reached the gates of Constantinople. In addition to the Eastern and Southern coastline of the Mediterranean Sea, the main islands, like Crete, Sicily, Cyprus, which were once under Roman rule fell under Arab authority. The Eastern capital of the Roman Empire was besieged by the Muslim army three times during the reign of the Umayyads and Abbasides.

Nevertheless, what appeared to be a continuation of hostilities did not represent the whole truth. Warlike expeditions did not form an insurmountable barrier to peaceful relations. This period was a long succession of war and peace, ruin and construction, enmity and friendship. There was no racial hatred. The Emperor Nicephorus was of Arabian origin. Under Leo III (A.D. 717— 741), a mosque was constructed in Constantinople, and a Greek chronicler refers to this Emperor as being Saracen-minded.'

It was indicated earlier that Muawiyah while he was governor of Syria had come to an agreement with the Byzantines, according to which he was to pay tribute to the Greek Emperor. Abdul Malek bin Marwan, the fifth Umayyad Caliph (A.D. 684-705), likewise concluded an agreement with Byzantium, on the basis of which he agreed to pay a weekly tribute to the Emperor.

During the reign of the Umayyads, Cyprus, which had been conquered by Muawiyah when he was still a governor of Syria, was bound by a treaty that recognized the dual loyalty of the Cypriots to both the Romans and the Arabs. According to this agreement, the Arabs would receive an annual tribute from the people of Cyprus, and would not object to the fact that the latter would continue at the same time, the payment of taxes to Byzantium. They were not required to fight with the Muslims against the Byzantines, but would warn them if the Romans were proceeding against them. Armenia was another example set by the Umayyads for a Byzantine province that came under the Arab sovereignty with the right to self-government.

During Al Rashid's reign the Cypriots committed, what could be considered as a breach of the treaty. The Abbaside governor of the buffer province (Al-Thughor), wanted to abrogate the treaty with them, but before doing so he wrote (in A.H. 173-A.D. 789) to eight known Muslim jurists (faqih), consulting them. The first one answered him, advising that he abrogate the treaty with the Cypriots, and supported his argument with a verse from the Quran that reads 'if thou fearest treachery from any group, throw back their covenant to them so as to be on equal terms.' Then he suggested that the inhabitants be offered one year to decide whether to join the Muslims or the Romans. The second jurist, Malek bin Anas, the founder of a school of the Sunni sect, wrote to the governor advising him to deliberate and not take a hasty decision, until he had enough proof against them. He cited the verse that reads 'so fulfil your engagements with them to the end of their term'. 'After that, if they do not improve their conduct', he said, 'and if you see them continue in their treachery, then you may deal with them accordingly, having warned them beforehand.' The third jurist cited precedents from the Prophet's (PBUH) time where people had violated their covenants and were dealt with accordingly. He then applied the rule that says, no commitment to those who broke their engagement, The fourth supported the view of the second. The fifth jurist pointed out that the Cypriots were pressed by the Byzantines, and the Muslims could not thus blame them for a stand that they had not taken out of their free will. It was for the Muslims to protect them from the Romans, but if they could not do so, the least that could be done was to keep their links with them.

Cultural and economic relations with Byzantium continued during this period, with some lapses. In spite of their frequency and intensity, the wars between the two states were not without breaks. During times of peace, the Empire and the Caliphate had enough time to realize the importance of establishing normal relations. Al Walid bin Abdul Malek (the sixth Umayyad Caliph A.D. 705-715) asked the Emperor to send him some Greek artisans to adorn the mosques of Damascus, Medina, and Jerusalem with mosaic. The Emperor sent him 1,00,000 grains (mithqal) of gold, one hundred artisans and forty loads of mosaics." The second Abbaside Caliph, Al Mansur, is said to have received in response to his request from the Byzantine Emperor, a number of books including Euclid. Al-Mamun, son of Al Rashid, dispatched emissaries to Constantinople in quest of Greek works. He sent one to a distinguished Greek mathematician, Leo, asking him to come to his court. It is related that the Byzantine Emperor Theophilus, hearing of this invitation, offered Leo a salary and appointed him as a public teacher to discourage his departure.

Commercial relations with Byzantium thrived during this period. In spite of the fact that Byzantium, after losing the Eastern provinces, had to abandon its control over trade with the East, but indirectly its advantages through commercial relations with the Arabs were quite large. According to Vasiliev, the thriving economic life in Syria and Palestine considerably helped the empire. Byzantine merchants appeared in many Arab cities, and Muslim traders came to Byzantium to transact business. The early merchants were Christians, Jews and Zoroastrians, but were later largely dominated by Muslim Arabs. Muslim merchants reached Morocco and Spain. A thousand years before De Lesseps, the Caliph Al Rashid entertained the idea of digging a canal through the Isthmus of the Suez. Al Masoudi, the Arab historian and geographer (who lived in the tenth century) described the numerous attempts to connect the Red Sea with the Mediterranean. Al Rashid made one last attempt at connecting the two seas, but his wazir, Yahya warned him against this as the canal would open the way for the Byzantine war vessels to reach the Holy Mosque in Mecca.' The Arabs of that period invented the mariner's compass and thus contributed to the flourishing international trade of that era.

Diplomatic relations with Byzantium were conspicuously manifested through Arab embassies to the court of the Emperor. Vasiliev relates that the ritual of the reception of Arab embassies sent to Constantinople 'was minutely elaborate, and the ambassadors were welcomed with all sorts of brilliant court ceremonies, diplomatic courtesies, and the astute display of military strength.' At the imperial table, the Arab 'friends' occupied higher places than the Frank 'friends' and the Eastern Arabs were placed higher than the Western. When Byzantine ambassadors made their appearance in Baghdad they were solemnly received by the Caliph with the full regalia of Oriental magnificence and military parade.

Relations with the Franks : Diplomatic relations between the Muslim State and the Franks began to develop during the reign of Harun al-Rashid. The common motive for this was the shared antagonism towards the Umayyad State in Spain and the Byzantine Empire. The reception of Frankish ambassadors in the court of Al-Rashid, was not the first of its kind. The Arab annalists ignored this question in their records, while the Latin historians gave details in theirs. One historian, Iorga, describes these contacts in the following words:

> Under Charles, son of Pepin, who was not at that time more than a meagre Christian king in the eyes of the Muslim Grand Chief, the Caliph Harun Al-Rashid, relations between Aix-La-Chapelle and Baghdad took place, because of the common antagonism towards the Byzantines, and it is said also, towards the Umayyads of Spain. In A.D. 796, three Frank ambassadors proceeded towards the court of the pagan emperor Aaron (Harun), a few months before the arrival of the Greek envoys charged with the mission of negotiating for peace with a new rival, who had just appeared to their master, in the person of Charlemagne.

In A.D. 799-800, a new exchange of ambassadors between the two courts took place. The Latin historian reports that the Caliph had put the holy places in Jerusalem under the authority of Charlemagne, by rendering the keys to the Holy Sepulchre and the Mount of Olive to him. Although such a concession on the part of Al-Rashid is doubted, the idea of offering certain privileges to the Latin clergy had been recorded.

The Umayyad State in Spain, which came into existence six years after the ascendance of the Abbaside Dynasty to the Caliphate in Baghdad, had more lively contacts with the Frankish Empire. A contemporary of Al-Rashid was the Umayyad Caliph, Abdur Rahman, who established the independent state in Spain in A.D. 756. Abdur Rahman discontinued the Khutba (Friday prayer) in the name of the Abbaside Caliph, but he never assumed the title Amir-al-Muminin (Commander of the Faithful) that the Caliph carried in Baghdad as a mark of respect for the seat of the Caliphate. He was content with the simpler title of Ameer (ruler or sovereign).

Abdur Rahman's relations with the Franks were not always friendly. In the beginning of his rule, Charlemagne invaded the Muslim territory and besieged Saragossa. By the time Abdur Rahman proceeded to meet him, Charlemagne sustained a disastrous defeat by the Muslim contingent in the area. The Umayyad Caliph decided not to pursue the defeated army, and instead, concentrated his efforts on subduing the rebellion within the State. Following this, a peace treaty was signed with the Franks.

The reports on who proposed the peace treaty are conflicting. According to Al-Maqqari, it was Charlemagne who came to the conclusion that Abdur Rahman was too hard to bend and it was wiser to coax him.' Therefore, he proposed peace, and offered Abdur Rahman his sister in marriage. Abdur Rahman acceded to the peace proposal, but declined the marriage. Other sources suggest that the Umayyad Ameer proposed peace in order to concentrate on internal problems. Abdur Rahman excused himself from the marriage proposal on the pretext of his health and advanced age, but concluded the treaty in the year A.D. 780.

During the reign of Abdur Rahman's son Hisham, hostilities with the Franks broke out more than once, and peace treaties were made twice. The last one was signed in A.H. 197 (A.D. 812). Again during the reign of the third Umayyad Ameer, hostilities and peace agreements were frequent.

In the year A.H. 252 (A.D. 866), after the two parties were exhausted, the Umayyad Ameer proposed a peace agreement to Charles, the Prankish King. The latter agreed to this proposal. He sent his envoys to the court of Cordova where they sealed the agreement, and from where they returned carrying valuable gifts and warm congratulatory messages.

During the period of Abdur Rahman An-Naser (A.D. 910-960), Cordova witnessed the peak of diplomatic activities of the Umayyad rule. In the year A.D. 947, envoys from Constantinople who came soliciting alliance with Al-Naser mingled with ambassadors from the King of the Slovenians, the Emperor of Germany, the King of France and another prince of the Franks from beyond the Pyrenees.

Relations with China : Arab relations with China go as far back as the pre-Islamic era. Arabs in China were known by the name of *Tashih'*, an expression that could have been derived from the Persian *Tazi* or *Tajik.* The latter word came either from the name of an Arab tribe *Tayy,* or the Arabic word *tajir* which means merchant. The Prophet (PBUH), encouraging the search for knowledge among his followers, enjoined the Muslims to go and look for it even if this quest took them as far as that land.

Propagating Islam was the reason which first gave the Arabs the opportunity to enter China *en masse.* They began to arrive in the late seventh century as missionaries of their newly-founded religion. During the rule of Othman (RA), the third orthodox Caliph, an Arab mission was received by the Chinese Monarch Kao Tsung. Before this mission, two others were reported by different sources. At the time of the Prophet (PBUH), it is related that Saad bin Abi Waqqas was sent as an envoy to China. Other sources mention the name of Ibn Hamza (son of Hamza, the uncle of the Prophet (PBUH)) as heading a delegation that called on the Emperor of China in A.D. 632, Between A.D. 651 and 798, more than thirty missions were sent by the Arabs to China. Likewise, Chinese missions visited the Muslim courts. Al-Masoudi records that Al-Mahdi, the Abbaside Caliph (A.D. 775-785) had granted audience to a Chinese delegation.

However, peaceful exchange of embassies and gifts was not always the norm of Arab-Chinese relations. Occasionally Arab representatives entered China by force, as they attempted to conquer Chinese territory in A.D. 715. On other occasions, the Arabs had to repulse Chinese forces as they did in A.D. 715. But most of the time, relations with China were at the level of friendly exchange of military assistance against a third party. In the year A.D. 751, during the transitional period of the Abbaside Caliphate, a Turkish province rebelled against the Abbaside authority and it requested the support of the Chinese Emperor. The latter refused, as he preferred not to cause damage to his relations with the Muslim State. On another occasion, the Chinese Emperor requested the help of the Arabs to suppress an internal revolt in A.D. 757. The request was complied with and Al-Mansur, the second Abbaside Caliph, sent twenty thousand soldiers, to help the Chinese monarch. During the third Muslim century (ninth century A.D.), Arab records tell of voyages by Sulayman Al-Basri, known as Sulayman Al-Tajir (the merchant), describing China and the route to it that came to be known as the great Silk Route. Accompanying one of these missions to China was a Muslim judge (Qadi) who stayed there to render justice in conformity with principles of the Quran, and who was treated on the same footing as the judges of the country. According to the same source, Muslims entering the Chinese territories had established a colony on the borders of China that served as a link in the Arab-Chinese relations.

The first military attempt to penetrate the Chinese territory, took place in the reign of the Umayyad Caliph Al-Walid bin Abdel-Malek. The course of diplomatic process that the encounter led to and the peaceful settlement that resolved the conflict are worth looking into. In the year A.H. 96 (A.D. 715), the Muslim Commander-in-chief, Qutaybah, tried to enter China after occupying several of its satellites. The Chinese Emperor sent a message to Qutaybah requesting that a delegation be dispatched to negotiate with the Emperor. Qutaybah, according to several Arab historians, selected a delegation of ten notables. He furnished them with the best outfits and equipment and requested them to convey to the Emperor the information that he had pledged not to return before he had set foot on Chinese soil and collected tribute from them.

For three consecutive days after their arrival, the delegation attended the court of the Emperor without opening discussions with him. On each of the three days, they were dressed in a different style. When they were invited again before the Emperor, who enquired about their different styles, the head of the delegation, Hubeirah, answered that on the first day they had put on feminine dress to indicate that they were woman-like before their people. On the second day they put on the dress in which they met their princes. The third outfit, with the war helmets, the swords and the spears, was what, they wore to face the enemy. During the discussion, the Emperor tried to divert them from their course by relating to them how great his Empire was and how strong his forces were compared to their limited number and armaments. Hubeirah countered this by asking how they could be considered small when the forepart of their cavalry was at the gates of his territory and the rear was in the land of olive trees. As to the possibility of death, he added, they did not fear or evade it. Then he disclosed to the Emperor that his commander had taken an oath and was determined to fulfil it. After deliberating on the matter, the Emperor came up with a solution. He proposed that he send Qutaybah some of his country's soil, so that the Muslim leader might step on it, and he would offer the Muslims gifts that would win their approval. The proposed compromise was acceptable to Qutaybah, who dispatched, in his turn, Hubeirah to report the settlement to the Caliph in Damascus.

Cultural and economic relations with China, which formed the other facets of political relations, developed to a great extent in this period. Through continuous contacts, both parties benefited from the knowledge and experience of each other. The Arabs brought to China, among other things, great knowledge of science and medicine. One of the first sciences to be accepted by the Chinese was astronomy. 'Muslim mathematical science' was also, taught in China. Arab medicaments were so widely used by doctors in China that some still retain their original names. On the other hand, the Arabs in the mid-eighth century, learned from the Chinese the process of making paper. Before the end of the century, Baghdad constructed its first paper-mill. Through Spain and Italy in the twelfth century, paper manufacturing became known in Europe. If the Muslims were not the original inventors of the mariner's compass, they would have learned about it from their contact with China, but certainly they introduced it to the benefit of international trade. Sulayman Al-Tajir in his book *Journey to China* indicated that the Chinese were the first to adopt the use of fingerprints as signature.

Arab and Chinese vessels exchanged goods at Aden, on the Red Sea, or in the Persian Gulf, to be transported to other parts of the world. Through the Arab intermediary, China was in contact with Africa and Europe.

22

Salient Features

Diplomacy, defined as 'the art and practice of conducting relations between nations', is both an instrument and a product of the process. To evaluate early Arab diplomacy and point out the principles and rules that governed its applications, one inevitably takes into account the principles and rules that directed the external relations of that period. The nature of these relations is shaped, necessarily, by the dominant cultural values and the recognized international traditions and laws.

At the time when the Muslim Arabs were expanding their rule over a vast portion of the old world, they were coming into contact with values and norms, which they did not try to put an end to. Neither did they try to create a completely new formula for the system of relations among states. Their concept was rather a link in the continuing chain of human civilization which they were influenced by, and influencing at the same time. The basic rules that governed ancient international relations were traditions and customs. For the Muslims, the most important rule for proper conduct is *al amr bil marouf wal nahy anil munkar* which, translated literally, means enjoining what is known *(Marouf)* and forbidding what is denied *(Munkar).* The word 'known', in a metaphorical sense meant the acceptable and the right.

It is true that the Islamic concept of the individual and state conduct is based on the divine theory that is embodied in the teachings of the Quran and the Prophet's (PBUH) Hadith. But the instructions of the Quran and Hadith do not cover all specific aspects of the national and international affairs. A wide margin in Islamic legislature is left for decision-making on the basis of unanimity, analogy, or wise judgement, provided that the last three sources of legislation are not contradicting the established rules specified in the Quran and Hadith. Generally accepted traditions and public interests are determining factors in formulating such rules and decisions. The same teachings of the Quran and Hadith include numerous rules that were practiced by the Romans, the Jews and the non-Muslim Arabs.

The Arabs coming from the desert with their spiritual values and social concepts came into contact with peoples and different cultures and advanced stages of civilizations. They neither adopted these cultures at face value, nor did they try to abolish them. The incessant interaction between the Arab concepts and values on the one hand and the other cultures and traditions on the other, formed what is called the Islamic civilization. This process could be seen as 'the clustering about a mobile magnetic center of particles, large and small, which by design, by accident or by their proper motion entered its field.'

The synthesis of this interaction was a civilization, in which Islamic thought played a dominant role in the determination of its structure and its course of action. The principles and the rules which characterized this civilization were the determinants in shaping and directing the external relations of the Islamic state and, consequently, the means and manners of conducting these relations. In other words, those were the principles and rules that were the guidelines for Arab diplomacy in the seventh to the ninth centuries.

Arab-foreign Relations

The basic rule that guides relations between Muslims and other people according to the Islamic concept is 'salam', i.e. peace. It is the term for greetings used by Muslims, and the salutation, by which all the letters addressed by the Prophet (PBUH) to the leaders of other nations began. The teachings of the Quran direct Muslims to approach other people in a friendly manner, and commend them to 'call unto the way of God with wisdom and fair exhortation, and (to) reason with them in the better way.'

Muslims are advised to 'repel the evil deed with one which is better, then he, between whom and thee, there was enmity, will become as though he was a bosom friend.' These teachings are directed to individuals as much as to groups and they become more specific in addressing relations between Muslims and peoples of other beliefs in the verses that read, 'God forbids you not, with regard to those who fought you not for your faith and drove you not out of your homes, that ye should show them kindness and deal justly with them. Lo! Allah loveth the just dealers.'

This concept of relations among nations is based on the belief that all people are created by God, and before Him they are equals. They are meant to meet and to know each other. The only distinction that classifies them before God is their conduct. 'O mankind! Lo! We have created you from a single pair of male and female and made you into nations and tribes, that you may know each other. Verily the most honoured of you in the sight of God is (he who is) the most righteous of you.'

Nonetheless, if peace was the basic rule of ordinary relations, war was not the exception. Islam was to evolve in an environment, where war was the dominant state of relations among peoples. The two super-powers, the Byzantine and the Persian, were in a continuous state of war. Parts of the Arab land were occupied by the Byzantines and the Persians. The Arab tribes were mostly fighting each other, the Qurayshites used force to drive the Muslims out of Mecca. Such were the circumstances that forced the Muslims to be in a state of war. In self-defence Muslims were allowed to fight back, but not to initiate hostilities. 'Fight in the cause of God, those who fight you, but begin not hostilities, for God loveth not aggressors.' In spite of the fact that they were drawn to hostilities which they did not begin, Muslims were to cease if the other party did so. 'But if they cease, let there be no hostilities except towards those who practice oppression.' 'But if they incline towards peace, incline thou to it, and trust in God.'

In case of hostilities among people, a just settlement was to be sought. Arbitration and mediation were and still are just two ways of settling conflicts. 'If two parties among believers fall to fighting, then make peace between them, and if one of them doeth wrong to the other, fight ye that which doeth wrong till it return unto the ordinance of Allah, then, if it returns, make peace between them justly and act equitably.'

Islam did not impose constraints only against the initiation of hostilities, but also established rules limiting the means and ways of fighting. It prohibited, in the course of war, assault against children, old men, and women who were not participating in the fighting, monks, and invalids. It forbids the destruction of temples, churches, trees, or animals—except for those slaughtered for the purpose of feeding the army.

All these rules could be counted as principles in theory, except that the early history of Islam proves that these rules were applied in practice. One good example of considering the Islamic principles of the Quran as the reference to the right conduct, is when Abu Obeidah wrote to the Caliph Omer (RA) requesting approval for the agreements he had reached with the cities conquered by the Muslims in Syria. In his reply to Abu Obeidah, Omar (RA) quoted a passage of the Quran as the reference to his judgment that could not be contested. He wrote:

> People have taken note of the information as regards the booty that God has delivered to you and of the conditions that you have covenanted with the inhabitants of the cities and towns. I have consulted with the Companions of the Apostle (God's prayers and peace be unto him) on this matter. And each one of them has offered a different view.

As for me, my view is based on the Book of God, the Most High, who said (that which Allah giveth as spoils unto His Messenger from the people of the townships).

The other example where these rules were applied, was when Al-Rashid's governor in the frontier province was faced with a violation of the treaty by the inhabitants of Cyprus. Before taking any action he consulted with eight well-known Muslim jurists. Each one of them, in reply to the governor's letter, quoted verses from the Quran and precedents from the Prophet's (PBUH) lifetime in support of his judgement .'

The early history of Islam is full of other such examples, that prove the strict application of the principles laid down in the Quran and Sunnah, by Muslim leaders in their dealing with other nations and peoples. Those principles formed handy guidelines for Arab envoys and negotiators in conducting their diplomatic missions.

Types of Relations

Relations between the Islamic state and other nations could be classified into three categories:

1. Relations with people with whom the Arabs were in a state of war. The rules that governed such relations could be outlined in the following:

Muslims were not allowed to fight their enemies before offering them three options. Either they adhered to Islam, in which case they would be like all other Muslims as to their duties and their rights; or if they were followers of heavenly religions likc Christianity and Judaism, they might accept paying a tribute (djizyeh) and thus keep their freedom and property. If these two alternatives were not acceptable, then the third option was war.

In case of conquest as a result of fighting, the procedure in the early phase was to confiscate the property and land of the conquered, but later during the rule of the second Caliph, Omer bin al-Khattab (RA), the conquered people could keep their property and land provided that they paid fixed taxes in proportion to their crops or their earnings. In any case no Christian, Jew or Sabiaan, who was a believer in God and in the hereafter, was to be forced into embracing Islam.

In case an enemy came to accept a peace agreement or a truce, then the terms of the agreement defined the kind of relations the non-Muslims would have with the Muslim party.

2. Relations with people to whom the Muslims were bound by a treaty of non-aggression or an alliance. An example of this type of relations is presented in the Hudeibiyah agreement that the Prophet (PBUH) concluded with the Qurayshites. According to this agreement, the Muslims would not go into Mecca for pilgrimage until the following year and both parties would abstain from any act of hostilities for the duration of ten years. The allies of either party would be treated under the same terms of the agreement that applied to their party.

3. Relations with dependant countries benefiting from the protection of the Muslim state. The treaty that Muawiyah concluded with Armenia in A.D. 653 is an interesting example of this type of relations. The Armenians who were previously under the domination of the Byzantines welcomed the Arabs in order to

secure their assistance in liberating them from the Byzantine pressure, and against the Khazares. According to this agreement, the Christian Armenians preserved their autonomy and their form of government, provided that they agreed to accommodate 15,000 Muslim cavaliers. The Caliph offered their leaders the same honours and the same ceremonies as those offered to the Muslim Amirs.

At the time of the death of Prophet Muhammed (PBUH), it appeared that the Muslim state had more enemies than friends. Abu Bakr (RA), the first Caliph after Prophet Muhammed (PBUH), insisted on dispatching the small army that the Prophet (PBUH) was preparing against the Romans in retaliation for the previous battle of Mutah, while he had to face the uprising of the apostate Arab tribes in the Arabian Peninsula. Then he resolved to dispatch an army to the Persian frontiers at the same time that other Muslim troops were fighting the Byzantines on four fronts. What seemed an odd strategy could not be explained just in military terms. Apparently, the Arabs were not facing the two major powers of that time only with comparable manpower or military equipments. Part of the credit for their success must go to the manner and methods, by which they conducted their relations with other people, which earned them more followers and friends than enemies. That may explain why 'in a few decades the new conquerors were able to do, by Islamizing and Arabizing the area (North Africa), more than what the earlier conquerors had been able to achieve in centuries by way of Romanizing or Hellenizing it.'

The Characteristics

The way the Arabs dealt with other people by applying the principles of Islam gave their diplomacy its credibility and force. 'The Quran commands to arbitrate with justice, to give true evidence, to fulfil one's contract and to return an item of trust or deposit to its owners, how one should act towards women and children, orphans and relatives, dependants and slaves.'

From the early days of the Islamic states, the Muslim tolerance towards Christians and Jews could be best represented by the first Umayyad Caliph. The wife of Muawiyah and mother of his son and heir, Yazid, was a Christian Arab. His chancellor and minister of finance, Ibn Sardjoun was a Christian. The court poet, Al-Akhtal was a Christian, who always wore a cross over his breast. The royal physician of Muawiyah, Ibn Uthal, was also a Christian.

Before Muawiyah, the Caliph Omer bin al-Khattab (RA) gave examples of respect for other religions when he abstained from saying his prayers in the Church of Sepulchre, in Jerusalem, fearing that some day the Muslims may claim this place, as Omer (RA) had prayed there.

Just as the Muslims were tolerant of other religions, they were indiscriminate as to race or colour of skin. The Prophet's (PBUH) Hadith says 'No advantage has an Arab over a non-Arab or a white man over a black one, except for piety.' It is claimed that the Umayyad Caliphate had favoured the Arabs and gave them priority, but when we study the four Caliphs, the standards prevailing become clear. The first priority was given to those, who immigrated to Medina, then to those Muslims who accommodated them in Medina, then to those who were the first to adhere to Islam and to donate more for its cause.

This was how the first Caliphs were elected to authority, for Abu-Bakr (RA) was from among the Muhajirin. Abu-Bakr (RA) himself declined to dispatch among the armies that were sent to Syria and Iraq, people belonging to the apostate tribes, who returned to Islam. The dividends of the spoils were distributed among Muslims according to this scale. If such a hierarchy existed among the Muslim Arabs, it is understandable then, that the Arabs in general were the first among nations to adhere to Islam, and the more privileged to comprehend its thoughts expressed in their language. Such privileges could have lasted for a certain period, but they did not last that long, as became apparent in the Abbaside epoch.

Rights of States

One other feature that characterized Arab relations with other nations in that early period of history was their recognition of the rights of other states to exist and to enjoy independence and sovereignty. It is a principle established in the Quran and practiced by the Muslim leaders to offer aid and protection to Muslims, who are under the sovereignty of another state. 'As for those Muslims who accepted the rule of a foreign state and chose not to emigrate from it, the Islamic State owes no duty of protection towards them.'

'As to those who believed, but came not into exile, ye owe no duty of protection to them. Until they came into exile. But if they seek your aid in religion, it is your duty to help them, except against a people with whom ye have a treaty'.

Interpreting the part regarding (aid in religion) offered to the oppressed Muslim community, Abdullah Yousuf Ali, explains that those who suffered voluntary exile on account of persecution were still bound to the duty of helping those staying behind. In a state of war with the persecuting state, the exiles would be free to fight against such a state.

Auxiliary Means of Diplomacy

Besides the three main institutions for conducting Arab diplomacy during the period under study, i.e. ambassadors, diplomatic correspondence and treaties, one can cite other auxiliary means, that ultimately would feed the main stream of diplomatic activities. These means may be restricted to the following three basic practices:

Economic and Commercial Relations

One may argue correctly that in the history of nations, commercial exchanges preceded diplomatic relations. The latter might have come to facilitate and to organize the former type of relations. This study already pointed out that the Qurayshites, in pre-Islamic history, had sent envoys to neighbouring countries to reach agreements with them in order to ensure the safety of their commercial caravans.

On the other hand, commercial and economic relations may serve, in the present, as they might have served in the past, the political and diplomatic plans of nations. With the expansion of the Islamic Empire the sphere of commercial relations expanded as well. The Arab historians, Al Masoudi and Abul-Fida, recorded that early Abbaside rulers discussed the possibility of boring a canal on the lines of the present Suez Canal, but they abandoned the idea out of fear that it might expose Hijaz to attacks from the enemy.' During this period, Damascus, and Baghdad became flourishing centers of commerce, that received traders from all over the territories surrounding the Islamic State. The Muslim traders reached lands where no Arab troops had set foot on.

Al Tabari relates that while Abu-Sufian (the Quraysh leader before embracing Islam) was in Gaza, heading a group of

Qurayshites, who came for trade, he was told to meet the Byzantine Emperor who happened to be then in Jerusalem. The meeting, that took place around A.D. 628, seemed to be devoted to the discussion of the new Islamic community in Medina and its leader.

Commercial relations with China commenced as early as the first century of Islam, but diplomatic relations with China preceded trade relations. The Chinese records of that period refer to Muslims under the name of Ta-shih, which could be related to the name of an Arab tribe Tayyi. Those traders had certainly carried with them and conveyed to the people they traded with, their beliefs and their political and social thoughts. A Muslim community was established on the periphery of China and served as an intermediary in the Arab-Chinese relations. It was also the Muslim traders, who carried Islam into the islands that later became known as Indonesia. The concept of benefiting from commercial relations in the service of diplomatic relations was not purely an Arab concept. Wilhelm Ensslin, in his study of Byzantine history of the same period, tells that the Byzantine government used to put commercial relations at the service of its diplomatic activities since every missionary, every merchant proceeding abroad, obtained information which could be of great value in dealing with the ruler of the countries visited.

Cultural Relations

In the previous paragraph it was pointed out that the Byzantine authorities used missionaries, as well as merchants in the service of their diplomatic relations. In the Byzantine-Islamic relations, warlike diplomatic and cultural contacts were actively shaping the relations between the two powers. Under Lieu III (A.D. 717-41) a mosque was constructed in Constantinople and he issued a decree by which he ordered the destruction of all images in churches, according to a concept which is not different from that of Islam 'so that one Greek chronicle refers to this emperor as the Saracen-minded.' The Nestorian, John of Damascus, who lived under the Umayyad Caliph Yazid II (A.D. 720-24) wrote the famous treatise 'Against Those Who Depreciate Holy Images'. Yet, John of Damascus was not hampered by the Muslims in his literary work while he was accused at the Iconoclast Council in A.D. 754 of being 'inclined to Mohammedanism'.

The cultural contacts between Byzantium and the Arabs went back to the first Umayyad Caliphs. The Caliph Walid I

(A.D. 705-15) 'asked the Emperor to send him Greek artisans to adorn with mosaics the mosques of Damascus, Medina and Jerusalem.' In the Abbaside epoch, Al-Mamun requested Theophilus, the Byzantine Emperor to permit Leo, a distinguished mathematician, to come to Baghdad for a short stay, offering in exchange 'lasting peace and two thousand pounds of gold'.

The impact of Arab culture on Byzantine diplomacy was evidenced in the way Arab envoys were treated in the Byzantine court. According to Ramboud in his chronicle *L'Impire Grec aux Dixieme Siecle*—a chronicle that describes the sympathetic treatment the Byzantines accorded to Arabs of the Orient, though 'infidels they certainly were, but courteous and civilized'—they were classified as a higher category than those 'unrefined co-religionists of theirs!'

Informational Activities

In the period that is being discussed, technical means of communicating information were not available, but the intent to influence public opinion and the employment of publicity to serve diplomatic ends existed. The Arabs resorted to different rudimentary means for the purpose of spreading information.

One important vehicle was poetry which was especially effective among the Arabs. A well composed poem would travel among the Arab tribes and would be remembered and retold, earning the admiration even of the enemies. Its effect would not be diminished except by a poem of equal or better standard countering it. In the ninth year of Hijra (A.D. 631), a delegation of Bani Tamim came to meet Prophet Muhammed (PBUH) in Medina. The head of the delegation asked Prophet Muhammed (PBUH) to let their orator and their poet compete with his people. When Otareh bin Hajeb delivered his oratory, on behalf of Bani Tamim, Thabit bin Qays responded, from the Muslim party, with an oration. Then the famous Muslim poet Hassan bin Thabit answered with a poem of his own, upon the request of the Prophet (PBUH). Another famous poet, who embraced Islam in the same year, was Kaab bin Zuhair. His poem praising Islam and the Prophet (PBUH) earned him the mantle 'burda' of the Prophet.

The Umayyad and Abbaside courts always had well-known poets. In addition to the court poets, other poets received generous treatment and rewards from the Caliphs and high officials.

23

Practical Diplomacy

In conducting their foreign relations, the Arabs in the early Islamic State resorted to four main instruments. They delegated envoys to other leaders and heads of states, they exchanged letters or concluded agreements and, furthermore, they benefited from commerce, culture and public information, to achieve their political and diplomatic ends.

Diplomatic Envoys

The terms 'Ambassador' and 'Embassy' are translated into Arabic as 'Safir' and 'Safarah', respectively. Both words are derived from the root verb Safera, which originally meant ' to exert efforts in bringing peace and reconciliation between two quarrelling parties.'

The present concept of the mission of a safir is still to bring peace into relations with other nations or to endeavour to maintain the existing peaceful relations. The term 'Safarah' could refer to the mission of the ambassador or the team accompanying him as well as to the residence of the mission. Some Arab historians refer to the mission that Abdul-Muttaleb, the grandfather of Prophet Muhammed (PBUH), took to the Abyssinian leader Abraha as Safarah. But, in general, the term was used in the period under study. The envoy could be 'Rasoul, or 'Mabouth', while a delegation was called 'Wafd'.

In that early period, there were no resident embassies. An envoy or a delegation could be dispatched for a particular mission and they would return as soon as this was accomplished. In fact, a long stay of an envoy was not favoured by the host party, lest he might know more than what was admissible.

During his lifetime, the Prophet (PBUH) sent envoys to the other Arab tribes, to the Abyssinian Negus, to the Patriarch of the Copts in Egypt, and to the monarchs of Persia and Byzantium. With the envoys he sent letters that could have served as credentials and verbal notes. In his letter addressed to the Negus of Abyssinia, he wrote, 'I am dispatching to you my cousin Ja'far, accompanied by a number of Muslims. At their arrival receive them with hospitality.'

In pre-Islamic history, it is recorded that Hashim, the greatgrandfather of the Prophet (PBUH) had been sent as envoy to the Roman ruler for Syria and to the King of the Ghassanid to secure their protection for the Quraysh commercial caravans. Hashim's brother Abd-Shams was sent to the Negus for the same purpose. Nawfal, another brother of Hashim, was sent to the Persians.

In the period of the Orthodox Caliphate and then the Umayyad and Abbaside Caliphates, messengers were dispatched to the rulers of neighbouring countries. The contemporary Arab historian, Hitti, refers to the legend that makes Saad bin Abi Waqqas, the conqueror of Persia, the first envoy of the Prophet (PBUH) to China, where the Muslims of China revere, to the present time, a tomb in Canton bearing his name. Until the mid-eighth century, several diplomatic missions had been exchanged with China. The Chinese document of that century refers to Amir al Muminin (the Arabic title of the Caliph) as Hami-Mo-Mo-Ni and to Harun as Al-lun. The missions of the Muslim Ambassadors were to:

- convey written or verbal messages,
- negotiate and conclude agreements,
- exchange war prisoners or to ransom captives,
- carry gifts to the heads of other states,
- carry out other duties.
- Harun Al-Rashid exchanged with Charlemagne both envoys and presents. The second Abbaside Caliph, Al

Mansur, is said to have received in response to his request from the Byzantine Emperor a number of books. As to the other duties of a diplomatic envoy, Nizam al -Mulk, the Minister of two Saljuki Sultans, wrote in the eleventh century a chapter in his book *Siyasat Nama* (the Book of Politics) on ambassadors and their treatment. In this chapter which describes an ambassador's mission and interests, as well as in other chapters of the book, the Minister accounts the experiences of the kings of the past. In the prologue of the book, he refers to 'functions which kings before (us) have performed' and to 'the laws and customs of past kings.'

Describing the mission of an ambassador he wrote: 'It should also be realized that when kings send ambassadors to one another their purpose is not merely the message or the letter which they communicate openly, but secretly they have a hundred other points and objectives.' The writer mentions that among these objectives was information that the ambassador sought to gather about roads and passes, the size of the army and quality of its officers, the protocols observed at court, the hobbies of the king, the standard of his table and the company he kept, as well as his personal qualities and manners and his designs and intentions.

The author advised the king that ambassadors should be received at the borders and accompanied on their way to the capital city. Local officers should offer them hospitality and courtesy at all the stops along this route. On their return the same procedure should be followed, so that they depart well satisfied. 'Whatever treatment is given to an ambassador, whether good or bad', he wrote, 'it is as if it were done to the king who sent him, and kings have always shown the greatest respect to one another.'

When Abu-Bakr (RA), the first Caliph, dispatched Yazid bin Abu Sufian at the head of an army towards Syria, he advised him, among other things, in his farewell speech, that 'in case envoys of the adversary come to you, treat them with hospitality and make their period of stay (residence) at your camps short, so that they quit while they are still ignorant. Let them not look about, so they may not see your weaknesses and know your disposition. (See to) it that they reside with the rich section of your troops.'

The ambassadors were granted immunities and certain privileges. They benefited from the principle of Aman, accorded to any foreigner, who sought safe entry into a Muslim country, and from the traditional immunity granted to foreign envoys.

The selection of an ambassador was based on two main specifications—capability and trustworthiness. The Quran puts it in the following terms: 'Truly the best of men for thee to employ is the man who is strong and trusty.' Nizam ul-Mulk suggests that an ambassadorship should be assigned to a person who is 'bold in speaking, but does not say too much, who has travelled widely, who has a portion of every branch of learning, who is retentive of memory and far-seeing, who is tall and handsome.'

According to Al-Tabari, in A.D. 715 (96 H.), when Qutaybah, the Muslim leader approached the Chinese frontiers, the Chinese monarch requested him to send him a delegation. Qutaybah selected a delegation of twelve persons, who were handsome, strong, eloquent, brave and wise. They were given the best arms, clothes and horses. Hubeirah Al-Kitabi, who was heading the delegation was known for his fluency and eloquence.

In other words, an envoy is meant to be convincing and impressive. For the same purpose, the reception of ambassadors at the court of the receiving state was to give the visiting envoys the impression of power and grandeur. Such qualifications are apparently not very different from the present practice.

Diplomatic Correspondence

Diplomatic correspondence was among the first instruments of diplomacy applied by the Arab state to their relations with foreign countries. When a group of Muslims immigrated to Abyssinia, in the pre-Hijra period, the Prophet (PBUH) sent a letter to the Abyssinian Negus, inviting him to convert to Islam and recommending to him, his cousin Jafar and the group of Muslims accompanying him. The letter reads: Prophet Muhammed, the Apostle of God, to al-Najashy, King of the Abyssinians.

I address to you the praise of God, the Sovereign Holy One, the Source of Peace, Guardian of Faith and Preserver of Safety, and attest that Isa (Jesus), son of Mariam is the Spirit of God and His Word that He passed to Mariam the Virgin, the Virtuous and

Chaste, who bore Isa and gave birth to him out of the spirit of God that was blown into him as, before, He created Adam by his hand. I call you to believe in and obey Allah, the Unique, who has no partner, and to follow me and believe in what I am entrusted with, for I am the Apostle of God, I have dispatched to you my cousin Jafar, accompanied with a number of Muslims. Upon their arrival, receive them with hospitality. I invite you and your troops to God, I have conveyed to you (the message) and advised you. Accept my advice. Peace be unto him who follows the right path.

The Prophet (PBUH) sent another message to the Negus and received answers to both messages. In the sixth year of Hijra (A.D. 628), Prophet Muhammed (PBUH) dispatched messengers to the Emperor of Byzantium, to the king of the Ghassanid, to Al-Moqawqas, the Patriarch of the Copts in Alexandria, to the Emperor of Persia and to the Arab tribes in the Peninsula. The Egyptian Chief responded with an amiable letter accompanied by a present consisting of two female slaves. Prophet Muhammed (PBUH) married one of them, Maria, who became the mother of his son Ibrahim. The Persian Emperor reacted with the worst diplomatic behaviour by tearing off the message in front of the Muslim envoy.

The Arab historians recorded letters addressed by the leaders of Arab armies to their opponents in the territories of Syria and Iraq, during the rule of the Orthodox Caliphs. At the same time similar correspondence between the Caliphs and the Arab leaders is reported to have been exchanged. By examining these, one can point out the following characteristics:

Language : The terminology and eloquence of these letters are not very different from those of the Quran. In a later stage it becomes easy to deduce that certain terms are no more in usage and that new expressions are inserted or came from common usage.

Style : The texts which are credited to be authentic among these letters are those which are precise, direct, forceful and exclusive. Any deviation from these principles subjects such correspondence to a legitimate doubt about its credibility.

Material : The subject matter of these letters was mainly to invite foreign leaders to adhere to Islam. If such invitation was refused, then, the Muslim leaders would guarantee the addressee safeguard and protection provided that the latter paid the djizyeh. During the period of Arab conquests, the third option was to declare war. These letters thus discussed duties, not privileges.

Length of the Text : The letters addressed by the Arab leaders during this period were relatively brief and precise in comparison with the letters of the later era. The longer a letter recorded from this period, the more its authenticity becomes doubtful. Such a judgement is based on two considerations. The first is that the style of expression of that period, as in analogy with the Prophet's (PBUH) Hadith, was short but expressive speech. The second is that the texts of those letters were relayed orally until they were recorded a few generations later by Arab historians.

In the Umayyad and Abbaside period, the language, the substance and the style of the diplomatic correspondence evolved. Muawiyah initiated the procedure of preserving a copy of his correspondence, before sealing and dispatching the original. By the time of Abdul Malek, the Umayyads had developed a state archives in Damascus. While diplomatic correspondence under the Orthodox Caliphs was brief and to the point, Abdul-Hamid Al Katib (the scribe of the last Umayyad Caliph died A.D. 750) introduced the elegant, 'long-drawn style with its conventional, polite phraseology betraying Persian influence.'

In the Abbaside period, a letter written in the name of Harun Al-Rashid to the Emperor of Constantinople may reveal the style of diplomacy of that epoch. The letter contains fifty pages, most of them discussing the faith of Islam and inviting the Emperor to embrace it. In case of the Emperor's refusal, the letter offers in its later part the other alternative, i.e. paying tribute in order to avoid war. The Caliph presents in the letter the advantages of peace and quotes passages from the New Testament to this effect. It ends with threats and reproaches for the untimely rupture of the treaty that was concluded with the Caliph Al-Mahdi.

The Negotiation

Negotiation is a diplomatic procedure in which representatives of states, in direct personal contact or through correspondence, engage in discussion of matters of mutual concern, and attempt to resolve disputes that have arisen between them. Its main objective is to reach an agreement, whether based on a treaty or on mutual understanding. As a flexible diplomatic instrument, negotiation is more suited to promote compromise and to induce a peaceful change of the legal *status quo.* Each party to a negotiation is assumed to be able to evaluate, on a numerical scale, the effectiveness of every conceivable outcome, including the possibility of no agreement. The criteria for a negotiated agreement are the following:

- Each party is presumed to have an alternative to a negotiated agreement.
- An agreement should obtain, through negotiation, certain advantages, in relation to no agreement.
- The bargaining set is to represent stature of each party. Fairness is one element conducive to a reasonable agreement.

To apply this concept of negotiation and the said criteria to negotiated settlements during the period of Arab history under consideration, the following examples are provided:

1. Through the negotiations conducted at Al-Hudeibiyah, Al-Qadsiya, Jerusalem, and on other occasions, the Muslims conceived the possibility of non-agreement with the option of fighting. In this case, they believed that they would achieve either martyrdom or triumph. In case they reached a negotiated agreement the scale of options included:
    - Acceptance of Islam or paving the path for spreading the faith.
    - Reaching a peace treaty by which the Muslims would offer their protection in exchange for payment of the djizyeh. In some cases both conditions were waived to obtain an available settlement.
2. For the inhabitants of the Byzantine and Persian occupied territories, the Muslims were offering a better option in replacement of the occupying regimes. Even during the process of negotiation at Al-Hudeibiyah, the Meccans were offered a share in the fruits of the triumph of Islam.

3. The bargaining set for the Muslims were: their determination that they made known to their adversaries; their faith that they would either win or enjoy martyrdom; their credibility and commitment to their conviction and their fair offer to the other negotiating parties. The similarity of the contexts of the peace agreements, that they concluded in the conquered territories testified to the fair dealing and unified measures which they applied. The terms regarding taxations were almost the same. People of the Holy Book were free to practice their religious duties. Those who elected to stay would be treated on equal terms. Those who preferred to depart would be protected until they reached their destination. Even after two hundred years of concluding an agreement with the inhabitants of Cyprus, the act of violation on the part of the Cypriots did not give the Governor of that province the justification to act, from a position of power, before he sought the legal judgement of the known jurists of that time.

Conclusion of Agreements

In the pre-state society of Islam, agreements could be concluded verbally as was done between the Muslims of Mecca and the Medina delegation before the immigration to Medina took place. In the Islamic State of Medina, legislative rules were being established. Muslims were directed to record their contracts in writing. 'Ye who believe, when ye deal with each other in transactions involving future obligations in fixed period of time, record it in writing.'

At present, as well as in the past, the rules of concluding agreements, observing their terms and abrogating them are and were subjected to the principles of international law and traditions. In the absence of the enforcing authority of such international principles, observing them, is a matter of mutual interest and political consideration. For the Islamic State such rules reflect the principles of Islam and are binding for religious considerations as much as for the necessity of adhering to acceptable international practice.

Several verses in the Quran commit Muslims to fulfil their obligations stipulated in an agreement. 'And keep the covenant. Lo, of the covenant it will be asked.' 'Excepting those of the idolators with whom Ye have a treaty, and who have since abated nothing of your right nor have supported anyone against you. (As for these) fulfil their treaty to them till their term. For God loveth those who keep their duty.' 'O Ye who believe! Fulfil your undertakings.'

Termination of a treaty could be the result of one of the following causes:

- Its term had come to an end.
- The other party had violated the terms of the treaty.
- The enemy had committed an antagonistic act against the Islamic State or its allies, or had indulged in a process that could be considered treacherous to the prevailing agreement. 'If thou fearest treachery from one group, throw back their covenant at them so as to be on equal terms.'

In the last two instances, the Muslim State was not free to act, without abrogating the agreement and informing the other party of absolving themselves of their commitment.

Abu-Bakr (RA), when bidding farewell to the Muslim army directed against the Byzantines, addressed the troops, ordering them 'not to commit perfidy, or betray, or transgress.

The substance of the treaty was in accordance with Islam. The terms of any agreement did not contradict the rules of Islam. When Abu Obeidah informed the Caliph Omer (RA) of the conquest of the cities in Syria and requested his advice as to the terms of peace that he should offer to the inhabitants there, Omer (RA) responded with a letter instructing Abu Obeidah to take the rules of Quran as his reference. The Caliph in his answer quoted more than one passage from the Holy Book to support his argument. On the basis of these verses he instructed Abu Obeidah to collect only djizyeh and to leave the properties to their owners. He also ordered him to give liberty to the people of the Book to practice their religion and to perform their religious ceremonies, provided that such practices did not affect the Muslim community living among them, or interfere with their prayers.

Treaties also specified duties and rights of either party to the treaty in unambiguous terms. Provisions of the treaty were to be mutually accepted. In times of peace the Islamic State had no right to exert pressure on another state to come to terms with it. In a state of war, concluding a peace treaty could be arguable from the subjugated state's point of view, whether its acceptance was considered as dictated by force or made out of its own free will. They could either opt for the continuation of war or, if the terms of the treaty seemed to be fair, enough, they could accept it.

As to the process of reaching an agreement with" another party, three steps were to be implemented:

1. The preliminary negotiation. Among the first agreements that the Muslims concluded with the Qurayshites was the Al-Hudeibiyah Treaty. The Islamic chronicles record that three delegates from the Quraysh came to negotiate with the Prophet (PBUH) a settlement that would give the Muslims access to Mecca. In the final stage, the Qurayshites sent a delegation of three members, headed by Sohail bin Amr, who conducted the negotiations for the Hudeibiyah Treaty. The purpose of the first three envoys was to explore the intentions, to evaluate the situation and probably, and to convince the Muslims to reconsider their plans. The last delegation was to discuss the terms of an agreement.

   Another example of such preliminary negotiation was when Amr bin al-Aas was leading an army in Egyptian territory. Al-Muqawqas of Egypt sent a delegation to Amr with a request for negotiations. The Arab leader kept the Egyptian delegation waiting for two days to demonstrate to them the power and determination of the Muslim troops. The Egyptian Chief sent another delegation with a similar request. Finally, Amr dispatched a delegation of ten persons to negotiate a peaceful settlement.

2. The next step is negotiating and composing the text of the treaty. Once again the Hudeibiyah Treaty presents a good example. Through the process of negotiation between Sohail bin Amr and the Prophet (PBUH), objections were raised as to the terms of the prologue, the credentials of the parties, and the provisions of the agreement.

The text of the treaty was recorded on two copies. Prophet Muhammed (PBUH) kept the original, and the other copy was delivered to the Qurayshites.

3. The third step of concluding an agreement is signing it and recording the witnesses. Prophet Muhammed (PBUH) fixed his seal on the document, Al-Hudeibiyah, which was attested by several witnesses from both parties. The number of witnesses varied from one treaty to another. In one case, there were thirty witnesses while, in another case there were only two.
4. One could add a fourth step to the process of finalizing an agreement, that is, the act of ratification. In case the Prophet (PBUH) or the Caliphs themselves retracted the covenant, the recording of several witnesses who were notables served as a ratification of the treaty. They were usually representatives of the notables *(Ahl-ul Hal wal Aqd).* In case an agreement was concluded by a representative of the Caliph, such an agreement would be transmitted to the Caliph for his ratification, as was the case when Abu Obeidah had to secure the approval of Caliph Omer (RA).

The types of agreements that were concluded by the Arabs in early Islamic history can be classified into the following three categories:

Treaties of Good Neighbourly Relations

The first treaty of this category was concluded in the first year of Hijra (Prophet's (PBUH) immigration to Medina). On his arrival in Medina Prophet Muhammed (PBUH) signed a convention that specified the kind of relations between the Muslims on one side and the other Arab and Jewish tribes in Medina on the other. The convention stipulated that the Jews who rallied themselves with the Muslims would earn the right to their aid without any indiscrimination, and the Muslims would not help other parties against them. The convention, further stipulated that the non-Muslim parties to this convention would not offer protection to any Qurayshite or to his property. Like all such treaties of good-neighbourly relations, either party is to disassociate itself from granting asylum to or helping an enemy of the other party.

Aman Agreement

The term 'Aman' could be interpreted as the right to protection, conduct, security or inviolability granted to individuals or groups by some party who was in a postion to offer it. The concept of 'Aman' existed before Islam as a moral commitment binding only on the party offering it. In the Islamic era this concept was institutionalized with two modifications:

- The Aman granted by an individual or the state is a binding commitment for all Muslims.
- Aman could be granted to individuals, to a group, or to the whole population of a city or region. Any Muslim, male, female or even slave could grant his protection to individuals from an opposing party, who were seeking his or her protection. For groups and inhabitants of a city or territory, this privilege was the responsibility of the leader or the state representative. The Quran and the Prophet's (PBUH) Hadith laid the principles for this concept. The Quran instructs Muslims 'If anyone of the idolaters seeketh thy protection, then protect him so that he may hear the word of God, and afterward convey him to his place of safety.' The Prophet's Hadith tells that 'the blood of Muslims is of equal value, and the humblest among them, grants their protection, and they are united against the others.'

Under this title we deal only with the general Aman that a Muslim leader or a representative of the Caliph could extend on the basis of an agreement. The protection of the Muslim State would include the population of the Aman territory and those, who are passing through it or temporarily residing in it. During war with other nations, two forms of restrictions could cease the acts of hostilities: the Aman Agreement or the peace treaty. The main difference between the two was that the latter was concluded by the heads of states or by representatives acting on their behalf. The Aman Agreement could be concluded by the Muslim leader on the spot and, generally, for a limited period. This could be transformed into a peace agreement if it was to be prolonged for a long or indefinite period.

Peace Treaties

These type of treaties are normally concluded at the end of a war, or during a war, when both parties reach a conciliatory agreement, or before the start of war to avoid hostilities. In other words, a peace treaty is concluded in relation to the state of war.

The ideological principle for this category of treaties is the Quranic verse that says 'If they incline to peace, incline thou also to it, and trust in God.' Peace treaties in regard to their duration could be:

- For a limited period, as in the case of Al-Hudeibiyah Treaty, which was for ten years, or the accord which the representative of the Umayyad Caliph, Abdul-Malek, reached with the king of Khurasan, that was to last for seven years. In both cases these agreements could be called truce agreements.
- For an indefinite period, as in the case of a treaty that the Caliph Muawiyah concluded with the Armenians.

  As to the substance of the peace treaties, one could classify them into five types:
- The treaties that stipulate the provision of tributes (djizyeh) to be paid to the Muslim State in exchange for peace and protection extended by the Islamic State to the contracting party.
- Peace treaties concluded with other parties without any financial obligations, provided that the other party may help the Muslim troops or facilitated their mission against a third party. Such agreements were concluded by Khalid bin al-Walid and the inhabitants of Ullays during the conquest of Iraq, and by Abu Obeidah and the people of Daluk (near Antioch) when fighting against the Byzantines in northern Syria.
- Peace treaties with hostages offered by one party, or exchanged by both parties as an assurance against treachery. Muawiyah, reached such an agreement with the Byzantines, who delivered hostages to the Muslim State. When the Byzantines violated the peace agreement,

the Muslims released the hostages saying 'It is better to counter treason with honesty than to reciprocate.' The rules regarding the preservation of hostages were:

- Hostages could not be released as long as hostilities did not break out.
- They were not to be killed or harmed.
- They had to be released in case the fighting resumed.
- If the hostages were men, they had to be safely conducted to the borders, but in case the hostages were women or minors, it was the obligation of the state to secure their reunion with their families.

- Peace treaties where a Muslim state would pay tribute to another state. Despite the fact that there is no clear legal principle in the teachings of Islam to this effect, in practice such agreements were frequently concluded. Muawiyah, his son Yazid, and later on, Abdul-Malek reached agreements with constantinople whereby they each paid a certain amount of money for maintaining peace with Byzantium during internal troubles.
- During the Abbaside rule, both states, the Byzantine and the Abbaside, were obliged at one time or another to conclude agreements, according to which, they had to pay ransom for the release of their prisoners.

24

Settlement through Arbitration

During the period of the Orthodox Caliphate, precedents of diplomatic conduct set the benchmark for the concept of Islamic diplomacy. Besides the model of diplomatic envoys, correspondence, negotiations and conclusion of treaties, other instruments of diplomatic practice had been explored and established. The expediency of peaceful settlements of disputes and arbitration had been manifested.

Until the rule of the fourth Caliph, Ali bin Abi-Taleb (A.H. 35-40—A.D. 656-661), the conduct of relations was between the Muslims world (Dar al-Islam) and the non-Muslims nations (Dar al-Harb). During the six years of the Caliphate of Ali (RA) a new phenomenon appeared which concerned relations between two Muslim communities. The Quranic provisions stipulated that the Muslim community is one Ummah, and that any act which could lead to the division of the Muslim Ummah is an infringement upon this principle. Such a situation should be amended, if not in a peaceful manner, then by force. 'And if two parties of believers take to fighting, then make peace between them. And if one party of them transgresses beyond bounds against the other, fight ye all against the one that transgresses till it return unto the ordinance of Allah, then, if it return, make peace between them, justly, and act equitably, for God loveth the equitable."

Ali's (RA) ascendance to the Caliphate was challenged twice. In the first instance by two of the Prophet's (PBUH) disciples together with Aisha, his widow, who contested the legitimacy of Ali supported by a community of Muslims. After all peaceful methods to appease the contenders and to preserve the unity had been exercised and proved futile, the Caliph had to resort to force. The rules that were applied during the course of battle and then to the process of reaching a settlement were different in many ways from those applicable to relations with non-Muslim communities. The rules of battle laid down that the act of deterring the contenders, should come after ample warning. The transgressors could be fought face to face, but not be pursued if they chose to escape. The wounded should not be killed, and their prisoners must be released after the battle, or during it, if they guarantee that they would not resume the hostilities. Their property would not be taken as booty. Muslims were not to ally themselves with non-Muslims against another Muslim party. As to the peaceful methods, mediation, conciliation, good offices and arbitration, were productive tools of diplomacy.

In the second instance of encounters between two Muslim communities, all these methods had been employed. On this occasion Muawiyah, the Governor of Damascus, contested the authority of Ali bin Abi Taleb (RA), and refused to announce his oath of fealty to the Caliph, on the ground that the latter should first deliver to him the murderers of Othman (RA) (the assassinated third Caliph).

In the revolt of Muawiyah against the Caliph Ali (RA)—who were both Qurayshites—Jareer bin Abdullah al-Bajliy proposed himself to Ali (RA) as a mediator. He mentioned that Muawiyah would accept him as a friend and a confidante. Ali (RA) accepted the proposal and handed him a message for Muawiyah. The message related to Muawiyah how all the Muhajeroun and the Ansar, i.e. the elite of the Muslims, had announced their allegiance to the Caliph. Then he reminded Muawiyah that he was one of those emancipated by the Prophet (PBUH) after the conquest of Mecca, which made him inferior in his state of precedency to the faithful of Muhajeroun and Ansar, and thus could not be a qualified contender to the Caliphate. Jareer, after delivering the letter to Muawiyah, was not given the chance to present his arguments and returned to Ali (RA) to convey the intransigence of Muawiyah and his supporters.

Ali (RA), then advanced to Syria with his troops and camped at a place called Siffin close to where the troops of Muawiyah were stationed. He then consulted with three notables of three different Arab tribes, and proposed to them that they call on Muawiyah and invite him to obey God and to preserve the unity of the nation. One of them suggested to Ali (RA) that he should reinstall Muawiyah as Governor of Damascus. Ali (RA), while not rejecting the compromise, asked the three delegates to proceed to Muawiyah and to explore the possibilities.

The conciliation committee met with Muawiyah on the first of Zil-Hijjah A.H. 36 (A.D. 10 April 658). Shabath bin Ribiy al-Tamimi (of the Tamim tribe) addressed Muawiyah and appealed to him to avoid the division of the Ummah, and to spare it unnecessary bloodshed. Muawiyah interrupted him and asked why he did not direct his advice to his man (the Caliph). The second delegate, Bashir bin Amr, intervened to emphasize the legitimate right of the Caliph, and his invitation to Muawiyah to resort to righteousness, which would protect him in his earthly life, and guarantee benevolence in the afterlife. Muawiyah asked, 'Are you telling me to abandon the blood of Othman (RA)?' and vowed that he would never do so. The third person Al-Hamadany, spoke in his turn, bluntly raising the following issues. He said:

> It is verily known to us what you are striving for. You could not find a way to incite the people, and to play on their sentiments better than to declare that the Caliph Othman (RA) was unjustly murdered and to claim that you are asking for his revenge. Thus you could have the support of the lowly and the ignorant. We are aware that you were hesitant in helping him, wishing that he was killed so that you may take the position you are taking now...Have some fear of God, and renounce what you have committed yourself to.

Muawiyah was angered by the latter's speech. He blamed him for interrupting his colleague 'the honourable, the descendant of a noble family and the chief of his tribe' and for meddling in matters that were not clearly known to him. He then dismissed the delegates telling them, that he would use the sword as judge in the matter.

The Caliph camping a short distance from Muawiyah commanded his troops to await the enemy's attack and not to initiate the fight. He called on Muawiyah to avoid confrontation and to meet him in a duel. But the Umayyad contender declined the challenge. Being the forbidden months (Zil-Hijjah and Muharram), both parties agreed to a truce until the end of Muharram.

At the beginning of Safar (the second month of the 37th year A.H.) the armies entered into combat. For ten consecutive days the parties carried on a bloody battle. The Syrian army was defeated in the last three successive encounters. Muawiyah was ready to leave the field when a trick suggested by his counselor, Amr bin al-Aas, saved them from destruction. He ordered his troops to raise copies of the Quran on the tips of their lances, and to shout for quarter. According to other Arab chronicles, men in the Syrian Army were shouting to the other party to make the Quran their reference and to let its provisions rule between them, so as to spare the blood of each other. Although the Caliph was not deceived by the trick, his soldiers desisted from pursuit, and many of his aides called upon him to respond to the call of peace. The resulting contacts between the two parties culminated in a mutual agreement to refer the dispute to arbitration.

Arbitration of Siffin

Among the peaceful methods for the settlement of disputes, arbitration and adjudication are considered to comprise the legal tools, while negotiations, good offices, mediation, and conciliation are political techniques. In this particular case, arbitration started with political motives, proceeded on the basis of diplomatic skills and ended with political manoeuvre. According to the preliminary agreement, each party was to authorize one arbitrator to represent it. The arbitrators were to be given a minimum period of eight months to come to a decision. Muawiyah delegated his confident and shrewd aide, Amr bin al-Aas, while the representative of Ali (RA), Abu Musa al-Ashaari, who lacked both qualifications, was imposed on him by his supporters. The Caliph, thus deprived of the fruit of his victory, retired with his army towards Kufa (his capital city in Iraq).

For Muawiyah, what could not be achieved through war had been pursued through diplomacy. His representative managed to attain more than one concession from his counterpart. When signing the protocol *(modus vivendi)* for the process of arbitration, he convinced Abu Musa to delete the title of Caliph after mentioning his name, this being a matter of dispute. The latter accepted this, recalling the precedent of Al-Hudeibiyah when the Prophet (PBUH) consented to the same intervention. The text proceeded to mention Ali (RA) as a contestant on behalf of the people of Kufa and Muawiyah as a contestant on behalf of the people of Syria. The third concession was implied in the consent of both parties to lay down their arms and not to resort to force for solving the conflict. The fourth provision stipulated the postponement of the process of arbitration until the month of Ramazan, eight months later. The accord was signed and witnessed by ten witnesses from each party. As could be deduced, Amr bin al-Aas succeeded in:

A. Denying the legitimacy of Ali (RA) as a Caliph and implying that he was a counterpart in the dispute on this matter. Knowing that Muawiyah had never before put any claim to this post, but that he merely introduced his condition for the recognition and allegiance to the newly acclaimed Caliph, the concession of this matter appears to be a departure from the original stance.

B. Mentioning Muawiyah and Ali (RA) on equal footing, and suggesting that each was representing a faction of the Muslims.

C. Laying down the arms and not resorting to force implied the preservation of the *status quo,* and guaranteed that the Caliph would never be able to employ his constitutional right of resorting to force to preserve the unity of the nation.

D. The postponement of the meeting of the arbitrators which gave Muawiyah ample time to strengthen his position, and to resort to manoeuvers that would weaken his opponents. It is to be recorded that Muawiyah had been occupying his position as the Governor of Syria for more than twenty years, where his authority was established and his means were abundant. On the other hand, Ali (RA) came to the seat of the Caliphate after a crisis (the revolt against Othman (RA) and his assassination) and was himself faced with more than one crisis. If he managed to avert the revolt of two companions and to gain momentum in the Battle of Siffin, the delay in ending the conflict was contrary to his interests.

Role of Arbitrator

The instructions given to the two arbitrators by their commanders may shed some light on the anticipated proceedings. Abdullah bin Abbas, the cousin of Ali (RA), advised Abu Musa before he proceeded for the meeting, drawing his attention to the fact that he was to meet the most astute among the Arabs, and reminding him of the rightful position of Ali (RA), who had the pledge of fealty from the same people, who had pledged their fealty to the three other Caliphs. On the other side, Muawiyah reminded Amr that his opponent was a man of oratory rather than of astuteness, and advised him to delay his decisions and not to disclose all his plans.

In the thirty eighth year of Hijra, each party dispatched a group of four hundred persons in addition to other un-committed observers to the place agreed upon, Dawmat Al Jandal. In the meeting, Amr displayed modesty and reverence to Abu Musa and insisted that the latter should start the discussion. Then he proposed that they document their proceedings in writing and agreed to dictate the proceedings to a scribe. After the preliminaries, Amr wanted to put down that they both testified to the fact that Abu Bakr (RA), Omer (RA) and Othman (RA) were the orthodox Caliphs to succeed the Prophet (PBUH). Hesitantly, Abu Musa consented to the insertion. Then Amr went on to record that Othman (RA) was unjustly murdered. Abu Musa protested, saying that this matter was not among the matters to be discussed. Amr affirmed that Othman (RA) was unjustly murdered, and that Muawiyah being a close relative of his was justified in being the rightful claimant for revenge for the blood of Othman (RA), a statement which Abu Musa could not deny. He went on to say that he could prove that Ali (RA) had participated in his assassination. Abu Musa protested again insisting that they had not met to discuss such irrelevant matters. He mentioned that since Muawiyah would not be agreeable to the Iraqis, and that Ali (RA), too, would not be accepted by the Syrians, why not then agree to depose both of them and select a third person to the seat of Caliphate. Amr accepted the proposition, and suggested that they leave the election of the new Caliph for further consultation (Shura). Abu Musa consented to the proposal and they both came out to announce their agreement.

Amr again insisted that Abu Musa speak first. Abu Musa accepting the courtesy, announced that he was deposing Ali (RA), and nominating Abdullah son of Omer ibn al Khattab (RA) for the post. Amr, speaking after him confirmed, what Abu Musa announced regarding the deposition of Ali (RA), and that he affirmed his consignor, Muawiyah, for the Caliphate. He supported his announcement by indicating that Abu Musa had established, in writing, the fact that Othman (RA) was unjustly murdered and that Muawiyah was the rightful claimant for his blood. He called on the conferrers to pledge their fealty to Muawiyah as a Caliph and as a claimant to the rights of Othman (RA). Although Abu Musa protested against this announcement together with the others within the party of Ali (RA), the meeting was adjourned without any final agreement.

In addition to the concessions that Muawiyah had obtained previously, he gained new advantages during the session of arbitration:

- It was established in writing that Muawiyah was the claimant for the blood of Othman (RA), implying his right to contest for that right.
- Both arbitrators according to the announcements agreed on the deposition of Ali (RA), but they differed on the status of Muawiyah.

- For the first time, Muawiyah was declared Caliph. Despite the fact that this was done by one party, he was still raised from the status of a rebel to the level of a rival, and Ali's (RA) position was lowered to the position of a pretender.
- The adjournment of the meeting without a final agreement created the *status quo*, and put Muawiyah in an advantageous position. Ali (RA) had to face disagreement and division within his party as to the wisdom of accepting arbitration, on the appointment of Abu Musa, and the process of arbitration. Muawiyah, already well established within his party, now had the time to work on the members of the adversary, and to try to win more supporters from among them.

Prophet's Example

The Islamic State, under the administration of the Prophet (PBUH), employed all diplomatic means known at present for the settlement of disputes. Negotiations, conciliation, mediation, good offices and arbitration, were instruments known and used by the Islamic State from an early date.

The Al-Hudeibiyah Peace Treaty was one example of the outcome of intensive negotiations. For the precedents of conciliation, mediation and good offices one can cite more than one example. In the year A.H. 1, a military expedition was sent by the Prophet (PBUH) to encounter the Meecans near the sea coast of Yanbu. Majdy bin Amr, who was an ally of both parties, successfully intervened with mediation. Another example is the case of Abdullah bin Ubbay Salul, who although a Muslim, but as an old ally of the Jewish tribe of Bani Qainuqa, pleaded with the Prophet on their behalf, and the dispute was peacefully settled.

Arbitration was a method widely practiced among the Arabs long before Islam. The Quran recognized this tradition and made it obligatory in case of a conflict between two Muslim communities or states. 'And if two parties of believers fall to fighting then make peace between them.' After returning from the Battle of the Trench (Al-Khandaq) in A.H. 5, the Prophet (PBUH) turned his attention directly to the Jewish community which had conspired with the Quraysh. After the capitulation of Bani Quraidha, their leaders asked for arbitration by one of their former allies, the Aus tribe. Both the Prophet (PBUH) and the leaders of Quraidha, accepted the arbitration of Saad bin Maaz, and the agreement was fully implemented.

Al-Aman

The non-Muslim who came under the protection of the Muslim community was called either Zimmi or Mustamen. The Zimmi was a Christian or Jew (Ahl-Al Kitab are Kitabis which means the people of the Holy Books), who lived within the Islamic State, and thus enjoyed the rights of citizenship. The Mustamen was a non-Muslim who entered the Muslim territory under the pledge of protection (Aman) granted by the Islamic State. Since the status of the Zimmi did not fall within the context of foreign relations, this study, then, will deal only with Mustamen.

The Arabic expression 'Aman' means security, protection, safeguard or guarantee. The Mustamen came within the jurisdiction of the Islamic State under the pledge of Aman. An example is the Aman given to the two envoys of Musailemah, who claimed prophethood, which codified a previously known tradition, of not harming envoys even if they professed an unacceptable view. The example of safeguarding the envoys also applies to the messengers of Kisra (Chosroes) who came to arrest Prophet Muhammed (PBUH) and to deliver him to the Persian court. They were not only protected, but were also presented with gifts on their departure.

An example of extending protection to women, children and the disabled during war time, is the order Prophet Muhammed (PBUH) gave to one of his leaders, Khalid bin al-Walid, during Hunain A.H. 8, prohibiting him from harming children, women, and disabled men.

The principle of Aman is laid down in the Quran and confirmed by the Sunnah and was practiced by the Prophet (PBUH) and his followers. The Quran instructs 'If any one of the pagans seeks thy protection, then grant it to him, so that he may hear the word of God, and afterward convey him to his place of safety.' The Prophet's (PBUH) Hadith tells us that 'the blood of Muslims is of an equal value', and that 'the protection of Muslims is one (indivisible), which could be granted by the humblest among them'.

Um Hanie, a cousin of Prophet Muhammed (PBUH), granted protection to two men at the conquest of Mecca. When Ali bin Abu Taleb (RA), her brother, threatened to kill them, she came to the Prophet (PBUH) to seek his support. His answer was 'We protect whom you protect'.

The Aman which could be granted to a group of people or a whole community is a prerogative of the leader. The example for this general Aman is the one conferred by the Prophet (PBUH) to the people of Mecca when it was conquered. The Prophet (PBUH) declared to Abu Sufian, the leader of Quraysh, when the latter professed his adherence to the faith, 'anyone who enters the house of Abu Sufian will be safe, any one who gets inside his own house is to be protected, and anyone who puts down his arms will be safe.'

25

The Encounters

During the Prophet's (PBUH) leadership in Medina, he had four major military encounters with the Qurayshites, and one significant peace treaty. The military encounters with the Qurayshites proved to be a proper stage for the diplomatic endeavours aimed at serving the political ends of both parties while the peace treaty (Al-Hudeibiyah) could be considered a truce agreement postponing the ultimate confrontation, and getting time for the organization or the accumulation of further military and political advantages.

The first military confrontation between the two cities of Mecca and Medina, the Battle of Badr, came after the Muslims had tried to block the way for a trade caravan belonging to the former. Although the caravan managed to escape, the Qurayshites used this incident as a *casus belli* to amass an army and to confront the Muslims in a battle that might put an end to the threat of the Medinians. When the Meccans lost the Battle of Badr in the second year of the Hijra (A.D. 623), they started their preparations for retaliation. They entered the territory of Medina with a large army in the third year of the Hijra. Though the Muslims lost a great number of lives in the Battle of Ohud (A.D. 624), the Meccans were not in a position to benefit from a victory and they retreated to Mecca.

In the fifth year of the Hijra, the Meccans again invaded Medina with a large army of 10,000 men. The Arab chronicles narrate that envoys from the Medina Jews of Bani Nadir went to Mecca to incite the Quraysh against the Medina Muslims, promising them their help. The envoys then went to the Ghatfan tribes instigating them against Prophet Muhammed (PBUH) and assuring them of the support of Quraysh. The two armies of Quraysh and Ghatfan marched towards Medina, with the aim of conquering it.

The Prophet (PBUH), being informed of the imminent offensive, consulted his followers and upon the advice of one, he dug a trench around the unprotected part of the city. The fight, that took place there, was known as the Battle of the Trench (Al-Khandaq) in relation to that defensive line, or the Battle of the Parties (Al-Ahzab) indicating the alliance of Quraysh and Ghatfan tribes. The tribes besieging Medina for a prolonged period made futile efforts to storm the city, but had to withdraw their forces in the end. This encounter proved to be a turning point in the balance of power in favour of the Muslims. The Prophet (PBUH) commented on the withdrawal of the Qurayshites saying 'from now on we shall be attacking them, but never will be attacked'.

The reference to these three major military encounters is necessary in order to point out the frequent diplomatic manoeuvers that preceded or coincided with each one of them. Before the Battle of Badr, and in accordance with the terms of the Medina Convention, the Muslim inhabitants of Medina were not under an obligation to participate in any fighting, except in defense of Medina. The raids and the military expedition that Prophet Muhammed (PBUH) launched against the Qurayshites were undertaken, until then, by the Muslim exiles on the grounds that the Qurayshites had driven them out of Mecca, and had confiscated their property. In the case of Badr, the Qurayshites were the aggressors, but in response to Muslim attempts to encounter the trade caravan, the Prophet (PBUH) first sought the advice of his followers from among the Muhajeroun, then addressed the whole Muslim community asking for their opinion. The Ansar realized that they were meant to commit themselves, when the convention did not commit them.

Before the Battle of Ohud, Abu Sufian, the leader of the

Quraysh, addressed the Medina Muslims, requesting them to disown Prophet Muhammed (PBUH) and to leave their cousin to them, since they were not inclined to fight. The same method was followed by the Prophet (PBUH) during the siege of Medina, in the Battle of Trench, when he sent a message to the leader of Ghatfan promising them one third of the Medina crop if they left. In his efforts to dissolve the alliance between the Medina Jews and the assailants, he sent a messenger to the Jews warning them against Ghatfan and Quraysh, who would leave them in the end to face Prophet Muhammed (PBUH), whether they won and departed with their spoils or lost and retreated to their home towns. He then advised them to request their allies to hand them, as a guarantee, a certain number of hostages from their noble families. The same messenger then informed the Qurayshites and Ghatfan leaders that the Jews were reversing their position and that as proof of their loyalty to Prophet Muhammed (PBUH), they offered to deliver to him a number of hostages from their notable families.

The fourth major encounter, which led to the conquest of Mecca by the Prophet (PBUH), in the eighth year of the Hijra, was an occasion for intensive diplomatic efforts. When the allies of the Qurayshites violated the peace treaty of al-Hudeibiyah, Abu Sufian was sure that the Muslims would respond forcefully to this act. He came to Medina and met with the immediate followers, companions or collaborators of the Prophet (PBUH), seeking their help for the confirmation, and probably extension, of the peace treaty. His mission was anticipated by the Prophet (PBUH) and the response was perceived. Abu Sufian met, first of all, his daughter, the wife of the Prophet (PBUH), then Abu Bakr (RA), and then Omer ibn al-Khattab. Not one of them gave him a warm reception, or a positive reaction. Ali (RA), the cousin of the Prophet (PBUH) and his son-in-law, advised him to go back.

Leading an army of 10,000 fighters on the way to Mecca, Prophet Muhammed (PBUH) camped at a short distance from the city. It is mentioned that Abbas, Muhammed's uncle, left the camp looking around for someone going to Mecca so as to inform him of the site of the Prophet's (PBUH) camp in the hope that the Meccans might approach the Prophet (PBUH) for a peaceful entry.

The Prophet's gesture was in the same vein, when he advised Abbas to take Abu Sufian to a spot at the neck of the valley where he could watch the procession of the Muslim army in a show of force that would support the diplomatic endeavours.

Peace Treaty

In the sixth year of Hijra, Prophet Muhammed (PBUH) declared his intention of making a minor pilgrimage (Ál-Umrah) together with his followers. This came one year after the Battle of the Trench when the Meccans lost any hope of conquering Medina and the Muslims were enhancing their powers and becoming true contenders against the Meccan pagans. There were around fifteen hundred pilgrims. With them they took seventy heads of cattle to be sacrificed there as a part of the pilgrimage ritual and as a proof of the peaceful nature of their march. On his way, Prophet Muhammed (PBUH) was informed that the Meccans had resolved not to allow him entry and that they had sent their forces to meet him ahead of Mecca. The comment of the Prophet (PBUH) on the said information sheds light on his concept of peace and war, and can be considered the yardstick for evaluating his relations with the non-Muslims. He said, 'How bad it is for Quraysh that they are obsessed with war, if they let me approach all the other people, if I lose, that would be what they hoped for, but if I succeed, then they may join the Islamic faith dignified and victorious. By God, I will continue my strife on the path of my commission until God bring it out, triumphant or I perish.' That saying may indicate the following:

- That war was neither his objective nor his preference, but rather he disliked this alternative.
- That his goal was to deliver the message of God to all people.
- The reference to his relations with other authorities was the stand they may take to allow or to obstruct his endeavours to communicate his message to all people.

To avoid the likelihood of confrontation with the Qurayshite forces, Prophet Muhammed (PBUH) decided to follow another road to Mecca. He halted his march at a place called Al-Hudeibiyah, nine miles from his destination. There, he received the first delegation from the Khuzaah tribe which was on peaceful terms with the Muslims. The delegation, headed by Budayl bin Warqaa, informed the Muslim leader that the Quraysh had grouped their men not far from there to prevent, by force, his entrance to Mecca. The Prophet (PBUH) explained to the delegation that he had not come to wage war, but to perform Umrah. It was the tradition among the Arabs that no confrontation should take place during the forbidden months. It was also the practice that no one should be prevented from entering Mecca to perform Umrah or Hajj. The Prophet (PBUH) expressed his readiness to reach an agreement with the Quraysh provided that, they would not obstruct his way.

The second delegation was headed by Urwah bin Masoud al-Thaqafi, from a tribe allied with the Quraysh. Urwah promised the Quraysh that he would try to confirm what Budayl had reported, and to obtain more information about the situation in the Muslim camp. He tried to convince Prophet Muhammed (PBUH) of the strength of his opponents, the weaknesses of his supporters and of the futility of his plan. He reminded him that Quraysh was his own tribe, and that he had no way of entering Mecca except by murdering his own people. The Prophet (PBUH) repeated to him what he had said to Budayl and reiterated his proposal of reaching an agreement with the Quraysh. On his return, Urwah described to the Quraysh the solidarity of their opponents and their resolve to defend Prophet Muhammed (PBUH) to the last man. He said:

I have been to the courts of Kisra (of Persia) of Heraclius (of Byzantium) and of Najashi (Negus of Abyssinia). By God, I never saw around them people who were more obedient to their kings than those around Prophet Muhammed (PBUH) to him. They would never look into his face or raise their voices in his presence, suffice it for him to gesture, and his wish would be fulfilled....I have seen the people who would care less for what they suffer in the defense of their man. Another envoy from Quraysh, Mikrez bin Hafs, met with the Prophet (PBUH). He returned with the same impression.

The next envoy from Quraysh, Al-Hulays bin Alqamah, was a leader of an allied group. When he came close to the Muslims' camp, they released the cattle they had brought for sacrifice. Al-Hulays returned to Quraysh without meeting the Prophet (PBUH). He described what he saw as a proof of the goodwill of the Muslims and their sole intention of performing the Umrah. He protested to the Quraysh saying that it was 'not within the terms of their agreement to obstruct the path to the House of the Lord, before those, who came in reverence to it, driving their cattle that were to be sacrificed...'

Diplomacy First

Prophet Muhammed (PBUH) sent more than one envoy to Quraysh hoping for a peaceful solution to the issues. First, he sent a Muslim from Khuzaah tribe on his own camel. The envoy, Khirash bin Umayah addressed the notables of Quraysh stating that the Muslims had come only for Umrah and that after performing it they would leave in peace. The Qurayshites stabbed his camel, and attempted to attack him. The Prophet (PBUH) later on sent another envoy, Othman bin Affan (RA) (who would become the Third Caliph). The selection of Othman (RA) as envoy was made because his clan of Quraysh was still among the Meccan pagans, and so he would be listened to, and protected. Othman (RA) conveyed the message and offered them multiple possibilities:

- To accept the faith of Islam that would ultimately prevail.
- To step aside, and let the message of Islam reach other people.
- To permit the Muslims, to perform Umrah, the only purpose for which they had come.
- Despite the fact that he was received with respect, and was offered the opportunity of performing the Umrah, which he refused, his proposition was totally rejected. His diplomatic mission, though, was not completely in vain. He managed to meet with a number of Muslims, who were staying in Mecca, and gave them encouragement and moral support.

The final phase of negotiations was set with the arrival of Sohail bin Amr, the representative of the Quraysh, at the Muslim camp. He started his argument with the request for a show of goodwill, demanding the release of prisoners held by the Muslims. Prophet Muhammed (PBUH) responded with a similar request, and then agreed to reciprocate. After discussing the issue and reaching an agreement on the main points, the negotiator went into a discussion of the specific terms of an agreement, which Sohail demanded to be put in writing. The Prophet (PBUH) agreed and requested the scribe to write what was dictated.

It is recorded that the Prophet agreed to the provision, which stipulated the obligation of sending back to the Quraysh those, who came to join the Muslims while Quraysh was under no obligation to send back those, who renounced the Islamic faith. Truce was concluded between the two parties for a period of ten years. The other tribes were to choose to ally themselves with either party. If any party to the agreement or one of its allies committed an act violating the provisions of the agreement, then such an act would be considered a breach of the agreement.

The Muslims were to return to Medina with the agreement that they would perform their Umrah the following year.

In the agreement, Prophet Muhammed (PBUH) accorded several concessions, which in the view of many of his companions, he should not have agreed to. He conceded to:

- Starting the document with a forepart used by the Qurayshite and not by the Muslims (In your Name, My Lord)
- The demand of his counterpart and erased, under protest of his followers, the phrase (the Messenger of God) after the name of the Prophet.
- The provision which stipulated returning to the Qurayshites those who would come to join the Muslims, without the condition of reciprocity.
- To return to Medina without performing the Umrah, with the pledge that he could perform it the following year.

It was apparent that Prophet Muhammed (PBUH) had taken it upon himself to yield to these concessions in spite of the vocal protestations of some of his close allies and the silent astonishment of some others. But soon enough, the advantages of this agreement became apparent. By concluding this ten-year non-aggression pact, the Prophet (PBUH) not only proved his inclination to peace in solving disputes, but he also accomplished the following:

- The formal recognition of Prophet Muhammed (PBUH), by the Quraysh as an equal, not a rebel, and their implied recognition of the Islamic State.
- Quraysh and its allies, recognized through the agreement, the rights of Muslims to perform their religious duties, and consequently Islam was acknowledged as an established religion.
- By neutralizing the Quraysh, Prophet Muhammed (PBUH) actualized the isolation of their former allies, the Jews of Khaiber.
- The signing of the treaty helped in creating a public opinion among the Arabs which compelled them to envisage Prophet Muhammed (PBUH) in a state of power that compelled the Quraysh to seek a peace agreement, that would secure peace for the period of ten years.'
- The Muslims, who were now secure on their southern boundaries, could devote more time and effort to the task of spreading the message of Islam. In the same year, Prophet Muhammed (PBUH) sent his ambassadors to the rulers of Persia, Byzantine, Abyssinia, Egypt, and some Arab leaders.
- The terms of the treaty that provided for the return of the Qurayshites, who embraced Islam, proved to work in favour of the Muslims' interests', as Abu Jandal and many others, who were sent back to Mecca after adhering to Islam formed a band of rebels working from within the Qurayshite community, assailing its trade caravans, and hitting at its vital interests.

On its conclusion, two copies of the Treaty were signed by both parties. Prophet Muhammed (PBUH) fixed his seal on the document. The Treaty also recorded the names of several witnesses from both sides.

Treaty with Najran

In the tenth year of the Hijra (A.D. 632), a delegation representing the Christians of Najran (in the south of the Peninsula) came to Medina, to negotiate a peace treaty with the Prophet (PBUH). The Arab chronicles record that the delegates, who came to meet the Prophet (PBUH) wearing long, magnificent dresses, with golden rings on their fingers, were not received by him. When they consulted with two of his companions, they were advised to return in their simple travel clothes before meeting him.

The two delegates reached an agreement that was recorded in the following terms:

In the name of Allah, the Gracious, the Merciful. This is what Muhammed (PBUH), the Apostle of God, has put in writing for the people of Najran upon whom he has the authority regarding their (crops of) fruits, their (money) yellow, white or black and their slaves. Being gracious to them he has relinquished all, for two thousand garments, of which one thousand is to be delivered in every month of Rajab and one thousand in every month of Safar (the seventh and the second months of the lunar calendar), each garment weighing one Owqiyeh (pound). Whatever garment of Kharaj weighs more or less than one Owqiyeh would be calculated. Whatever may be collected, in other kind, of shields, horses, mounts or other objects should also be calculated.

The Najranites will receive and shelter my envoys for a maximum period of one month, and the envoys will not be kept for more than one month.

In case of an act of treachery in Yemen, the Najranites will lend my envoys thirty shields, thirty horses and thirty camels, and whatever may perish of the horses or the mounts that my envoys had borrowed, they will guarantee their return.

To the Najranites, and to those living among them, the protection of God, and the pledge of Muhammed, the Prophet (PBUH) and the Apostle of God, is conferred upon them their faith, their land and their properties, upon those, who are absent or present, upon their caravans, their sanctuaries and their sacred possessions.

Nothing that they used to have will be altered, and no right they used to enjoy will be withdrawn. No bishop will be prevented from his bishopric, and no monk will be displaced from his monastery. No one will carry the burden of the past (Al-Jahilyeh) or will be charged in retaliation for blood from that period.

They will not be recruited for fighting, nor will they be taxed for the one tenth, and their land will not be flocked by any army.

If anyone among them raises a claim for a right, then justice and equity will be asserted. No oppression there will be or oppressors in Najran. Any one who will practice usury, after this date, will be abjured from my pledge. No person among them will carry the responsibility for the mischief of another person.

For the contents of this document, they have the safeguard of Allah, and the pledge of Muhammed the Prophet (PBUH) for ever, and until the judgement of God materializes, as long as they discharge fairly and properly of their obligations, without imposing on them any unjustifiable demand.

Witnessed by: Abu Sufian bin Harb, Ghailan bin Amr, Malik bin Auf, of (the tribe of) Bani Nasr, Al-Aqraa bin Hubis Al-Hanzaly, Al-Mughirah bin Shubah'.

Diplomatic Correspondence

The Prophet (PBUH), during the sixth year of the Hijra sent envoys with messages to the monarchs and rulers of Byzantine, Persia, the (Arab) Ghassanid, and the Patriarch of Alexandria. Similar messages were sent to the governors of Oman, Bahrain, Ailah (Aqaba Port on the Red Sea) and the Najranites. In his letter to Heraclius, the Prophet (PBUH) wrote:

In the name of Allah, the Gracious, the Merciful. From Muhammed (PBUH) the servant of Allah and Apostle (PBUH), to Heraqle, the Grand Chief of Byzantines: Peace be unto those who followed the right path. Thence I call upon you with the call of Islam, submit (to Islam) and you will be safe, (if you do) God will reward you twice, if you decline, then you would be liable of the sins of peasants. 'O people of the book! come to common terms as between us and you, that we worship none but God, that we associate no partner with Him; that we erect not, from among ourselves, lords and patrons other than God. If they turn back, say ye: Bear witness that we are Muslims (They who have surrendered).'

The letter delivered to Chosroes (Emperor of Persia) reads, as follows:

In the Name of Allah, the Gracious, the Merciful. From Muhammed the Messenger of God (PBUH), to Chosroes, the Grand Chief of the Persians:

> Peace be unto him, who follows the right path and believes in God and His Messanger, and testifies that there is no god but Allah, and that Muhammed (PBUH) is His Servant and Apostle (PBUH), I call upon you to the call of God, that I am the envoy of God sent to all peoples, to give admonition to any who are alive, and that the word may be fulfilled against the disbelivers. Submit (to Islam) and you will be safe, but if you decline, then you will be liable for the sins of Magus'.

In the letter addressed to the Patriarch of the Egyptian Copts, Prophet Muhammed (PBUH) invited him to adhere to Islam, and promised him a two-fold reward by God for his acceptance and for those, who would follow in his footsteps and warned him, if he declined, of being accountable for himself and for all the Copts. The letter goes on to read.

O people of the Book, come to the common terms between us and you, that we shall worship none but Allah, and that we shall ascribe no partner unto Him, and that none of us shall take others for lords beside Allah. And if they turn away, then say: Bear witness that we are they who have surrendered unto Him.

The text of the letter addressed to the Persian Governor of Bahrain starts with the same salutation and calls for adherence to Islam as those which were addressed to the other rulers then and continues:

> God is aware of what is within your hands, and be it known that this faith will come out triumphant all over, to the confines that heel or the hoof can reach.

The Arab historians record that Heraclius received the envoy of the Prophet (PBUH) cordially, and he read the letter before his audience, but did not respond to his call. The Persian Emperor reacted with anger and tore up the letter. He then dispatched a message to his governor in Yemen, ordering him to summon Prophet Muhammed (PBUH) to his court. The envoys of the governor of Yemen were received by the Prophet (PBUH), and there they were informed of the assassination of their Emperor. The Prophet (PBUH) requested them to deliver a message to their leader in Yemen calling on him to embrace the faith, and apprising him, that he would be then re-instated. Before departing, the envoys were presented with a girdle made of gold and silver as a gift.

The envoy to the Egyptian Patriarch was received warmly, and later on was sent back with four female slaves as a present to the Prophet (PBUH). One of the maids, Maria, became the mother of his son Ibrahim. Ibn Khaldoun writes that at the time Prophet Muhammad (PBUH) dictated his message addressed to Heraclius of Byzantine, he was told that foreign monarchs would not recognize a formal letter if it was not properly sealed. The Prophet (PBUH), saw to it that a ring made of silver was prepared as his seal on which was engraved 'Muhammad, the Apostle of God'. The words were inscribed in three lines. The same seal was used later on by his successors, the three Caliphs Abu Bakr, Omer and Othman (RA).

Delegations in Medina

After the bloodless conquest of Mecca in the eighth year of the Hijra, delegations from all over the Arabian Peninsula started to arrive in Medina. The ninth year of the Hijra was known as the 'year of delegations.' In a delegation from Thaqif, six delegates representing the different clans of Taif and headed by Abd Yalil came to Medina. The delegation was received by Al-Mughirah, who acquainted them with the formalities of greeting the Prophet (PBUH), advice which they ignored. The preliminary contacts were made with considerable caution. An intermediary went back and forth between them and the Prophet (PBUH), until a written agreement was concluded. When they were offered their meals, the intermediary would taste the food before the envoys ate it. They declared their readiness to adhere to Islam, with certain conditions, and negotiated stubbornly for concessions, such as being exempted from prayers, or postponing the demolition of their idols. At the conclusion of the agreement, the delegation returned accompanied by two delegates from the host party, who were authorized to destroy the idol of Thaqif. Another delegation from the tribe of Bani Tamim came to Medina in the same year. Among the delegation were two persons, who had already embraced Islam. On their arrival at the home of the Prophet (PBUH), the delegates called loudly for him to come out to them, a behaviour which was considered highly unbecoming. A verse in the Quran was revealed which reads:

> Ye who believe! Put not yourselves forward before God and his Apostle; but fear God, for God is He who hears and knows all things.
>
> Ye who believe! Raise not your voices above the voice of the Prophet (PBUH), nor speak aloud to him in talk, as ye may speak aloud to one another.

Those who shout out to thee from without the inner Apartments, most of them lack understanding.

The delegates invited Prophet Muhammed (PBUH) to a competition, and asked permission for their poet and their orator, to speak on their behalf. The Prophet permitted them and requested a Muslim orator to reply to theirs and a well-known poet Hassan bin Thabit to reply to their poet. The dialogue, expressed through verses and oratory, ended in an agreement, and the delegation received gifts before leaving.

The delegation from the rulers of Hemyar (in Yemen) came to Medina to show their adherence to Islam. The Prophet (PBUH) handed them a message for their rulers, in which he instructed them to follow the rules of Islam: ...and that God had guided you to his truth, provided that you behave righteously, and you obey God and His Apostle, and perform your prayers, that you pay the tithe and deliver the one fifth... and if one of the Jews or the Christians embraces Islam then he is of the faithful. He has what rights they have and he carries what obligations they carry.

He who is of the Jewish or the Christian faith, will not be deterred from his religion, but he will pay the djizyeh (the tax). Every mature individual, male or female, free or enslaved, would pay one (full) dinar, or its equivalent in garments. If he pays that duty to the Prophet then he will have the guarantee of God and the pledge of His Apostle...'

The letter indicates that Muslims have to follow the principles of Islam, and pay the tithe (Zakat) from their surplus property at the rate of 2.5 per cent and deliver the share of one fifth (20 per cent) of what they gain from their enemies. The message also prohibited Muslims from forcing Jews or Christians to reject their own religion. The latter were exempted from the duties imposed on Muslims, but they were to pay the djizyeh at the rate of one dinar per mature person. The message expressed the pledge the Prophet (PBUH) gave to safeguard the rights of Kitabis (Jews and Christians).

Among the other delegations received in Medina, one delegation came to the Prophet (PBUH) representing Musailemah bin Khabib, from Yamameh (Najd) who claimed to be a prophet. The two delegates delivered a message which said: 'From Musailemah, the Apostle of God, to Muhammed the Apostle of God. Peace be unto you. I, then, inform you that I have been associated with you in this mission, and that we have half of the territory, and Quraysh has the other half, but Quraysh is an aggressive community.' The Prophet Muhammed (PBUH), after receiving the message, asked the two envoys: 'What say you (of this matter)?' The delegates replied: 'We say what he has said.' The Prophet (PBUH) replied: 'By God, if it were not the tradition that envoys could not be killed, I would have severed your heads.'

The influx of delegations into Medina during the last two years of the Prophet's (PBUH) life, and after the conquest of Medina, was recorded in the Quran in the following text:

> When comes the help of God, and victory, and thou dost see the people enter God's religion in crowds, celebrate the praises of thy Lord, and pray for His forgiveness: For He is oft-returning in grace and mercy.

26

The Ambassadors

In the fifteenth year of Hijra (A.D. 636) and before the decisive battle of Al Qudsiya (in Iraq), the Persian Commander-in-chief, Rustam, asked the Muslim leader, Saad bin Abi Waqqas, to send him a delegation for a possible negotiation. Saad assigned this mission to Al Mughirah bin Shubah. On arrival at the headquarters of the Persian army, bin Shubah headed directly to seat himself beside Rustam. When Rustam's aides indicated their displeasure, he addressed them saying, 'Truly my seat in this place would do me no honour, and be sure it would not degrade that of your chief.'

Delegation to Iran

The talks began with Rustam asking, 'Do tell me, what is it that brought you out of your country. After all, you are few in number, and possess very little armament.' To that Al Mughirah replied, 'We were people of ignorance and mischief, until God sent us His Apostle, through whom He guided us (to the right path).' The talks went on until Rustam threatened to annihilate them altogether, when Al Mughirah interrupted him to say, 'If we are killed while fighting you, then to heaven we believe we will go, but if you are killed, hell would be your fate, unless you agree to pay the djizyeh.'

According to other sources, the Muslim delegate was not allowed to take his seat alongside Rustam, and the Persian chief offered the Muslims 'food enough to satisfy their hunger and to send them back with what would please them', assuming that they had come to fight because of poverty, and were driven by the hardships they suffered in their lands to do so.

It is recorded, too, that Omer (RA) ordered his Commander-in-chief, Saad, before entering into battle to approach the Emperor himself. Saad, according to these records, sent a delegation of fourteen persons to the court of the Emperor after passing through the headquarters of Rustam. On their arrival, they were kept waiting while the emperor Yazdjard consulted with his ministers and his commander of the army. When they were given audience, the Emperor questioned them about the motive for the Muslim presence in his territory. 'Is it because we were occupied and distracted from showing concern, that you were emboldened against us?' he asked. Al Nu'man bin Al Muqrin, after requesting permission of the other delegates to speak on their behalf answered: 'God conferring his mercy on us had sent us His Apostle enjoining us to do what is right, and forbidding us from committing what is sinful....' Al Nu'man related to the Emperor how the call for the Islamic faith spread through the Arabian Peninsula and how the Prophet (PBUH) pointed out that the message should be delivered to all other nations, starting with those nearer to them. He then said:

> So we call on you to adhere to our faith that upholds what is right and condemns what is wrong. If you decline to do so, then you may opt for the next alternative, which is to pay the djizyeh. And if you refuse to do both, then your only option is to fight us. If you choose to embrace the faith, we would leave with you the Book of God, the provisions of which shall guide your judgement, and then we would withdraw and leave you in control of your land and of your affairs. If, otherwise, you opt to pay the djizyeh, then you will have our protection. If neither (proposal) is acceptable, then it is the fighting.

Yazdjard told the delegation : I have never known a nation that is worse in misery and fewer in numbers than yours. If it is a delusion of your own strength that you are suffering from, then stop being so conceited. If it is hardship that makes you act this, then we will help you by sustaining you until you have favourable weather and your land is fertile again, so that you are no longer in want. Furthermore, we will treat your notables with honour, and also assign a governor, who will treat you with kindness.

After a moment of silence, another one of the delegates stood up to reply to the Emperor's statement. He said:

> Your Majesty, those are the chiefs of the Arabs and their notables. They are distinguished people, who conduct themselves with modesty before your notables. It is the men of honour, who glorify and pay due respect to other men of honour. Not all that they have been commissioned to convey, has been said, and not all you have stated has been responded to...it is true what you say about our condition. It could have been worse than what you described, but God has sent His Apostle....

The speaker, Al Mughirah bin Zurareh, continued, repeating what the previous spokesman of the delegation had said, and the three proposals he had offered. The Emperor ended the talks saying, 'If it were not (the tradition) that envoys should not be punished, I would have committed you to death. You will have nothing from me. He then ordered that a load of dust be hung from the neck of the most notable among the delegates, and told them to go back to their chief (Saad) and to warn him that he would be sending Rustam to bury him together with his men in Al Qadsiya, and then Rustam would advance into their country, to get them occupied with the worst that they could have.

In the twentieth year of the Hijra, Amr bin al Aas was dispatched to Egypt by Omer bin al Khattab, leading a Muslim army. Al Muqawqas, the chief of the Copts, sent him two delegates to negotiate a peaceful settlement. Amr kept the Egyptian envoys waiting before sending them back without talking to them. When they returned to their chief they gave account of the high morals of the Muslims, of their modesty and of their unity. When, for the second time, Al Muqawaqas sent his envoys to the Muslims' camps inviting their leader to send a delegation, 'with whom to discuss what is of interest to both sides', Amr sent a delegation of five members headed by Obadeh bin al Samet, who was of dark complexion and considerable height. When Obadeh stepped forward to address the Egyptian chief, the latter requested that someone else 'other than that black man' do the talking. The delegates with Obadeh answered that 'this black one is the wisest among us and the most benevolent. He is our commander, who has precedence over everyone of us. We all revert to what he opines and to what he utters.' The negotiations that proceeded then, were lengthy and intensive, but nevertheless they ended with a peace agreement.

Al-Tabari, relates that Amr had requested the envoys to convey a message to the Copts which included the following: 'The Prophet (PBUH) has advised us to deal kindly with the Copts, that they are our kinsmen'. The reference to kinship indicated the relationship of the Arabs, the descendant of Abraham through his Egyptian wife Hagar.

The Chinese historian, Feng Chia Sheng, records that in the year A.D. 651 (A.H. 30), an official Arab mission which was sent by Othman bin Affan (RA), bearing gifts to the Chinese monarch, was received by the Chinese Emperor Kao Tsung. It was not the only Arab delegation that reached the Chinese territory in expression of peaceful cooperation. Up to the end of the eighth century more than thirty missions were sent to China.

Letters of Pledges

Kitabis (people of the Books) could maintain peaceful relations with the Muslim State and be guaranteed of its protection provided, they paid the djizyeh. However, there were certain cases established, during this period, where this obligation would be forfeited. One example was set when Abu Obeidah paid back the djizyeh collected from the inhabitants of Horns, because the Muslim army, being pre-occupied with the Byzantine, could not provide the protection pledged to the population of that city. Another instance of abolishing the tribute was, when the Kitabis could not afford to pay it. The third instance was, when the Muslims came to an agreement with a community, whereby the latter pledged to offer some kind of assistance to the Islamic State.

The following are some examples of where the Muslim commanders documented such pledges in letters addressed to the population of those regions.

In the 18th year of the Hijra (A.D. 640), the commander of the Muslim forces which marched to Azerbaijan, under the rule of Omer bin al-Khattab (RA), reached an agreement with the people of that region, whereby he offered them Aman, provided that they would help the Muslims. In the letter of pledge he wrote:

> In the name of God, the Gracious, the Merciful. This is what Otbeh bin Farqad, Agent of Omer bin al-Khattab (RA) Amir al-Muminin, has pledged to the inhabitants of Azerbeijan, of its plains and mountains, of its centers and confines, to all the inhabitants of different creeds and races. He has pledged to offer all of them the Aman for themselves, their property and their faith, provided that they pay the djizyeh that they can afford, excluding the children, the women, the aged persons and those who consecrate their time for worshipping... and those who fight along with the Muslims, would be exempted from paying the djizyeh for the year, wherein they were recruited. Those who preferred to stay would have the same (duties and rights) like all other residents; those who choose to depart, would be safe and protected until they reach their safe destination. Written by Jundub, and witnessed by Bakir bin Abdullah al-Laithi and Semak bin Kharshed al-Ansari, in the eighteenth year.

Suraqeh bin Amr, the leader of the Muslim army sent to Armenia, concluded a similar agreement with Shehre Biraz, the Persian governor of Armenia, attested by Omer bin al-Khattab (RA). The letter started with contents similar to those of the aforementioned letter, with the provision of conferring Aman to the people of Armenia, 'provided that they would rise to assist in case of raids', the djizyeh would be waived for those, who responded to the call of recruitment, but those who chose to avert it would have the same (duties and rights) as those of the inhabitants of Azerbeijan.

In the same year another commander of the Muslim army, Suweid bin Muqrin, addressed a similar letter to the chief of Gorgan which included the text referring to ' those, who assisted us will be compensated, instead of being taxed' and the letter ends with naming the witnesses and the date.

Treaty of Jerusalem

The four Muslim armies which were dispatched to Greater Syria (Biladu-Sham) by Caliph Abu Bakr (RA) were assigned different tasks, but they were to cooperate under the general command of Abu Obeidah. Amr bin al-Aas who was charged with the conquest of Palestine won a number of victories against the Roman governor Artabin. The latter, leaving large contingents of troops at Jerusalem, Gaza and Ramleh, assembled the bulk of his forces in Ajnadin, a village near Jerusalem. As per their military tactics, the Arab armies grouped their forces when facing a major encounter. The Roman army faced disastrous defeat in Ajnadin and the few, who escaped found refuge within the walls of Jerusalem. The city of Jerusalem, garrisoned by a heavy force, resisted for some time. According to a number of Arab chronicles, the siege of Jerusalem lasted for four months.

It is worthwhile to note that Jerusalem, even then, had a very special significance for the Muslims. When still in Mecca, before their exile to Medina, the Muslims were ordered to pray facing Jerusalem. It was in Mecca, that a Sura of the Quran was revealed to the Prophet (PBUH) describing his (spiritual) transporation to Jerusalem, 'where the farthest Mosque (Al-Aqsa Mosque), whose precincts God did bless.'

The Arab historian, Al-Waqidi, records that Abu Obeidah had sent a message to the Patriarch of Jerusalem (then known as Ilyae) inviting him to accept Islam and to avoid bloodshed. But all Arab historians agree that Sophronius, the Bishop of Jerusalem, had proposed to Abu Obeidah a peace treaty with the condition that the Caliph Omer bin al Khattab (RA) himself be present to conclude it. When Abu Obeidah conveyed the proposal to Omer (RA), the Caliph consulted his allies. Othman (RA) advised him to reject the proposal. This was to indicate the weakening of the besieged city and the implication of ignoring the request, was an expression of confidence that, surrender was imminent. Ali bin Abi Taleb (RA) suggested that the Caliph proceed to Jerusalem so that they would attain the target without bloodshed. He warned against the possibility of the arrival of support to the besieged city if, the Muslims chose to refuse the offer and to wait for its surrender. Omer (RA) accepted the advice of Ali (RA) and headed for Jerusalem.

The Caliph travelled with a single attendant, without escort and without ceremony, and arrived at Jabia, where he was met by a deputation from Jerusalem. When Omer (RA) entered Jerusalem and met the Bishop Sophronius in his modest clothes, the Greek historian, Theophanes, claims that the Bishop exclaimed 'Truly, this is the abomination of desolation spoken of in Daniel the Prophet as standing in the Holy Place."

The fact that the Caliph himself came to conclude the agreement of peaceful entry into Jerusalem, in response to the request of its Bishop, is a unique case in the annals of Islamic conquests. Much more so, considering that the besieged city was without enough military force after the escape of Artabin to Egypt, and that the siege took place after the decisive defeat of the Byzantine armies. The people of Jerusalem might have feared that their concession to the Arab commanders would lead to acts of reprisal from those, who were still living in a condition of war. On the Arab side, inspite of their confidence in the imminent surrender of the city, they were proving that they would not forgo any attempt at peace. At the same time they were expressing their conviction that Jerusalem, the city 'of the farthest mosque, whose precincts God did bless' had a sacred place in their faith. Furthermore, they indicated that they were fighting the military foreign power in the Arab territories, and felt no antagonism against the inhabitants of the city.

Before the arrival of Omer (RA), the Muslim leaders, as preparatory work for the peaceful settlement, wanted first to make sure of the real intentions and to test the sincerity of the desire of the inhabitants for a peaceful settlement. Al-Yaquobi, the Arab historian, narrates in this regard, that the Arabs presented one of their commanders, Khalid bin al-Walid, as being Omer bin al-Khattab (RA), for the resemblance between them was strong. Sophronius recognized the difference and insisted on the presence of Omer (RA) in person to conclude the agreement. The Arab Commander-in-chief, Abu Obeidah, proceeded then to the second phase of negotiating on the principles and the guarantees that the peace treaty would be concluded on the arrival of the Caliph.

Arab chronicles present different versions of the peace treaty, its language, the length of the text, the indirect or direct quotation and some other details. Al-Yaquobi presents the shorter text that reads:

> In the name of God, the Gracious, the Merciful. This script written by Omer bin al-Khattab (RA) is addressed to the people of Beit Al-Maqdis (Jerusalem). You would be safeguarded as to your blood, your properties and your churches, that would not be lodged or damaged, unless an act of violation is committed.

Al-Tabari presents a more detailed text, whose context, many other Arab historians accept and quote. The text states:

> In the name of God, the Gracious, the Merciful. This is what Abdullah (slave of God) Omer bin al-Khattab (RA), commander of the believers, has conferred protection on the inhabitants of Ilyae. He offered them safety over their persons, their properties, their churches and their crosses, over all the inhabitants, the healthy and the sick. Their churches would not be inhabited, or demolished or decreased in area, neither their crosses nor properties would be damaged. They would not be forced to reject their faith, and none of them would be treated unjustly. No one of the Jews would be allowed to dwell in Ilyae. The people of Iiyae would pay the djizyeh according to the same terms the djizyeh is being paid by the people of Al-Madaen. They should deport the Romans from their city. Those who depart would be safeguarded, together with their properties until they reach their safe destination. Those who stay would be protected, and

> they would have to pay what the people of Ilyae have to pay of djizyeh... to the contents of this script, the oath of God is given and the pledge of His Apostle, of the Caliphs and of the faithfuls....Witnessed by Khalid bin al-Walid, Amr bin al-Aas, Abdul-Rahman bin Auf and Muawiyah bin Abi Sufian. Prepared and written in the year 15 A.H. (637 A.D.).

The text of the treaty, which has become known as the Omeri Pact,' includes, in addition to the basic mutual agreement of conferring Aman and setting the djizyeh, certain additional terms. One of the conditions was to deport the Romans and the outlaws of the city. The second provision entailed the prohibition of the dwelling of the Jews inside the city. The third provision dealt with other ethnic groups within the city, who were given the free choice of staying and sharing with the other inhabitants the same rights and duties, or leaving with the departing Romans, and being protected until they reached their safe destination. It seems likely that the first two provisions were inserted in the text upon demand by the Christian leadership of the city. To get rid of the Byzantine foreign presence was a demand voiced in other cities of the region. As to the clause regarding the prohibition of the Jews from residing within the city, one should recall that Jerusalem at that time was not inhabited by a Jewish community. During the Persian-Roman War, the Jews were accused of conspiring with the Persians and of assisting their thrust into the area. When, later on, the Byzantines had the upper hand, they punished the Jews by expelling them from the city and forbidding their re-entry there. It is easy then, to conceive the fear of the Christian inhabitants of Jerusalem, that the act of the Persians might be repeated by the Muslim Arabs.

Law for Foreign Relations

In the period of the Umayyad and Abbaside Caliphates, a new branch of studies in Islamic jurisprudence (fiqh) came into existence. The Muslim jurists researching in this field, called it Al Siyar. Al-Sarakhsi, a scholar who dealt with this topic defined Al Siyar as 'the study that is concerned with relations of the Muslims with other communities, living in the territories of the enemies or to whom the Muslims are bound by treaties: the Mustaminin (who were pledged the protection of the Muslim State), the Zimmis (people of the Book who live within the State), the apostates and Ahlul-Baghy (dissident Muslim community).'

In the early days of Islam, the Arabs, who were surrounded by the two occupying powers, Persians and Byzantines, viewed the world as consisting of two parts: that of the Muslims which they called Dar-ul-Islam, and that of the warring powers which they called Dar-ul-Harb. At a later stage they came to realize that there were other communities with whom they had to subsist. Their relations with these entities were complex and multi-faceted, to the extent that they needed to legislate clear rules and laws based on Islamic principles to conduct these relations.

In the early eighth century, there were Muslim jurists, who devoted chapters of their works to the subject of foreign relations of the Islamic State. Al Shaabi (died A.D. 723) and Abu Sufian Al Thawri (died A.D. 718) had considerable influence over the thoughts of the well-known scholar Abu Hanifah. Among the jurists, who produced independent works devoted to the subject, were Al-Awzaie (died A.D. 774), Abu Hanifah, and his two disciples, Abu Yousuf and Al-Shaibani.

Abu Hanifah (died A.D. 768), the founder of the Al-Hanafi school of thought, was the first to put down a set of rules and legislations to regulate the conduct of foreign relations on the basis of Islamic principles and mainly the principle of Qiyas (analogy). Abu Yousuf had compiled the views and judgements of Abu Hanifah on this subject, in a book titled *Al Asil* (the source). He is also known for another book written at the request of the Abbaside Caliph Al Rashid, under the title *Kitab Al Kharaj* (the book on land taxation). This well-known book studied the rules of Islam regarding the taxes on land belonging to non-Muslims (Al Kharaj), and also other rules that regulate the Muslim State's relations with other communities.

Al-Shaibani (A.D. 750-804) who was the disciple of both Abu Hanifah and Abu Yousuf, had authored several books on the question of the state's relations with other societies. Some of these books have survived to this day through scholars, who quoted him or commented on his works. A typical example is Al-Shaibani's book titled *Kitab Al-Siyar Al-Kabir* (the large book on Al-Siyar) which survived through the work of Al-Sarakhsi under the title *Shark Kitab Al-Siyar Al-Kabir* (interpretation of the large book on Al-Siyar).

To acquaint oneself with the main features of these legislations, one should recall that before Islam, there existed several systems of international law. Each system was concerned with a family of nations belonging to the same civilization. The basic rules of each system were the extension of the national laws of the civilization based on its common moral values and traditions. These systems of international laws lacked the two main principles accepted in the present international law— equality and reciprocity.

Islamic international law was an extension of Islamic jurisprudence and was binding on the state as much as on the individual Muslim. Its rules stem from the same sources that other religious and legal codes are derived from, namely the Quran, the Prophet's (PBUH) Sunnah (traditions), the Ijmaa, (consensus), Qiyas (analogy) and Ijtihad (best judgement). To these sources, one may add five other sources that comprise the references for codifying the Islamic Law of Nations. These are the provisions of the treaties that the Muslim State had concluded with other states, the conduct of other states, or principle of reciprocity, the arbitral awards, the traditional norms and customs, and the Caliphs' decrees and practices. In comparison with the present concept of international law, the Islamic Law of Nations is not very different. One of the modern definitions of international law describes it as the system of rules on the rights and duties of states in their mutual relations. International law is based on the concept of sovereign equality of states and rests ultimately on agreement among them. The sources of international law include: (1) treaties (2) international customs (3) general principles of laws based on such ideas as justice, equity, and morality recognized by civilized nations, and (4) a subsidiary source of law found in judicial decisions and in the teachings of the recognized legal publicists of the various nations. On the concepts of universality of the Islamic international law and equality of nations, one may quote the first source of Islamic legislation, namely, the Quran. Although the Islamic faith is addressed to all nations and Muslims have the duty to spread Islam to all parts of the world, the Quran recognized the fact that there are different nations that will never cease to exist. It says: 'And if the Lord had so willed, He could have made mankind a single nation, but they will not cease to differ.' In another verse, the Quran points to the concept of relations among nations which are equal, with a common origin, whom God created and made into different nations so that they may know each other, 'O mankind! We created you from a single (pair) of male and female. And made you into nations and tribes, that you may know each other. Verily the most honoured of you in the sight of God is (he who is) the most righteous among you'.

Bibliography

Antonio Cassese : *The Self-determination of Peoples,* Columbia University, New York, 1981.

Antony G.N. Flew : *Wants or Needs : Choices or Commands,* Paris, 1953.

Arnold, T. W. : *Preaching of Islam,* London, 1913.

Asborn Eide : *Human Rights in World Society,* Oslo, 1977.

Assemani, J. S. : *Bibliotheca Orientalis,* Rome, 1719-1728.

Aurobindo, Sri : *The Foundations of Islamic Culture,* New York, 1973.

Bar Hebraeus : *Chronicon Ecclesiasticum,* Louvain, 1872.

Baral, Lok Raj : *Regional Migrations, Ethnkity and Security,* Bombay, 1995.

Baumstark, A. : *Ceschichte der Syrischen Literatur,* Bonn, 1922.

El-Beladhuri : *Kitab futuh al-buldan, Liber expugnationis regionum,* London, 1868.

Bergestrasser, G. : *Risalat Hunayn ibn Isltaq,* Leipzig, 1925.

Bevan, E. R. : *House of Seleucus,* London, 1902.

Boer, T. J. : *Geschichte der Philosophie im Islam,* Stuttgart, 1901.

Browne, E. G. : *History of Arabian Polity,* Cambridge, 1921.

Caetani, L. : *Annali dell' Islam,* Milano, 1905.

Cajori, F. : *A History of Muslims,* New York, 1954.

Carra De Vaux : *Penseurs d' Islam,* Paris, 1921.

Dhagamwar, Vasudha : *Law, Power and Justice: Protection of Personal Rights under Islam*, Bombay, 2001.

Doughty, C.M. : *Travels in Arabia Deserta*, London, 1923.

Duchesne, L. : *Early History of the Christian Church*, London, 1914.

Dutt, Nalinaksha : *Early Monastic Buddhism*, Calcutta, 1941.

Haskins, C.H. : *Arabic Science in Western Europe*, in *Isis*, 1925.

Hauser : *Ueber das Kitab al-hijar*, Erlangen, 1922.

Heath, T. L. : *Aristarchus of Samos*, Oxford, 1913.

Hffele, C, J. : *History of the Christian Church Councils*, Edinburgh, 1871.

Hogarth, D. G. : *The Nearer East*, London, 1905.

Houtsma, T. and others : *Encyclopaedia of Islam*, London, 1934.

Inge, R. : *Philosophy of Plotinus*, London, 1918.

Inostranzev : *Iranian influences on Moslem literature*, Bombay, 1918.

Mas'udi : *Muruj adh-Dhab*, de Courteille, Paris 1861-71.

Mathew Thomas : *"Political Economy of Etimic Conflict"*, School of International Studies, Jawaharlal Nehru University, New Delhi, 2003.

Merivale, C. : *History of the Romans under the Empire*, London, 1896.

Meherhof, H. : *New Light on Hunayn ibn Ishaq*, in *Isis*, 1956.

Mommsen, T. : *Provinces of the Roman Empire*, London, 1909.

Muir, Sir William : *The Caliphate, its Rise, Decline, and Fall*, London, 1891.

Muller, A. Der : *Islam im Morgen-und Abehnland*, Berlin, 1885-7.

Muni, S.D. and Kalim Bahadur : *Domestic Conflicts in South Asia*, South Asia Publishers, New Delhi, 1986.

Murthy, T.S. : *Assam: the Difficult Years*, Himalayan Books, New Delhi, 1983.

Musil, A. : *The Manners and Customs of the Rwala Bedounis*, New York, 1928.

Myron Weiner : *Sons of the Soil: Migration and Ethnic Conflict in India*, University Press, Prineton, 1978.

Nicholson, R.A. : *Literary History of the Arabs*, London, 1922.

Poole, Lane, S. : *The Mohammedan Dynasties*, London 1895.

Purgiter : *Ancient Indian Historical Tradition*, 1922.

Ray, Samirendra : *Judicial Review and Fundamantal Rights*, Eastern Law House, Kolkata, 2002.

Saxena, K.P. : *Human Rights: Perspective and Challenges*, Lancers Books, New Delhi, 1996.

Sharma Sastri R. : *Kautilya's Arthasastra*, Raghuveer Press, Mysore, 1951.

Smith, D. E. : *History of Iran and Turkey*, New York, 1923-25.

Smith, V.A. : *Early History of India*, Oxford, 1914.

Socrates : *Ecclesiatica Historia*, Oxford, 1844.

Stapleton & Azo-Hussain : *Polity in Iraq and Persia*, Calcutta, 1927.

Steele, R. : *Practical Diplomacy*, New Delhi, 1952

Tarn, W. W. : *The Greeks in Bactria*, Cambridge, 1938.

Thomas, J. : *Selections Illustrating the History of Greek Polity*, 1941.

Warmington, E. H. : *The Commerce between the Roman Empire and Arabs*, 1939.

Wiberg, J. : *The Anatomy of the Brain in the Works of Galen and 'Ali' Abbas, Janus*, 1914.

Wiedemann, E. : *Uber Thabit ibn Qurra, sein Leben und Wirken*, Erlangen, 1922.

Winer, L. : *Contributions towards a History of Arabico-Gothic Culture*, New York, 1917.

Index

J

N

Q

Y

Z

□□□